Principles of Computer-aided Design

This book is one part of an Open University
it is therefore related to other material availa
evoke the critical understanding of students. Opinions expressed in it are not
necessarily those of the course team or of the University.

8

Principles of

Computer-aided

Design

Edited by
Joe Rooney and Philip Steadman
at the Open University

Pitman Publishing

in association with The Open University

PITMAN PUBLISHING
128 Long Acre, London WC2E 9AN

First published in Great Britain 1987

© The Open University 1987

British Library Cataloguing in Publication Data

Rooney, Joe
  Principles of computer-aided design.
  1. Engineering design—Data processing
  I. Title   II. Steadman, Philip
  620′.00425′0285   TA174

ISBN 0 273 02672 0

Typeset by Mathematical Composition Setters Ltd, Salisbury, UK
Printed in Great Britain at The Bath Press, Avon

Contents

Contributing authors

		Chapter
Dr. M. S. Bloor	Computational Adviser Geometric Modelling Group Leeds University	5
Prof. A de Pennington	Professor of Computer-Aided Engineering Geometric Modelling Group Leeds University	4
Mr. J. R. Dodsworth	Lecturer Geometric Modelling Group Leeds University	9
Mr. M. Dooner	Lecturer The Design Discipline Faculty of Technology The Open University	12
Dr. C. F. Earl	Principal Lecturer Department of Engineering Bristol Polytechnic	2 16
Dr. I. D. Faux	Director of European Studies Computer-Aided Manufacturing — International (CAM-I) Poole, Dorset	7 8
Mr. R. J. Goult	Lecturer Department of Applied Computing and Mathematics Cranfield Institute of Technology	10
Mr. G. E. M. Jared	Senior Research Officer Department of Applied Computing and Mathematics Cranfield Institute of Technology	9

Mr. K. G. Pasquill	Applications Consultant Engineering Computer Services Lichfield, Staffs	17
Mr. M. J. Pratt	Director of Research Department of Applied Computing and Mathematics Cranfield Institute of Technology	6 11
Dr. J. Rooney	Lecturer The Design Discipline Faculty of Technology The Open University	0 1 5 15
Mr. A. Saia	Lecturer Geometric Modelling Group Leeds University	4 5
Dr. J. P. Steadman	Reader The Design Discipline Faculty of Technology The Open University	0 3 4 13 14
Mr. P. Wallace	European Technical Manager Computer-Aided Manaufacturing — International (CAM-I) Poole, Dorset	12
Dr. P. R. Wilson	General Electric Company Schenectady New York, USA	17

Introduction

P Steadman and J Rooney

1   Origins of computer-aided design

Intro

Computer-aided design (CAD) is barely twenty years old, yet in the 1980s it is transforming the working practices of designers in many industries and has become a huge world-wide industry itself.

If we were to try to locate a single historical point of origin for CAD, then it would surely have to be the revolutionary SKETCHPAD system developed by Ivan Sutherland at the Massachusetts Institute of Technology (MIT) in 1962/63 [Sutherland 1965]. Computers had been used before that for making

Fig. 0.1   Detail of the displayed image of the SKETCHPAD III system on the TX-2 computer of Lincoln Laboratory, MIT, showing a perspective view and three orthographic projections of a chair

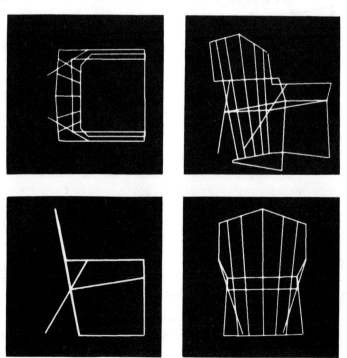

analytical calculations in engineering design. What was new in SKETCHPAD was that the designer could for the first time *interact* with the computer *graphically,* via the medium of display screen and light-pen.

Designs — of a rather rudimentary kind — could be input directly to the machine by drawing them. The computer then made some analyses of their performance automatically. For example, the stresses in the members of a bridge structure could be calculated and displayed. Or the responses of an electrical circuit to the introduction of voltages and currents could be simulated.

Sutherland's first version of SKETCHPAD was limited to drawing in two dimensions. A later version of the system by T. E. Johnson [1963] allowed for objects to be modelled in three dimensions, so that perspective views could be displayed of the design from different viewpoints (Figure 0.1).

A few years earlier, again at MIT, there had been developed the world's first numerically-controlled milling machine, capable of machining parts automatically from instructions coded on punched tape. These data were at first prepared by hand from conventional engineering drawings. Later the APT (Automatic Programming of Tools) language was developed to speed up this very time-consuming process of 'part programming'.

The logical next step was to link the computer-aided design of a component directly to its manufacture, in what has become known as CADCAM (Computer-Aided Design and Computer-Aided Manufacture). In the case of machined parts this means producing numerical-control (NC) tapes automatically, from the geometric model of the design created in the computer. However, making this link proved more difficult than was originally envisaged in the 1960s. Only in the 1980s is it becoming a practical commercial reality.

Most of the elements of modern CAD systems were thus present in embryonic form in this pioneering work of the late 1950s and early 1960s: two-dimensional *computer draughting*; three-dimensional *computer modelling*; automatic *analysis* of the performance of designs; and at least the potential for *integrating design with manufacture,* in CADCAM.

Because of the cost of the computer hardware, the first commercial users of CAD in the early 1960s were the big car and aerospace companies, with such firms as General Motors, Boeing and Lockheed–Georgia among the leaders. At the same time large electronics firms like Fairchild and Motorola began using computer techniques for designing printed circuit boards and integrated circuits. Slightly later came civil engineering and architectural applications, especially for large projects in the public sector, where government departments were able to make available the necessary capital investment. During the 1970s CAD spread widely into other application areas such as graphic and textile design, television and film animation, and typography.

2 Structure of the design and manufacturing process

How do these various uses of the computer fit into the design and manufacturing process viewed as a whole? Many authors have tried to describe the typical structure of the design process, and to set out in some formal scheme or diagram the various activities which designers undertake in their work [Archer 1965; Jones 1970; March 1976; Pahl & Beitz 1984]. These authors differ widely in their terminology. There are good reasons too for expecting that the nature of the design process itself will vary considerably between different design professions and industries. For example: the geometry of the type of artefact in question is of a different character in each case; the nature of the manufacturing process varies, and this in turn affects the design process; in some engineering fields the technical specification for a design is very tightly defined, whereas in other areas such as architecture or graphics designers may have much more freedom of action. Furthermore, individual designers within the same profession will go about their work in many different ways.

Fig. 0.2 Schematic structure of the design and manufacturing process

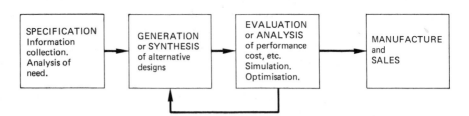

Nevertheless, it is still possible to identify some basic features common to most accounts of the design process, and to pick out some activities which are common to the designer's job in many industries (Figure 0.2). The first activity is usually that of **specification**. Here the designer's task is set out, and criteria for the performance of the designed object are laid down. The designer will probably be involved here in collecting many different kinds of information, about existing products of a similar type, about the potential market, about manufacturing constraints, about legal requirements and standards, and so on.

The second phase is that of **generation** or **synthesis** of alternative designs. This is the very heart of the design process. It is where the designer's creativity and inventive powers are brought into play. Often a new design may in fact be only a modification of an existing artefact. We might call this 'evolutionary design', in which small incremental changes are made in each new 'generation' of a certain type of product. In other cases a new design is created by permuting and recombining components or elements in a completely new configuration. In the extreme case the result may be sufficiently novel to qualify as a patentable invention.

The third activity is that of **evaluation** or **analysis**. Here the alternative designs which have been generated are tested in turn and compared to see if they meet the specification. The tests will probably be theoretical ones in the first instance, made in the designer's imagination or by means of calculations. Later on there may be practical tests made using physical models or actual prototypes.

The kinds of performance criteria which different artefacts might have to meet could be of an almost infinite variety. But for example these might be tests of the strength of mechanical components or structures. The architect might want to analyse the flow of heat through the rooms and walls of a building. The electronics designer would want to test the logic or simulate the behaviour of a circuit. The mechanical engineer might want to simulate the geometric motions of a mechanism. The designer of a consumer product would need to assess the product's visual appearance and make some aesthetic evaluations. Furthermore in all cases it would be important to estimate the costs of materials and manufacture.

It is useful conceptually to decouple these activities of synthesis and analysis, of generation and testing. In practice they are not so distinct. In the flowchart of Figure 0.2 they are shown connected in a loop. The designer generates some alternative possibilities, subjects these to analysis, and as a result rejects some of the alternatives, makes modifications to others, and tests them again. Many writers on design have agreed about this essentially cyclic or iterative nature of the design process. Among these perhaps the most perceptive is Herbert Simon [1969] who speaks of designing as involving 'first the generation of alternatives and then the testing of these alternatives against a whole array of requirements and constraints. There need not be merely a single generate–test cycle, but there can be a whole nested series of such cycles.'

The most primitive kind of generate-and-test process, says Simon, is that employed by the proverbial monkeys trying to type Shakespeare. However, 'generate-and-test processes of practical interest proceed more subtly and selectively than this. They are constrained so that any object they generate is already guaranteed to satisfy a certain subset of the design requirements.' A great part of the art of design as practised by skilled professionals appears to lie in the way in which they are able to organise and balance these 'generate-and-test cycles' mentally. Attempts to automate the process of design must grapple, it seems, with ways of formalising whole sequences of these generators and tests, and of allocating computational resources between them.

2.1 Hierarchical nature of design problems Advantage/disadvantage of cad.

It would be a mistake to think that *complete* designs are produced for whole artefacts, and only then are tests applied. Rather, the designer tries to break down the problem hierarchically into several smaller sub-problems, often working in turn on the separate components of a machine or structure, generating alternative designs for these relatively discrete parts, and subjecting them to separate tests.

The design of a large and complex artefact such as an aeroplane or major building is the work not of one person but of a team. Here the sub-division of the whole problem into smaller parts corresponds broadly to the division of labour among the members of the team. The completed component designs are assembled together and further tests of performance applied to the assembly as it is built up. The results of these tests may show that it is necessary to go back and redesign some of the components again.

Although the parts into which the overall design problem is decomposed might often correspond to spatially separate components, in other cases the hierarchical breakdown of the problem might not be of this character. In the design of a building for example, the architect, the structural engineer and the mechanical engineer would work on different *systems* or *aspects* of the design

— the room layout, the structural systems, the heating and ventilating systems — not all of which correspond necessarily to distinct, geometrically separable physical entities. This is analogous to a description of human anatomy in terms of tissues rather than in terms of organs.

The design process goes on then at several levels: on the level of the artefact as a whole, on the level of separate systems or components, and on intermediate levels between these. Always the designer or design team will move back and forth between consideration of the parts and consideration of the whole. It is nevertheless possible to distinguish different *styles* of designing: for example, a process which works predominantly from the *bottom up*, starting with the detailed design of the components and then putting these together, in an essentially additive way; or a process which works predominantly from the *top down*, making decisions about the overall scheme first, before considering more closely the details of the parts. Simon [1969] compares these alternative styles of design process with the choices of compositional style which are made by workers in other creative professions. Composers of music 'must decide how far the architectonics of a musical structure will be evolved before some of the component musical themes and other elements have been invented. Computer programmers face the same choices, between working downward from executive routines to subroutines or upward from component subroutines to a coordinating executive.'

In comparing the top-down and bottom-up approaches it is important to realise that neither approach can succeed without the other. Thus a high-level decision made about an overall design scheme depends crucially on the form, properties, function and availability of lower-level components. Indeed a high-level design specification may be impossible to realise: because it violates the laws of physics; because it is currently too costly or too complicated; or because the 'necessary' components have not yet been developed or invented.

Similarly, low-level decisions made about the detailed design of components, and/or their interconnection in systems, depend crucially on the required form, (emergent) properties, reliability of function, and constructability of higher-level sub-assemblies and assemblies. Low-level design will not by itself prevent interference or adverse interaction between components; nor will it indicate mutual incompatibility between sub-systems; nor will it determine the suitability and reliability of the system as a whole.

In some ways the bottom-up approach is to be preferred in that a detailed component design in conjunction with a scheme for generating higher-level systems based on precise rules of construction and assembly, should lead to more reliable (and more modular) systems. However, the size and type of system must be restricted (if we are to avoid producing a 'combinatorial explosion' of possible designs) and this unavoidably entails high-level specifications.

One further characteristic of these alternating phases of synthesis and analysis in design is that they tend to move from the general and tentative, to the more specific and definite. At first the designer considers preliminary outline ideas or sketch proposals. The evaluations made here are perhaps of a rather informal and approximate kind; later the preferred design or designs are fleshed out in more detail, and analyses of performance and cost are made with greater precision. This fact has important consequences for CAD, since it is extraordinarily difficult to allow for vagueness, sketchiness or ambiguity in a computer program. For this, as well as other reasons, most computer aids produced to date serve the later rather than the earlier stages of the design process.

To return once more to the schematic diagram of the design process in Figure 0.2: the last stage, when the design is finalised, is the transfer of a description of the design to the manufacturers or builders who will make it.

2.2 People involved in design and manufacture

We can use the basic structure of Figure 0.2 to organise a picture of the various *people* involved in the design and manufacturing process, and of how (typically) they exchange information with each other (see Figure 0.3). The designer will of course be centrally concerned with the activities of synthesis and analysis. In many industries the design, as mentioned, is the product of a team of designers, some with specialised skills, who must communicate amongst themselves. The specification for the design may come in part from market research in the case of a mass-produced consumer product, or from an individual client or client organisation in the case of a building or specialised engineering project.

Fig. 0.3 People involved in the design and manufacturing process, and some of the patterns of information flow between them

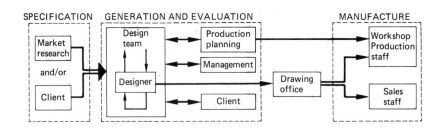

During the course of the design process proper, the designer will usually continue to consult with the client or clients to show them the developing design and to solicit further information. The designer will also probably discuss with management and production planners the manufacturing, marketing and cost aspects of the design. In the traditional design and manufacturing process, the designer passes information about the completed design to the drawing office staff, who prepare detailed working drawings for the workshop and production staff in the case of an industrial product, or for the construction firm in the case of a building.

2.3 The transmission of information in design

Design information may be transmitted via a number of different media. Much of the information will be exchanged verbally of course, and in written documents. But the description of the geometrical form and of the visual appearance of the designed object will (in the traditional design process) be conveyed in the form of drawings and perhaps also in the form of physical models. The drawings will be of many kinds, depending on the intended *receiver* of the information conveyed, and on the particular *properties* of the object represented by the drawing.

The designer may personally use sketch drawings to externalise ideas at the conceptual stages of design; and members of a design team will similarly use sketches to communicate amongst themselves. These sketch drawings may represent many properties of the design: form, appearance, structure, kinematic behaviour and so on. Drawings and models intended for lay clients or for use in sales literature will probably place emphasis on the realistic depiction of visual appearance. The working drawings by which the design is communicated to workshop and production staff, or to the builders of a building, will obviously seek to convey precise information about shape and size, together with details of materials and manufacturing methods.

3 The role of the computer in design and manufacture

With the help of the above simplified picture of the design and manufacturing process and of the flows of information between the people involved (as these exist in traditional practice), we can now begin to identify where the various past, present and possible future applications of computers lie.

Fig. 0.4 The place of computer draughting in the design and manufacturing process

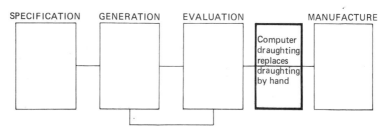

Historically the first area of application, and today the most widespread in industry, is **computer draughting** (Figure 0.4). This automates the production of the detailed working drawings by which the finished design is communicated for manufacture. In this area the central activities of design, those of synthesis and analysis, remain essentially unaffected, although it is possible that designers themselves might use such a draughting system, in the later stages of the design process proper. However, the representation remains strictly two-dimensional, and the machine has no 'understanding' of the three-dimensional geometry or the physical properties of the object which lies behind the drawings.

The next step in CAD has been the development of a great variety of separate computer programs or 'packages' for carrying out **analyses of performance** (Figure 0.5). Thus packages have been produced for structural analysis, for thermal analysis, for kinematic analysis, for the drawing of perspective images and for many other applications. Other programs allow the behaviour of designs to be **simulated**, for example: the simulation of electronic circuits; the simulation of robot manipulator arms moving in their workspaces; or the simulation of the movement of lifts in high-rise buildings. Where the constraints on design can be formally stated, and some performance objective can be quantified, then it may be possible to use mathematical methods to **optimise** the design with respect to that objective.

7

Fig. 0.5 The place of separate analysis packages in the design and manufacturing process

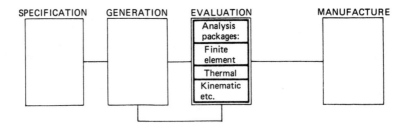

Fig. 0.6 The place of integrated solid modelling, analysis and draughting in the design and manufacturing process

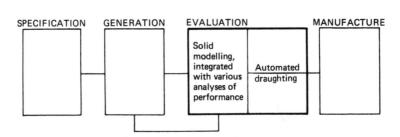

These programs are intended again mainly for use in the later stages of the development of a design, rather than at the early conceptual stage, since they tend to require detailed (input) data on shape, dimensions, materials and so on in order to yield precise quantitative analytical (output) results. One intrinsic problem with all these separate applications programs, however, is that these data have often had to be taken from paper drawings by hand and entered to a different program for each type of analysis. This can be a time-consuming process: one which is avoided entirely by taking the next logical step, which is to **model** the design in the computer, and to integrate this model directly with the automated analyses (Figure 0.6).

Solid modellers form one type of modelling system and they have been developed primarily for use in mechanical engineering, and in architecture. They allow the designer to work in a sculptural way, building up complex three-dimensional forms from combinations of simpler 'primitive' shapes. Within the subject of three-dimensional design generally, different industries will be concerned with different classes of geometrical object. Thus the geometry of buildings is largely a geometry of rectangular blocks. The forms of many mechanical parts will be composed from combinations of simple solids such as cuboids, prisms, cylinders and spheres. The products of some industries have complex sculptured surfaces, such as: the bodies of cars and aircraft; the hulls of ships; the shapes of bottles and of shoes, and so on. Solid modelling systems for the various different industries reflect to some extent these geometrical differences.

Once a three-dimensional description of a design has been built up in the machine, then, in principle, geometric data can be passed automatically to any of a number of linked analysis packages. The same data can be used also to generate electronic and paper drawings, both realistic perspective views, and detailed working drawings for manufacture.

The next development is the linking of computer-aided design with **computer-aided manufacture,** in CADCAM (Figure 0.7). The description of the design is transferred electronically to the production processes, and paper drawings can be dispensed with. As mentioned earlier, it has taken until the

Fig. 0.7 Computer-aided design and manufacture as it exists in its most advanced form in the mid-1980s

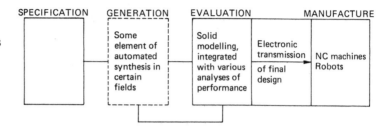

SPECIFICATION	GENERATION	EVALUATION		MANUFACTURE
	Some element of automated synthesis in certain fields	Solid modelling, integrated with various analyses of performance	Electronic transmission of final design	NC machines Robots

early 1980s for this CAD–CAM link to be achieved. Indeed it is still practicable only in some quite limited areas of design and manufacture, such as: in the machining of components by NC tools; in the preparation of photographic masks for fabricating printed circuits and micro-chips; and in the direct production of printing plates in the newspaper and publishing industries. We are also seeing some links made between computer-aided design and the programming of robots to carry out assembly operations. But we are a long way yet from the complete automation of the assembly process for complex products with many components. Moreover, in some cases, for instance in the building industry, it is difficult to see how any significant automation of assembly will ever come about. Here, for the foreseeable future at least, paper drawings will continue to play their traditional role.

'Integrated' CADCAM systems incorporating solid modellers and linked analysis packages represent the most advanced and comprehensive types of computer aid commercially available in the mid 1980s. As we have noted however, it is still necessary to bring to such a system a substantially well-developed design scheme or schemes, before these can be modelled and analysed. Furthermore, computer aids have hardly begun to touch the activity of synthesis (the generation of alternatives in design), which still remains the province of human designers and their imaginations. In some restricted areas there have certainly been attempts at automated synthesis: in kinematic design; in room layout in architecture; and in the layout of tracks on electronic circuit boards. But, for the most part, computer aids to synthesis in design are subjects for future research, and are especially problematic subjects at that.

Some of the difficulties arise from the intrinsic vagueness and conceptual abstraction of the early stages of design, as already discussed. Others come from the complex structure of the process of design, the way it moves between hierarchical levels, balancing generators and tests in many repeated cycles of synthesis and analysis. If the processes of testing are to be completely automated, this must involve the formal representation in the computer of a large body of analytical engineering science. Meanwhile, the automation of the process of synthesis requires the representation of a different kind of knowledge (Figure 0.8). This is knowledge (which the human designer certainly possesses), of formal possibilities, of 'worlds of possible designs', of the kinds of overall compositions which may be generated by applying certain rules of construction, or by certain procedures for combining together elementary parts. Such knowledge, however, is very rarely set down or formalised explicitly. Indeed it would need a considerable programme of research to elicit knowledge of this type from designers, or to infer it from a study of the artefacts themselves. In computing terms, these topics take us into the realms

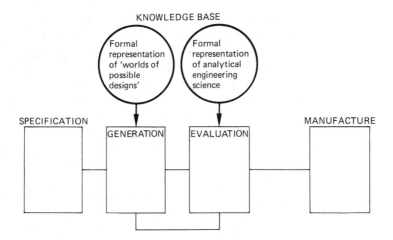

Fig. 0.8 The 'knowledge base' on which future developments in automated synthesis and automated evaluation will have to build

of expert systems and artificial intelligence (with their problems of knowledge acquisition, etc.). Some people might question the desirability or practicability of even trying to emulate in the computer these highly creative faculties of the human mind.

4 Structure of this book

The previous sections have offered an outline of the complete design and manufacturing process, and a review of existing and possible future applications of the computer in design. We now turn to the question of how these topics are treated in the present book.

As the title signals, the emphasis throughout is on principles. The reader will find here only some rather brief mentions of computer hardware, and certainly no review of currently available equipment or commercial software. There are no sample programs and little discussion of any strictly computing science issues. The book focuses rather: on what 'computer aids' mean for the practice and theory of design; on the ways in which various tasks and procedures in design can be formalised for CAD; and on the ways in which geometrical and other properties of designed objects may be represented in the machine. Computer-aided design is changing very rapidly both as an industry and as an academic subject. By concentrating on principles we hope to offer a treatment of the subject which will not date quite as quickly as it otherwise might.

The book is in four parts. The first part (Chapters 1–3) lays some *conceptual and mathematical foundations* for what follows. Basic ideas are introduced relating to ways of describing, manipulating and viewing representations of geometrical objects in the computer.

The second part (Chapters 4–9) is concerned principally with *geometric modelling*; although the introductory chapter provides an account of two-dimensional draughting systems, and moves from this to the simplest type of wire-frame three-dimensional models. Two chapters deal with the mathematics and modelling of curves and surfaces. Other chapters examine the constructive operations by which models of complex solids can be built up from primitive shapes and different techniques by which the resulting geometrical forms can be described in computing terms.

The third part of the book (Chapters 10–13) is devoted to the topics of *analysis and synthesis*, with the greater emphasis being placed on analysis. We have necessarily had to be highly selective here. We have chosen to look at four areas: finite element methods, which were originally developed for structural analysis (but now also have widespread applications in other areas, such as fluid mechanics and vibration analysis); kinematic analysis; logic, simulation and spatial layout problems arising in electronics; and spatial layout methods in architecture. This last chapter raises some of the difficulties of automated synthesis, which are explored further in the final part of the book.

In the fourth part (Chapters 14–17) we have again not tried to be comprehensive, but have instead picked out some current research areas in CAD. Of these the best-developed area is the creation of highly realistic images by computer graphic techniques.

Representing objects 1

J Rooney

1 Introduction

Design is concerned fundamentally with the generation and with the processing of information. Much of this information relates to 'real' (or realisable) objects and systems: it describes their **form** and/or their **function,** for the purposes of specifying, creating, analysing, synthesising and communicating design solutions.

Both form and function have long been discussed, as to which comes first, and as to which is the more important in the design activity. Depending on the particular design profession or industry (architectural, mechanical, electronic, and so on) and on the individual approach of the designer, one or the other aspect is given more prominence. For our purposes it is convenient to give them equal weighting and to view the form–function duality rather like the wave–particle duality occurring in modern physics. Then all designed objects have form and function, but attention to one or the other aspect is suppressed, depending on the circumstances.

In this book we concentrate mainly on representing the form of an object. This is the area where much progress has been made recently, particularly in the context of computer-aided design (CAD). In attempting to represent the form of an object or system, designers are inevitably faced with the inherent problems of defining and recognising objects, and of constructing 'faithful' representations of objects. With the advent of CAD systems these problems have become even more acute, and, in order to solve them, designers have developed elaborate formalised techniques and constructions. As a result, this has, in one sense, restricted the variety of possible forms of objects that may be considered, but, in another sense, it has liberated designers from many onerous tasks, and allowed much more complex objects to be constructed.

2 Objects and attributes

The physical objects that have been (and are being) designed range, in scale, from tiny micro-electronic circuits to whole cities, and, in complexity, from simple objects, such as a paper-weight, to vastly complex ultra-computers. In between these extremes lie motor cars, bridges, buildings, supertankers, supersonic aeroplanes, robots, chemical processing plants, machine-tools, desk-lamps, chairs, and so on, as well as consumer products, such as televisions, calculators, watches, refrigerators, cookers and clothes.

In addition to these physical objects, there is also a large class of less tangible designed 'objects'. These range from organisational structures for government and multinational companies, through communication networks and air-traffic control systems, to computer programs and software systems.

With most designed artefacts (such as those listed above), fashion and/or technical developments lead to continual changes in form, so that it is often meaningless to discuss a single 'fixed form' or 'final form' for an object. Moreover, it is often the case that widely different designed objects have apparently very similar forms. Using a biological analogy, designs 'evolve' in form and give rise to both *homologous* forms and *analogous* forms.

Homologous forms

In the field of biology, genetically related organisms generally have very similar underlying physical structures, but often have dissimilar superficial appearances. These organisms, which are fundamentally of the same generic type, are said to be homologous in form. By analogy with this situation we might consider two designed objects, which have essentially the same or similar (functional) form, but different appearances, to have homologous forms. There are many examples of this in design and Figure 1.1 illustrates two such *homologues* sharing the (functional) form — 'motor car'.

Fig. 1.1 Design homologues sharing the form — 'motor car'

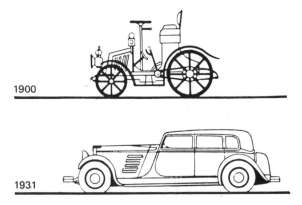

1900

1931

Analogous forms

Again in biology, genetically unrelated organisms often have very similar superficial appearances. These organisms, which are fundamentally of different generic type but which, through environmental factors (for example), have 'converged' in evolutionary terms, are said to be analogous in form. By

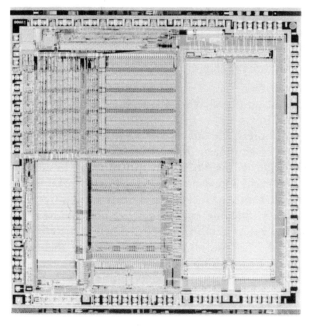

The Inmos Transputer

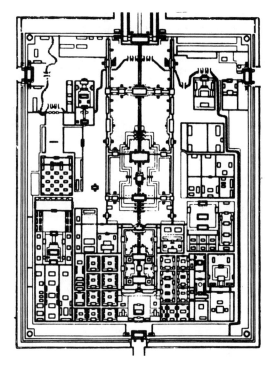

The forbidden city of Peking

Fig. 1.2 Design analogues sharing the constraint — 'organisation of flow'

analogy with this situation we might consider two designed objects, which have essentially different (functional) forms, but similar appearances, to be analogous forms. Again there are many cases of this in design and Figure 1.2 illustrates a striking example of *analogues* provided by a micro-chip circuit and a city plan. Here the similarity in superficial appearances arose partly because of similar functional constraints, namely: the organisation of information flow and the organisation of the flow of people.

Although we have not defined the terms 'homologue' and 'analogue' rigorously for design purposes, the concepts are implicitly used widely in design. Thus, homologues occur in several guises, for example parameterised shapes (Chapter 3), and analogues are indispensable for the purposes of simulation.

The above two biological metaphors have been introduced, simply to highlight some of the problems arising in trying to define and to recognise objects. For a CAD system this is especially problematical, and often the user is required to indicate painstakingly and laboriously every detail and feature associated with an 'object' created on screen.

The idea of an 'object' has been the subject of much discussion in the past and one that is still highly relevant in the context of CAD. The main difficulty concerns the relationship between **objects** and **attributes** (such as shape, colour, texture, physical state and so on). In particular at least four aspects of this relationship continue to cause problems, namely:

- an object is defined essentially by its attributes;
- an attribute only has real existence in relation to objects;
- an attribute is defined essentially by the objects which share it;
- an object (or an attribute) can be represented by many possible different forms.

The first aspect suggests that an object is to be identified with the set of attributes which it possesses. However, physical objects seem to have a real existence apart from their attributes. The difficulty lies partly in the problem of specifying *all* the attributes of an object. In practice this has to be a finite task yielding a finite (preferably small) set of attributes, although intuitively we feel that the set should be infinite (and perhaps uncountably so).

The second aspect is concerned with the fact that attributes such as 'round', 'square', 'rigid', 'hot', 'strained', 'moving', and so on, are not like the parts of an object, which are themselves objects. An object defined as a collection of attributes is not composed of those attributes in the sense that it is composed of component parts. Each attribute must relate to an object.

The third aspect suggests that an attribute is to be identified with the set of objects which possess it. However, this set is continually changing, and intuitively we feel that it should be infinite (at least potentially), though in practice it has to be finite, or at least finitely specified.

The fourth aspect raises the question as to whether there is an underlying special (or **canonical**) representation for each object (and for each attribute), from which all others can be derived. If not, how then are the various different representations interrelated? For instance, the base of a circular cylinder has the attribute 'elliptical' in many different two-dimensional projections (representations), but it has the single canonical attribute 'circular' in one special projection, and all others can be derived from this.

We do not attempt to pursue any of these deep philosophical aspects further but nevertheless we have introduced them here because they must each be addressed (albeit on a smaller scale) if objects and their attributes are to be represented and modelled on a computer system for the purposes of computer-aided design.

3 Representing and modelling

In attempting to describe an object or system for the purposes of design, analysis, or simulation, designers are inevitably faced with the problems of how to identify and of how to represent the component parts, their properties, their behaviour and their interrelationships. In a sense, representations and models are simply analogues, or analogous descriptions, of the represented objects. However, in the context of CAD such analogues must be precisely formulated or constructed.

Everyday language is too imprecise to provide a suitable basis for a description, and so we naturally adopt mathematical concepts and techniques for this purpose. When using such techniques it is important always to be aware of the *limitations* (as well as of the capabilities) of mathematical language. In particular the mathematical description of an object or system is always a limited one and must not be confused with the real object or system. All types of representation describe a *limited set of attributes* — mathematics describes these more precisely.

Having said this, it is, of course, possible to create an artificial (limited) world of mathematically generated objects, and in this sense to have a complete description of such objects. However, if these are ever to be realised as physical objects or systems we must then accept that the real objects will have a host of atributes which were not foreseen. An example might be an electronic circuit design, generated using precise rules of geometrical layout, but which fails as a real design because of heat problems or capacitive cross-talk — attributes not incorporated in the original representation.

Subsequent inclusion of these factors in the model does not necessarily solve the underlying problem, and in some cases it can lead to an infinite regress of more and more unforeseen attributes.

In this book several different types of representation or model are introduced in the context of design, analysis and synthesis. The main emphasis in all of these is on the representation of spatial forms and in particular on the geometry of these forms. Since all physical objects are embedded in three-dimensional space, geometrical representations are of primary importance, even where non-geometrical aspects or behaviour are the subjects of the design activity. However, there are several general problems associated with the representation of geometrical form, of which we now briefly discuss two.

Faithful forms

As previously discussed, depending on which attributes of an object are identified, a representation is an approximation, to a greater or lesser extent. A *faithful* representation is one which incorporates all those attributes necessary to the design or analysis being performed. As an example, consider a box-shaped object (Figure 1.3). We represent this in three different ways: as a wire-frame model (Chapter 5); as a surface model (Chapter 6); and as a solid model (Chapter 9). Figure 1.3 illustrates the distinction between the three representations by considering a transverse cross-sectional plane.

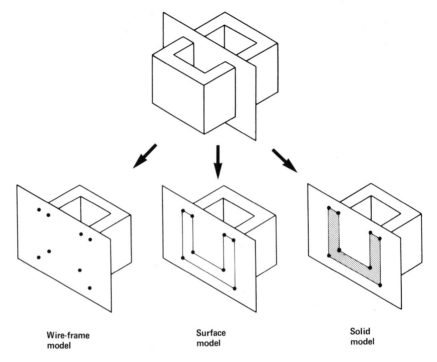

Fig. 1.3 Faithful wire-frame, surface and solid representations of a box

Wire-frame model

Surface model

Solid model

For the wire-frame model the box is represented as a collection of corner points and edge lines — its cross-section is just a set of disconnected (edge) points. This representation is faithful if we are only interested in the general shape, position, orientation or appearance of the box, for example.

For the surface model the box is represented as a collection of corner points, edge lines and face surfaces — its cross-section is now a set of (edge) points and (face) lines. This representation is faithful if we are interested in the appearance of the external surfaces, or if we wish to machine those surfaces from a (blank) solid shape, for example.

Finally, for the solid model the box is represented as a collection of corner points, edge lines, face surfaces and interior volumes — its cross-section is now a set of (edge) points, (face) lines and interior (section) plane segments. This representation is faithful if we are interested in mass properties (such as weight, moments and products of inertia, etc.), dynamic properties (such as momentum, angular momentum, etc.), or material properties (such as opacity, stress/strain characteristics, and so on), although, for some of these, extra non-shape-related attributes must be incorporated. In addition, the solid model enables the interference and/or interaction of two or more objects to be determined — a wire-frame model is relatively useless here, since two such wire-frame objects can easily interpenetrate without their corners or edges being affected.

Indeterminate forms
Often a simple representation, which is considered to be adequate for the task in hand, can give rise to unexpected problems. Such is the case with some two-dimensional representations of three-dimensional objects. A standard form of this type is the first angle or third angle projection of an object (Chapter 3). In general, the three orthographic two-dimensional views of the object can be

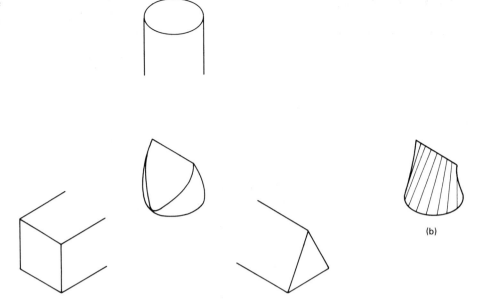

Fig. 1.4 Indeterminate representation of form. (a) Screwdriver tip. (b) Conoid

(b)

(a)

considered to be three prismatic 'solids' which mutually intersect and so define the three-dimensional object. But indeterminate forms can occur. The example shown in Figure 1.4 illustrates the situation.

Here, the three views are an isosceles triangle, a square and a circle, giving rise to three prismatic solids — a triangular prism, a square prism and a circular cylinder, respectively. The resulting mutual intersection is an object with the shape of the tip of a screw-driver. Unfortunately this is not the only object which has these three orthographic views, since the conoid, shown in Figure 1.4(b), also gives rise to these. In fact any object, lying between the screw-driver tip and the conoid in shape and volume, will also satisfy these conditions provided its three views have the same triangular, square and circular profiles. Clearly the two-dimensional views must contain more information in order to represent faithfully a particular object from this infinite collection.

4 Declarative vs. procedural representations

There exist two fundamentally different approaches to the problem of describing objects and systems, namely: **declarative** representations and **procedural** representations. The difference between them is essentially that between a description of the *state* of the object, and a description of the *process* needed to obtain the object. It is a bit like the difference between the physical shape of a cake and the recipe for making the cake, or between a knitted garment and the knitting pattern for producing the garment.

A more relevant comparison here is that between an object represented by its geometrical shape (in terms of points, lines, surfaces and so on), and one represented by the numerically-controlled (NC) machine-tool cutter path instructions for machining it. However, the distinction is not just one between design and manufacturing, or between CAD and CAM, as might be supposed from the above. Both types of representation occur solely within CAD, and particularly within geometric modelling. Thus a wire-frame model of a tetrahedron (Chapter 5) can be constructed as a *set* of four vertices and six edges (declarative representation), or as an ordered *sequence* of six directed edges to be traversed in tracing out its shape (procedural representation). This is illustrated in Figure 1.5.

Fig. 1.5 Declarative and procedural forms of a tetrahedron

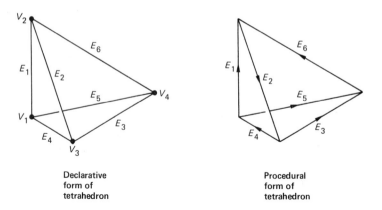

Declarative
form of
tetrahedron

Procedural
form of
tetrahedron

Notice that, in general, a polyhedral shape cannot be traced out *unicursally* (that is, in one unbroken sequence of different edges) and so its procedural representation would consist of more than one sequence of directed edges (consider the cube, for example). Of course, this is also true of declarative representations, since often a shape is described by more than one set of vertices and edges, etc., particularly if it is constructed or assembled from simpler primitive shapes (Chapter 9).

Declarative form
A declarative representation of an object or system is rather like a noun in that it is characterised by *labels* (such as variable *names,* etc.), and by *statements* about those labels (such as *equations* relating the variable names, etc.). Generally a declarative form involves: *extrinsic* attributes and properties of the

object, such as its position and orientation relative to an external frame of reference (Chapters 3 and 11); *global* geometry, with respect to a 'world' coordinate system (Chapters 3 and 5); and *implicit* spatial relations, such as constraint equations expressing relationships between the coordinates of points on the object (Chapters 7 and 8).

The declarative form of an object generally must represent both topological and geometrical aspects. Usually this is achieved in terms of various **primitive declarative forms** and attributes which include:

- *vertices, edges* and *faces*;
- *points, lines, surfaces* and *volumes*;
- *position* and *orientation*;
- *equality* and *inequality*.

Most of these are expressed using an *algebraic analytical* formulation.

Procedural form

A procedural representation of an object or system is rather like a verb in that it is characterised by *actions* (such as spatial *movements*, etc.), and by *instructions* about those actions (such as *rules* specifying the spatial movements, etc.). Generally a procedural form involves: *intrinsic* attributes and properties of the object, such as its shape relative to an internal frame of reference (Chapters 2 and 16); *local* geometry, with respect to a local coordinate system (Chapters 6, 7, 8 and 11); and *explicit* spatial relations, such as parametric equations or rules specifying relative movements of points, lines or surfaces, in terms of some parameter(s) (Chapters 2, 7 and 8).

The procedural form of an object generally must represent both topological and geometrical aspects. Usually this is achieved in terms of various **primitive procedural forms** and attributes which include:

- *paths* and *cycles*;
- *pointers* and *records*;
- *translation* and *rotation*;
- *algorithms* and *procedures*.

Most of these are expressed using an *iterative* (or *recursive*) *synthetical* formulation.

5 Mathematical tools and techniques

In this section we briefly present some important mathematical tools and techniques used in both declarative and procedural representations of spatial form.

5.1 Graphs

In modelling the *interrelationships* of the component parts of an object (Chapters 5 and 9), the *spatial relations* of the component objects of a system (Chapters 2, 9, 11 and 12), or the *interconnections* of the components of an assembly (Chapters 9, 11 and 13), it is generally useful to introduce the concept of a *graph*. This is not the familiar graphical relationship between two or more variables, illustrating a mathematical function. Instead, here a graph consists of a set of elements, usually denoted by points and termed **vertices**, together with a list of unordered pairs of these elements, usually denoted by lines and termed **edges** (Figure 1.6(a)). Each vertex then represents an object (or component) and each edge joins a pair of vertices if and only if the two objects these represent are related (or connected).

Fig. 1.6 (a) A graph consisting of vertices and edges. (b) A digraph consisting of vertices and directed edges

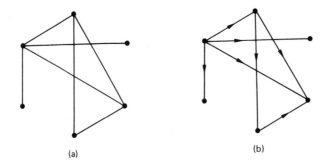

(a)   (b)

In a graph the set of vertices is referred to as the **vertex-set** or **vertex-list**, whereas the list of edges is naturally termed the **edge-list** (Chapters 2, 5, 9 and 13). Often it is useful to consider each edge to be *directed* so that it becomes an *ordered* pair of vertices. In this case the directed edges (or **arcs**) usually indicate some precedence, or ordering, amongst the vertices, such as is present in a hierarchy of component parts and sub-assemblies of a system. The graph is then termed a directed graph or **digraph** (Figure 1.6(b)). Both graphs and digraphs can have labels associated with their vertices (or their edges), to distinguish them or to indicate physical attributes or constraints, such as *mass, strength* of relationship, *type* of connection, and so on. They are then naturally referred to as **labelled (di)graphs**. Similarly, if either consists of just one connected set of vertices and edges, it is termed a **connected (di)graph**.

Certain aspects of graphs and digraphs are especially relevant in the context of CAD. In particular the concepts of a path and of a cycle occur frequently. A **path** is a connected sequence of edges in which all edges are distinct and in which all vertices are distinct. A **cycle** is a closed path such that the first vertex and the final vertex are the same.

Paths arise in procedural forms to indicate the tracing (or in CAM, the cutting) of a shape. They also occur in the context of searching (or traversing) a graph (Chapter 17).

Cycles arise in several situations but particularly in declarative forms where special types of cycle — the **faces** of an object — are singled out (Chapters 5 and 9). They also occur in jointed mechanical assemblies, as kinematic loops (Chapter 11).

One final aspect to be mentioned is the *degree* of a vertex in a graph. This is simply the number of edges meeting at the vertex. It is then often convenient and useful to list the degrees of all the vertices in a graph in 'non-decreasing' order of magnitude. Such a list is termed the *degree-sequence* of the graph, and it can be used to represent the topology of an object (Chapter 9).

Two important types of graph arise frequently in CAD, namely **bipartite graphs** and **trees.**

Bipartite graphs

A bipartite graph is a graph whose vertex-set can be split into two disjoint subsets, such that each edge of the graph joins a vertex of one subset to a vertex of the other subset (Figure 1.7(a)). Each pair of vertices within one of the subsets is *not* joined by any edge. Bipartite graphs are useful in CAD for representing the relationships of inputs to outputs, such as occurs in electronic design, for example (Chapter 12).

Fig. 1.7 (a) A bipartite graph. (b) A tree graph

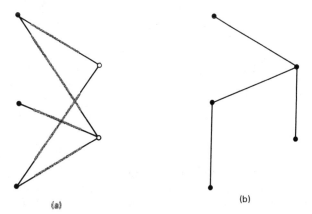

(a)　　　　　　　　　　　(b)

Trees

A tree is a connected graph which contains no cycles (Figure 1.7(b)). There is then only one path from any one vertex to any other within the tree. Trees are useful in CAD for representing the relationships amongst primitives or amongst objects in an assembly (Chapter 9) and for representing hierarchical designs, data structures and databases (Chapters 13, 16 and 17). In CAD these tree structures are constructed using various computational tools, such as pointers and records.

For a tree, if the number of vertices is n then the number of edges must be $(n - 1)$.

5.2 Coordinates

In modelling the geometry of objects, components or systems (see most chapters) an indispensable mathematical tool is that of a **coordinate system,** particularly for declarative representations. Essentially a coordinate system provides a framework for labelling basic geometrical entities such as points, lines and surfaces. It enables individual points, for example, to be recognised and/or distinguished from one another, but in addition, it achieves this in a systematic way so that, in a sense, it is more than just a labelling system.

There are two general ways in which coordinate systems are used in CAD, namely:

- to label the points of (empty) space, and so to provide a reference *world coordinate system* for locating the positions and orientations of objects, and for describing their movements (Figure 1.8(a));
- to label the points of objects, and so to provide a reference *local coordinate system* for describing the shape of objects, and for monitoring changes of shape (Figure 1.8(b)).

Fig. 1.8 Coordinates used: (a) to label the points of space; (b) to label the points of objects

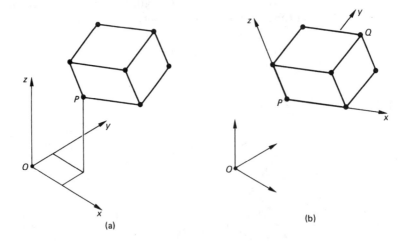

Coordinates can be used to label: an uncountably infinite set of points (such as the points on a line, surface or volume); a countably infinite set of points (such as the integer points along a line or the intersection points of a grid); or a finite set of points (such as the pixel locations on a computer graphics screen).

The coordinates of a point consist of an ordered set of numbers locating the point with respect to some reference point (the *origin*) and some reference lines (the coordinate *directions*).

Usually a point in one-dimensional space is specified by a single coordinate; a point in two-dimensional space by two coordinates; and a point in three-dimensional space by three coordinates. However, it is often convenient to use more than the minimum number of coordinates to label points in order to clarify the representation, or in order to simplify some subsequent operations of transformations on the points. Thus in a two-dimensional isometric projection of an object (Chapter 3), the points are often labelled with *three* coordinates (corresponding to the three directions on the underlying isometric grid). Similarly, points in three-dimensional space are often labelled with *four* (homogeneous) coordinates in order to provide a unified representation for rotations, translations and projections of objects.

Many different coordinate systems have been devised but we briefly consider only the following three types.

Cartesian coordinates

The cartesian coordinate system is perhaps the most familar type. In two-dimensional space, points are labelled with two cartesian coordinates — the *x*-coordinate and the *y*-coordinate — and are represented by the ordered *pair* of variables (x, y).

The *x*- and *y*-coordinates of a point are evaluated with respect to: a chosen origin; two mutually orthogonal axes intersecting at this origin; and a specified scale for measuring distance (Figure 1.9(a)).

The value given to the *x*-coordinate (*y*-coordinate) of a particular point is then its distance along the *x*-direction (*y*-direction) from the origin. Alternatively the value is given by the distance of the point from the *y*-axis (*x*-axis), but note that, in a more refined treatment of cartesian coordinates, this value would not be the same as the previous one in general (consider, for example, an oblique coordinate system).

Fig. 1.9 Coordinate systems in two-dimensional space: (a) cartesian coordinates; (b) polar coordinates; (c) homogeneous coordinates

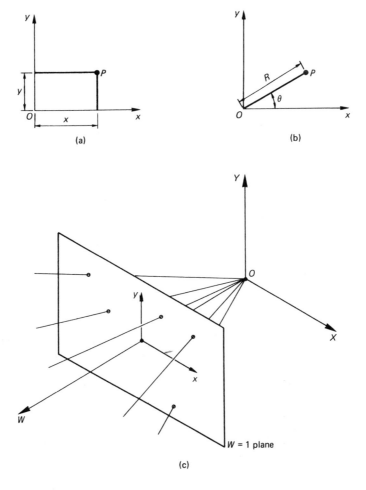

(a)

(b)

(c)

The above two-dimensional cartesian coordinate system extends in a natural way into three-dimensional space, where a point is then represented by an ordered *triple* of coordinate variables (x, y, z).

Cartesian coordinate systems are ubiquitous and often form the basis on which other systems are constructed. In particular, many other types of coordinate system are specified in terms of cartesian systems by relating the 'new' coordinates to the equivalent 'old' cartesian coordinates.

Polar coordinates

Polar coordinate systems are also a very familiar type. They are used in situations where the positions of points are more conveniently specified in terms of a *range* and a *bearing* (that is, the distance and the direction from some fixed origin), or where there is some form of *central symmetry* in the represented objects and/or their positions.

In two-dimensional space, points are labelled with two polar coordinates, R and θ, and they are represented by the ordered pair (R, θ). The R-coordinate of a point is evaluated as the radial distance of the point from a chosen origin point. The θ-coordinate is evaluated as the angle between some fixed axis through the origin and the radial line from the origin to the point (Figure 1.9(b)).

The polar coordinates of a point in two-dimensional space are related to its cartesian coordinates by the relationships

$$x = R \cos \theta$$

$$y = R \sin \theta \tag{1}$$

where cos and sin are the cosine and sine trigonometric functions, respectively.

Polar coordinates can be extended into three-dimensional space in several ways. Thus **cylindrical polar coordinates** introduce the third dimension essentially by 'extruding' the two-dimensional polar coordinate system in an orthogonal (z) direction. Points are then represented by the ordered triple of coordinate variables (R, θ, z), and this system is useful for describing prismatic or axially symmetric shapes and relationships. Cylindrical polar coordinates are related to the equivalent cartesian coordinates by

$$x = R \cos \theta$$

$$y = R \sin \theta$$

$$z = z \tag{2}$$

The other common system is **spherical polar coordinates** which introduce the third dimension essentially by 'tilting' the two-dimensional polar coordinate system out of its plane by an angle ϕ. Points are then represented by the ordered triple of coordinate variables (R, θ, ϕ), and this system is useful for describing centrally symmetric shapes and relationships. Spherical polar coordinates are related to the equivalent cartesian coordinates by

$$x = R \sin \phi \cos \theta$$

$$y = R \sin \phi \sin \theta$$

$$z = R \cos \phi \tag{3}$$

Homogeneous coordinates

Homogeneous coordinates were originally introduced as a device to facilitate a unified treatment of various geometrical transformations, particularly those arising in projective geometry, such as perspective, linear, affine and rigid transformations (Chapters 3 and 14). The approach is based on the idea of replacing each point of a space by an associated line in a space of higher dimension.

Figure 1.9(c) illustrates the situation for a two-dimensional space. This xy-space is identified with the $W = 1$ plane of an XYW three-dimensional space. Then each point of the two-dimensional space is associated with the straight line joining it to the origin of the three-dimensional space. The association is one-to-one and it has the advantage that relatively complicated transformations on the points of the two-dimensional space can often be replaced by simpler transformations on the associated lines in the three-dimensional space.

Fig. 1.10 A transformation using homogeneous coordinates

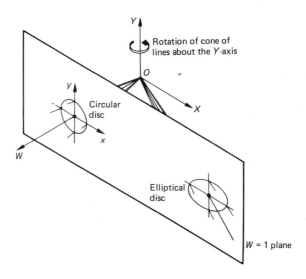

An example of this is illustrated by Figure 1.10, where we show a circular disc transformed into an elliptical 'disc', and displaced in position. In terms of the points defining the disc in the two-dimensional space, the transformation is relatively complicated. But in terms of the associated lines in the three-dimensional space the transformation is a simple rotation.

Homogeneous coordinates are essentially based on cartesian coordinates. But in the current example it is *not* the cartesian coordinate system of the two-dimensional space that is used, but rather the cartesian coordinate system of the three-dimensional space (Figure 1.9(c)). A point with two coordinates (x, y) in the two-dimensional space is represented by the *three* homogeneous coordinates (X, Y, W) of some point on the associated line in the three-dimensional space. Any such point on the line can be used, since it is the whole line that is associated, but this then implies that the homogeneous coordinates (X, Y, W) of the point in two-dimensional space are *not* unique. However, although the triple of coordinates (X, Y, W) is different for each point on the line, the two ratios X/W and Y/W will be the same for every such point. This

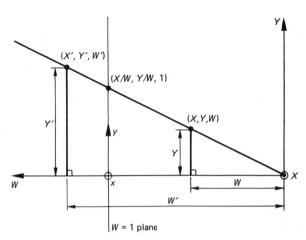

Fig. 1.11 Any two sets of homogeneous coordinates (X, Y, W) and (X', Y', W') for the same point in two-dimensional space have the same ratios, so that $X/W = X'/W'$ and $Y/W = Y'/W'$

is easily demonstrated using similar triangles and it depends on the fact that the line passes through the origin of the three-dimensional space (Figure 1.11).

In the same way it is easily seen that if the point with coordinates (X, Y, W) lies on the line, then so also does a point with coordinates $(\lambda X, \lambda Y, \lambda W)$ for any choice of λ. By choosing $\lambda = 1/W$, we obtain the unique point with coordinates $(X/W, Y/W, 1)$ which clearly lies on the $W = 1$ plane (the original two-dimensional space). It is convenient to use this point, wherever possible.

From the above discussion we are now able to relate the homogeneous coordinates (X, Y, W) of a point in two-dimensional space to its cartesian coordinates (x, y). The relationship is

$$x = X/W$$
$$y = Y/W \tag{4}$$

Homogeneous coordinates can be extended into three-dimensional space using similar ideas, and a point with cartesian coordinates (x, y, z) is then represented by *four* homogeneous coordinates (X, Y, Z, W). The relationship between these again has the form

$$x = X/W$$
$$y = Y/W$$
$$z = Z/W \tag{5}$$

5.3 Vectors

Many physical quantities and attributes, such as force, velocity, acceleration, angular velocity, momentum and angular momentum, have both a *magnitude* and a *spatial direction* associated with them. Such quantities are usually termed **vectors** and are represented geometrically by straight-line segments with an arrowhead on one end indicating the sense of the direction. The length of the line segment represents the magnitude of the physical quantity, and two such vectors are equal if and only if they have the same magnitudes *and* the same directions.

In a similar way many purely geometrical entities, such as lines tangent to curves (Chapter 7), lines normal to surfaces (Chapter 8), and axes of rotation (Chapter 11), can also be modelled by vectors. In these cases there is a direct association between the vector-line segments and the geometry being represented.

Perhaps the best-known archetypal vector is the **position vector** of a point in space with respect to some origin. This is simply identified with the straight-line segment joining the origin to the point, and it faithfully represents the position or the displacement of the point relative to the origin (Figure 1.12). Its magnitude is just the distance of the point from the origin.

Fig. 1.12 The position vector **r** of a point in two-dimensional space

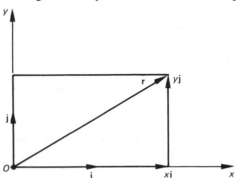

Conventionally a position vector is written **r**, with its magnitude denoted $|\mathbf{r}|$. In two-dimensional space it can be expressed in terms of the cartesian coordinates (x, y) of the point, in the form

$$\mathbf{r} = x\mathbf{i} + y\mathbf{j} \qquad (6)$$

where **i** and **j** are vectors of *unit* magnitude in the directions of the x- and y-axes, respectively. Equation (6) and Figure 1.12 together indicate that a direct displacement from the origin to the point is equivalent to two *component* displacements consisting of a move through a distance x in the x-direction, followed by a move through a distance y in the y-direction. The standard addition symbol '+' is used for this combination of moves and the idea generalises to allow any two vectors to be added. Geometrically, the line segments corresponding to two vectors form two sides of a triangle, and their sum is simply the third side of the triangle. To add two vectors we therefore 'complete the triangle'.

Strictly speaking this 'triangle law' is part of the definition of a vector. Those quantities which have magnitude and direction but which cannot be added consistently using this triangle addition are not vectors. An example of such a 'failed vector' is afforded by the angular displacement of an object in three-dimensional space. This has magnitude (the angle turned through), and direction (the axis of rotation), but two such angular displacements do not combine in the manner required by the triangle law.

In three-dimensional space a position vector **r** can be expressed in terms of the cartesian coordinates (x, y, z) of the point, in the form

$$\mathbf{r} = x\mathbf{i} + y\mathbf{j} + z\mathbf{k} \qquad (7)$$

where $\mathbf{i}, \mathbf{j}$ and $\mathbf{k}$ are vectors of unit magnitude in the x-, y- and z-directions, respectively. This time the vector is expressed as the sum of *three* component displacements but the situation is essentially the same as before.

By analogy with the position vector and its components, we consider any vector to have two (three) components in two-dimensional (three-dimensional) space. For example, a force (such as weight) acting on an object, might be represented in three-dimensional space by the vector

$$\mathbf{F} = F_x\mathbf{i} + F_y\mathbf{j} + F_z\mathbf{k} \tag{8}$$

where F_x, F_y and F_z are its three components in the x-, y- and z-directions respectively. Two such vectors are then equal if and only if their respective x-, y- and z-components are individually equal.

Often a single vector will suffice to represent an attribute of an object (its velocity, for example), but in more complicated situations a collection of vectors (a **vector field**) is required. Such is the case for fluid motion, where each individual fluid element has a different velocity, for example. The same is true for the field of tangent vectors along a curve (Chapter 7), or of normal vectors across a surface (Chapter 8).

In such cases each vector in the vector field must be considered to be *bound* at its tail end-point, and only vectors sharing the same tail end-point can be added or combined. Here, although those vectors at 'adjacent' or 'nearby' points *cannot* be combined, they *are* usually related in some systematic pattern which can be specified mathematically (usually in terms of derivatives or rates of change).

Less restrictive constraints on a vector sometimes occur where the vectors are bound to lines rather than to points. These **line vectors** arise in rigid body motion where they represent axes of rotation, lines of action of forces and so on (Chapter 11).

The least restrictive situation occurs in the case of **free vectors**. One of the simplest examples of this is afforded by a rigid body moving with uniform velocity in a straight line. All points of the body have the same velocity, and so a single (free) velocity vector will suffice to represent the motion.

For bound vectors more information must be included in the representation than just the vectors themselves. Thus, for example, the points or lines, to which the vectors are bound, must be represented, as also must the relationships amongst the vectors.

The dot product

We have so far shown how vectors are added (and subtracted) using the triangle law to give another vector. But it is also possible to 'multiply' vectors in various ways. The first type of multiplication we consider is termed the *dot product*. For two vectors **a** and **b** this is defined by

$$\mathbf{a} \cdot \mathbf{b} = |\mathbf{a}||\mathbf{b}| \cos \theta \tag{9}$$

where θ is the angle between the line segments denoting **a** and **b** (Figure 1.13(a)). If the dot product of two non-zero vectors is zero, then the vectors are mutually perpendicular.

This product is not strictly a true multiplication since the dot product of two vectors is not another vector but just a number (a scalar). However, it is very useful in practice particularly for deriving vector expressions, or for denoting relationships amongst vectors (Chapters 7 and 8).

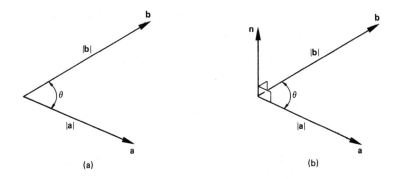

Fig. 1.13 Multiplying vectors: (a) the dot product; (b) the cross product

(a) (b)

The cross product

Another type of multiplication for vectors is termed the *cross product*. For two vectors **a** and **b** in three-dimensional space, this is defined by

$$\mathbf{a} \times \mathbf{b} = |\mathbf{a}||\mathbf{b}| \sin \theta \ \mathbf{n} \tag{10}$$

where θ is the angle between the line segments denoting **a** and **b**, and **n** is a vector of unit magnitude which is orthogonal to both **a** and **b** (Figure 1.13(b)). The sense of direction for **n** is defined to be such that the three vectors **a, b** and **n** form a *right-handed system,* so that rotating **a** through angle θ into **b** would advance a right-handed screw in the direction of **n**. If the cross product of two non-zero vectors is zero, then the vectors are parallel or anti-parallel.

Although the cross product of two vectors yields another vector it is still not a true multiplication in the normal sense, because it is both

non-commutative, that is $\mathbf{a} \times \mathbf{b} \neq \mathbf{b} \times \mathbf{a}$, and

non-associative, that is $(\mathbf{a} \times \mathbf{b}) \times \mathbf{c} \neq \mathbf{a} \times (\mathbf{b} \times \mathbf{c})$

However, like the dot product, it is very useful in the derivation of vector relationships and equations (Chapters 7 and 8).

A true multiplication operation for vectors is possible only in two-dimensional space. In three- and higher-dimensional spaces such a product has been proven to be impossible to define consistently, and we do not discuss this further here.

Row vectors and column vectors

The position vector **r** discussed previously was written in terms of its components in equation (7). In this particular case the components can be considered to be the cartesian coordinates of the point, normally written as the ordered triple (x, y, z). The **i, j** and **k** unit vectors are implicitly understood here from the ordering. In a similar way we can write the components of a force vector **F** (equation (8)) as an ordered triple (F_x, F_y, F_z), where again **i, j** and **k** are understood from the ordering.

When vectors are written in this form as an ordered sequence or row of their components they are termed **row vectors**. Often an alternative similar form is used where the components are written as a column, and this is the **column vector**.

In terms of row vectors, the addition, subtraction, dot product and cross product of two vectors

$$\mathbf{a} = (a_x, a_y, a_z) \quad \text{and} \quad \mathbf{b} = (b_x, b_y, b_z)$$

are given respectively by

$$\mathbf{a} + \mathbf{b} = (a_x + b_x, a_y + b_y, a_z + b_z)$$

$$\mathbf{a} - \mathbf{b} = (a_x - b_x, a_y - b_y, a_z - b_z)$$

$$\mathbf{a} \cdot \mathbf{b} = a_x b_x + a_y b_y + a_z b_z$$

$$\mathbf{a} \times \mathbf{b} = (a_y b_z - a_z b_y, a_z b_x - a_x b_z, a_x b_y - a_y b_x) \tag{11}$$

Similar expressions exist for column vectors.

These row and column forms are very useful for the purposes of CAD since they are easily implemented on a computer and provide a natural scheme for combining, manipulating and transforming vectors.

5.4 Matrices

There are many situations in representing objects and systems where a rectangular array of quantities arises, and such arrays are termed **matrices.** In the previous sub-section we considered two special cases of this, namely: a row vector (a (1×3) array) and a column vector (a (3×1) array) in three-dimensional space. In general a matrix is an $(n \times m)$ array and the individual quantities comprising the matrix are termed its **elements.** In its simplest form a matrix is just a convenient tabulation of quantities (cf. the truth tables in Chapter 12). However, various special types of matrix have been constructed which are used in CAD, and we now consider some of these.

Adjacency and incidence matrices

As previously discussed, a graph is often used for representing the interrelationships amongst objects and components. Usually two different types of matrix are then constructed to provide a formal description of the graph. The **adjacency matrix** is set up as a representation of the adjacency relationships of the graph (that is, representing which vertices are directly connected via single edges). The **incidence matrix** is set up as a representation of the incidence relationships of the graph (that is, representing which edges are incident at which vertices).

For a graph with n vertices the adjacency matrix is an $(n \times n)$ square array with each column and each row representing a vertex. Then if, for example, an edge connects vertex 2 to vertex 3 on the graph, we place a 1 at the intersection of row 2 and column 3 in the matrix. If no edge connects these vertices we place a zero at this position. An adjacency matrix is therefore a square matrix of zeros and ones. For the wire-frame model of the tetrahedron (Figure 1.5) the graph has four vertices and an adjacency matrix is

$$\begin{bmatrix} 0 & 1 & 1 & 1 \\ 1 & 0 & 1 & 1 \\ 1 & 1 & 0 & 1 \\ 1 & 1 & 1 & 0 \end{bmatrix}$$

Notice that usually for physical objects, no vertex is connected to itself, so that this matrix has only zeros on the leading diagonal. Notice also that for a graph (rather than a digraph) if vertex 2 is connected to vertex 3 by an edge then so also is vertex 3 connected to vertex 2. This symmetrical relationship is reflected in the symmetry of the adjacency matrix about the leading diagonal.

For a graph with n vertices and m edges, the incidence matrix is an $(n \times m)$ rectangular array with each row representing a vertex and each column representing an edge. Then, if edge 4 meets vertex 2 on the graph, we place a 1 at the intersection of row 2 and column 4 in the matrix. Otherwise we place a zero there. For the tetrahedron of Figure 1.5 the graph has four vertices and six edges, so an incidence matrix is

$$\begin{bmatrix} 1 & 1 & 1 & 0 & 0 & 0 \\ 1 & 0 & 0 & 1 & 0 & 1 \\ 0 & 1 & 0 & 1 & 1 & 0 \\ 0 & 0 & 1 & 0 & 1 & 1 \end{bmatrix}$$

In general, neither adjacency matrices nor incidence matrices are unique for a particular graph since they depend on how the vertices and edges are labelled, and associated with rows and columns.

Coefficient matrices

The other major area in which matrices are used widely is as **coefficient matrices**, representing spatial relationships between pairs of objects, or representing transformations of particular objects and spaces. The archetypal situation arises where an object is moved or transformed in space and its new position has 'new' coordinates related to the 'old' (before the move) coordinates by linear mathematical relationships (that is, expressions containing terms of no higher than the first power). As an example consider a simple rotation in two-dimensional space (Figure 1.14).

Fig. 1.14 A rotation through angle θ about the origin in two-dimensional space

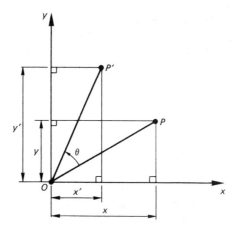

Here the new cartesian coordinates (x', y') of a point are related to the old coordinates (x, y) by the linear relationships

$$x' = \cos \theta \ x - \sin \theta \ y$$

$$y' = \sin \theta \ x + \cos \theta \ y \tag{12}$$

where θ is the angle of rotation. This is a special case of the more general linear transformation involving shear, scaling and reflection, as well as rotation, but not translation (Chapter 3), which has the form

$$x' = a_1 x + b_1 y$$

$$y' = a_2 x + b_2 y \qquad (13)$$

The standard mathematical form for expressing this involves the coefficients a_1, b_1, a_2 and b_2 in a coefficient matrix, and we write equation (13) as the matrix equation

$$\begin{bmatrix} x' \\ y' \end{bmatrix} = \begin{bmatrix} a_1 & b_1 \\ a_2 & b_2 \end{bmatrix} \begin{bmatrix} x \\ y \end{bmatrix} \qquad (14)$$

We can interpret this on the simplest level as just a convenient shorthand for equation (13) but on a higher level it has given rise to powerful matrix techniques for representing and processing geometrical transformations (Chapters 7 and 8). In addition, matrix techniques have spread into many other non-geometrical areas as useful computational tools (Chapter 10).

The basis for all these techniques is the interpretation of equations like (14), as a *matrix product*. Thus the coefficient matrix (pre)multiplies the column matrix of old coordinates to produce a column matrix of new coordinates, using equations like (13) to interpret (or define) how to perform the matrix multiplication. The situation has been generalised for larger sets of linear equations in more variables, and an algebra for matrices has been constructed to enable equations such as (13) to be solved purely in terms of the coefficient matrices (Chapter 10). Many powerful computational procedures have also been derived to assist in processing matrices, since they have a very convenient and natural form for computation.

Matrix algebra and matrix computational techniques enable matrices to be added, subtracted (both in a component- or element-wise fashion), multiplied (as above) and inverted (the equivalent of division) in general. Two matrices are equal if and only if they have the same size and 'shape' and corresponding elements are equal. Two matrices can be multiplied if and only if they are compatible in shape. Thus an $(n \times m)$ matrix can only (pre)multiply an $(m \times p)$ matrix, and so on.

5.5 Rates of change

In modelling the shapes of objects, the concepts of 'continuity', of 'curvature', and of 'smoothness' of shape arise naturally. Similarly, the representation of many physical attributes of objects, such as their spatial deformations under mechanical or thermal stresses, or their temporal responses to various external mechanical, thermal or electrical stimuli, involve the idea of a rate of change of some quantity. Such aspects as smoothness, continuity and rates of change are generally modelled in terms of the calculus, which involves the techniques of *differentiation* and *integration* of mathematical functions. We do not intend to deal with these techniques here, but instead we briefly introduce some of the concepts used. Later chapters (notably Chapters 7, 8 and 10) then make use of these concepts, without derivation.

If a shape is described by a mathematical function we can also describe the

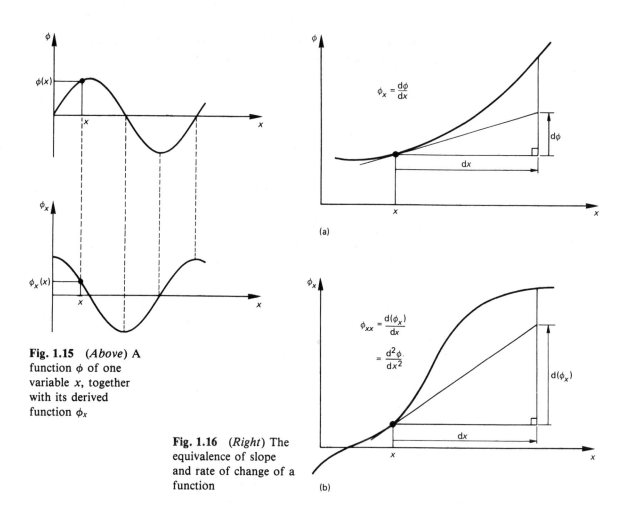

Fig. 1.15 (*Above*) A function ϕ of one variable x, together with its derived function ϕ_x

Fig. 1.16 (*Right*) The equivalence of slope and rate of change of a function

$$\phi_x = \frac{d\phi}{dx}$$

(a)

$$\phi_{xx} = \frac{d(\phi_x)}{dx}$$

$$= \frac{d^2\phi}{dx^2}$$

(b)

continuity, the curvature and the smoothness of the shape by *differentiating* this function, and examining the resulting *derived function*. We represent a 'one-dimensional' shape (such as the stretched string of Chapter 10) by a function ϕ of one variable, say x (Figure 1.15).

By referring to Figure 1.15 we see that the value of ϕ at some point with coordinate x is denoted by $\phi(x)$, and that all such values collectively define the shape. The derived function, or **derivative** of ϕ, with respect to x, is then another function of x, denoted by ϕ_x, and *its* value at the point with coordinate x (that is, $\phi_x(x)$) represents the *rate of change* of ϕ with respect to x, at that point. Thus if ϕ_x suffers a relatively large (small) change in value as we move through a relatively small (large) change in the x-coordinate, then ϕ has a high (low) rate of change in that particular vicinity of x.

Geometrically, if the shape represented by the function ϕ rises or falls steeply (gently) then ϕ has a high (low) rate of change. Figure 1.16 illustrates the equivalence of *slope* and rate of change, in terms of the tangent line to the curve. The steepness of this tangent line is specified by considering it to be the hypotenuse of any right-angled triangle with a 'vertical' side and a 'horizontal' side, as shown. The slope is then given by the *ratio* of the length of the vertical side to that of the horizontal side. If these lengths are denoted by $d\phi$

(indicating a *change* in the ϕ-direction) and by $\mathrm{d}x$ (indicating a *change* in the x-direction), respectively, we can write the derived function ϕ_x as the ratio $\mathrm{d}\phi/\mathrm{d}x$. This latter form is a very common notation for derivatives.

The above ideas can be extended, so that we can consider taking the derivative of ϕ_x to produce the second derived function of ϕ. This **second derivative** is denoted ϕ_{xx}, and its value at the point with coordinate x is written $\phi_{xx}(x)$. The function ϕ_{xx} describes the rate of change of the rate of change of ϕ with respect to x, and it can be used to represent the *curvature* and the *smoothness* of the shape.

Figure 1.16 illustrates the basis on which ϕ_{xx} is commonly written as a ratio. Thus as with the first derivative we construct a right-angled triangle, but this time for the ϕ_x curve rather than for ϕ. The length of the vertical side is denoted by $\mathrm{d}(\phi_x)$ or by $\mathrm{d}(\mathrm{d}\phi/\mathrm{d}x)$ (to indicate a *change* in the $\mathrm{d}\phi/\mathrm{d}x$-direction), and the length of the horizontal side is denoted again by $\mathrm{d}x$ (indicating a *change* in the x-direction). The slope of the tangent line to the ϕ_x curve is then given by the ratio

$$\mathrm{d}(\mathrm{d}\phi/\mathrm{d}x)/\mathrm{d}x \quad \text{or more simply in the form} \quad \mathrm{d}^2\phi/\mathrm{d}x^2$$

This is the common notation for second derivatives.

Further derived functions can be obtained by differentiating ϕ_{xx} to obtain ϕ_{xxx} (usually written as $\mathrm{d}^3\phi/\mathrm{d}x^3$), and so on, but we do not pursue this further here. Instead we briefly discuss the situation where ϕ is a function of two variables, say x and y, representing a two-dimensional shape (Figure 1.17).

Fig. 1.17 A function ϕ of two variables x and y

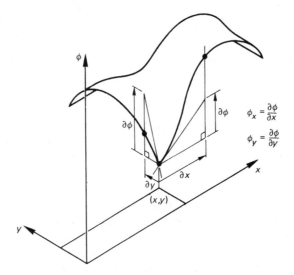

We can now consider the derivative of ϕ with respect to either x or y (or some combination) depending on whether we are interested in the rate of change of ϕ in the x-direction or in the y-direction (or in some other direction in the xy-plane) respectively. As before, the derivative of ϕ with respect to x is denoted by ϕ_x and at the point (x, y) this has the value $\phi_x(x, y)$. Similarly, the derivative of ϕ with respect to y is denoted by ϕ_y, and this has the value $\phi_y(x, y)$ at the point (x, y). The derivative ϕ_x is obtained by differentiating ϕ as if it were a function of only x (that is by ignoring y), and similarly for ϕ_y.

Derivatives with respect to some other direction are obtained as combinations of ϕ_x and ϕ_y. Second (and higher) derivatives ϕ_{xx} (and ϕ_{yy}) can be obtained, as with functions of one variable, but it is now also possible to obtain 'mixed' or 'cross' derivatives, ϕ_{xy} or ϕ_{yx}, etc., which define for example the rate of change in the y-direction of the rate of change in the x-direction of the function ϕ. These cross derivatives are useful in representing the twist or torsion of a two-dimensional shape (Chapter 8).

In discussing the derivative of a function of one variable we introduced the common notation $d\phi/dx$. In the case of a function of two or more variables, however, a slightly different ratio notation is used, which incorporates the symbol '∂' rather than 'd'. Thus $\phi_x, \phi_y, \phi_{xx}$ and ϕ_{xy} are written $\partial\phi/\partial x$, $\partial\phi/\partial y, \partial^2\phi/\partial x^2$ and $\partial^2\phi/\partial y\partial x$, respectively, if ϕ is a function of more than one variable, and they are also then referred to as **partial derivatives**. (If ϕ is a function of only one variable we refer to ϕ_x or $d\phi/dx$ as an **ordinary derivative**.)

An equation involving ordinary (partial) derivatives of functions is termed an ordinary (partial) differential equation. Several examples of these occur in Chapter 10. The solution to such differential equations involves a process which is in many cases the *inverse* of differentiation — that is, *integration*. Single, double and, in general, multiple integrals (analogous to first, second and multiple derivatives) arise depending on how many such inverse operations of integration are performed. These, together with some special types of integral (that is, *line* integrals), also occur in Chapter 10.

Finally we note that if a function is a vector-valued function (such as a variable position vector tracing out a curve or surface), then its derivative, with respect to x, with respect to y or with respect to any other variable or parameter that it is expressed in terms of, is usually another vector-valued function. In other words, the derivative of a vector is usually another vector and, in general, both its magnitude and its direction will differ from those of the original vector (Chapters 7 and 8). However, there are some situations where a vector is obtained by differentiating a scalar (that is a non-vector) function. Such is the case for the gradient, or **grad**, vector operator considered in Chapter 8. And conversely there is an operator (the divergence or **div**) which produces a scalar-valued function by differentiating a vector-valued function.

Representing relations

2

C F Earl

1 Introduction

The previous chapter examined how the shape and geometry of objects are represented for the purposes of computer-aided design (CAD). In order to create these representations within the computer, information must be supplied by the CAD user. This is accomplished using interactive graphics and by invoking commands from CAD software. These commands may do many things, from drawing a line between specified points to displaying different views of objects.

This chapter will examine two operations that the CAD user will want to perform on objects. First, the user may want to *move* objects (perhaps retrieved from a previously created library or file) into different configurations or arrangements. For example, in designing a kitchen layout, standard components such as cookers, sinks, cupboards and worktops are arranged and rearranged in the search for a suitable overall design. Second, the user may want to *create* complex objects from simpler ones. For example, in creating a design for a bottle we might use three different simple shapes for the neck, shoulder and body and 'join' them to form the complete bottle. To do this the three (previously created) simple shapes are moved into the desired relative positions and a command to join them is invoked. This chapter is called 'Representing relations', because in moving and combining objects we are primarily interested in their **spatial relations** to one another. The information required to specify moves and spatial relations will be examined as well as the kinds of representation used within a CAD system. However, in order that these functions of CAD can be used interactively in design it is vital that both the simple objects and the composite objects can be viewed from different angles and at different scales by the user. This requires an interactive computer graphics facility, an aspect which will be examined in the next chapter. For the moment we assume that some means of displaying the objects being designed is available.

2 Moving an object

A triangular prism (object A) is shown in Figure 2.1, together with a list of the (x, y, z)-coordinates (with respect to some reference frame) of its six corner points (vertices). The triangular prism is not just a set of vertices, since it also has edges and faces, which may be expressed as lists of vertices. Edges are expressed as pairs of vertices so that, for example, the pair $\langle P_2, P_3 \rangle$ represents the edge joining vertex P_2 to vertex P_3. Similarly, the list $\langle P_1, P_3, P_4, P_6 \rangle$ represents the face which is parallel to the yz-plane.

Fig. 2.1 A triangular prism

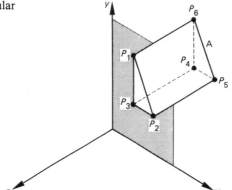

Corner points	Coordinates
P_1	(2, 4.5, 1)
P_2	(3, 2.5, 1)
P_3	(2, 2.5, 1)
P_4	(2, 2.5, −2)
P_5	(3, 2.5, −2)
P_6	(2, 4.5, −2)

When an object is moved, the *coordinate* description of the object changes. However, in other respects the description will remain unchanged. For rigid objects and rigid moves the incidence relations amongst faces, edges and vertex points remain the same, as do the distances between points and the angles between lines.

Before object A is moved, notice that in its initial position the edges $\langle P_3, P_4 \rangle$, $\langle P_1, P_6 \rangle$ and $\langle P_2, P_5 \rangle$ are parallel to the z-axis, whilst edges $\langle P_1, P_3 \rangle$ and $\langle P_4, P_6 \rangle$ are parallel to the y-axis.

We consider two types of move: namely **translation** and **rotation**. Translations move the object along some direction, whereas (in three-dimensional space) rotations turn objects about some line — the axis of the rotation.

2.1 Translation

Figure 2.2 shows object A translated by four units in the direction of the x-axis. This changes the coordinate description of object A. It adds four units to each x-coordinate in the object description, but leaves the y- and z-coordinates unchanged. The move changes coordinates according to the *rule*

$$(x, y, z) \mapsto (x + 4, y, z)$$

The rule specifies that a general point in the object, with initial coordinates (x, y, z), has coordinates $(x + 4, y, z)$ after the move.

A further translation by one unit in the y-direction changes coordinates by the rule

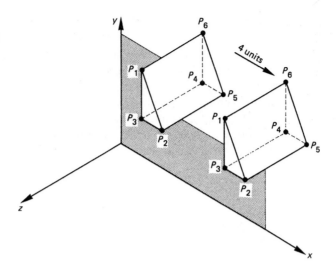

Fig. 2.2 Translating the prism by four units in the x-direction

Corner points	Original coordinates	New coordinates
P_1	(2, 4.5, 1)	(6, 4.5, 1)
P_2	(3, 2.5, 1)	(7, 2.5, 1)
P_3	(2, 2.5, 1)	(6, 2.5, 1)
P_4	(2, 2.5, -2)	(6, 2.5, -2)
P_5	(3, 2.5, -2)	(7, 2.5, -2)
P_6	(2, 4.5, -2)	(6, 4.5, -2)

$$(x, y, z) \mapsto (x, y + 1, z)$$

The combined move changes the coordinates of object A according to the rule

$$(x, y, z) \mapsto (x + 4, y, z) \mapsto (x + 4, y + 1, z)$$

The overall move

$$(x, y, z) \mapsto (x + 4, y + 1, z)$$

has two parts — the translation along four units in the x-direction and the translation along one unit in the y-direction.

A general translation through a units in the x-direction, b units in the y-direction and c units in the z-direction is represented by the rule

$$(x, y, z) \mapsto (x + a, y + b, z + c)$$

In particular, the rule for the translation which moves the point P_3 in object A (Figure 2.1) to the origin is

$$(x, y, z,) \mapsto (x - 2, y - 2.5, z - 1)$$

2.2 Rotation through right angles

We will concentrate on rotations whose axes are parallel to the z-axis. For example, consider a rotation of object A (Figure 2.3) about the z-axis, through $90°$. Before proceeding we explain a convention we will use for rotations. Rotation through a positive angle will take place in a *clockwise* sense when looking along the positive direction of the axes from the origin. To visualise this may require a bit of mental gymnastics, but it is vital to maintain such conventions.

Fig. 2.3 Rotating the prism through $90°$ about the z-axis

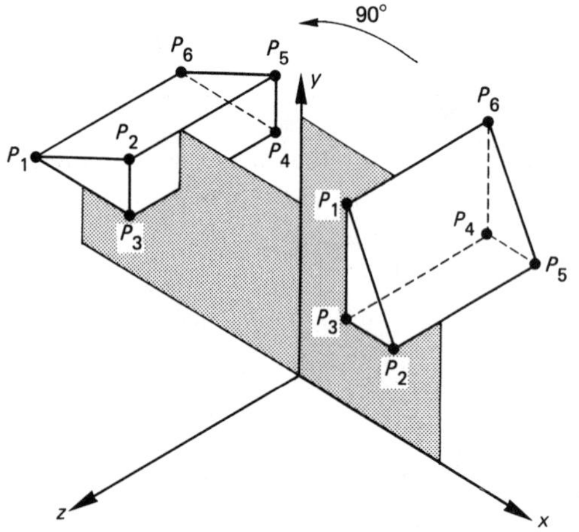

Corner points	Original coordinates	New coordinates
P_1	(2, 4.5, 1)	(−4.5, 2, 1)
P_2	(3, 2.5, 1)	(−2.5, 3, 1)
P_3	(2, 2.5, 1)	(−2.5, 2, 1)
P_4	(2, 2.5, −2)	(−2.5, 2, −2)
P_5	(3, 2.5, −2)	(−2.5, 3, −2)
P_6	(2, 4.5, −2)	(−4.5, 2, −2)

In the rotation through $90°$ (Figure 2.3), all the points on object A have been changed and hence their coordinates have also been changed. The table accompanying Figure 2.3 shows how the coordinates of all the vertex points are changed. However, we would like to represent the move as a rule, similar to that used previously for translations. A suitable rule which produces all of the vertex point moves in Figure 2.3 is

$$(x, y, z) \mapsto (-y, x, z)$$

This rule states that each new x-coordinate is equal to the negative of the old y-coordinate, each new y-coordinate is equal to the old x-coordinate and each z-coordinate remains unchanged.

Now consider a rotation through $90°$ about an axis which is parallel to the z-axis but which passes through the point with coordinates $x = 2$, $y = 2.5$, $z = 0$ (Figure 2.4). When specifying that the axis of rotation is parallel to the z-axis, we assume that this parallel axis has the same positive direction. A rotation through $90°$ will take place in a clockwise sense when looking along the positive direction of this axis from P_3. We are rotating the object about the edge $\langle P_4, P_3 \rangle$. In performing this move all the points on the object change their coordinates, except those on the edge $\langle P_4, P_3 \rangle$, which remain unaltered.

How are the coordinates of the other points on the object changed? We might try to construct a rule for changing coordinates from the list of coordinate changes in Figure 2.4. However, it is quite tricky to find a simple rule which satisfies all the changes. We now show a way of constructing the appropriate rule.

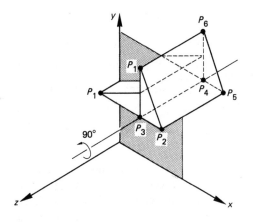

Corner points	Original coordinates	New coordinates
P_1	(2, 4.5, 1)	(0, 2.5, 1)
P_2	(3, 2.5, 1)	(2, 3.5, 1)
P_3	(2, 2.5, 1)	(2, 2.5, 1)
P_4	(2, 2.5, −2)	(2, 2.5, −2)
P_5	(3, 2.5, −2)	(2, 3.5, −2)
P_6	(2, 4.5, −2)	(0, 2.5, −2)

Fig. 2.4 Rotating the prism through 90° about a line parallel to the z-axis

We begin by dividing the move into three simpler subsidiary moves (Figure 2.5), which are together equivalent to the required rotation, namely:

1 Translate using the rule

$$(x, y, z) \mapsto (x - 2,\, y - 2.5,\, z)$$

so that the edge $\langle P_4, P_3 \rangle$ of the object lies along the z-axis.

2 Rotate through 90° about the z-axis using the rule

$$(x, y, z) \mapsto (-y,\, x,\, z)$$

Fig. 2.5 Dividing a 90° rotation move into three simpler moves

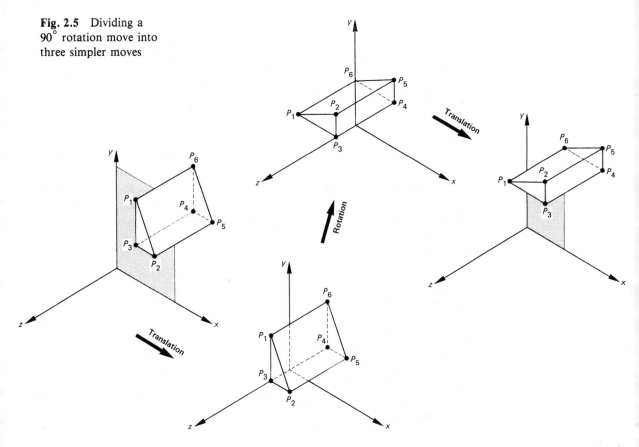

3 Translate using the rule

$$(x, y, z) \mapsto (x + 2, y + 2.5, z)$$

which takes the axis of rotation back to its original position.

The required rule for the rotation is then constructed by combining or composing the rules for these three moves to give:

$$(x, y, z) \mapsto (x - 2, y - 2.5, z) \mapsto (-y + 2.5, x - 2, z) \mapsto (-y + 4.5, x + 0.5, z)$$

[translation]　　　　　　　　[rotation]　　　　　　　　[translation]

The application of the rotation rule above may require some explanation. The rule is stated as $(x, y, z) \mapsto (-y, x, z)$. However, we want to apply this rule to $(x - 2, y - 2.5, z)$. In words, the rule tells us to change the x-coordinate into the negative of the original y-coordinate. The original y-coordinate is given by $y - 2.5$, thus the new x-coordinate is $-(y - 2.5) = -y + 2.5$. The rule also tells us to change the y-coordinate into the original x-coordinate. The original x-coordinate is $x - 2$, thus the new y-coordinate is $x - 2$. Finally the z-coordinate remains unchanged.

2.3 General rotations about the z-axis

In the previous section we discussed rotations through the particular angle, $90°$, and derived appropriate simple rules. However, a rotation about the z-axis through a general angle θ (which may take any value) is given by the more complicated rule

$$(x, y, z) \mapsto (x \cos \theta - y \sin \theta, x \sin \theta + y \cos \theta, z)$$

We will not derive this rule, but by substituting particular values for the angle θ it can be verified easily. For example, we have shown that a rotation through $90°$ about the z-axis, has the corresponding rule

$$(x, y, z) \mapsto (-y, x, z)$$

Looking at the general rule and putting $\theta = 90°$ (which gives $\cos 90° = 0$, $\sin 90° = 1$) we obtain $(x, y, z) \mapsto (-y, x, z)$, and so verify the general rule in this case.

A rotation θ about an axis which is parallel to the z-axis and which passes through the point with coordinates $x = a$, $y = b$, $z = 0$ is more complicated. As before we can decompose this rotation into three subsidiary moves:

1 Translation using

$$(x, y, z) \mapsto (x - a, y - b, z)$$

to make the axis of rotation coincide with the z-axis.
2 Rotation using

$$(x, y, z) \mapsto (x \cos \theta - y \sin \theta, x \sin \theta + y \cos \theta, z)$$

about the axis.
3 Translation using

$$(x, y, z) \mapsto (x + a, y + b, z)$$

to bring the axis of rotation back to its original position.

The complete rule is obtained, after combining the three subsidiary rules, as

$$(x, y, z) \mapsto ((x - a)\cos \theta - (y - b)\sin \theta + a, (x - a)\sin \theta + (y - b)\cos \theta + b, z)$$

We can check this general rule, by again considering the particular rotation though $90°$ about an axis through $x = 2$, $y = 2.5$ and $z = 0$. In this case $a = 2$, $b = 2.5$, $\theta = 90°$ and the rule becomes

$$(x, y, z) \mapsto (-y + 4.5, x + 0.5, z)$$

which agrees with the previous expression.

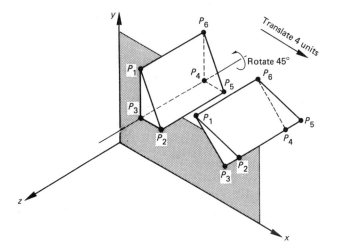

Fig. 2.6 A $45°$ rotation followed by a four-unit translation

The general rotation rule can be applied to represent other moves of the object. For instance, in Figure 2.6, the object is rotated about an axis along one of its edges (through $x = 2$, $y = 2.5$, $z = 0$) by $45°$ and then translated in the x-direction by 4 units. The general rotation is represented by the rule:

$$(x, y, z) \mapsto \left(\frac{(x - 2)}{\sqrt{2}} - \frac{(y - 2.5)}{\sqrt{2}} + 2, \frac{(x - 2)}{\sqrt{2}} + \frac{(y - 2.5)}{\sqrt{2}} + 2.5, z \right)$$

that is

$$(x, y, z) \mapsto \left(\frac{(x - y + 0.5)}{\sqrt{2}} + 2, \frac{(x + y - 4.5)}{\sqrt{2}} + 2.5, z \right)$$

(Note that $\cos 45° = \sin 45° = 1/\sqrt{2}$.) The translation is represented by the rule

$$(x, y, z) \mapsto (x + 4, y, z)$$

and the complete move is therefore given by

$$(x, y, z) \mapsto \left(\frac{(x - y + 0.5)}{\sqrt{2}} + 6, \frac{(x + y - 4.5)}{\sqrt{2}} + 2.5, z \right)$$

In composing these latter two rules we performed them in the order: 'general rotation followed by translation'. What happens if we apply them in the reverse order: 'translation followed by general rotation'? Figure 2.7 shows that a different move is obtained. The important lesson here is that we must be very careful to specify the order in which rules are to be combined in the

45

Fig. 2.7 A four-unit translation followed by a 45° rotation

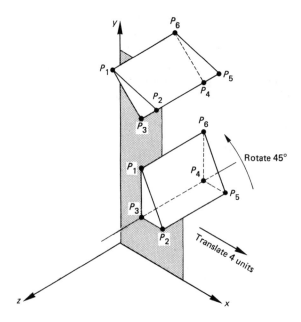

compositions, since the resultant moves they represent are themselves dependent on the order in which the subsidiary moves take place.

General rotations about axes parallel either to the x-axis or to the y-axis can be obtained in the same way and are each represented by a rule having a similar form to that considered above for general z-axis rotations. General rotations about arbitrary axes are more complex, and give rise to more complicated rules. It can be helpful to express such moves in terms of matrices and the composition of such moves by the multiplication of matrices. This and other representations of rules for moves will be considered in a later chapter.

3 Relations between objects

We have seen how to describe translations and rotations of objects by changes in the coordinates of their points. Objects can be moved around in the reference coordinate frame by using combinations of these translations and rotations.

In computer-aided design, one aim of moving objects is to bring them into a specific spatial relation required in a design. For example, in designing a gearbox we might start from a library of gears, each described in some standard position with respect to the reference frame. During the design phase, representative images or models of the gears are moved to required positions in the final assembly. Being able to move representations of objects thus allows us to create designs of assemblies.

We might also want to construct composite shapes, perhaps the gearbox

Fig. 2.8 Joining a truncated cone to a cylinder

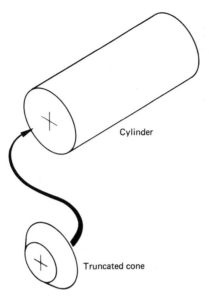

Cylinder

Truncated cone

housing, from primitive shapes. To do this we bring objects into a specific spatial relation and apply an operation which joins the two objects to make a single object. For example to obtain a shaft with a chamfered end (Figure 2.8) we might take a cylinder and a truncated cone as primitive objects and move them so that they touch end to end. A joining operation would then be invoked. The essential aspect of creating assemblies or compound objects is the moving of separate objects into a specified relation. We now show how to represent these relations and how to realise them by moves of the objects.

3.1 Local coordinate frames

To express a spatial relation we can define local coordinate frames in objects. The idea is quite simple. A coordinate frame is (rigidly) fixed in each object, and so it moves as the object is moved. An example of a local coordinate frame is shown in Figure 2.9, for the object A. We call this frame F_A denoting the fact that it is attached to object A.

Fig. 2.9 A local coordinate frame for the prism A

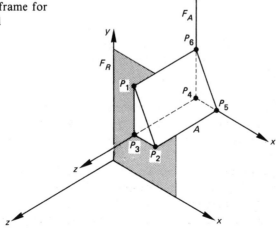

Corner points	Coordinates in F_A
P_1	(0, 2, 3)
P_2	(1, 0, 3)
P_3	(0, 0, 3)
P_4	(0, 0, 0)
P_5	(1, 0, 0)
P_6	(0, 2, 0)

Object A can be described with respect to the local frame. This local description then remains the same as the object is moved. As an example, for the frame F_A in Figure 2.9, the coordinates of the vertex points are listed in the accompanying table.

3.2 Describing the local coordinate frame

The local frame may itself be described by a move (albeit a rather artificial one), which brings a copy of the reference frame F_R into coincidence with the local frame F_A. For the object A in Figure 2.9 this move is particularly easy to specify. The copy of F_R is translated by 2 units in the x-direction, by 2.5 units in the y-direction and by 2 units in the negative z-direction. The move is represented by the rule

$$(x, y, z) \mapsto (x + 2, y + 2.5, z - 2)$$

The relation of the local frame F_A to the reference frame is therefore represented by this rule.

The coordinates of the points of object A in the reference frame F_R can be calculated by applying the rule

$$(x, y, z) \mapsto (x + 2, y + 2.5, z - 2)$$

to their coordinates expressed in the local frame, F_A. Table 2.1 illustrates the relation arising in this case.

Table 2.1

Point	Coordinates in F_A (x, y, z)	Coordinates in F_R $(x + 2, y + 2.5, z - 2)$
P_1	$(0, 2, 3)$	$(2, 4.5, 1)$
P_2	$(1, 0, 3)$	$(3, 2.5, 1)$
P_3	$(0, 0, 3)$	$(2, 2.5, 1)$
P_4	$(0, 0, 0)$	$(2, 2.5, -2)$
P_5	$(1, 0, 0)$	$(3, 2.5, -2)$
P_6	$(0, 2, 0)$	$(2, 4.5, -2)$

As another example, recall the move of object A shown in Figure 2.6, consisting of a rotation through $45°$ about an axis through $x = 2$, $y = 2.5$, $z = 0$, followed by a translation along the x-direction through four units.

The new position of the local frame F_A is described by a composition of two rules; namely the rule

$$(x, y, z) \mapsto (x + 2, y + 2.5, z - 2)$$

which represents the original position of F_A, composed with the rule representing the move of F_A:

$$(x, y, z) \mapsto \left(\frac{(x - y + 0.5)}{\sqrt{2}} + 6, \frac{(x + y - 4.5)}{\sqrt{2}} + 2.5, z \right)$$

It is important to note that all of these moves are considered with respect to the reference frame F_R.

3.3 Relations between two local frames

We have seen how to represent the spatial relation between the local frame F_A and the reference frame F_R as the move which brings a copy of F_R to coincide with F_A. The same idea can be used to represent the relation between two objects, each with their own local coordinate frames. For example, consider the two objects A and B shown in Figure 2.10 with local frames F_A and F_B respectively. The relation between F_A and F_B expressed in F_A is represented by the rule

$$(x, y, z) \mapsto (x + 4, y, z)$$

Fig. 2.10 The relation between two local coordinate frames

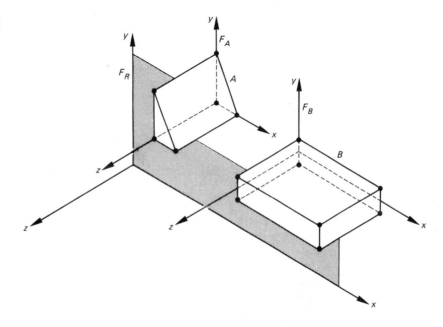

The same relation expressed in F_B is represented by the rule

$$(x, y, z) \mapsto (x - 4, y, z)$$

The relation between two objects can also be represented by that move in the reference frame which takes one local frame into the other. However, in considering how objects are assembled, the desired final *goal spatial relation* will probably be specified in one of the local frames. Thus for representing relations between objects A and B we mainly consider relations between local frames. These relations can be expressed as rules. Conversely, for representing moves we generally use the reference frame.

As an example, the objects A and B from Figure 2.10 are shown in some required goal spatial relation prior to applying a 'join' operation (Figure 2.11). In Figure 2.6 we saw how to move the object A into this relation, which is described by a rotation about the z-axis through $+ 45°$ in the frame F_B but through $- 45°$ in the frame F_A. In the frame F_B the relation is represented by the rule

Fig. 2.11 Joining the two objects A (a prism) and B (a cuboid)

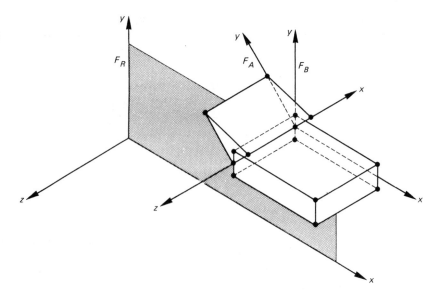

$$(x, y, z) \mapsto \left(\frac{x}{\sqrt{2}} - \frac{y}{\sqrt{2}}, \frac{x}{\sqrt{2}} + \frac{y}{\sqrt{2}}, z \right)$$

We denote the relation between A and B as (B, A) when expressed in frame F_B and as (A, B) when expressed in frame F_A. The relation (A, B) is called the *inverse* of (B, A).

3.4 Moves and goals

In manipulating objects it is often convenient to move them into a goal relation. The CAD system accepts the required goal relation as input and calculates the move that must be made to bring this about. In the example above, the move required object A to be taken from the initial relation

$$(x, y, z) \mapsto (x - 4, y, z)$$

to the goal relation

$$(x, y, z) \mapsto \left(\frac{x}{\sqrt{2}} - \frac{y}{\sqrt{2}}, \frac{x}{\sqrt{2}} + \frac{y}{\sqrt{2}}, z \right)$$

These relations are each expressed in the local frame F_B. The move required of object A to achieve the change in relation will be described in the reference frame. We thus want to calculate the corresponding rule in the reference frame.

To clarify the situation we introduce Figure 2.12 which illustrates the various interrelationships schematically. In the diagram, coordinate frames are represented by vertices, whereas transformations from one frame to another are represented by edges directed out from the frame in which the relation is described. The final position of F_A is denoted by $F_{A'}$ in Figure 2.12, and the relation of $F_{A'}$ to F_R is described by the composition of relations (F_R to F_B) and (F_B to $F_{A'}$). In the notation introduced above, these relations are written more simply as (R, B) and (B, A') respectively (Table 2.2).

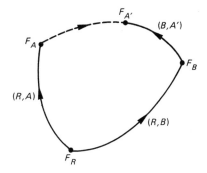

Fig. 2.12 Schematic diagram of interrelationships amongst reference and local coordinate frames

Table 2.2

Relation	Rule
(R, B)	$(x, y, z) \mapsto (x + 6, y + 2.5, z - 2)$
(B, A')	$(x, y, z) \mapsto \left(\dfrac{(x - y)}{\sqrt{2}}, \dfrac{(-x + y)}{\sqrt{2}}, z \right)$

It is important to note that the latter relation is described relative to the local frame F_B. To calculate the $F_{A'}$ in F_R we *cannot* 'compose' the rules in the order: first (R, B), and then (B, A'), as we have done previously for moves in the reference frame.

For this example we can see directly that the relation (R, A'), is given by a rotation

$$(x, y, z) \mapsto \left(\frac{(x - y)}{\sqrt{2}}, \frac{(x + y)}{\sqrt{2}}, z \right)$$

followed by a translation

$$(x, y, z) \mapsto (x + 6, y + 2.5, z - 2)$$

giving the rule

$$(x, y, z) \mapsto \left(\frac{(x - y)}{\sqrt{2}} + 6, \frac{(x + y)}{\sqrt{2}} + 2.5, z - 2 \right)$$

However, composing the rules in the local frames in order gives

$$(x, y, z) \mapsto (x + 6, y + 2.5, z - 2) \mapsto \left(\frac{(x - y + 3.5)}{\sqrt{2}}, \frac{(x + y + 8.5)}{\sqrt{2}}, z - 2 \right)$$

which is incorrect.

To obtain the correct relation form for the relation (R, A') from the local relations is actually quite simple — we must compose the relations in *reverse* order. We can write this composition of relations (or strictly the corresponding rules) as $(R, B)(B, A')$, assuming that the rule on the right is applied first. This gives the correct composite rule.

To find the move in the reference frame which brings object A to the goal relation (B, A') in the reference frame, consider the diagram in Figure 2.12. We require the move between F_A and $F_{A'}$ in the reference frame shown by a dotted line. From the diagram this is equivalent to the *inverse* of (R, A) (i.e. (A, R)) followed by (R, A'). We have seen that (R, A') is expressed as $(R, B)(B, A')$, thus the move required to attain the goal relation is the composition of three relations giving the composite relation $(R, B)(B, A')(A, R)$. The relation on the right of such expressions is applied first. Since (R, A) is represented by the rule

$$(x, y, z) \mapsto (x + 2, y + 2.5, z - 2)$$

its inverse (A, R) is represented by

$$(x, y, z) \mapsto (x - 2, y - 2.5, z + 2)$$

Thus the rule which represents the move of object A to its goal position is finally

$$(x, y, z) \mapsto \left(\frac{(x - y + 0.5)}{\sqrt{2}} + 6, \frac{(x + y - 4.5)}{\sqrt{2}} + 2.5, z \right)$$

4 Combining objects

Consider the pair of objects A and B in the relation in Figure 2.13. They are distinct but overlap. We can form new objects from this pair, by taking unions, intersections and differences.

4.1 Shape operations

Figure 2.13 shows the union $A \cup B$, the difference $B - A$, and the intersection $A \cap B$ of the objects A and B. These shape operations construct more complex objects from simple or primitive objects. Objects are first moved to the required relation and then these shape operations are applied. The new object can be described in the local frames F_A or F_B or in some new frame. The details of constructing the representation of such a new object will be covered later in the book. We note here that in order to apply these operations it is not necessary to impose any restriction on the relations between objects. Thus, for example, two objects which do not overlap have a union which is just the original two objects, although they may now have a common name. Such a pair of objects has an empty intersection.

4.2 Structure of compound objects

Recall that the relation between two objects A and B is represented by the relations (A, B) or (B, A) between their local frames. The representation of compound objects is in two parts, namely: the relation between primitive objects, and the shape operations.

The relations between primitive objects are represented by pairwise relations. Consider three objects A, B and C. The relations (A, B) and (B, C) are sufficient to describe the relation

$$(A, C) = (A, B)(B, C)$$

Note that to find the rule representing the relation (A, C), we first apply the rule (B, C) followed by the rule (A, B).

The shape operations can be represented in graph form (Figure 2.14). Suppose we form the union of A and B and then take their intersection with C. This is represented by the tree structure.

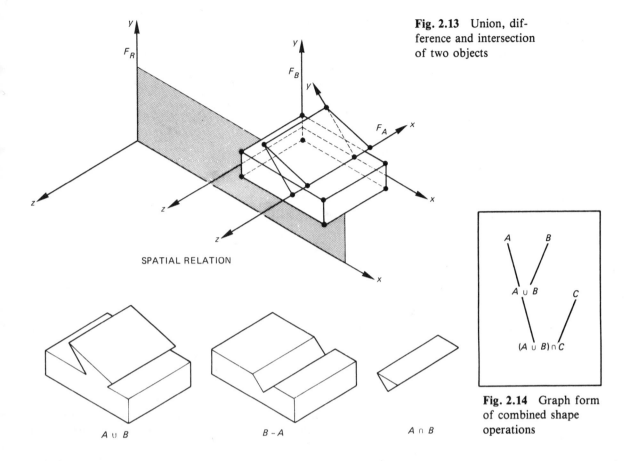

SPATIAL RELATION

Fig. 2.13 Union, difference and intersection of two objects

$A \cup B$ $B - A$ $A \cap B$

Fig. 2.14 Graph form of combined shape operations

5 Assemblies

Let us look at the relations between objects in assemblies. These relations do not include interpenetrations. What kind of relations are they? In an assembly objects touch one another. This occurs in a number of ways.

Recall from the previous chapter that one way to represent objects is by configurations of vertices, edges and faces. Just as a single object is represented by relations between these elements, so the representation of assemblies is given by similar relations between vertices, edges and faces of the assembled objects. However, in an assembly, components may move and so these relations may be variable.

5.1 Variable relations

Consider assembly relations in which the faces of one object are in contact with another. We restrict the type of 'face' to be plane, cylindrical or spherical surfaces for the purpose of this chapter.

Fig. 2.15 Two objects obtained as the union of A and B, and the difference of A and B respectively

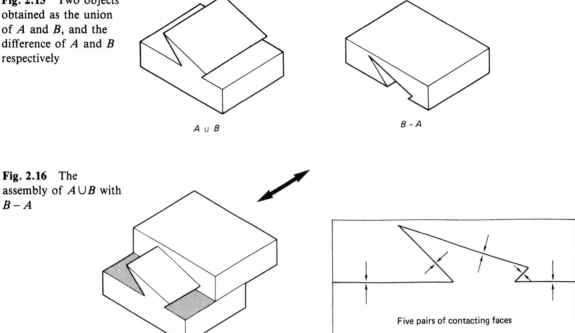

$A \cup B$

$B - A$

Fig. 2.16 The assembly of $A \cup B$ with $B - A$

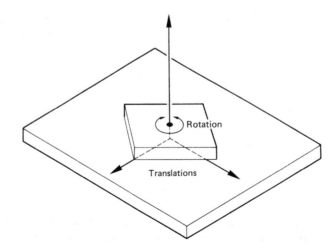

Five pairs of contacting faces

Consider object $A \cup B$ and other copies of A and B in the relation shown (Figure 2.15). Perform the difference operation $B - A$ to obtain a block with a groove.

Assemble $A \cup B$ in the groove in $B - A$ (Figure 2.16). Consider the face–face relations between the two compound objects. Five pairs of faces are in contact so there are five face–face relations.

There are three independent relative motions (Figure 2.17) possible between two planes in contact. These are translations (in either of two directions in the plane of contact) and rotations (about an axis perpendicular to the plane of

Fig. 2.17 The three independent relative motions of two planes in contact

Rotation

Translations

contact). These possible relative motions are not all realised in the final assembly which only allows one sliding motion. The satisfying of all five relations simultaneously thus imposes restrictions on the possible motions of each individual relation. The motion in the final assembly — sliding up and down the groove — is common to all five face–face relations.

We have seen how the relations between objects in assemblies can be variable and represented by variable rules. The interaction of a number of variable relations between objects and how they restrict actual variation is generally a difficult problem.

5.2 Dependent relations

Another example of variable relations occurs in mechanisms. Consider a planar quadrilateral (Figure 2.18) hinged at its vertices. There are four objects A, B, C, D connected in pairs (A, B), (B, C), (C, D), (D, A) which may be considered to be variable relations allowing rotation about the axes of the hinges. These variable relations interact because the bodies are connected in a loop. In fact the rotations between objects are dependent, in the sense that given any one relation we can deduce the other three.

Fig. 2.18 A hinged planar quadrilateral

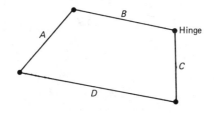

5.3 Composing relations

We have seen how a number of relations between objects can form loops and restrict their potential variation. Consider the more general case in which a number of variable relations between pairs of objects can be composed to give *greater* variation.

Four bodies A, B, C, D without the connection between D and A are shown in Figure 2.19. The relation (D, A) is unconstrained. The relation between D and A is, roughly speaking, composed of the relations (A, B), (B, C) and (C, D).

Fig. 2.19 A hinged assembly of four bodies

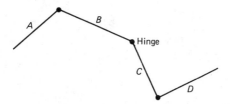

Such considerations arise in the design and control of robot manipulators. A robot used for assembly should be capable of holding and placing an object in a range of spatial relations with other objects. This range is achieved by composing 'simple' variable, but controllable, relations among the components (or links) of the robot. A robot moves physical objects just as the transformations described above move representations of objects.

Graphical techniques 3

P Steadman

1 Introduction

Designers generally use *drawings* to represent the object which they are designing, and to communicate the design to others. Of course they will also use other forms of representation — symbolic and mathematical models, and perhaps three-dimensional physical models — but the drawing is arguably the most flexible and convenient of the forms of representation available. Drawings are useful above all, obviously, for representing the geometrical *form* of the designed object, and for representing its *appearance*. Hence the importance in computer-aided design (CAD) of the production of visual images by computer, that is **computer graphics.**

Currently there are two quite distinct situations in CAD. The first and most widespread use of computers in design at present (the mid 1980s) is solely for the production of drawings, by means of **computer draughting systems.** Each drawing may depict some solid object, but there is no corresponding three-dimensional model of the object in the machine; there is nothing so to speak 'behind the drawings' on the screen. In this case the operator of the draughting system is concerned only with moving two-dimensional shapes in the plane of the drawing.

In the second situation, a description of the designed object is built up in the machine, by one or other of the geometrical modelling techniques described in later chapters. Two-dimensional drawings are then generated automatically by the computer, *from* that model. Engineering and architecture deal for the most part with three-dimensional objects and so **solid modellers** are now commonly used in these fields. In other fields the object being designed may itself be essentially two-dimensional: a textile pattern, a work of graphic art, a printed circuit layout or micro-chip. However, it is still useful to make the distinction in this two-dimensional case between the internal *model* of the design which the machine holds, and the visual image of the design which is displayed at any time.

We examine two-dimensional design and drawing first. The principles and practical applications of computer draughting systems are described in more detail in the following chapter. Here we will just consider some of the basic geometrical operations involved.

2 Computer graphics

In computer graphics we are generally concerned with images drawn on display screens. (**Hard copies** can then be made of these images if needed, using various types of plotting device.) There are several ways in which these images can be constructed and different types of display device use a range of imaging techniques to achieve acceptable visual representations.

2.1 Screen coordinates

In order to specify the positions of points (and hence lines, polygons and other features) in a displayed image it is necessary to refer these to some system of **screen coordinates** (x, y). The convention is for x-values to increase from left to right, and for y-values to increase from bottom to top, in the normal way. The origin of this coordinate system might be taken typically either at the bottom left corner of the screen, or at the centre of the screen (Figure 3.1).

Fig. 3.1 Screen coordinates

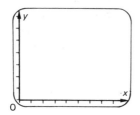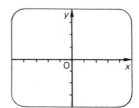

2.2 Vector graphics

The way in which drawings are built up on the screen, and are plotted out in hard copy, is related to the hardware used. Drawings can be constructed from *lines* — more precisely, from straight-line segments — defined by the coordinates of their end-points. These may be linked together to form chains of lines, and the chains can be closed to form polygons. Curved lines can be approximated as chains of short straight-line segments; the number of these segments then depends on the required closeness of the approximation and on the resolution of the display device (Figure 3.2).

Such line drawings are specially suited to **vector displays.** In a vector display a steerable electron beam draws the line segment (the 'vector') by tracing the actual path of the required line across the screen surface. Hard copy can similarly be produced on a plotter which draws with a pen on paper or plastic drawing film. Different colours and thicknesses of line are obtained by using

Fig. 3.2 Approximation of curve by chain of straight-line segments

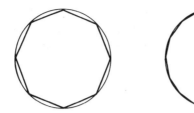

different pens. A plotter of this type is comparable with a vector display in that it draws line segments by moving the pen along the actual path of the required line — just as a draughtsman would.

In both cases (the vector display and the pen plotter) it is necessary to store, manipulate and draw only the positions of the lines, while the areas left blank in the image can be ignored.

2.3 Raster graphics

A second possibility is that the drawing be constructed from *dots* rather than lines. This option has grown in popularity with the widespread introduction from the early 1970s of the **raster-scan display.** Here the electron beam scans continuously along a series of horizontal lines which fill the screen, similar to those on a television set. Each such horizontal **scan-line** is itself sub-divided into a number of elements across the screen. The effect is to divide the whole screen into a rectangular array of 'picture elements' or **pixels** (Figure 3.3). Each pixel can be uniquely identified by a pair of screen coordinates (x, y) at its centre. Each pixel may then be set to display some tone or colour. It is, of course, possible to draw (straight or curved) lines on a raster-scan display — but they must first be converted into suitable rows of dots. This can involve some approximation, especially where a line runs diagonally across the screen at either a steep or a shallow angle (Figure 3.4).

Fig. 3.3 Sub-division of raster-scan display screen into scan-lines and pixels. The scan is *interlaced*: it follows alternate lines on a first pass (solid arrow) and then fills in the remaining lines on a second pass (dotted arrow)

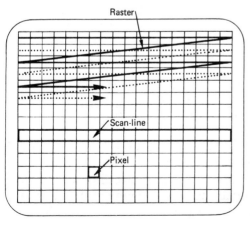

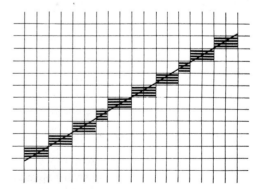

Fig. 3.4 'Staircasing' effect in diagonal line on raster-scan display

The number of pixels in the *x*- and *y*-directions defines the resolution of the display. Typical resolutions (in the mid 1980s) are 512×512 or 1024×1024 pixels. A complete picture is stored by the machine as an array of pixel values, in a **frame buffer** (also referred to as a frame store or a memory map). Notice how this means that, for any picture, a value is stored for *every* pixel in the screen, whether it corresponds to part of a line, an infill or a background colour, or whatever.

Some plotting devices work on similar principles, and form printed images on paper with arrays of dots (a dot-matrix). These include electrostatic printers which work on the principle of the Xerox copier; and ink-jet plotters which deposit very fine droplets of ink onto the paper. Electrostatic printers are generally limited to a single colour; ink-jet plotters can plot many colours by suitable combinations of three inks.

(It is quite possible to plot drawings made up of vectors, on such a dot-matrix-type plotter; but the vector representation must first be converted to dot-matrix form.)

2.4 Vector versus raster

Vector displays are suitable for many applications in design, such as architectural plans, conventional engineering drawings or electronic circuit diagrams, where line drawings in one or a few colours will suffice. They are not well-suited, however, to displaying more realistic images, in which various areas are shaded or coloured in naturalistic colours. This is where raster-scan displays come into their own. The possibilities for producing very realistic computer images using raster displays are explored further in Chapter 14.

The disadvantage of the raster display is that, in effect, a value must be stored, as mentioned above, for every pixel in the screen; and, especially if the pixel may take any of a number of colours, the problems of storing such a large amount of data can become very serious. (There are ways of making economies here, but the storage problem still remains formidable.) The number of pixels is a function of the resolution: the higher the resolution, the greater the number of pixels and so the greater the storage problem. If, on the other hand, the resolution is decreased to make storage more manageable, then the approximations in the rectangular pixel-array representation become visually more obtrusive. Diagonal lines tend to have the 'staircase' appearance familiar in low-cost micro-computer displays and video games (Figure 3.4). In practice some compromise must be reached between economy in storage and an acceptable level of resolution.

3 Two-dimensional graphics

Constructing computer graphics images for three-dimensional objects is a fairly involved process, so we first restrict our attention to the simpler two-dimensional case. We need to consider: the representation of the shape; how we might alter or transform it; and how we view it. For present purposes we consider the shape to be represented as an arrangement of either dots or lines, as discussed above.

3.1 Transformations

Once a shape is formed, from lines or dots, it is convenient to be able to transform it in the plane. We can distinguish six simple types of two-dimensional transformation:

Translation This is a movement in the plane, from one position to another position, which preserves the shape and does not alter its orientation (Figure 3.5). In general, this transformation changes the position of all points of the shape.

Fig. 3.5 Translation of a shape by T_x units in the direction of the x-axis and T_y units in the direction of the y-axis

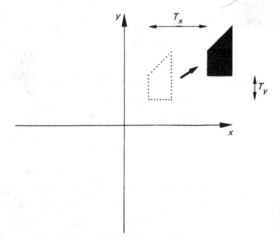

Rotation This is a movement in the plane, from one position and orientation to another position and orientation, which preserves the shape (Figure 3.6). In general, this transformation leaves just one point (not necessarily within the shape) fixed in position. This fixed point is the centre of the rotation.

Fig. 3.6 Rotation of a shape by θ degrees anti-clockwise. The dot marks the centre of rotation

Fig. 3.7 Reflection of a shape about the y-axis. The broken line marks the mirror line

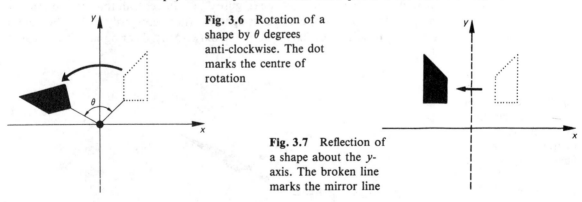

Reflection This is a 'movement' in the plane, from one position and orientation to another position and orientation, which produces a congruent mirror image shape from the initial shape (Figure 3.7). In general, this transformation leaves all the points on just one straight line (not necessarily within the shape) fixed in position. This fixed line is the 'mirror line'.

Scaling This is a 'movement' in the plane which produces a (geometrically) similar shape from the initial shape but which preserves the orientation of the shape (Figure 3.8). In general, this transformation leaves just one point (not necessarily within the shape) fixed in position. This point is the centre of the scaling and it is located at the origin.

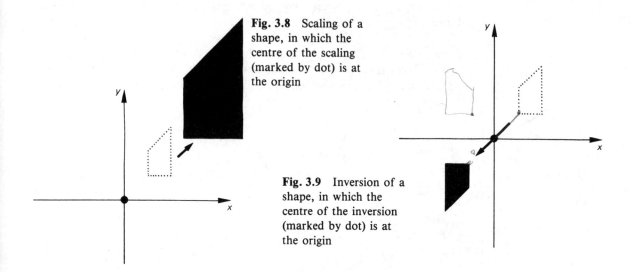

Fig. 3.8 Scaling of a shape, in which the centre of the scaling (marked by dot) is at the origin

Fig. 3.9 Inversion of a shape, in which the centre of the inversion (marked by dot) is at the origin

Inversion This is a 'movement' in the plane, from one position and orientation to another position and orientation, which preserves the shape (Figure 3.9). This transformation leaves just one point (not necessarily within the shape) fixed in position. This fixed point is the centre of the inversion and it is located at the origin.

Shearing This is a 'movement' in the plane which produces a shape having the same area as the initial shape (Figure 3.10). In general, this transformation leaves all the points on just one straight line (not necessarily within the shape) fixed in position. This fixed line is the axis of the shearing and it is located along the x-axis.

Fig. 3.10 Shearing of a shape, in which the axis of the shearing (marked by broken line) is along the x-axis

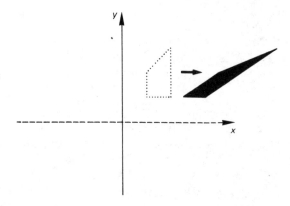

These six types of two-dimensional transformation are particular examples of **linear transformations**; so-called because they each transform all *straight* lines within the initial shape into corresponding *straight* lines within the final shape. Other *non-linear* (or *curvilinear*) transformations are possible but we do not consider them in this chapter.

If we consider a single point with initial position (x, y) in the shape, then the effect of applying some transformation (linear or otherwise) is to generate a new position (x', y'); and similarly for all other points. (Of course, not all new positions need be different from their corresponding initial positions.) For a linear transformation the new coordinates are related to the old coordinates by an algebraic expression which is itself linear (that is, it only contains variable terms of the first degree).

A *translation* is given by

$$x' = x + T_x$$

$$y' = y + T_y$$

where T_x and T_y are the distances which the shape is moved in the directions of the x- and y-axes respectively (Figure 3.5). If T_x and T_y are both zero, then a zero translation occurs and all new positions of points are identical to their initial positions.

For *rotation*, if we consider the simplest case, of rotation about the origin of the coordinate system (Figure 3.6), then a rotation by θ degrees anticlockwise is given by

$$x' = x \cos \theta - y \sin \theta$$

$$y' = x \sin \theta + y \cos \theta$$

For *reflection,* if we again consider the simplest case, of reflection about one of the axes; then a reflection about the y-axis is given by reversing the sign of all the x-values whilst leaving the y-values unchanged (Figure 3.7):

$$x' = -x$$

$$y' = y$$

whereas a reflection about the x-axis is given by reversing the sign of all the y-values and keeping the x-values unchanged:

$$x' = x$$

$$y' = -y$$

A reflection about *both* axes is produced by

$$x' = -x$$

$$y' = -y$$

This 'double reflection' in the x- and y-axes is identical to an inversion (Figure 3.9).

A general *scaling* is given by

$$x' = xS_x$$

$$y' = yS_y$$

This multiplies all x-values by the scaling factor S_x, and all y-values by the scaling factor S_y. The effect is to scale the shape *relative to the origin* as in Figure 3.8; it becomes larger and moves away, or it becomes smaller and moves nearer to the origin. If we wish to keep some point in the shape (other than the origin) in some fixed position, while altering the scale, it is necessary to apply both a scaling transformation and a translation. Normally the values of S_x and S_y would be equal (as in Figure 3.8) in which case the scaled shape is geometrically similar to the original. But this is not necessary, and if S_x and S_y are unequal, then the shape will be stretched or compressed in the x- or y-directions (Figure 3.11).

Fig. 3.11 Scaling of a shape by unequal scaling factors in the x- and y-directions

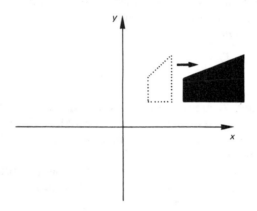

Finally, a *shearing* is given by

$$x' = x + \sigma y$$

$$y' = y$$

This shifts each point in a direction parallel to the x-axis through a distance directly proportional to the y-value of the point (Figure 3.10). It leaves all y-values unchanged.

Each of the above six transformations is a special case of the general linear transformation

$$x' = a_1 x + b_1 y + c_1$$

$$y' = a_2 x + b_2 y + c_2$$

where the coefficients a_1, b_1, c_1, a_2, b_2 and c_2 take on the appropriate (different) form for each different special case. In CAD it is common practice to express this general transformation (and hence also all the particular special cases) in a more convenient (square) **matrix** form, suitable for computational purposes. The matrix is simply the array of coefficients augmented with an extra row of two zeros and a one to form the square (3×3) arrangement:

$$\begin{bmatrix} a_1 & b_1 & c_1 \\ a_2 & b_2 & c_2 \\ 0 & 0 & 1 \end{bmatrix}$$

This matrix transforms each point from its initial position to its new position by operating on the position vector of the point, expressed in terms of homogeneous coordinates (see Chapter 1), as follows:

$$\begin{bmatrix} x' \\ y' \\ 1 \end{bmatrix} = \begin{bmatrix} a_1 & b_1 & c_1 \\ a_2 & b_2 & c_2 \\ 0 & 0 & 1 \end{bmatrix} \begin{bmatrix} x \\ y \\ 1 \end{bmatrix}$$

The original rectangular (2×3) matrix of coefficients (without the 0 0 1 row), and the position vector expressed without homogeneous coordinates, *cannot* be used together in this way because the resulting matrix product would be

$$\begin{bmatrix} a_1 & b_1 & c_1 \\ a_2 & b_2 & c_2 \end{bmatrix} \begin{bmatrix} x \\ y \end{bmatrix}$$

This is not a valid matrix product since a (2×3) matrix cannot operate on a (2×1) matrix — they are incompatible. Hence an augmented matrix and homogeneous coordinates are used.

The fact that a shape can be defined in the computer, and can then be subjected repeatedly to these various transformations, provides one of the main reasons for the relative speed and economy of computer draughting compared with manual techniques. Any repeated feature or symbol need be built up line by line only once; it can then be moved, scaled if necessary, and copied automatically in all the required positions. If a design has overall *reflected* symmetry, say, then only one half need be drawn. This half can then be reflected to make the complete drawing (Figure 3.12). Similarly a view of a mechanical component may possess *rotational* symmetry (Figure 3.13). To make such a drawing, again only one sector need be drawn and then suitably rotated and copied the appropriate number of times about the centre point.

Fig. 3.12 View of a mechanical component with reflected symmetry. [*Courtesy* General Drafting System, Applied Research of Cambridge Ltd.]

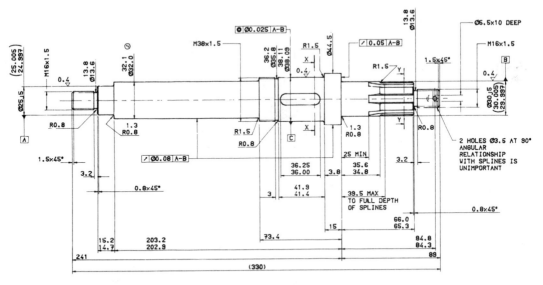

Fig. 3.13 View of a mechanical component with rotational symmetry

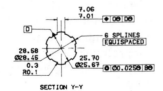

SECTION Y-Y

Fig. 3.14 Concatenation of a translation, a rotation about the origin, and a second translation, to achieve a rotation of a shape about a centre (marked by cross) which is not the origin

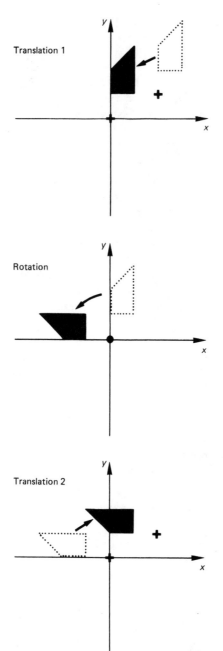

Different transformations can be combined together, or *concatenated*, to produce some combination of moves. For example, suppose we wish to rotate a shape about some point which is not the origin. This can be achieved by translating the shape such that the required centre of rotation (relative to the shape) coincides with the origin; rotating the shape about the origin; and then using a second translation (the inverse of the first) to move the rotated shape back to its correct position (Figure 3.14).

Fig. 3.15 Rotation of a shape (*above left*) followed by a reflection (*below left*) produces a different result from the same transformations carried out in the reverse order (*right, above and below*)

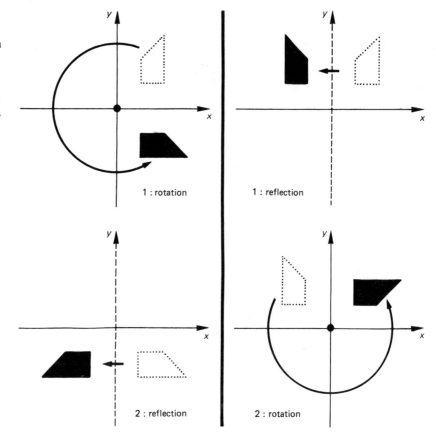

1 : rotation

1 : reflection

2 : reflection

2 : rotation

Notice that it is very important in which order the transformations are carried out. In many cases the same transformations applied in a different sequence will have a different effect. For example, a rotation followed by a reflection can produce a different end-result from the same reflection followed by the same rotation (Figure 3.15).

3.2 Windows and viewports

One purpose for which the scaling transformation is particularly useful is for enlarging or reducing the size of the visual image as a whole. For an architectural or engineering drawing it will be convenient to measure in units of, say, metres or millimetres; for the layout of a micro-chip, perhaps in units of micrometres. But to *display* these images, the units of measurement must somehow be related to the coordinates of the screen itself. For this reason a distinction is usually made between the screen coordinate system, and a system of **world coordinates** which describe a notional two-dimensional world (of potentially infinite extent) in which the design or drawing as a whole is represented.

It is possible to define some **window** relative to the world coordinates corresponding to that part of the design or total image which we wish to display (Figure 3.16). The world coordinates of this window are then scaled

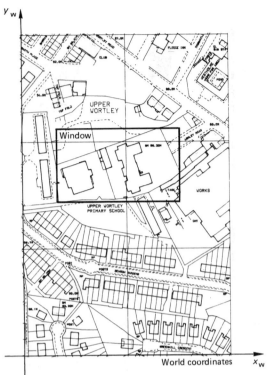

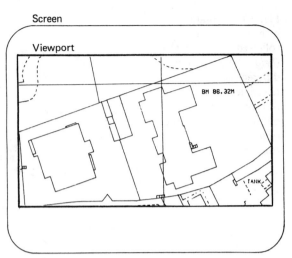

Fig. 3.17 Scaling of the window of Figure 3.16 to a viewport in the display screen

Fig. 3.16 Window on an image, defined relative to world coordinates

appropriately so as to fit that part of the design or drawing, contained by the window, into the display screen (Figure 3.17). The window may be the same shape as the display screen, and scaled to fill the screen completely. However, this is not the only possibility.

Another option is to define some smaller rectangular part of the screen, known as a **viewport;** and then to scale the window to fill just this viewport. The screen may be divided into several viewports, showing different parts of the same design or drawing (or perhaps different drawings), possibly at different scales. If a (rectangular) viewport is *not* the same shape as the corresponding (rectangular) window, then the scaling in the *x*-direction must differ from that in the *y*-direction, and the image will be compressed or stretched accordingly.

The use of windows and viewports makes it possible to achieve something like the effects of 'zooming' and 'panning' with a film camera. If progressively smaller parts of a drawing are scaled up to fit the same viewport, the effect is that of zooming in. If windows spaced at intervals across the drawing are displayed in sequence through the same viewport, the effect is that of panning laterally.

(*Warning:* some computer manuals use 'window' to mean 'viewport' as defined here.)

3.3 Clipping

One consequence of the use of windows is that some lines or polygons in the drawing at the edge of a window may be only partly visible and others completely invisible. If the attempt is made to display those invisible parts whose screen coordinates actually fall outside the screen or viewport area, then faults in the display will occur. For this reason it is necessary to **clip** off and discard the invisible parts of the drawing.

A number of different clipping techniques have been devised. It is especially easy to clip points, since an examination of the values of their world coordinates relative to the coordinates of the edges of the window can readily determine whether they will be visible or invisible. The problem here is that to test every point in a drawing for visibility is much too time-consuming.

One well-known algorithm for clipping lines is that due to Cohen and Sutherland. This relies on the fact that for any straight line in the picture there can only be at most one visible segment (given that the screen or viewport is rectangular). The first part of the algorithm decides whether or not a line lies completely inside or completely outside the window. The latter can then be discarded. To do this the edges of the window are extended to form nine regions (Figure 3.18). Any line whose end-points both fall in the central region must obviously be completely visible. Any line whose end-points *both* lie either to the left of, or to the right of, or above or below the extended edges of the window, must be completely invisible. Any other line may potentially intersect the window, and is dealt with by the second part of the algorithm. This divides each such line into visible and invisible parts, by finding its point(s) of intersection with the edge(s) of the window. The invisible part(s) are then discarded.

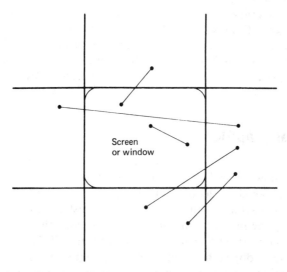

Screen
or window

Fig. 3.18 Edges of a screen or window extended to form nine regions (heavy lines), of which the window forms the central region, in the line-clipping algorithm of Cohen and Sutherland. End-points (dots) of lines in picture (thin lines) must fall in one or other of these regions

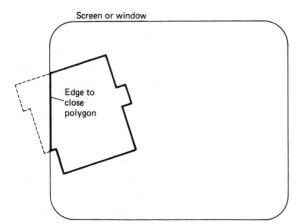
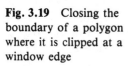

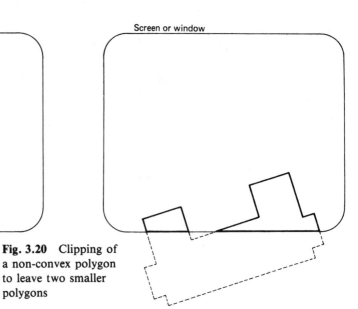

Fig. 3.19 Closing the boundary of a polygon where it is clipped at a window edge

Fig. 3.20 Clipping of a non-convex polygon to leave two smaller polygons

Other clipping techniques have been devised: for clipping curves (by breaking them into short straight-line segments and proceeding as before for each short segment); for clipping text characters; and for clipping polygons. This last problem poses special difficulties. If a polygon is described by listing in order the line segments which make up its boundary, and it is clipped, the resulting outline will no longer be closed. It must be re-closed by adding in appropriate sections of the window edge (Figure 3.19). Moreover, if a non-convex polygon is clipped, it may become split into two or more smaller polygons (Figure 3.20). Because of this it is not possible to clip polygons, described in terms of their boundaries, using a line-clipping algorithm, since information is lost about which line belongs to the boundary of which polygon; and special polygon-clipping techniques are therefore needed.

4 Three-dimensional graphics

We now consider the situation where the computer contains a three-dimensional model of some designed object, and visual images are produced by the machine from that model. To construct a faithful image we must think about the interrelationships of three things: the *object* itself; the position of the observer who views the object, specifically the observer's *eye-point*; and, between object and eye-point, the required flat *plane of the image*. The situation is conceptually at its simplest with perspective images. Imagine a person looking at the scene through a window (Figure 3.21). This was the way in which the Renaissance discoverers of perspective thought about the subject. (The word itself refers to the act of 'looking through'.) Here the eye-point

Fig. 3.21 The basic geometry of perspective projection, in which an object is viewed through a 'window' corresponding to the image plane. The viewer's eye-point is at *E*. The dotted lines correspond to rays of light

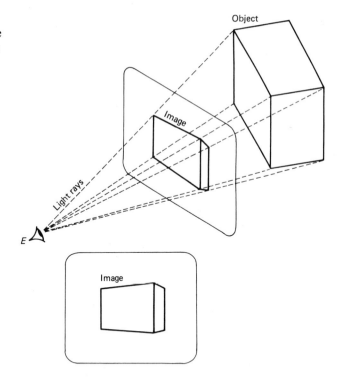

corresponds to the position of one of the viewer's eyes — we can imagine the other eye closed. The plane of the image is the glass pane of the window. Light rays (dotted lines in Figure 3.21) are reflected off the object and travel in straight lines, passing through the glass (we ignore refraction) to meet the eye.

4.1 Perspective images

Consider a point *P* on the object (Figure 3.22). The light ray passes from this point to the eye, and on its way meets the required plane of the image (the glass) at *P'*. This marks the position of the *image* of *P* in the total image.

Fig. 3.22 The perspective image *P'* of a point *P* in the object. *P* is joined to the eye-point *E* by a ray or projector (shown dotted) which meets the image plane at *P'*

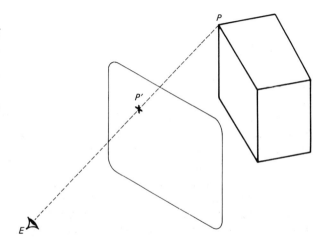

The images of all other points on the object are similarly obtained from appropriate rays. *A perspective image is like the image seen through a window* (with one eye, kept in a fixed position). A perspective drawing produces geometrically the same image on the viewer's retina as that obtained by looking at the actual scene from the same eye-position. It gives a naturalistic impression of appearances.

The geometry of photography is essentially equivalent, with the place of the eye being taken by the lens of the camera, and the plane of the image corresponding to the plate or film. The difference here is that the 'eye-point' of the lens is *between* the object and the image plane, and as a consequence the image is formed upside-down. But otherwise a photograph and a correct perspective drawing from the same viewpoint will be geometrically similar.

In computer graphics the plane of the image corresponds, obviously, to the surface of the display screen itself, and the eye-point to the eye of the operator, usually at 500 mm or so distance, and directly facing the centre of the screen. (Of course, we normally view computer screens with both eyes open, and from various positions, but this makes little practical difference.) If a correct perspective is then displayed, the observer will have the illusion of seeing the actual object, somewhere in space *beyond* the display screen.

4.2 Perspective and parallel projection

The production of visual images from computer models is a matter of **projection** of the three-dimensional object onto the two-dimensional image plane. To do this we need several systems of coordinates. It will be convenient to take the origin of the *screen coordinate* system at the centre of the screen. The object will be described in its own three-dimensional system of *world coordinates*. Suppose then that a third system, of *eye coordinates,* is defined, whose origin is at the eye-point E (Figure 3.23). Let us assume that the eye is

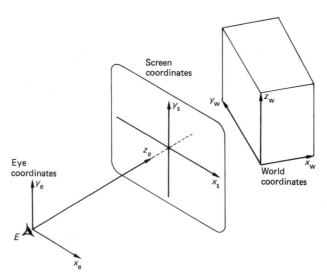

Fig. 3.23 System of world coordinates (x_w, y_w, z_w) defining the object; system of screen coordinates (x_s, y_s) with origin at the centre of the screen; and system of eye coordinates (x_e, y_e, z_e) with origin at the eye-point E. The z-axis of the eye coordinates passes through the origin of the screen coordinates, normal to the plane of the screen

directly facing the centre of the screen, and that the z-axis of the eye coordinates passes through this centre point normal to the plane of the screen. The x-axes of eye and screen coordinate systems are parallel, as are their y-axes.

The object can then be moved in its system of world coordinates, relative to this system of eye coordinates, using appropriate *three-dimensional transformations* (Chapter 2). The effect might be, for example, to rotate the object relative to the eye-point, or move it closer to or further away from the eye. The perspective view obtained of the object would change accordingly.

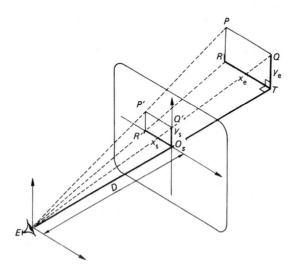

Fig. 3.24 Point P on the object, with eye coordinates (x_e, y_e, z_e), joined by a ray or projector to the eye-point E. E is at a distance D from the screen. The perspective image P' of the point P has screen coordinates (x_s, y_s)

Suppose that the object has been manoeuvred into some desired position for viewing. Imagine a point P on the object whose eye coordinates are (x_e, y_e, z_e). This point is joined by a straight line to the eye-point E (Figure 3.24). The line corresponds to the 'ray of light' — in geometrical terms it is a *projector*. The projector meets the screen at the point P', whose screen coordinates are (x_s, y_s). P' marks the perspective image in the screen of the point P in the object. Let the distance of the eye-point from the screen be D. Consider the whole arrangement in the ERT plane as shown in Figure 3.25. The triangles ERT and $ER'O_s$ are similar, giving

$$x_s/D = x_e/z_e$$

Fig. 3.25 The similar triangles ERT and $ER'O_s$ (refer to Figure 3.24)

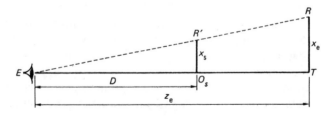

so that

$$x_s = Dx_e/z_e \tag{1}$$

Considering the arrangement in the EQT plane as in Figure 3.26, the triangles EQT and $EQ'O_s$ are similar, and so

$$y_s/D = y_e/z_e$$

thus

$$y_s = Dy_e/z_e \tag{2}$$

This therefore gives us the screen coordinates (x_s, y_s) of the point P' in terms of x_e, y_e and z_e. It is convenient in practice to divide x_s and y_s by a suitable scaling factor S, to suit the size of the screen such that the values of the screen coordinates lie between 0 and 1.

Fig. 3.26 The similar triangles EQT and $EQ'O_s$ (refer to Figure 3.24)

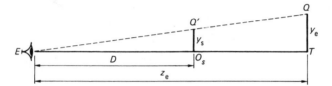

Notice how the values of x_s and y_s depend on the value of D, the theoretical distance of eye from screen. To obtain a natural-looking perspective view it would be necessary to set D roughly equal to the *actual* distance at which the viewer's eye(s) would be positioned from the screen (about 500 mm, as mentioned). If the notional position of the object relative to the screen is kept fixed, however, but D is altered, then different kinds of perspective view will result. If D is small, the effect will be that of a photograph taken with a wide-angle lens, and distortions will begin to occur in the picture. For this reason it is usual to maintain the angle subtended by the edges of the screen at the eye at not much greater than $30°$. If D is large, the effect will be more like that of using a telephoto lens.

As the eye-point becomes more distant, so the angle between the projectors becomes smaller; that is to say, the projectors become more nearly parallel. If the (notional) eye-point is taken to infinity, then the projectors become exactly parallel (Figure 3.27). In equations (1) and (2) the ratio D/z_e tends to 1, and so $x_s = x_e$ and $y_s = y_e$.

This marks the crucial distinction between the two principal methods of projection used in technical drawing: **perspective** (sometimes called conical) projection, in which the projectors converge to a single point, the eye-point, and meet the image plane at varying angles; and **parallel** (sometimes called cylindrical) projection, in which the projectors are all parallel and meet the image plane at the same angle. A parallel projection can be thought of as like a perspective with an infinitely distant eye-point.

A special case of parallel projection is produced when the projectors meet the image plane at right angles, as shown in Figure 3.28. This is an **orthographic** projection. It is particularly simple to construct orthographic projections by computer since, as we have seen, the (x_s, y_s) values of the screen coordinates for the image of any point in the object are then just *equal* to that point's eye coordinates (x_e, y_e) while the z_e coordinate is ignored.

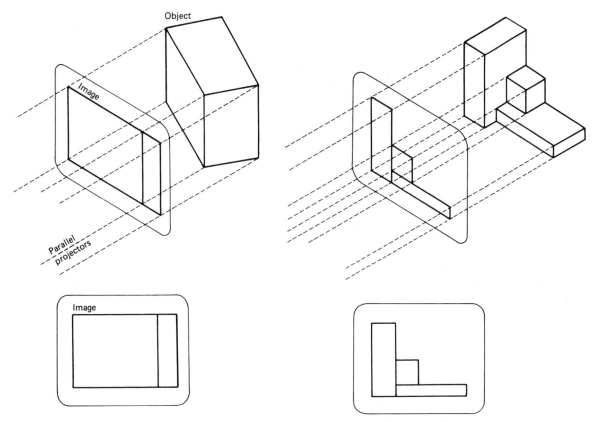

Fig. 3.27 The basic geometry of parallel projection, in which the notional eye-point is infinitely distant from the object, and the rays or projectors (shown dotted) are all parallel

Fig. 3.28 Object of rectangular geometry set with its front faces parallel with the image plane, in orthographic projection. These faces are projected at their true shape and size

Orthographic projections have, until the advent of computer graphics, been the most widely-used type of drawing in engineering and architectural practice. The reasons are that orthographic drawings are easier to draw by hand than perspectives, and that under appropriate conditions they preserve the true size and shape of the face of an object, and so can be used directly for measurement. Thus consider an object of broadly rectangular geometry, set such that its 'front' face or faces are parallel with the image plane (Figure 3.28). It is clear that these front faces will be projected orthographically without changing their shape or dimensions. On the other hand, the front faces in a corresponding perspective projection will be reduced in size, and, generally, *foreshortened* in the image depending on their distances and positions relative to the eye-point. Meanwhile other rectangular faces in the object, at right angles to the image plane, will, nevertheless, be visible in the image (unlike the orthographic projection) and will be transformed in shape (Figure 3.29).

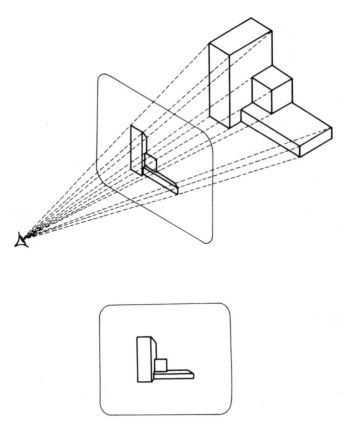

Fig. 3.29 Object of rectangular geometry set with its front faces parallel with the image plane, in perspective projection. These faces are foreshortened, and other faces perpendicular to the image plane are visible in the image (unlike orthographic projection; compare Figure 3.28)

4.3 Orthographic multi-views

It is usual in engineering to describe an object of rectangular geometry by means of a set of orthographic projections or **multi-views**. In the convention widely used in Britain and the United States known as **third angle**, these views can be imagined as projections onto the six faces of a notional 'glass box' surrounding the object (Figure 3.30). The projections are then viewed from the *outside* of this box. When the views are set out in an engineering drawing on a single sheet of paper, they are positioned relative to one another as if the box had been unfolded and laid flat. If the view from the front is set at the centre of the sheet, then the view from the right will be at the right, the view from the top at the top, and so on. In practice, for a largely symmetrical object it is often sufficient to draw three views only, and sometimes fewer than that. Some CAD systems for engineering design divide the screen into four quarters and show three multi-views in three of these viewports (Figure 3.31). The fourth viewport can then be used for text or for some other type of view, such as a perspective or isometric view.

In the architectural case the side views are the *elevations* of the building, and the top view is a *roof plan*. (These are not usually set out however in third angle convention, but drawn on separate sheets.)

The alternative convention for arranging multi-views, used sometimes in Britain and on the Continent, is that known as **first angle.** Here again we can think of the object as set inside a box, and orthographic projections formed onto the six faces of the box — the difference being this time that the box is opaque and the drawings are as if viewed from the *inside* of the box (Figure 3.32). The arrangement of different views on a single sheet then follows from 'unfolding' the box and laying it out flat as before.

Fig. 3.30 Conventional arrangement of orthographic multi-views in third angle

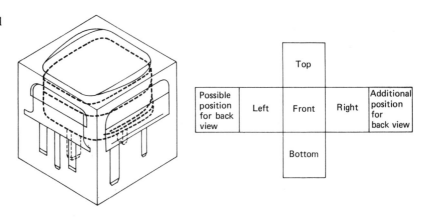

Possible position for back view	Left	Top		
	Left	Front	Right	Additional position for back view
		Bottom		

Fig. 3.31 Display screen divided into four viewports, to show three multi-views in first angle, plus a fourth pictorial view. [Euclid solid modeller, Matra Datavision.]

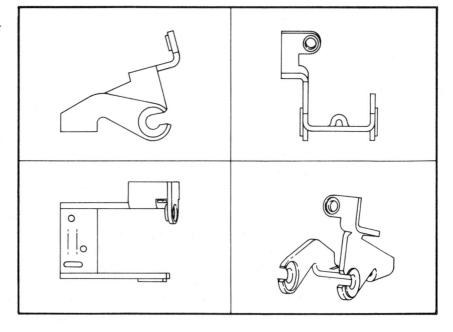

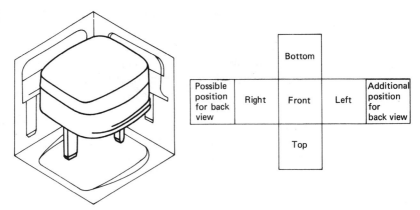

Fig. 3.32 Conventional arrangement of orthographic multi-views in first angle

		Bottom		
Possible position for back view	Right	Front	Left	Additional position for back view
		Top		

4.4 Sections

In all these cases the plane of projection is taken somewhere outside the object. However, another very useful type of orthographic view is the **section,** where the projection plane is taken *cutting through* the object. Naturally, this is most appropriate where the object has holes or interior features which are not visible from the outside. When the projection plane is outside the object, we assume obviously that the direction of view is towards the object. But when the projection plane cuts through the object in a section view, there are two alternative directions of view, and it is necessary to specify which is taken (Figure 3.33).

In architecture, because buildings are by their very nature hollow objects with complex interior detail, the use of sections is especially important. These can be taken in the vertical plane, in which case they are referred to simply as sections. Meanwhile, architects' *floor plans* are in effect sections in the horizontal plane, taken usually at about window height on each floor.

4.5 Doubly-curved surfaces represented by sections

Complex doubly-curved surfaces present special problems for conventional engineering drawing. Surfaces of this kind are to be found in the hulls of ships, the fuselages of aircraft, the bodies of cars, or the uppers of shoes. In later chapters we will see how these surfaces may be modelled mathematically for the purposes of CAD. Before the introduction of computer methods, however, there were only two ways of representing these kinds of surfaces: either by means of physical models of clay or wood; or by using section drawings. The technique, evolved originally in ship design, was to take sections (similar to contours) on a series of equally-spaced parallel planes in three perpendicular directions (Figure 3.34). Intermediate points on the surface could then be interpolated from these sections. As described in Chapter 6, computer methods for representing such doubly-curved surfaces have their origin in the practices of ship design, and are now highly developed.

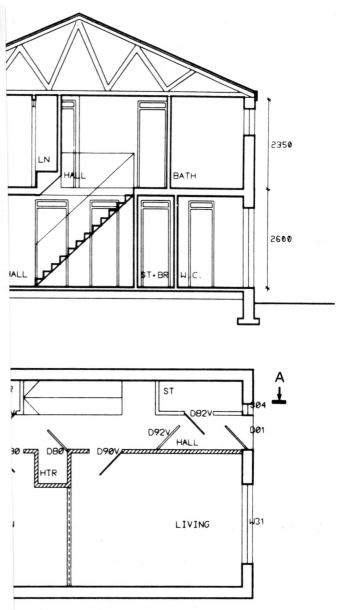

iew showing section plane and direction of view (marked by
A-A). The material cut by the section plane is shown in heavy
cottish Special Housing Association by Edinburgh University
litectural Design group.]

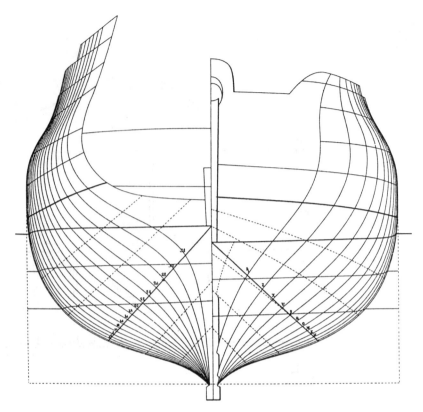

Fig. 3.34 Hull shape of 18th century French frigate described by a series of sections on regularly-spaced parallel planes

4.6   Comparative merits of perspective and orthographic projections

Because they preserve the true shapes of faces parallel to the given plane of projection, orthographic drawings are used almost universally for conveying information about dimension and shape from designer to manufacturer or builder. On the other hand, their drawback is that it is difficult for the designer — and even more so for the layman — to conceive the three-dimensional form and appearance of the object from a set of orthographic multi-views. For these purposes perspectives are more suitable. However, in the past the very great labour of producing perspectives by hand has limited their use in engineering.

For this reason a number of techniques have been devised for drawing 'pictorial' views, which are simpler to construct than perspectives. These are all special cases of parallel projection, but with the front faces of the object now set *at an angle* to the image plane. The best-known are the **isometric** projection, which is a special type of orthographic view in which x-, y- and z-axes of the world coordinate system describing the object all make equal angles with the image plane (Figure 3.35); and various forms of **oblique** projection, in which the projectors meet the image plane at some angle other than 90° (Figure 3.36). For all their merits, however, such projections neither correspond in general to natural appearances (like perspective), nor do they

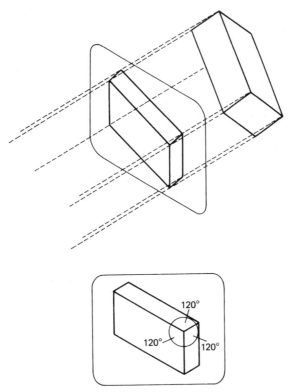

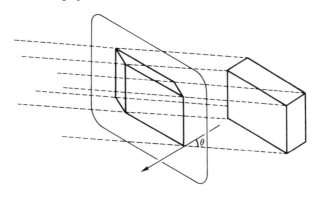

Fig. 3.35 The basic geometry of isometric projection, which is a class of orthographic projection where the x-, y- and z-axes of the world coordinate system all make equal angles with the image plane. As a result, the angles between the *images* of these axes, in the image plane, are all $120°$

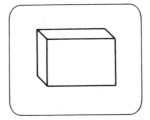

Fig. 3.36 The basic geometry of oblique projection, which is a class of parallel projection where the projectors meet the image plane at some angle θ other than $90°$

completely preserve true shape and size to scale in the visible faces (like orthographic multi-views).

With the introduction of computer-aided design, the designer can have the best of both worlds. Once a geometrical model of the designed object has been built in the machine, the cost of producing perspectives automatically from any chosen eye-point is trivial in computing terms. (Isometric and oblique projections are unlikely to survive in CAD, as a consequence.) Meanwhile, traditional orthographic multi-views can also be produced if required. Here there is a further advantage. Since the various orthographic projections are all made from the *same* three-dimensional model of the object, there is no possibility of geometrical inconsistency between the views — something that often occurs in orthographic drawings made by hand.

Draughting systems 4

P Steadman, A de Pennington and A Saia

1   Draughting system configurations

The development of interactive computer display technology has made possible the *computer-aided draughting system,* which essentially computerises the production of engineering, architectural, electronics and other technical drawings. Computer draughting now represents one of the most widespread uses of computers in design, and a large number of commercial systems are available. These computer-based draughting packages use an interactive display terminal and plotter to replace the drawing board and pencil.

A typical computer draughting workstation consists of a *graphics terminal* with screen and keyboard, and a *graphics tablet.* The screen displays either a part or the whole of the drawing, as it is being developed or modified. The keyboard is used to enter commands, instructions and data to the system, and also to input any text, labelling, titles or notes which are to appear in the drawing. In some systems two screens are employed, one an alphanumeric display (the dialogue monitor) for text and commands, the other capable of displaying graphics. Increasingly the trend is towards the adoption of raster graphics and the use of colour.

The tablet is used to enter the (x, y)-coordinates of points, by moving a *puck* or *stylus* over the tablet surface. The position of the stylus on the tablet is echoed by the position of a *cursor* symbol (often a flashing cross) on the screen. Currently other possibilities are for the movement of the cursor to be controlled by a *joystick, tracking ball, mouse, thumb-wheels, light-pen,* or special *cursor keys* on the keyboard. Screen positions can also be selected or located using faint, on-screen, (x, y) *cross-hairs* instead of a cursor symbol.

In some cases, coordinates must be transferred from an existing paper drawing — for example, a contoured site plan for a civil engineering or architectural project. This is done by taping the drawing to a *digitising board* and moving a puck over the required points or lines to input their positions.

Many draughting systems (and indeed computer-aided design systems generally) make use of *menus*, whereby a part of the screen or tablet is divided up into segments, each labelled with the name of a frequently-used command or action. A command is then activated by moving the stylus or cursor symbol to the relevant entry in the menu and entered typically by pressing a key. This has often proved to be more convenient for the user than typing, since the same 'pointing' instrument can be used to enter both commands and the positions of points.

Screen menus offer greater flexibility than do printed menus on tablets, since they can be organised hierarchically. A main menu can be displayed first, from which the user selects one of a number of *sub-menus,* each containing a related group of specific commands. Thus the user only sees on screen those commands which are relevant to what is being done.

Completed drawings can be *stored* as data in files on magnetic tape or disc, and paper copies made on plotters or printers, or photographic copies made on microfilm. Full-colour drawings on paper can be produced using ink-jet plotters. Engineering drawings of varying complexity might typically occupy between 0.1 and 0.4 megabytes of memory. Thus some three hundred drawings might be stored on a disc of 60 megabyte capacity. A tape typically has an even greater capacity. In addition to any on-line use, both magnetic tapes and discs provide compact archival facilities for the storage of all types of technical drawing.

2   Draughting system functions and facilities

Existing draughting systems vary considerably in the range and type of detailed functions which they provide. However, the following functions are representative of most current commercial packages.

All systems will have basic system control functions which allow: new drawings, graphical 'objects' or symbols to be entered, named and filed; old drawings or symbols to be called up from file, edited and redrawn; and finished drawings to be refiled or despatched for plotting.

Then there are the functions by which the drawing is actually put together. Engineering drawings convey essentially two kinds of information. The first kind of information is *geometrical* and relates to the shape and size of the object depicted. The second kind of information relates to *manufacturing* aspects (such as surface finish, tolerances and fits, and machining data), and this is generally conveyed in the form of notes, machining symbols, etc. (Figure 4.1).

2.1   Geometrical constructions

The geometrical parts of most engineering drawings are made up from straight lines, circles and arcs of circles, ellipses and perhaps higher-degree curves. All draughting systems provide functions for entering such shapes and moving or manipulating them on the screen, using the two-dimensional transformations described in the previous chapter (Figure 4.2).

A straight line might be entered by specifying the coordinates of two points

Fig. 4.1 Geometrical information and manufacturing information. [Drawing created with General Drafting System, Applied Research of Cambridge Ltd.]

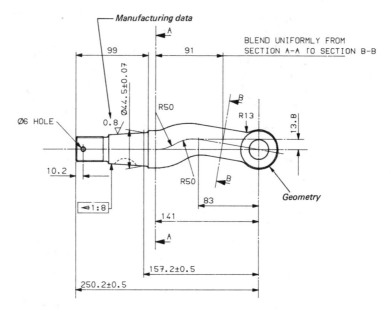

Manufacturing data

BLEND UNIFORMLY FROM
SECTION A-A TO SECTION B-B

Geometry

Fig. 4.2 (*Below, and page 86*) Selected examples of draughting system functions for geometrical constructions, from General Drafting System [Applied Research of Cambridge Ltd.]

straight line constructions

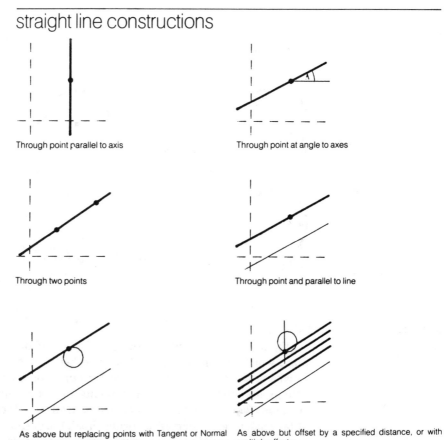

Through point parallel to axis

Through point at angle to axes

Through two points

Through point and parallel to line

As above but replacing points with Tangent or Normal relationship to existing graphics.

As above but offset by a specified distance, or with multiple offsets.

circles

Through three points

Through two diametrical points

By radius and two points on the circumference given in sequence

By radius, point on circumference and line on which centre must lie

By radius and centre

By point on circumference and centre

circular arcs

Through three points given in sequence

By start point, line through end and centre

By radius, start and end point given in sequence

Point on arc, line through start and line through end

on the line, or by specifying the coordinates of one point together with the angle which the line makes with some other line. A circle might be specified by giving the coordinates of its centre point together with its radius, or by giving the coordinates of three points on its circumference. A series of functions would provide for such geometrical constructions as: drawing lines at tangents to given curves; drawing circular arcs to join pairs of straight-line segments tangentially; drawing lines parallel to other lines at specified offset distances; creating regular polygons, particularly squares; and fitting curves through specified series of points.

The user might be helped in these geometrical operations in a variety of ways. First, the system might allow for temporary *construction lines* to be set out and erased again at a later stage. Secondly, it might be possible to impose a *regularly-spaced grid* of lines or points on the screen (either visible or invisible). The system then accepts the nearest grid-point to the current cursor position as the designated point (Figure 4.3). Thus points and lines are

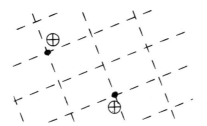

Fig. 4.3 Points automatically snapped to intersections of grid. The cross-in-circle indicates the actual cursor position, and the dot the grid-point accepted by the system

automatically 'snapped to' the grid. Such a facility might be useful, for example, in the design of a floor plan for a modular building. Thirdly, 'on-screen rulers' might be displayed to aid in the spacing of points or lines. Fourthly, the coordinates of the cursor position might be displayed, for the same spacing purpose.

Finally, all systems will allow for lines and other features to be erased selectively. It may be possible also to step back automatically through a sequence of lines in the reverse order to that in which they were drawn, in order to locate the one to be deleted.

2.2 Standard symbols

Once a complete drawing or part of a drawing has been created, it can be named and filed as a graphical 'object', to be recalled for use at any future time. Although any arbitrary collection of lines can be so designated, this facility is especially useful for drawing standard components or symbols, such as nuts, bolts, springs and screw-threads, electronic symbols, or the top views of furniture and fittings as shown in building plans. Many suppliers of draughting systems offer *libraries* of such ready-drawn symbols. These take the place of stencils and adhesive transfers in traditional draughting. These symbols can be rotated, reflected or scaled if necessary, and copied into the drawing in the required positions. One very useful graphical object is the standard frame and title box which a company uses for all its drawings.

In Britain, engineering drawings are ideally required to conform to the standards laid down in British Standard 308 (BS308), *Engineering drawing practice*. This specifies, amongst many other things, a series of standard line types, of differing widths and styles (continuous, chained, dashed) to show outlines, centre lines, dimension lines, hidden detail and so on. Any draughting system for engineering applications will provide functions for drawing lines in these styles. It will also provide facilities for the automatic hatching of sectioned parts (Figure 4.4).

Fig. 4.4 Automatic hatching of sectioned parts in various styles. [General Drafting System, Applied Research of Cambridge Ltd.]

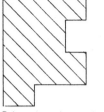

Polygons may be any shape

Polygons may be detached

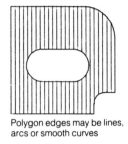

Polygon edges may be lines, arcs or smooth curves

2.3 Automatic dimensioning

Some more powerful draughting systems allow dimensions to be added automatically to a drawing. In a drawing made by hand, there is no necessary or inherent correspondence between the dimensions of the drawn outline and the intended dimensions of the object which it represents, until a scale has been specified. Moreover, the dimensional accuracy of the outline depends on the skill of the draughtsman. However, in a computer-generated drawing the actual coordinate values of points are entered explicitly and the image is generated *from* these. The machine can therefore calculate dimensions of length and angle from the coordinate information directly, and attach dimensional notations to the drawings, in the style laid down in BS308 for arrowheads, leaders, and the positioning and size of lettering. This is not, however, a trivial task, since it requires some judgement and skill on the part of the human draughtsman — which the machine must emulate — to decide where to place lettering and leaders so that these are clear and legible.

Computer drawings, unlike drawings made by hand, do not have to be constructed to some fixed scale. The actual dimensions of the required object are entered, and the drawing is displayed in a screen window at some arbitrary scale suited to the window size. The user can zoom in on selected parts of the drawing, in order to work on finer detail and to overcome the problem of the limited resolution of the screen. A fixed scale need only be decided when the finished drawing is despatched for plotting.

2.4 Layering

In many systems the data by which a drawing is represented are organised into a number of separate *layers*. From the user's point of view these can be thought of as a series of transparent sheets which are superimposed to make up the complete drawing. Thus the actual outline of a component might be on one layer; construction lines on another; dimensional annotations on a third; other notes and labels on a fourth; hatching on a fifth; and so on.

Different layers can be 'switched' on or off, and various different combinations of layers can be displayed or plotted. This method of organising the data makes for increased flexibility in the selective editing and layout of different parts of a drawing. Furthermore, the layering facility may be used in a different way to create, for example, a layered assembly drawing by bringing together appropriate existing drawings of all the components in the assembly, each of which can be scaled, positioned and edited where necessary on its own distinct layer. Yet another use of layers might be in the production of a version of a drawing with all the text translated into a foreign language and stored on a separate layer. Finally, some layering facilities allow security levels to be associated with different layers, so that 'locks' can be put on to restrict the viewing of certain commercially confidential features.

2.5 Parameterised descriptions of parts

One particularly powerful feature offered by some draughting systems is the ability to define shapes or symbols *parametrically*. A master shape is described in general terms by means of dimensional parameters identified by labels. The user can then assign specific values to these parameters, so as to produce a particular dimensioned instance of the shape (Figure 4.5). The effect is that one master parametric description can serve to represent a whole family of

Fig. 4.5 Master parametric definition of symbol (*top*), and three actual symbols generated from the master (*below*). [Micro Aided Engineering]

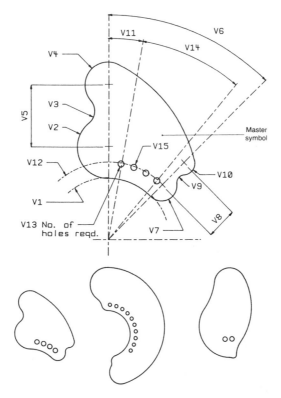

related shapes. These shapes may in principle be related not just by the kind of simple scaling and shearing transformations described in the last chapter, but by more complex transformations in which perhaps only the topological property of 'connectedness' is preserved for each member of the family of related 'shapes'. In practical terms this means that one parameterised definition can represent the drawings of a whole range of components of some standard type, such as bearings, ball-races or shafts (Figure 4.6). In certain cases the production of a complete component drawing will then involve nothing more than assigning appropriate parameter values to the master parametric shape and adding annotations.

Fig. 4.6 Drawing of a ball-race, produced automatically by assigning some twenty parameter values to a parameterised part description

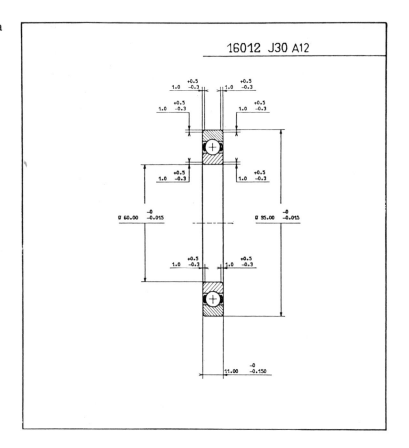

2.6 Integration of modelling with draughting

This chapter has concentrated solely on computer-aided draughting, and considered this essentially to be a two-dimensional application area. In contrast, the following chapters describe various different approaches to the computer modelling of objects in three dimensions. However, once a three-dimensional design has been created by such methods, there will in many cases still come a need to produce detailed paper drawings for the purposes of manufacture. Certainly this will be true of the drawings needed for buildings and civil engineering projects. In these circumstances the modelling and draughting functions must be linked together into a single integrated system, so that the drawings can be generated automatically from the geometrical data stored in the model (Figures 4.7 and 4.8). One advantage of integrating modelling with draughting in this way is that there is then no possibility of geometrical inconsistency between the various two-dimensional views of the object.

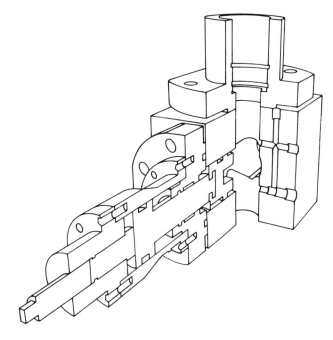

Fig. 4.7 Cut-away perspective view generated by NONAME solid modeller. [Geometric Modelling Project, Department of Mechanical Engineering, University of Leeds, and NEI Clarke Chapman Ltd.]

3 Traditional vs. computer draughting methods

The main advantages claimed for computer draughting over traditional drawing board methods are increased productivity and greater accuracy (although drawing office productivity may actually drop temporarily when a system is first installed, while staff go through a learning process). Computer draughting is generally faster than drawing by hand for a number of reasons already mentioned. Many geometrical constructions which would require elaborate and careful manual operations using instruments are made rapidly and automatically by the machine. Tedious hatching and dimensioning tasks are automated. The use of libraries of symbols and parameterised descriptions of parts means that much of the laborious repeated drawing of the same shape, involved in traditional methods, is avoided. When a revised version of an old drawing is required with some alterations, there is no need to re-trace the unchanged portions, and the parts to be revised can be erased or modified on screen before the final drawing is output on a plotter.

Historically one of the purposes of the conventions for engineering drawing laid down in the British Standard has been to reduce the labour of draughting by hand. For example, conventions are used to indicate symmetrical or repeated features without actually drawing these in full. Thus only one half of a bilaterally symmetric view of a component would be drawn, or only one radial sector of a view of a component with rotational symmetry. Other conventions are used to avoid the necessity for hand-rendering large areas of hatching or surface texture. In computer draughting, however, these constraints no longer need apply, and so we are seeing already the

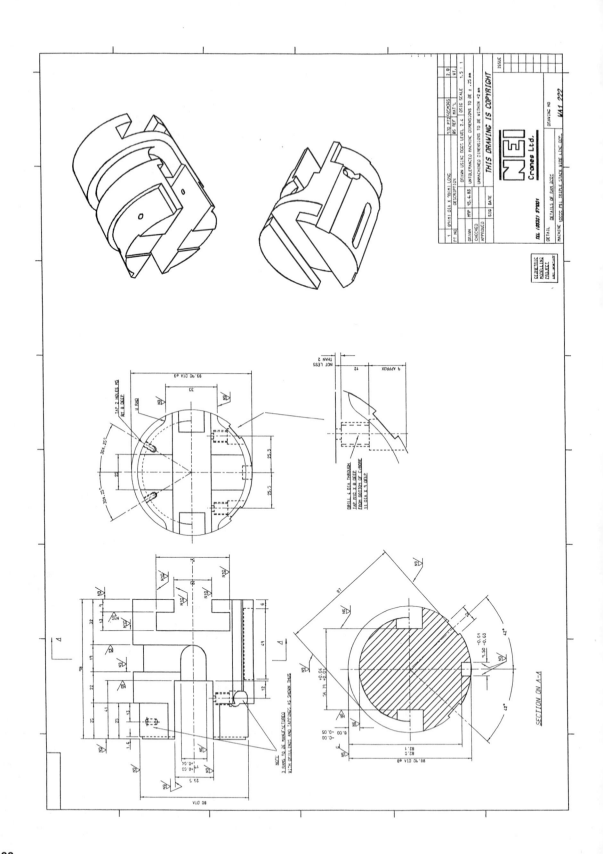

SECTION ON A-A

Fig. 4.8 Orthographic multi-views and perspectives generated by NONAME solid modeller. [Geometric Modelling Project, Department of Mechanical Engineering, University of Leeds, NEI Clarke Chapman Ltd, and PAFEC Ltd.]
(*see opposite on p. 92*)

reintroduction of 'labour-intensive' styles of engineering drawing, reminiscent even of 19th century practice (such as the use of colour and texture and the representation of shadows) where these can aid legibility and comprehension.

On the negative side, computer draughting systems do not always offer the flexibility of hand drawing methods. Furthermore, in the recent past the capital investment required in both hardware and software to set up a computer draughting installation has been considerable; though with the introduction of powerful micro-computer based systems this situation is changing. And, finally, from a non-commercial perspective, computer draughting of course, like some other computing applications, takes away a manual skill which has been a source of pride and pleasure to many workers.

Wire-frame modelling

5

J Rooney, M S Bloor and A Saia

1 Introduction

In order to create or to change a design, designers must have at their disposal some means for representing two-dimensional and three-dimensional objects. Traditionally, the method most commonly used for constructing and/or communicating such designs involves the use of various types of drawing and associated types of projection of three-dimensional geometrical information onto a two-dimensional medium.

Very often designers also build physical models to help in the visualisation of a design. This may require the construction of 'skeleton' models using wires to represent the edges of an object or component. *Wire-frame modelling*, as used currently in computer-aided engineering techniques, is the computer-based analogue of this process, and is used not only to model objects but also to facilitate the production of various projected views to aid visualisation.

Essentially, a **wire-frame model** consists of a finite set of points together with the edges connecting various pairs of these points, so that a drawing of these points and edges aids the visualisation of the object. The usefulness and ubiquity of wire-frames in computer-aided engineering drawing stems from the computer's ability to calculate quickly and accurately the positions of the points (and hence also the edges) on the screen or plotter-paper, when a view of a wire-frame object is required from some viewpoint. Objects represented by point (and associated edge) data can be manipulated to produce any required orthographic, isometric or perspective projection with equal ease. Since these projections make visualisation easier, and since point and edge data are always available for even the most rudimentary manual drawing of a three-dimensional object, wire-frame models have entered the standard tool kit of the computer-aided designer.

Although in some ways a draughting system is a two-dimensional wire-frame modeller, the actual geometric information implicitly used by designers when draughting, or when producing orthographic projections (say), is usually

95

greater than that used to define a wire-frame model, since (for draughting) they use their knowledge of the 'solidity' of the object and of its bounding surfaces. Thus a designer may draw a dotted line on a front view of an object to show that a particular (rear) edge cannot be seen, but only a human reader could interpret this as a hidden line. The computer draughting system has no three-dimensional model of the object with which to make any inference of this kind. Even a wire-frame model does not usually embody this type of additional information about the 'real' object. It is a representation which lies somewhere between that of a typical engineering drawing (whether produced manually or by a draughting system) and the more complex object representations which embody knowledge of surfaces and underlying solidity.

There are two important aspects to the use of wire-frame models in computer-aided design. The first is the computer representation of an object, and this is concerned with the structure needed to encode a wire-frame model. The second is concerned with the computational procedures needed to produce and manipulate the viewing or visualisation of this representation. We will concentrate here entirely on the first of these aspects. The viewing aspect is dealt with in Chapters 3 and 14.

2   Wire-frame representation

A wire-frame representation of a three-dimensional object consists of a finite set of points and connecting edges which define the object 'adequately' and facilitate subsequent visualisation. The term 'edge' does not necessarily imply that it is a straight-line segment. An edge may well be an arc of a circle or any other well-defined space curve (see Chapter 7) which is required for a 'good' wire-frame representation.

The geometric complexity of the representation of an object is dependent on a trade-off between what can be represented and computed easily and quickly, and what is required for a reasonably faithful and useful representation. The wire-frame offers a relatively simple three-dimensional modelling technique for relatively small computing resources and overheads. However, there are certain disadvantages associated with wire-frame modelling techniques (such as *ambiguity* and *lack of validity*) which make this type of representation unreliable in general. We will return to a discussion of these disadvantages later, but first we discuss the details of a wire-frame representation using several simple objects.

A computer representation of a wire-frame structure consists essentially of two types of information. The first is termed 'metric' or 'geometric' data which relate to the three-dimensional coordinate positions of the wire-frame 'node' points in space. The second is concerned with the 'connectivity' or 'topological' data which relate pairs of points together as edges.

2.1   Wire-frame with linear edges

As previously mentioned, the edges of a wire-frame model need not be straight-line segments but, clearly, these are the simplest type and we deal with them first. We refer to them as *linear* edges.

The tetrahedron

A simple illustration of a wire-frame model is afforded by the tetrahedron. The tetrahedron consists of four (vertex) points in space, with six linear edges joining pairs of these points.

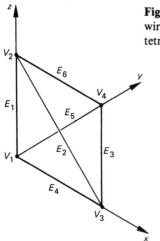

Fig. 5.1 Linear wire-frame model of a tetrahedron

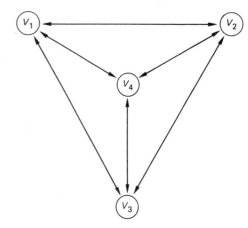

Fig. 5.2 Data structure for a tetrahedron

Vertex list	Edge list	Edge type
V_1 (0,0,0)	E_1 $<V_1, V_2>$	Linear
V_2 (0,0,1)	E_2 $<V_2, V_3>$	Linear
V_3 (1,0,0)	E_3 $<V_3, V_4>$	Linear
V_4 (0,1,0)	E_4 $<V_3, V_1>$	Linear
	E_5 $<V_1, V_4>$	Linear
	E_6 $<V_4, V_2>$	Linear

In Figure 5.1 the geometry of the tetrahedron is represented by a **vertex list** giving the (x, y, z)-coordinates of its vertices. The topology is similarly represented by an **edge list** giving each edge as a pair of vertices (its endpoints). If the edges were required to be more complex (that is, circular arcs, general curves, etc.) then a further tabulation could be associated which defines what each edge represents. The actual method used for representing these geometric and topological data within a computer is dependent on the particular coding facilities available (records, pointers) and on the types of viewing algorithms which will access these data. For example, Figure 5.2 shows the same (wire-frame) tetrahedron represented by a data structure using records and pointers.

This description represents the simplest level of wire-frame modelling. Extensions to this can be incorporated which progressively embody more information regarding the solidity of the object concerned (the aim of this is partly to allow the computation of more realistic images for visualisation). For example, a first step in building a more sophisticated model might be to add further topological data by defining a **face list** (that is, a list of sets of three edges to represent faces of the tetrahedron). These *faces* can then be considered to be surfaces, effectively extending the wire-frame model into a surface model which could subsequently be used to derive hidden line views (see Chapter 14), thereby further enhancing the visualisation of the object.

The cube

As a second simple example of a wire-frame model we consider the cube. This consists of eight (vertex) points in space, with twelve linear edges joining pairs of these points.

Fig. 5.3 Linear wire-frame model of a cube

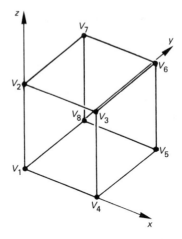

Vertex list	Edge list		Face list
V_1 (0,0,0)	E_1 $<V_1, V_2>$	E_7 $<V_7, V_8>$	F_1 $<E_1, E_2, E_3, E_{11}>$
V_2 (0,0,1)	E_2 $<V_2, V_3>$	E_8 $<V_8, V_1>$	F_2 $<E_7, E_6, E_5, E_{12}>$
V_3 (1,0,1)	E_3 $<V_3, V_4>$	E_9 $<V_2, V_7>$	F_3 $<E_1, E_9, E_7, E_8>$
V_4 (1,0,0)	E_4 $<V_4, V_5>$	E_{10} $<V_3, V_6>$	F_4 $<E_3, E_{10}, E_5, E_4>$
V_5 (1,1,0)	E_5 $<V_5, V_6>$	E_{11} $<V_1, V_4>$	F_5 $<E_8, E_{12}, E_4, E_{11}>$
V_6 (1,1,1)	E_6 $<V_6, V_7>$	E_{12} $<V_8, V_5>$	F_6 $<E_9, E_6, E_{10}, E_2>$
V_7 (0,1,1)			
V_8 (0,1,0)			

In Figure 5.3 the geometry of the cube is again represented by a vertex list and the topology by an edge list. However, notice that, unlike the case of the tetrahedron, the edge list for the cube does not contain all pairs of vertices, since each pair of diagonally opposite vertices on each face, for example, does not form an edge.

We can extend this simple wire-frame model of the cube by defining a face list from sets of four edges (since the faces are square). However, it is not true that any four edges define a face for the cube (consider diagonally opposite pairs of edges, for example). So, as with the edge list, the face list for the cube does not contain all possible sets of four edges.

The tesseract

As a further example of a linear wire-frame model we consider the framework shown in Figure 5.4. This has sixteen (vertex) points, with thirty-two linear edges joining pairs of these points. The framework has the same topology (that is, edge list) as the well-known four-dimensional 'cube' — the tesseract — but we treat it here as a three-dimensional 'image' of the original, potentially representing a solid box, for example.

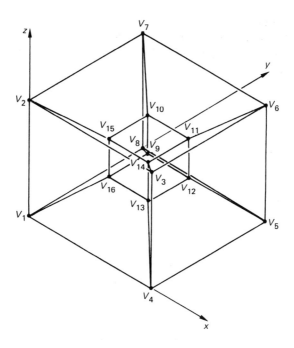

Fig. 5.4 Linear wire-frame model of a tesseract

Vertex list			
V_1	(0,0,0)	V_9	(1,2,1)
V_2	(0,0,3)	V_{10}	(1,2,2)
V_3	(3,0,3)	V_{11}	(2,2,2)
V_4	(3,0,0)	V_{12}	(2,2,1)
V_5	(3,3,0)	V_{13}	(2,1,1)
V_6	(3,3,3)	V_{14}	(2,1,2)
V_7	(0,3,3)	V_{15}	(1,1,2)
V_8	(0,3,0)	V_{16}	(1,1,1)

The geometry of the tesseract is again represented by a vertex list (Figure 5.4) and the topology by an edge list. As with the cube, the edge list for the tesseract will not contain all pairs of vertices. Similarly, if we construct a face list of sets of four edges, not all such sets would form valid faces, again as with the cube. (Extending this concept a little further it is actually possible to construct a **volume list** for the tesseract from sets of six faces, if we revert to considering it as a four-dimensional object, but we will not pursue this here.)

Considered as a three-dimensional object, the tesseract is interesting in that some of its edges and faces are inside the bounding cube. This illustrates the inadequacy of wire-frame modelling, since we cannot immediately determine whether or not the wire framework is enclosing a volume and so defining a solid object. This is clearly still a problem even though we have defined a face list — the faces do not necessarily form the boundary of an enclosed volume. Furthermore it is possible to interpret the tesseract as a solid object with a hole (rather like a doughnut or one of the links in a chain) in which case it is a non-convex solid, and some of the specified faces would be sets of four edges forming the boundary of a rectangular (or square) hole, rather than of a rectangular surface.

2.2 Wire-frames with curvilinear edges

Many (if not most) solid obects have curved boundaries and so are best represented in wire-frame form by *curvilinear* edges.

The cone

Perhaps the simplest illustration of a curvilinear wire-frame model is afforded by the cone. This consists of a single vertex point (the apex) and a circular base. The apex is joined to the base by an infinite set of straight-line segments (the generators of the cone).

Fig. 5.5 Curvilinear wire-frame model of a cone

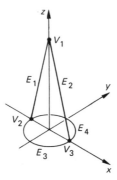

Vertex list	Edge list	Edge type
V_1 (0,0,,3)	E_1 $<V_1, V_2>$	Linear
V_2 (−1,0,0)	E_2 $<V_1, V_3>$	Linear
V_3 (1,0,0)	E_3 $<V_2, V_3>$	Semi-circular
	E_4 $<V_2, V_3>$	Semi-circular

In representing the geometry of the cone (Figure 5.5) the simplest vertex list contains just three vertices — the apex and two other vertices, one on either end of a diameter across the circular base. The edge list then contains just four edges — two linear edges from the apex to the base, and two semi-circular edges forming the circular base. (Actually we could have just one vertex on the base, but this would complicate the edge list, since the base edge would then be a complete circle and be specified by a single vertex, or pair of identical vertices.) Of course, the edge list must be augmented by a specification of the form of the curvilinear edges (in this case, semi-circles). The trouble with this wire-frame model is that the resulting cone only looks like a cone from certain viewpoints and any faces that we may define by a face list are not easily perceived.

An improvement can be achieved by dividing up the base circle with more vertices. This produces both a longer vertex list and a longer edge list, and the curvilinear edges become shorter circular arcs. As the number of vertices is increased, so the wire-frame model becomes (in appearance at least) more realistic until, in the limit, with an infinite number of vertices on the base circle, we obtain all the generators of the cone and have thus represented the entire curved surface as an infinite set of linear edges.

A simplified form of the cone can similarly be obtained by dividing up the base circle with many vertices (as before), but then joining these with linear edges (chords of the circle) instead of curvilinear edges (circular arcs). Any face list that we then construct would consist mainly of flat triangular faces — the cone becomes facetted.

The cylinder

Another simple illustration of a curvilinear wire-frame model is afforded by the cylinder. This consists of a circular top and a circular base joined by an infinite set of parallel straight line segments (the generators of the cylinder).

Fig. 5.6 Curvilinear wire-frame model of a cylinder

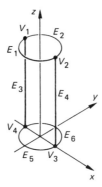

Vertex list	Edge list	Edge type
V_1 (-1,0,3)	E_1 $<V_1, V_2>$	Semi-circular
V_2 (1,0,3)	E_2 $<V_1, V_2>$	Semi-circular
V_3 (1,0,0)	E_3 $<V_1, V_4>$	Linear
V_4 (-1,0,0)	E_4 $<V_2, V_3>$	Linear
	E_5 $<V_3, V_4>$	Semi-circular
	E_6 $<V_3, V_4>$	Semi-circular

The simplest vertex list contains just four vertices — two on the top and two on the base (Figure 5.6). The edge list then contains just six edges — two linear edges from top to base, and four semi-circular edges. Again the edge list must be augmented by a specification of the form of the curvilinear edges.

As with the cone, more vertices can be introduced on both top and base circle to produce a more realistic model. A facetted wire-frame model can similarly be produced by using linear edges (chords) around top and base circles. In this case any face list constructed for the facetted cylinder would consist mainly of flat rectangular faces, and the cylinder would become essentially a prism.

The sphere

A final example of a curvilinear wire-frame model is provided by the sphere. In the case of both the cone and the cylinder, the solid objects have bounding surfaces which can be generated from straight lines (they are *ruled* surfaces). As a consequence, the corresponding edge lists in their wire-frame models contain a mixture of linear and curvilinear edges. However, for the sphere this is not the case, since its bounding surface is doubly curved (and hence not ruled). A wire-frame model of the sphere therefore contains only curvilinear edges in its edge list, unless some approximation (such as facetting) is imposed.

Fig. 5.7 Two curvilinear wire-frame models of a sphere

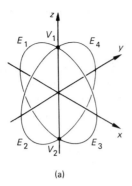

(a)

Vertex list	Edge list
V_1 (0,0,1)	E_1 $<V_1, V_2>$
V_2 (0,0,-1)	E_2 $<V_1, V_2>$
	E_3 $<V_1, V_2>$
	E_4 $<V_1, V_2>$

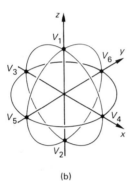

(b)

Vertex list	Edge list
V_1 (0,0,1)	E_1 $<V_1, V_3>$
V_2 (0,0,-1)	E_2 $<V_1, V_4>$
V_3 (-1,0,0)	E_3 $<V_1, V_5>$
V_4 (1,0,0)	E_4 $<V_1, V_6>$
V_5 (0,-1,0)	E_5 $<V_2, V_3>$
V_6 (0,1,0)	E_6 $<V_2, V_4>$
	E_7 $<V_2, V_5>$
	E_8 $<V_2, V_6>$
	E_9 $<V_3, V_5>$
	E_{10} $<V_5, V_4>$
	E_{11} $<V_4, V_6>$
	E_{12} $<V_6, V_3>$

Actually a vertex list for a sphere is somewhat problematical since there are no obvious vertex points to select. All points on the surface of a sphere are essentially equivalent, so we must arbitrarily choose some as our vertices. Many different possible choices exist, but perhaps the simplest is to select a 'north pole' and a 'south pole' as just two vertices and then to form an edge list of curvilinear edges consisting of a set of *meridians* (Figure 5.7).

This choice has two odd consequences. First, all meridian edges have the same end-points, so that the edge list consists of repeated copies of the pair of north and south pole vertices. Each edge differs from the next only in its *curvilinear* specification. Secondly, any face list we construct will consist of faces bounded by just *two* edges (cf. the base of the cone, and the top and base of the cylinder).

Any number of meridians can be introduced into this wire-frame model (resembling a segmented orange) to produce a more (or less) realistic appearance, but facetting in terms of flat polygonal faces is not possible without introducing more vertices along the meridians between the poles.

A better, simple wire-frame model of the sphere is obtained by constructing a vertex list consisting of six vertices symmetrically disposed at the corners of a regular octahedron (Figure 5.7(b)). The edge list then consists of twelve curvilinear edges (quarter-circle arcs), and a face list of eight sets of three such edges can easily be specified. This time a crude facetted approximation can also be derived by replacing the quarter-circle arcs with straight-line chords to obtain an octahedron.

3 Real objects and wire-frame models

Interesting (and perhaps not so interesting) wire-frame structures can be created and manipulated as entities without any consideration for the object(s) they may be used to represent. However, in most cases three-dimensional wire-frames are used to model objects in the real world, providing (amongst other things) a tool to aid object visualisation. In general this modelling process can be likened to the increasing use of constraints which limit the allowable data structures available to represent true objects. A general wire-frame such as each of those given in the previous examples usually has associated low-level constraints. Thus each point must have three coordinate values, and each edge must be associated with only two points, which must both be defined in the point list. Additionally, real object representation effectively involves further constraints on the wire-frame structure. These constraints may be left to the user to maintain (often leading to error), or, more commonly, they may be embodied in checking algorithms, which process a wire-frame structure in order to determine its suitability in representing an object. A third possibility is that they can be built into the interactive tools used to create the wire-frame.

Again, referring to our previous examples, we can embody the constraint that edges must form closed loops, which effectively define the faces of the object. Of course, these edge-loops (forming the faces) should not be self-intersecting and should be in one piece (that is, multiple loops are not allowed). All of these types of object-related requirements imply much more sophisticated representations than simple wire-frames provide, and they require accompanying creation and consistency facilities in the wire-frame builder.

Even supposing that all of these requirements are satisfied, three-dimensional wire-frames still have failings in two major areas: *lack of validity* and *ambiguity*. Consider the object shown in Figure 5.8. This can be

Fig. 5.8 A wire-frame nonsense object

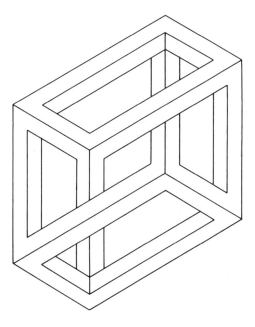

represented by the type of structure described above, consisting of simple (vertex) points and linear edges. Each point is well-defined in three-dimensional space; each edge is associated with just two end-points; the face edges all form closed loops; and no faces are self-intersecting. However, despite these constraints, this wire-frame is essentially a nonsense. We would never be able to manufacture such an object. In other words, the wire-frame does not represent a valid solid entity. We could argue that imposing further constraints such as 'faces form closed volumes' would not allow such objects to be defined, but this is effectively moving away from what we may term pure wire-frames into the area of solid modelling, where the requirement from the outset is the creation of representations of real solid objects within computers.

The second failing is that of ambiguity. Essentially it is possible to produce a general wire-frame which can be interpreted to represent more than one real object. An example is shown in Figure 5.9. Again this wire-frame conforms to the constraints mentioned earlier, and in addition we can argue that the faces formed by edge-loops do in fact form closed volumes, but which volumes are they? The wire-frame is ambiguous and can represent any of the other real objects shown in the figure. Again we can argue further that more sophisticated constraints can be built into the wire-frame structure which eliminate this type of ambiguity, but this takes us into the realm of solid modelling theory which was originally driven by such problems in wire-frame modelling for real object representation.

Fig. 5.9 An ambiguous wire-frame object

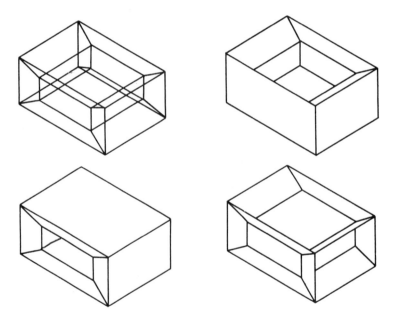

One final point to be made is that a simple wire-frame model incorporating curvilinear edges produces several difficulties when we wish to view it. The most serious is the problem of its *silhouette, horizon,* or *profile curve.* Generally this will not be the same as one (or a collection) of the edges and it must be calculated separately from a knowledge of the wire-frame edges and the proposed viewpoint. The difficulties are best understood by referring to Figure 5.10. This illustrates the wire-frame cylinder as viewed from two

Fig. 5.10 Silhouette curves for a wire-frame cylinder

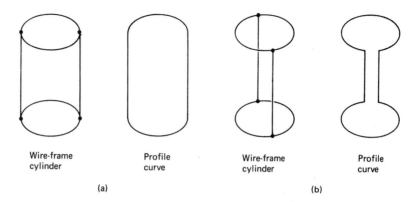

Wire-frame cylinder

Profile curve

Wire-frame cylinder

Profile curve

(a)

(b)

different viewpoints. In the first, the silhouette is clearly the same as the desired shape of the cylinder. In the second, however, the silhouette gives only a partial view of the modelled cylinder. Similarly the sphere, shown in Figure 5.7 and represented by six vertices and twelve quarter-circle edges, will clearly have a complete circle as silhouette when viewed from directly above one of the vertices. In reality, when viewed from directly above any other position it should still have a circular profile. However, the wire-frame edges will give at best an elliptical silhouette and in general a more complicated profile with cusps. The true profile must therefore be calculated before displaying the object and for more general shapes this can be a complex task.

Surface modelling 6

M J Pratt

1 Background

Historically, the first systems to be developed for computer-aided geometric design were surface systems. Their line of development can be traced back to before the Second World War to methods used in the aircraft and shipbuilding industries. At that time curvilinear shapes such as fuselages and ship hulls were defined by means of sets of curves in three orthogonal planes; the terms 'section lines', 'waterlines' and 'buttock lines', which originated in the shipyards, are still often used for these curves. Traditionally, they were drawn out full size in the loft of the shipyard; this gave rise to the term 'lofting', which remains in use today to describe the specification of a curved form in terms of families of plane curves.

Lofting was a lengthy and tedious process, because although the shapes being designed were three-dimensional the lofters were restricted to working in terms of plane curves. The shape was not defined satisfactorily until the three families of curves had been adjusted to form a spatial network in which the curves intersected each other as though they had been drawn on the desired surface. However, a first attempt usually led to a set of waterlines which did not intersect with the section lines, for example. A meticulous and time-consuming iterative manual process was required for achievement of the desired intersecting network.

This was essentially the situation in the early 1940s. The pressures of wartime production, particularly in the aircraft industry, led to changes in the way the geometry was represented. It was found possible to avoid working to full size, and to represent fuselage cross-sections in terms of mathematically defined curves such as conics. Subsequently, mathematical techniques were devised allowing these cross-sections to be blended or interpolated into a smooth surface. Thus the 'network of curves' approach was gradually superseded, becoming replaced by methods which actually described a complete surface. A book by Liming [1944] explains many of the techniques used at this time.

The transition to a more mathematical procedure naturally brought with it a demand for increased computation. This was initially met by the use of mechanical or electro-mechanical desk calculators, but with the advent of powerful electronic digital computers the methods became increasingly automated. Lidbro [1956] describes a system used by Saab-Scania in Sweden in the 1950s, a developed version of which was still in use on mainframe computers in the 1980s, based closely on the approach described.

The major conceptual change which has taken place since the development of these early surface systems lies in the modern use of parametrically defined geometry, which has largely replaced the use of classical geometry expressed in terms of conventional cartesian coordinates. The use of parametric techniques demands greater computing resources but has numerous advantages, as will be described. Such methods became popular in the 1960s, largely due to the pioneering work of Coons [1964]. One of their most important features is that the mathematical formulation of curves and surfaces defined parametrically does not change under transformations such as translation, rotation or reflection. All that changes is a set of numerical coefficients in the defining equations. The designer effectively works in terms of these coefficients, which have been described as the 'handles' on the design system. Various ingenious, but essentially equivalent, ways have been devised of providing 'handles' to allow a designer to take advantage of the freedom available in design with no requirement for advanced mathematical training.

Corresponding technological changes have occurred during the same period. Quite apart from the enormous increase in computing power, we now have inexpensive computer graphics systems. In the earliest days surfaces were defined by sets of numbers on paper; later they were defined by sets of numbers in the computer, but it was not until comparatively recently that graphical feedback to the designer became a commonplace reality. In the 1960s surface generation was essentially a batch process, and the output had to be judged by interpretation of tables of numbers. Nowadays, however, computers are fast enough for surface design to be an interactive process, and the graphics terminal allows designers to judge the acceptability of their results as they proceed.

Once a mathematical representation of a shape has been computed and stored, it may be used in various ways. For example, the computer can readily convert between different units of measurement. It can compute cross-sectional curves or areas automatically. It can output shape information not only to a graphics screen but also, for example, to a draughting machine, to a finite element mesh generator or to a numerically-controlled (NC) machine tool used in the manufacture of the surface. Surface systems were, in fact, the first CAD systems to raise the possibility of integrating the whole industrial process of design and analysis through to production and quality control, using the computer as an intermediary.

Although the earliest surface systems were developed within the aircraft industry and demanded very large and expensive computer installations, modern systems are used in a wide spectrum of industrial applications and now have comparatively modest hardware requirements by present-day standards. Their use is widespread in shipbuilding, automotive manufacture and the shoe industry, and they are rapidly spreading into numerous small and medium-sized companies manufacturing forgings, castings and moulded products.

Many such articles, including a wide range of commonplace household products, are characterised by smoothly curved shapes with blended edges which are not easily represented by conventional engineering drawings. Furthermore, it is difficult for designers to obtain good visualisations of their ideas from wire-frame models of this type of artefact, whereas the surface modeller is ideal for the design of such products since the entire surface is represented, allowing the computer to generate very realistic shaded surface pictures.

Once the product has been (surface) modelled, its geometry may be used directly in the design of the mould or die in which it is to be made. Essential calculations can usually be performed automatically by the computer such as, for example, the determination of the volume enclosed by a mould or by a pair of dies. This gives an immediate estimate of the volume of raw material needed to make the product. For applications such as this, the surface modeller has manifest advantages over the wire-frame modeller. On the other hand, there would be little virtue in carrying all the overheads associated with true solid modelling, described in later chapters, especially since most existing solid modelling systems are not as yet very well developed in free-form surface representation.

2   The nature of parametric curve and surface geometry

To demonstrate some of the virtues of the parametric approach we consider a parametric equation for the straight line joining two distinct points having position vectors $\mathbf{p}_1, \mathbf{p}_2$ with respect to some origin (Figure 6.1).

Fig. 6.1 Parametric form of a straight line

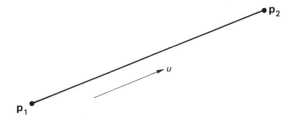

Only one independent parameter is needed to parameterise a curve (for example, the length along the curve from some fixed point on it). For a straight line joining the points $\mathbf{p}_1$ and $\mathbf{p}_2$, the position of a general point on the line is specified by its position vector, $\mathbf{r}$ (Chapter 1). The simplest mathematical expression for $\mathbf{r}$ in terms of a parameter u has the form

$$\mathbf{r}(u) = (1 - u)\mathbf{p}_1 + u\mathbf{p}_2$$

where $\mathbf{r}(u)$ is the variable position vector depending on u. This is a linear combination of the position vectors $\mathbf{p}_1$ and $\mathbf{p}_2$, but it is not the most general linear combination since the two coefficients u and $(1 - u)$ sum to 1. This ensures that the $\mathbf{r}(u)$ so generated lies on the straight line joining $\mathbf{p}_1$ to $\mathbf{p}_2$ rather than being a general point in the plane defined by the position vectors $\mathbf{p}_1$ and

$\mathbf{p}_2$. It is clear that $u = 0$ gives $\mathbf{r}(0) = \mathbf{p}_1$ while $u = 1$ gives $\mathbf{r}(1) = \mathbf{p}_2$. These are the end-points of the straight-line segment. As u increases from 0 to 1 the point defined by $\mathbf{r}(u)$ moves along the line from one end-point to the other. Note that if it is desired to apply some transformation such as translation or rotation to the line, it is only necessary to transform the points $\mathbf{p}_1$ and $\mathbf{p}_2$, i.e. the defining data. The mathematical form of the line representation in terms of the parameter u remains unaltered. This is an important and very useful property which is possessed by many of the parametric representations of CAD geometry, but which is frequently lacking in other types of representation.

The linear functions $(1-u)$ and u used in the line definition are the simplest cases of what are called **blending functions.** They blend the defining data together to give the required geometric entity, in this case the straight-line segment interpolating two given points. Suppose now that we have two lines defined in the manner described:

$$\mathbf{r}_1(u) = (1 - u)\mathbf{p}_1 + u\mathbf{p}_2$$

$$\mathbf{r}_2(u) = (1 - u)\mathbf{p}_3 + u\mathbf{p}_4$$

where $0 \leqslant u \leqslant 1$

If we now use a further two linear blending functions $(1-v)$ and v, in terms of a second parameter v, we can interpolate a surface between the two original lines with the same type of linear mathematical expression:

$$\mathbf{r}(u, v) = (1 - v)\mathbf{r}_1(u) + v\mathbf{r}_2(u)$$

Clearly $v = 0$ gives the first line and $v = 1$ the second. As v varies from 0 to 1 the line moves in space between $\mathbf{r}_1(u)$ and $\mathbf{r}_2(u)$, sweeping out a surface as shown in Figure 6.2.

Fig. 6.2 A parametric bilinear surface

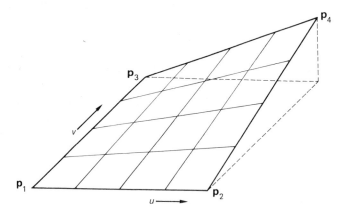

All four boundaries of the surface are straight lines. It is known as a **parametric bilinear surface,** since it is expressed in terms of linear functions of both u and v (namely u, $1 - u$, v and $1 - v$). If the straight lines $\mathbf{r}_1(u)$ and $\mathbf{r}_2(u)$ lie in the same plane, the surface $\mathbf{r}(u, v)$ will be a plane segment, but in general it will be a segment of a hyperbolic paraboloid, one of the class of quadric surfaces.

By substituting into the equation for $\mathbf{r}(u, v)$ the expressions for $\mathbf{r}_1(u)$ and $\mathbf{r}_2(u)$, we can obtain an expression for the surface in terms of the four position vectors defining the original two line segments. This has the form

$$\mathbf{r}(u, v) = (1 - v)(1 - u)\mathbf{p}_1 + (1 - v)u\mathbf{p}_2 + v(1 - u)\mathbf{p}_3 + vu\mathbf{p}_4$$

As with the straight line, this surface region is specified entirely in terms of point data, $\mathbf{p}_1, \mathbf{p}_2, \mathbf{p}_3, \mathbf{p}_4$. It may be transformed very simply by applying the required transformations to these defining points; the mathematical formulation in terms of the blending functions remains unchanged. Most other types of surface representation do not have this desirable property.

Two parameters, u and v, have been used in defining the surface region described. In fact these parameters provide a natural curvilinear coordinate system embedded in the surface. Lines for which u is constant and lines for which v is constant form a mesh lying on the surface as shown in Figure 6.2. The existence of these constant parameter lines in the surface is of great importance (as will be seen later) in the computation of cutter paths for NC machine tools when machining the surface. Since the corners of the region have parameter-pair values $(0, 0), (0, 1), (1, 0)$ and $(1, 1)$, it can be thought of as a deformation of the unit square $0 \leqslant u, v \leqslant 1$ (in the two-dimensional (u, v)-plane) into three-dimensional (x, y, z)-space.

Although bilinear surfaces of the type described above illustrate the nature of parametric surface geometry in general, they are not much used in practice because they possess very little flexibility for surface design. It has been found that a practical basis for this purpose results if the two linear (first-degree) blending functions, u and $(1 - u)$, introduced earlier for curves, are replaced by four cubic (third-degree) blending functions of the parameter u. This gives a **cubic parametric curve**, which can occur in several different mathematical forms. The following expression is a typical form due to Bézier [1971]:

$$\mathbf{r}(u) = (1 - u)^3\mathbf{p}_1 + 3u(1 - u)^2\mathbf{q}_1 + 3u^2(1 - u)\mathbf{q}_2 + u^3\mathbf{p}_2$$

As can be seen, for defining such a cubic curve the position vectors of four points (rather than the two required previously for the straight line) are now needed. These are the original end-points $\mathbf{p}_1$ and $\mathbf{p}_2$, together with two extra points $\mathbf{q}_1$ and $\mathbf{q}_2$ associated with these end-points respectively. All four points are known as **control points**. Each position vector is multiplied by a different one of the four cubic blending functions and the products summed to give the curve representation. An appropriate choice of blending functions can be made so that the curve segment defined by the parameter range $0 \leqslant u \leqslant 1$ approximates in some sense the polygonal arc obtained by joining the four control points $\mathbf{p}_1, \mathbf{q}_1, \mathbf{q}_2$ and $\mathbf{p}_2$ by three straight lines, as shown in Figure 6.3.

Fig. 6.3 A Bézier cubic parametric curve

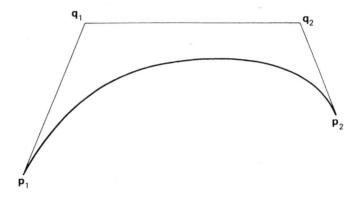

This then allows the user to manipulate the curve in a predictable way by moving the control points. The well-known Bézier and B-spline techniques are based on this type of approach. They and certain other formulations of the cubic parametric curve are mathematically equivalent, differing only in the way in which the various degrees of freedom available for changing the shape are presented to the user defining the curve. For example, the user may be required to work solely in terms of control points, or alternatively may have to specify the end-points together with the end tangent directions of the curve segment.

Curve representations have also been devised using $n + 1$ blending functions which are each polynomials of degree $n > 3$. The extra degrees of freedom may be presented to the user as more control points to manipulate or as additional conditions which can be imposed at the end-points of the segment.

Just as in the linear case first described, it is possible to introduce a second parameter v, and extend these more general curve definitions into definitions of surface regions in terms of u and v. Such regions, which in many cases are bounded by the range of parameters $0 \leqslant u \leqslant 1, 0 \leqslant v \leqslant 1$, are often called **surface patches.** This extension of the cubic curve segment governed by four control points gives rise to a **bicubic surface patch** governed by sixteen control points $\mathbf{p}_1, \ldots, \mathbf{p}_4, \mathbf{q}_1, \ldots, \mathbf{q}_{12}$, arranged in a (4×4) spatial mesh as shown in Figure 6.4. As in the case of the curve, the surface patch can be manipulated by moving the control points.

Fig. 6.4 A Bézier bicubic parametric patch

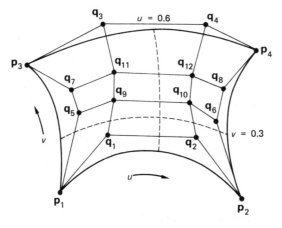

A more detailed account of the properties of the types of curves and surfaces briefly discussed here is given in Chapters 7 and 8, while a full discussion may be found in Faux and Pratt [1979].

3 Practical aspects of surface modelling systems

Individual surface patches of the kinds described do not generally possess sufficient freedom for the representation of the shape of a complete artefact. It is almost invariably necessary to use an assembly of such patches; a complete car body, for example, may need several hundred patches. In general, the lower the polynomial degree of the patches used, the more patches will be needed. Fortunately techniques are available for ensuring continuity of position and of surface slope across boundaries between adjoining patches. Conversely, if a slope discontinuity is required, as for example along a crease-line on a car body, then this is also easy to arrange.

From the user's point of view there are three fairly distinct methods for defining composite patched surfaces in existing commercial systems. These are as follows:

1 The designer works initially in terms of a set of plane cross-sectional curves, not necessarily all in parallel planes. The system then automatically lofts or blends the cross-sections to give a smooth surface which contains all of them. This is the method most closely related to traditional practice. The system DUCT [Sturge 1983] exemplifies this approach.

2 The designer initially sets up an array of points in space, such that a family of m curves can be interpolated through them in one direction and a family of n curves through them in another direction, to give a regular curvilinear mesh of four-sided cells. The original points lie at the intersections of the two families of curves. The system then automatically constructs surface patches to fit each mesh cell, subject to slope continuity across all patch boundaries unless otherwise specified. Indeed, it is even possible to obtain curvature continuity between patches using polynomial surfaces of degree as low as three. The system POLYAPT [Clarke 1982] uses this method.

3 The designer again defines a network of curves on the surface, but this time generates an irregular mesh which may contain three-sided patches. Surface patches are then individually fitted to the boundaries thus defined; it is in some cases possible to specify a least-squares fit to data points in the patch interiors also. This type of technique is suited to the definition of car bodies, which are fitted to point data measured from a clay model. The feature lines of the surface are first fitted with curves, and then the resulting mesh is used as the framework for the composite surface. The Advanced Surface Design facility in the well-known Computervision system can be used in this way.

From the traditional designer's point of view some of these methods present unfamiliar features. The lofting approach usually gives rise to fewer conceptual difficulties, since it is based on the use of plane cross-sections. If these cross-sections all lie in parallel planes the situation is comparatively straightforward, but considerably more flexibility is gained by the use of non-parallel cross-section planes, which permit the definition of objects such as the pump volute shown in Figure 6.5.

The use of a lofting system with this capability requires a good facility in three-dimensional conceptualisation on the part of the user. The systems based

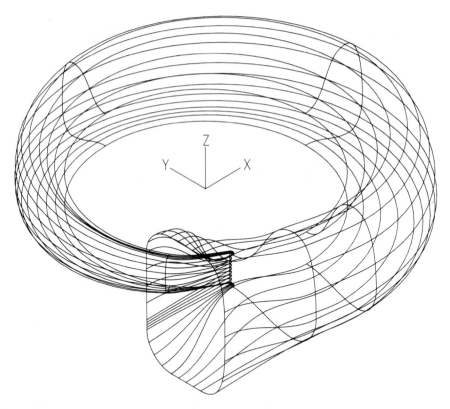

Fig. 6.5 A surface model of a pump volute. [DUCT System, courtesy Delta CAE Ltd.]

on curve networks also demand skills of this type for advantage to be taken of their full powers. Fortunately, most surface systems are graphically interactive, providing visual feedback and various means for interactive modification of the surface until an acceptable result is obtained.

Although the necessity to develop new skills for the design of three-dimensional surfaces may be irksome to the designer, there are ample rewards once the surface design is finalised. A wide range of calculations may then be performed automatically by the computer, including calculations of the area and of the volume subtended by the surface. Moreover, since the surface is based on a network of curves, it is easy for the computer to sub-divide the mesh cells further to obtain a finite element mesh such as that shown in Figure 6.6.

Most importantly, instructions for the NC machining of the surface can often be generated almost entirely automatically. This last point will be illustrated by reference to Figure 6.4. The surface patch shown there has two constant parameter lines ($u = 0.6$ and $v = 0.3$) drawn on it. It is possible to define families of such lines in either the u- or the v-direction, as closely spaced as desired. These lines lying in the surface may be used as cutter contact paths for machining the surface. A common strategy is to machine in zigzag fashion along lines of constant u, incrementing u by (say) 0.1 for each pass. The choice of increment is, in practice, a compromise between cusp height on the machined surface and total machining time. The method may be extended also to the machining of composite patched surfaces which is particularly easy

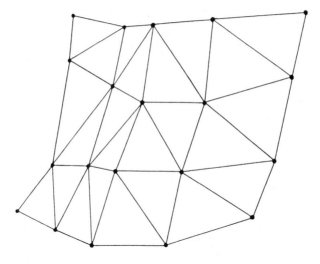

Fig. 6.6 A finite element mesh on a parametric surface

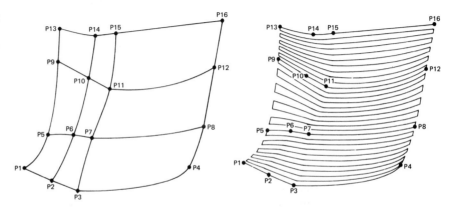

Fig. 6.7 Cutter contact paths on a parametric surface. [CAM-I Sculptured Surfaces System.]

when the overall surface is made up of a regular assembly of four-sided patches. Figure 6.7 shows a set of computer-generated cutter contact paths on a patched surface (CAM-I Sculptured Surfaces System).

The advantages mentioned above are most apparent when just one surface is dealt with at a time. However, most engineering objects are bounded by several surfaces, and manufacturing processes must be concerned with the way in which these surfaces intersect with each other to generate edges of the object. Many surface systems do not calculate these intersections, and very few systems store information about the way in which the various faces of the object are connected together to form its boundary.

Information of this latter kind is loosely referred to as 'topological', and it lies within the province of the solid modelling systems to be discussed in later chapters. In the absence of such data the user has the responsibility for ensuring that a cutter moving on one surface, for example, does not gouge one of the other surfaces, since it will not know of the relationship between the two surfaces unless informed of this by the user. As will be seen, a true solid modeller enables responsibility for such matters to rest with the modelling system itself. Unfortunately most solid modelling systems do not completely implement the parametric surface types discussed earlier, and these are urgently needed for the modelling of the subtle blends and fillets exhibited by many engineering objects. The marriage of surface and solid modelling is a current topic of research, and some approaches to a solution of the problem are discussed by Várady and Pratt [1984].

Geometry of curves 7

I D Faux

1 Introduction

Informally, we may define a two-dimensional curve as the locus of a point constrained to move in a two-dimensional space. Whilst we can, in general, consider curves which lie on a curved surface, the most familiar examples of two-dimensional curves are the familiar plane curves — the straight line, circle and conic sections. We shall use these examples to introduce the concepts which will lay the foundation for more complex curves, including three-dimensional space curves, and the development of parametric surface geometry in the following chapter.

2 The representation of two-dimensional curves

Two-dimensional or plane curves have been represented mainly in two distinct ways:

Explicitly: by equations of the form $x = X(u)$, $y = Y(u)$ which enable us to obtain the x- and y-coordinates of points on the curve by direct substitution of values of the parameter u. In general, these are known as **parametric** or **freedom equations** for x and y. In the particular case where we choose $x = u$, we get the familiar explicit curve equation $y = Y(x)$.

Implicitly: by a **constraint equation** $F(x, y) = 0$ which expresses a relationship between the coordinates x and y of each point in two-dimensional space. This equation does not permit us to obtain points directly. We must either solve the equation analytically to obtain the explicit form, or resort to a numerical procedure to generate approximate points on the curve.

We shall now illustrate these two approaches by means of familiar examples.

2.1 The straight line

Several different equations exist to represent a straight line, based on different descriptive definitions. The most familiar form, perhaps, is that based on the slope–intercept description:

$$y = mx + c \tag{1}$$

where the line is defined by its intercept c on the y-axis and by its slope m, given by the tangent of the angle between the line and the positive x-axis (see Figure 7.1).

Fig. 7.1 Slope–intercept form of a straight line

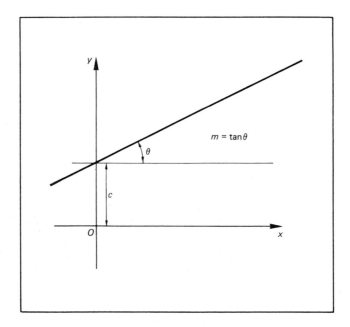

This example is familiar from plotting experimental results and choosing (usually by eye) a best-fit straight line through the experimental points. More sophisticated linear regression techniques, of fitting a straight line through data points, are also based on this explicit form. One drawback of this form is that vertical lines cannot be represented due to their infinite slope value. Similarly, the 'inverse' form $x = ny + d$ can represent vertical, but not horizontal, lines.

Another familiar form is based on the description of a straight line as the locus of points collinear with two given points P_1 with coordinates (x_1, y_1), and P_2 with coordinates (x_2, y_2), as illustrated in Figure 7.2. The corresponding equation is given by

$$(x_2 - x_1)(y - y_1) = (y_2 - y_1)(x - x_1) \tag{2}$$

This equation is now an implicit form, and can represent all lines regardless of slope. Points on the line can be obtained by selecting a value of x and solving the equation for y, or vice versa.

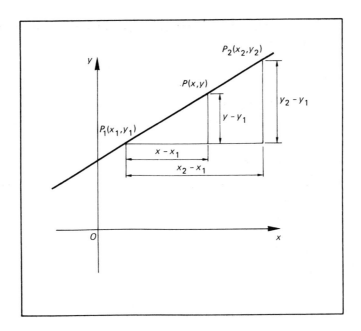

Fig. 7.2 The straight line through the two points P_1 and P_2

Equation (2) is not a *unique* implicit representation for the line, since the points P_1 and P_2 may be any two distinct points on the line. Even the more neutral implicit form

$$ax + by + c = 0 \qquad\qquad (3)$$

is not unique, since any multiples λa, λb and λc of the coefficients will represent the same straight line. To obtain a unique implicit representation, the coefficients may be scaled such that $a^2 + b^2 = 1$ and $c < 0$.

Although the special handling of vertical (or nearly vertical) lines, and the uniqueness of representation are easily dealt with when solving problems manually, they add unnecessary complexity to the programming of computers to perform the same tasks automatically.

A parametric equation for the straight line described by equation (2) can be derived from Figure 7.2 by defining a parameter u equal to the ratio PP_1/P_2P_1. We can then show that

$$x = (1 - u)x_1 + ux_2$$
$$y = (1 - u)y_1 + uy_2 \qquad\qquad (4)$$

In this parametric equation, we have used a natural parameter based on the distance between the variable point $P(u)$ and the start-point P_1, normalised (that is, confined to the range $0 \leqslant u \leqslant 1$) by the distance P_1P_2 between the start-point and end-point of the line segment. As with the implicit equation (2), the parametric representation (4) is not unique, since the start- and end-points may be chosen freely. Moreover, in the parametric form, we can choose other parameters such as the angle subtended at the origin by the variable point P. Such parameterisations do not usually produce simple (in this case, linear) functions of the parameter u. However, in the case of the straight line, we do have the unique combination of a natural (and simple) length parameterisation which also results in the simplest parameterisation functions.

For computational purposes, we shall see that simple polynomial (or rational polynomial) functions are to be preferred for the design of general curves and surfaces, but that these generally result in the use of parameters which do not correspond to a natural parameterisation of the point P in terms of, for example, arc length, subtended angle, etc.

2.2 General plane curves

We are all familiar with the use of equations of the form $y = Y(x)$, where $Y(x)$ is a computable or tabulated function of x, such as a polynomial or trigonometric function. The problem with such representations is that they are unsatisfactory for automatic computation on curves with vertical tangents, and especially on curves for which the function $Y(x)$ would have to be multiple-valued, such as on closed curves (for example, the circle, ellipse, etc.). The following discussion of the equations of a **circle** will illustrate this point and indicate how the implicit and parametric equations overcome the problem.

The implicit equation of a circle of radius R and centre at the point P_c, with coordinates (a, b), is well-known:

$$(x - a)^2 + (y - b)^2 = R^2 \tag{5}$$

In order to obtain an explicit equation, we must divide the circle into two segments, such that the corresponding functions $Y_1(x)$ and $Y_2(x)$ are single-valued. We could choose the function

$$y = b + [R^2 - (x - a)^2]^{0.5}$$

for the upper segment, and the function

$$y = b - [R^2 - (x - a)^2]^{0.5}$$

for the lower segment. Apart from the remaining problem that these segments have vertical tangents at each end, it is inconvenient to have to break the curve into two segments in this way, unless this can be performed in the context of a general treatment of segmented curves which is amenable to automatic computation.

A well-known parametric equation for this circle is given by the use of trigonometric functions, as shown in Figure 7.3:

$$x = a + R \cos \theta$$

$$y = b + R \sin \theta \tag{6}$$

Once again, we have chosen a natural parameter — the angle subtended at the centre P_c — and in the case of the circle this is directly related to arc length s along the curve by the equation $s = R\theta$. However, we can see that the resulting parameterisation involves more complicated functions (requiring the evaluation of series approximations) than those required for a straight line. Segments of the circle can be described by defining their start and end parameter values θ_1 and θ_2.

The circle may be parameterised in terms of simpler polynomial functions (approximately) or by rational polynomial functions (exactly). However, these choices of parameter are not simply related to natural parameters such as arc length.

Fig. 7.3 A parametric description of the circle

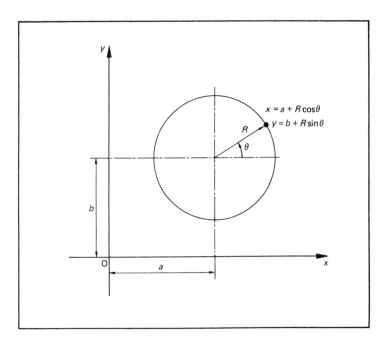

The implicit equation of a general **two-dimensional curve** takes the form $F(x, y) = 0$, and we usually require the existence and continuity of the function F and its partial derivatives $\partial F/\partial x$ and $\partial F/\partial y$ in the vicinity of the curve, for the purposes of numerical procedures which are used to plot the curve automatically. It is also desirable that $\partial F/\partial x$ and $\partial F/\partial y$ should not vanish simultaneously at any point near the curve in order to avoid tangent discontinuities. It is at least desirable to be aware of the presence of such singular points in order to take appropriate measures. Henceforth for convenience we adopt the standard notation

F_x for $\partial F/\partial x$ and F_y for $\partial F/\partial y$

A general two-dimensional curve has parametric equations of the form

$x = X(u), y = Y(u)$

where $X(u)$ and $Y(u)$ are single-valued functions defined on some real closed interval $I[u_1, u_2]$ of the parameter u which corresponds to the segment of the curve of current interest. It is usually desirable for $X(u)$ and $Y(u)$ to be at least continuous at all points on the interval I, and for dX/du and dY/du not to vanish simultaneously on I, except at points where this is specifically intended. Such points are known as *singular* points on the curve, whereas all other points are said to be *regular*.

As with the implicit equation, the parametric type of representation treats the coordinates x and y symmetrically, and is capable of representing a wide range of curve types including curves with vertical tangents, closed curves, curves with cusps and even self-intersecting curves. This great flexibility will be seen later to be useful in curve and surface design, but the occurrence of unwanted cusps and loops in curves must be carefully monitored.

2.3 Derived entities and properties of curves

We now present, without proof, the standard equations and formulae for derived entities such as tangents, normals and intersection points, as well as derived properties such as curvature. For comparison, these are tabulated for both the implicit and the parametric forms in Table 7.1.

Table 7.1 Summary of defined entities and properties of curves.

Entity/property	*Implicit*	*Parametric*
Curve itself	$F(x, y) = 0$	$x = X(u)$ $y = Y(u)$
Tangent line	$F_x(x_1, y_1)(x - x_1)$ $+ F_y(x_1, y_1)(y - y_1) = 0$	$x = X(u_1) + \lambda X_u(u_1)$ $y = Y(u_1) + \lambda Y_u(u_1)$
Normal line	$F_y(x_1, y_1)(x - x_1)$ $- F_x(x_1, y_1)(y - y_1) = 0$	$x = X(u_1) + \lambda Y_u(u_1)$ $y = Y(u_1) - \lambda X_u(u_1)$

Intersection point:
   Solve...
   with ...
   for ...
	$F_1(x, y) = 0$
	 $F_2(x, y) = 0$
	 x and y
		$X_1(u_1) = X_2(u_2)$
		 $Y_1(u_1) = Y_2(u_2)$
		 u_1 and u_2

Curvature	$\dfrac{F_{xx}F_y^2 - 2F_{xy}F_xF_y + F_{yy}F_x^2}{(F_x^2 + F_y^2)^{1.5}} =$	$\dfrac{X_u Y_{uu} - Y_u X_{uu}}{(X_u^2 + Y_u^2)^{1.5}}$

3 The parametric representation of three-dimensional curves

Parametric representations of three-dimensional or space curves are usually defined in terms of vector functions of a single parameter, say u, and can be expressed in component form by three scalar parametric equations $x = X(u)$, $y = Y(u)$ and $z = Z(u)$, in much the same way as plane curves were described in the previous section by two scalar parametric equations.

Using vector notation, we may collect these three scalar equations together into the single equation

$$\mathbf{r} = \mathbf{R}(u)$$

where $\mathbf{r}$ is now the position vector of a variable point $P(u)$ on the curve, with parameter u, and $\mathbf{R}(u)$ is a vector-valued function of u.

As is the case with the two-dimensional curves described earlier, the functions $X(u)$, $Y(u)$ and $Z(u)$ should be single-valued functions defined on some real closed interval $I[u_1, u_2]$ of the parameter u corresponding to the segment of the curve we wish to consider. We again require the functions to be at least continuous on the interval I, and the first derivatives dX/du, dY/du and dZ/du not to vanish simultaneously at any point of I, except by intent.

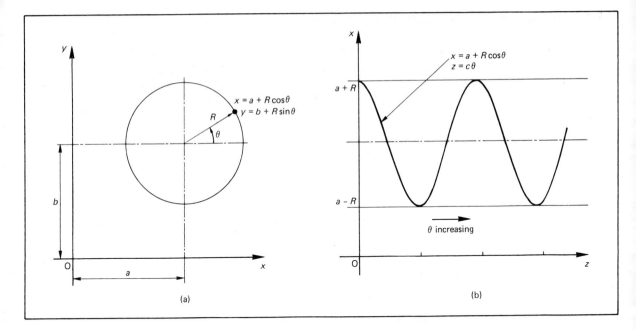

Fig. 7.4 The circle considered as a particle moving along the circumference at a constant angular velocity about the centre

Once again, points where $d\mathbf{R}/du = \mathbf{0}$ are known as singular points, the remainder being termed regular points of the curve.

In order to illustrate these concepts, we first take the equation (6), of a circle described in two dimensions, and rewrite this in vector notation as

$$\mathbf{r} = (a + R\cos\theta)\mathbf{i} + (b + R\sin\theta)\mathbf{j} \qquad (7)$$

This represents a circle in the Oxy-plane, traced in an anti-clockwise direction in the view shown in Figure 7.4(a). The complete circle can be represented by the interval $0 \leqslant \theta \leqslant 2\pi$.

In describing informally the properties of a space curve, it is often helpful to visualise the curve as the trajectory $\mathbf{r} = \mathbf{R}(t)$ of a moving particle, and, for example, to relate the direction of the curve's tangent to the velocity vector of the particle. In this case we consider the parameter u to be the time t.

If we visualise the circle as the trajectory of a particle which traces this circle continuously in the anti-clockwise direction (viewed from the positive z-direction) at a constant angular velocity $\omega = \theta/t$, then we can see that the effect of adding an extra linear motion in the z-direction with a constant speed $c\omega$ will be to stretch out the two-dimensional trajectory into a three-dimensional helical curve given by

$$\mathbf{r} = (a + R\cos\theta)\mathbf{i} + (b + R\sin\theta)\mathbf{j} + c\theta\mathbf{k}$$

The view in the Oxz-plane is shown in Figure 7.4(b).

Continuing the analogy with the motion of a particle, we see that the velocity vector of the particle is given by:

$$\mathbf{v} = \frac{d\mathbf{r}}{dt} = \omega\frac{d\mathbf{r}}{d\theta} = \omega[-(R\sin\theta)\mathbf{i} + (R\cos\theta)\mathbf{j} + c\mathbf{k}]$$

and $\mathbf{v}$ 'points' in a direction tangential to the helix.

The speed of the particle is the magnitude of this velocity vector, but it is also equal to ds/dt, where s is the arc length from some fixed point on the trajectory to the variable point $P(\theta)$. This speed has two components. The first is tangential to the original circle and hence is parallel to the xy-plane — its magnitude is $R\omega$. The second is parallel to the z-axis, along the axis of the helix — its magnitude is $c\omega$. The resultant speed ds/dt is therefore given by

$$(c^2\omega^2 + R^2\omega^2)^{0.5}$$

since the two component magnitudes are at right angles and we can use Pythagoras' expression for the resultant.

The *unit tangent vector* **T** can therefore be seen to be given by

$$\mathbf{T} = \frac{\mathbf{v}}{|\mathbf{v}|} = \frac{d\mathbf{r}}{dt} \div \frac{ds}{dt} = \frac{d\mathbf{r}}{ds}$$

$$= \frac{[-(R\sin\theta)\mathbf{i} + (R\cos\theta)\mathbf{j} + c\mathbf{k}]}{[c^2 + R^2]^{0.5}}$$

For a two-dimensional plane curve, a single well-defined normal line exists at each point on the curve. In the case of a space curve, however, every vector normal to the tangent vector at the given point on the curve can be considered to be a normal to the curve at that point.

It is therefore conventional to define just two particular normal vectors at each point on the curve, which together span the space of all normal vectors. The first of these is termed the *principal normal* vector **N**, and it is chosen or defined to be in the direction of $d\mathbf{T}/ds$ and to be of unit magnitude. This happens to be the direction from the given point on the curve to the *centre of curvature*, which is also the centre of the *osculating circle* at the point. (If we take three distinct points on the curve within an arc distance δs of the given point and construct the circle which passes through them, then the osculating circle is the limit of such constructed circles as $\delta s \to 0$.) The other singled-out normal vector is the *binormal* vector **B**, defined by the relationship $\mathbf{B} = \mathbf{T} \times \mathbf{N}$. The three vectors **T**, **N** and **B** form the so-called *moving trihedral*, illustrated in Figure 7.5.

In terms of our helix example

$$\frac{d\mathbf{T}}{ds} = \frac{d\mathbf{T}}{dt} \div \frac{ds}{dt} = \omega \frac{d\mathbf{T}}{d\theta} \div \omega[c^2 + R^2]^{0.5}$$

$$= \frac{[-(R\cos\theta)\mathbf{i} - (R\sin\theta)\mathbf{j}]}{[c^2 + R^2]}$$

Now it can be shown that the magnitude of the vector $d\mathbf{T}/ds$ is equal to the inverse of the radius of curvature ρ. This inverse is known as the curvature, denoted by $\varkappa$. Since the principal normal vector **N** is also a unit vector, we have $d\mathbf{T}/ds = \varkappa\mathbf{N}$, and so in our example

$$\mathbf{N} = -(\cos\theta)\,\mathbf{i} - (\sin\theta)\,\mathbf{j}$$

and

$$\varkappa = \frac{R}{[c^2 + R^2]}$$

Fig. 7.5 The moving trihedral at a point on a space curve

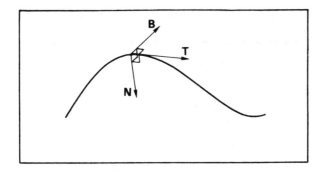

The centre of curvature P_c for each point on the curve is located at distance ρ along this principal normal, at the point with position vector $\mathbf{r}_c = \mathbf{r} + \rho \mathbf{N}$. The binormal vector is given, for our helix example, by

$$\mathbf{B} = \mathbf{T} \times \mathbf{N} = \frac{1}{[c^2 + R^2]^{0.5}} \begin{vmatrix} \mathbf{i} & \mathbf{j} & \mathbf{k} \\ -R\sin\theta & +R\cos\theta & c \\ -\cos\theta & -\sin\theta & 0 \end{vmatrix}$$

$$= \frac{[(c\sin\theta)\,\mathbf{i} - (c\cos\theta)\,\mathbf{j} + R\mathbf{k}]}{[c^2 + R^2]^{0.5}}$$

This binormal vector is normal to the plane of the osculating circle, which is known as the osculating plane. In the case of a plane curve, the binomial vector is constant, so that the vector $d\mathbf{B}/ds$ provides a measure of the deviation of a space curve from a plane curve. It can be shown that $d\mathbf{B}/ds$ is parallel to $\mathbf{N}$, and by convention we write

$$d\mathbf{B}/ds = -\tau\mathbf{N}$$

where τ is known as the *torsion* of the curve.

In our helix example

$$\frac{d\mathbf{B}}{ds} = \frac{[(c\cos\theta)\,\mathbf{i} + (c\sin\theta)\,\mathbf{j}]}{[c^2 + R^2]}$$

so that the torsion of the helix is given by

$$\tau = \frac{c}{[c^2 + R^2]}$$

3.1 The Frenet-Serret formulae

The important results illustrated above may be summarised by the so-called Frenet-Serret formulae. These are tabulated in Table 7.2 in terms of the arc length parameter s, and a general parameter u.

For our purposes, when we are considering a space curve with general parameter $\mathbf{r} = \mathbf{R}(u)$, the corresponding results are best written in terms of the derivatives of $\mathbf{R}$ with respect to u. For convenience we shall henceforth denote these derivatives by the standard subscript notation. Thus

$d\mathbf{R}/du$ is denoted by $\mathbf{R}_u$

$d^2\mathbf{R}/du^2$ by $\mathbf{R}_{uu}$

Table 7.2   The Frenet-Serret formulae for a space curve.

$$\frac{d\mathbf{R}}{ds} = \mathbf{T}$$

$$\frac{d\mathbf{T}}{ds} = \varkappa\mathbf{N}$$

$$\frac{d\mathbf{N}}{ds} = \tau\mathbf{B} - \varkappa\mathbf{T}$$

$$\frac{d\mathbf{B}}{ds} = -\tau\mathbf{N}$$

$$\mathbf{T} = \frac{\mathbf{R}_u}{s_u}$$

$$\varkappa\mathbf{B} = \frac{(\mathbf{R}_u \times \mathbf{R}_{uu})}{s_u^3}$$

$$\mathbf{N} = \mathbf{B} \times \mathbf{T}$$

$$\tau = \frac{\mathbf{R}_u \cdot (\mathbf{R}_{uu} \times \mathbf{R}_{uuu})}{s_u^6 \varkappa^2}$$

$$s_u = |\mathbf{R}_u|$$

and so on. This notation is used throughout Table 7.2.

The use of these Frenet-Serret formulae will be seen in the following section on curve design.

A full mathematical treatment of the differential geometry of space curves (and parametric surfaces) will be found in Willmore [1959]. A fuller account from the CADCAM point of view is given in Faux and Pratt [1979].

4   Curve design

Whereas parametric curves are generally considered to be defined over an infinite range of parameter values u, it is always necessary to limit these to a finite interval when modelling shapes on the computer, since physical objects always have finite dimensions, and computers can only store finite numbers to a finite number of decimal places.

Quite apart from these considerations, it also useful to be able to sub-divide the shape to be designed into **segments** which may be adjusted independently.

We shall therefore begin by discussing the properties of some of the more commonly used curve segments, and follow this by considering the various ways in which these segments are combined to form composite curves and splines. A fuller treatment of curve design will be found in Faux and Pratt [1979].

4.1 Cubic polynomial segments

A curve divided into segments may have each of its segments approximated by an expression, giving the position vector of a variable point on the approximate segment in terms of a set of polynomial (basis) functions of some parameter u, together with a set of vector 'coefficients'. These approximate segments are termed polynomial segments and a **cubic polynomial segment** consists of four basis functions and four vector coefficients.

All the cubic polynomial segments (including the Ferguson, Bézier and uniform B-spline types considered here) correspond to the same basic family of curves which have the form

$$\mathbf{r} = \mathbf{R}(u) = \mathbf{a}_0 + u\mathbf{a}_1 + u^2\mathbf{a}_2 + u^3\mathbf{a}_3 \tag{8}$$

where the highest degree polynomial function is a cubic u^3, and where the segment is traditionally bounded by the parameter interval $0 \leqslant u \leqslant 1$.

This simple form is readily manipulated algebraically, and easily differentiated, but the vector coefficients (that is, $\mathbf{a}_0, \mathbf{a}_1, \mathbf{a}_2$ and $\mathbf{a}_3$) do not all have direct physical significance, and are not convenient 'handles' for adjusting the segment shape or its incorporation into a composite curve.

Ferguson curve segment

The Ferguson form of the cubic polynomial segment replaces the simple polynomials $1, u, u^2$ and u^3 by more complicated cubic functions and the vector coefficients $\mathbf{a}_0, \mathbf{a}_1, \mathbf{a}_2$ and $\mathbf{a}_3$ by the more physically meaningful values $\mathbf{R}(0)$ and $\mathbf{R}(1)$ of the position vector at each end of the segment, together with its derivative values $\mathbf{R}_u(0)$ and $\mathbf{R}_u(1)$ at these end-points, giving

$$\begin{aligned}
\mathbf{r} = \mathbf{R}(u) = {} & \mathbf{R}(0)(1 - 3u^2 + 2u^3) + \mathbf{R}(1)(3u^2 - 2u^3) \\
& + \mathbf{R}_u(0)(u - 2u^2 + u^3) + \mathbf{R}_u(1)(-u^2 + u^3)
\end{aligned}$$

Just as the functions $1, u, u^2$ and u^3 form the simplest basis for the space of cubic polynomials, so the four functions above form another basis of the same space (in fact the basis for Hermite interpolation over the interval $[0, 1]$). The form can be conveniently adjusted to yield various shapes of curve segment by altering one or more of $\mathbf{R}(0)$, $\mathbf{R}(1)$, $\mathbf{R}_u(0)$ or $\mathbf{R}_u(1)$ appropriately.

The Ferguson form can be expressed in terms of the basis matrix $\mathbf{M}$, relating its basis functions

$$(1 - 3u^2 + 2u^3), (3u^2 - 2u^3), (u - 2u^2 + u^3), (-u^2 + u^3)$$

to the simple polynomial basis, $1, u, u^2, u^3$, as follows:

$$\mathbf{r} = \mathbf{UMA} = [1 \; u \; u^2 \; u^3]
\begin{bmatrix}
1 & 0 & 0 & 0 \\
0 & 0 & 1 & 0 \\
-3 & 3 & -2 & -1 \\
2 & -2 & 1 & 1
\end{bmatrix}
\begin{bmatrix}
\mathbf{R}(0) \\
\mathbf{R}(1) \\
\mathbf{R}_u(0) \\
\mathbf{R}_u(1)
\end{bmatrix} \tag{9}$$

$$\underset{\mathbf{U}}{\uparrow} \qquad\qquad\qquad \underset{\mathbf{M}}{\uparrow} \qquad\qquad\qquad \underset{\mathbf{A}}{\uparrow}$$

where $\mathbf{A}$ is the column matrix of 'coefficient' vectors.

The derivatives $\mathbf{R}_u(0)$ and $\mathbf{R}_u(1)$ are proportional to the tangent vectors $\mathbf{T}(0)$ and $\mathbf{T}(1)$ at the two end-points, and the magnitudes of these derivatives influence the fullness of the segment when they are increased or decreased simultaneously. The larger the tangent magnitude at either end, the greater the tendency to follow the end-value of the curve tangent before turning away to pass through the other end-point in the tangent direction there.

Fig. 7.6 The variation of segment shape when the magnitudes α_0 and α_1 of the derivatives $\mathbf{R}_u(0)$ and $\mathbf{R}_u(1)$ respectively are varied (a) symmetrically, (b) asymmetrically

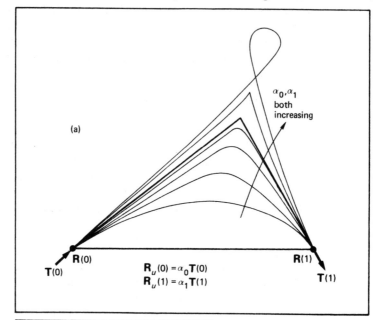

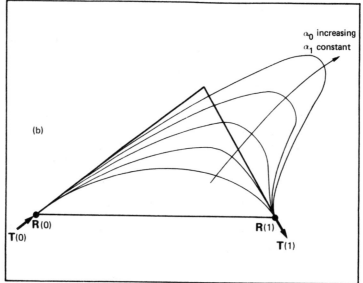

Figure 7.6 illustrates the variation of the segment shape when the magnitudes are varied symmetrically or asymmetrically. It can be seen that the curve may become so full that kinks or loops form. This usually occurs if the tangent magnitudes become too great.

This form of the cubic polynomial segment was introduced by Ferguson [1963] for the definition of curves and surfaces in aircraft design.

Bézier cubic curve segment

The Bézier form of the cubic segments uses a different set of basis functions from the Ferguson form. These segments are based on the Bernstein cubic basis functions

$$(1 - u)^3, 3u(1 - u)^2, 3u^2(1 - u), u^3$$

This leads to the following expression for the position vector $\mathbf{r}$ of a point on the segment:

$$\mathbf{r} = \mathbf{R}(u) = (1 - u)^3\mathbf{r}_0 + 3u(1 - u)^2\mathbf{r}_1 + 3u^2(1 - u)\mathbf{r}_2 + u^3\mathbf{r}_3$$

where, once again, the segment is defined on $0 \leqslant u \leqslant 1$.

As with the Ferguson form, the Bézier form may also be expressed in terms of the basis matrix $\mathbf{M}$ as follows:

$$\mathbf{r} = \mathbf{UMA} = [1\ u\ u^2\ u^3] \begin{bmatrix} 1 & 0 & 0 & 0 \\ -3 & 3 & 0 & 0 \\ 3 & -6 & 3 & 0 \\ -1 & 3 & -3 & 1 \end{bmatrix} \begin{bmatrix} \mathbf{r}_0 \\ \mathbf{r}_1 \\ \mathbf{r}_2 \\ \mathbf{r}_3 \end{bmatrix} \qquad (10)$$

$$\underset{\mathbf{U}}{\uparrow} \qquad\qquad \underset{\mathbf{M}}{\uparrow} \qquad \underset{\mathbf{A}}{\uparrow}$$

Fig. 7.7 The Bézier cubic segments for various choices of the characteristic polygon

This time the column matrix $\mathbf{A}$ consists of a different set of vector coefficients. In the Bézier form, these coefficients are the position vectors of four points

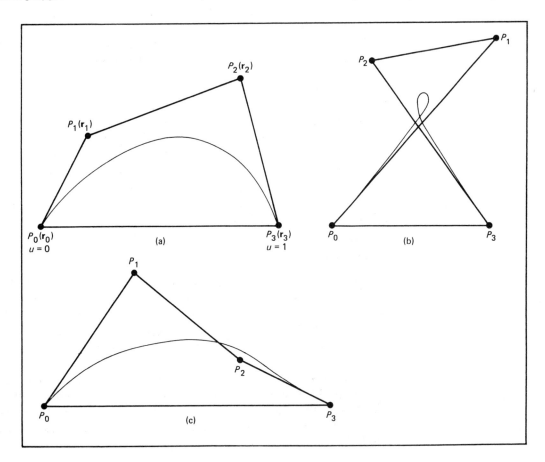

P_0, P_1, P_2 and P_3 which form the so-called *characteristic polygon* of the segment. The curve passes through the points P_0 and P_3 at parameter values 0 and 1, and the tangents at these points are in the directions of the lines P_0P_1 and P_2P_3 respectively. This is illustrated by Figure 7.7.

Furthermore, the length of each tangent vector is proportional to the length of the corresponding line segments P_0P_1 or P_2P_3, so that the positions of the interior points P_1 and P_2 regulate both the directions of the end-tangents and also the fullness of the segment in the vicinity of each end, as shown in Figure 7.7.

Because all the coefficients are *position* vectors, the whole curve may be transformed by applying a transformation once and for all to these coefficients, rather than transforming the evaluated points **r** for each value of u required.

Moreover, the four polygon points form the vertices of a tetrahedron in general, and the curve segment lies entirely within this tetrahedron over the interval $0 < u < 1$. This property is known as the **convex hull property**, and is a most useful property in relation to algorithms used to calculate curve intersection and other applications where spatial bounds on the curve segment are required.

Finally, by taking second derivatives, curvature properties of the curve can also be shown to depend closely on the shape of the characteristic polygon [Faux and Pratt 1979].

The history and application of the Bézier curves and surfaces can be found in Bézier [1970].

The Bézier cubic curve segment discussed above is a special case of the more general Bézier polynomial curve segment which takes the form

$$\mathbf{r} = \mathbf{R}(u) = \sum_{i=0}^{n} {}^nC_r u^i (1 - u)^{n-i} \mathbf{r}_i \tag{11}$$

where ${}^nC_r$ represents the standard binomial coefficients and where $\mathbf{r}_i$ $(i = 0, \ldots, n)$ are the position vectors of the $n + 1$ vertices of a generalised characteristic polygon. The first pair and the last pair of points in this general polygon have the same significance and properties as they do in the special case of the cubic curve.

Other special cases of this general Bézier segment are the straight line ($n = 1$) and the parabola ($n = 2$) given below:

Straight line: $\mathbf{r} = \mathbf{R}(u) = (1 - u)\mathbf{r}_0 + u\mathbf{r}_1$
Parabola: $\mathbf{r} = \mathbf{R}(u) = (1 - u)^2\mathbf{r}_0 + 2u(1 - u)\mathbf{r}_1 + u^2\mathbf{r}_2$

Although the higher (than cubic) degree Bézier segments do allow more flexibility in the design of curves, the relationship between the curve characteristics and the polygon is weaker and less helpful to the designer, since geometrical properties of the curve such as curvature are non-linear functions of the derivatives (see Table 7.2), and hence non-linear in terms of the polygon points also.

In terms of the Bézier form, we have seen that the straight line and parabola can be exactly represented as lower (than cubic) degree polynomial segments. For convenience, a design system based on Bézier cubics will represent these as degenerate cases by appropriate selection of the polygon points [Faux and Pratt 1979].

Uniform cubic B-spline

This form of the cubic segments uses a third set of basis functions different from both the Ferguson and the Bézier types.

A cubic B-spline curve is a special case of the spline curves based on the work of Schoenberg, Cox and de Boer and further developed by Gordon and Riesenfeld [1974]. We shall illustrate this method by describing a uniform cubic B-spline curve based on a sequence of n cubic segments each defined on the interval $0 \leqslant u \leqslant 1$.

For this purpose we introduce (without derivation) $n + 3$ polygon control points P_i, with corresponding position vectors $\mathbf{r}_i$, for $i = -1, 0, 1, 2, \ldots, n + 1$, and we use these to define n cubic segments of the form

$$
\begin{aligned}
\mathbf{r} = \mathbf{R}_i(u) = {} & \tfrac{1}{6}(1 - 3u + 3u^2 - u^3)\mathbf{r}_{i-2} \\
& + \tfrac{1}{6}(4 - 6u^2 + 3u^3)\mathbf{r}_{i-1} \\
& + \tfrac{1}{6}(1 + 3u + 3u^2 - 3u^3)\mathbf{r}_i \\
& + \tfrac{1}{6}u^3\mathbf{r}_{i+1}
\end{aligned}
\tag{12}
$$

As with the previous Ferguson and Bézier types, these expressions can be written in matrix form as

$$
\mathbf{r} = \mathbf{R}_i(u) = \mathbf{UMA} = [1 \ u \ u^2 \ u^3] \ \tfrac{1}{6}
\underset{\underset{\mathbf{M}}{\uparrow}}{\begin{bmatrix} 1 & 4 & 1 & 0 \\ -3 & 0 & 3 & 0 \\ 3 & -6 & 3 & 0 \\ -1 & 3 & -3 & 1 \end{bmatrix}}
\underset{\underset{\mathbf{A}}{\uparrow}}{\begin{bmatrix} \mathbf{r}_{i-2} \\ \mathbf{r}_{i-1} \\ \mathbf{r}_i \\ \mathbf{r}_{i+1} \end{bmatrix}}
\tag{13}
$$

for $1 \leqslant i \leqslant n$.

When the control points are distinct, this curve is continuous in slope and curvature between successive segments, but it does not pass through any of the polygon (control) points, as can be seen in Figure 7.8.

The uniform cubic B-spline segment is particularly suitable for free-form design, since it has the advantage that any of the control points may be moved without affecting slope and curvature continuity, and only four spans of the overall curve will be affected by the change. Moreover, by allowing two

Fig. 7.8 A uniform cubic B-spline curve with nine cubic segments and twelve control points

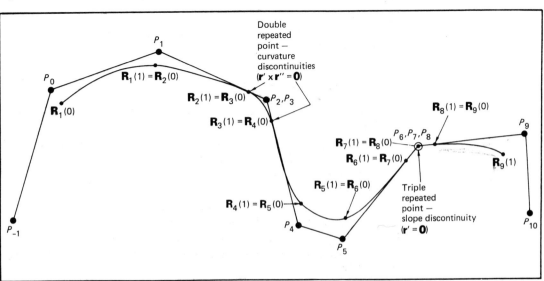

control points to coincide, it is possible to create a curvature discontinuity, and a slope discontinuity can similarly be induced by choosing three successive control points to be coincident.

Each cubic B-spline segment also possesses the simple transformation and convex hull properties noted in relation to the Bézier segments.

Some other B-spline formulations make adjustments to the end-segments to ensure that they pass through the end-points of the controlling polygon and have their tangents in the direction of the first and last edges of the polygon. B-spline curves are also used for exact interpolation of data points, but it is then necessary to solve equations to determine the control points.

Other refinements allow for variable parameter intervals (that is, not necessarily $0 \leqslant u \leqslant 1$) for the different segments, and these modifications lead to more satisfactory curves when splines are used to fit data points with irregular spacing.

By further generalising these curves using rational cubic segments, exact reproduction of circular and other 'conic' segments of the curve can be obtained. This gives the *non-uniform rational B-spline* which combines the benefits of many of the major curve types.

4.2 Rational polynomial segments

We have noted that the cubic curve segment can also model straight-line and parabolic segments exactly. However, circular segments must generally be approximated to the required accuracy by dividing the whole segment into a sufficient number of smaller segments.

An alternative approach which does permit exact representation of circular and other conic curves is based on the use of the **rational quadratic segment** which has the form

$$r = R(u) = \frac{(1-u)^2 w_0 r_0 + 2u(1-u)w_1 r_1 + u^2 w_2 r_2}{(1-u)^2 w_0 + 2u(1-u)w_1 + u^2 w_2} \tag{14}$$

This represents a conic segment contained within the triangle $P_0 P_1 P_2$ defined by the three position vectors r_0, r_1 and r_2. The segment starts at the point P_0 with direction $P_0 P_1$ and ends at the point P_2 with direction $P_1 P_2$. The fullness of the curve is controlled by the ratio

$$w_0 w_2 / w_1^2 = k^2$$

The cases $k < 1$, $k = 1$ and $k > 1$ correspond to an hyperbola, a parabola and an ellipse respectively.

Higher-degree rational polynomial segments can similarly be defined. Thus the *rational cubic* form is

$$r = R(u) = \frac{(1-u)^3 w_0 r_0 + 3u(1-u)^2 w_1 r_1 + 3u^2(1-u)w_2 r_2 + u^3 w_3 r_3}{(1-u)^3 w_0 + 3u(1-u)^2 w_1 + 3u^2(1-u)w_2 + u^3 w_3} \tag{15}$$

By using a rational cubic form of this type, it is possible to subsume in a single form all of the classical conic curves together with the cubic segments described earlier, leading to a uniform treatment of most major curve types.

A fuller discussion of rational curves is given in Faux and Pratt [1979].

4.3 Composite curves and splines

It is possible to represent complex curve shapes by considering **composite curves** constructed from individual segments. Bézier segments may be joined with position continuity by choosing the start-point of the second segment coincident with the end-point of the first, but in general slope and curvature continuity can only be ensured by applying further conditions to the inner polygon points, as described in Faux and Pratt [1979].

Automatic position *and* slope continuity can be ensured for Ferguson segments by additionally taking equal derivative vectors at the join. Each segment then shares two common vector coefficients with its neighbouring segments.

For the uniform B-spline segments, position, slope and *curvature* continuity can be guaranteed by taking the last *three* control points of the first to form the first three of the next segment.

Note that continuity of slope only requires continuity of the tangent direction, whereas continuity of the derivative $R_u(u)$ at the join implies also that the magnitude of this vector is continuous [Faux and Pratt 1979]. We shall now consider the requirements we need to impose on Ferguson segments when curvature continuity is required.

Ferguson parametric splines

If we consider two consecutive Ferguson segments with equal values of R and R_u at their join, together with the following expression for R_{uu}:

$$R_{uu}(u) = \begin{cases} 6[R(1) - R(0) - 4R_u(0) - 2R_u(1)] & \text{at } u = 0 \\ -6[R(1) - R(0) + 2R_u(0) + 2R_u(1)] & \text{at } u = 1 \end{cases}$$

we may derive the following relationship between the first derivative vectors, which ensures continuity of the second derivative and hence of the curvature

$$R_u(i-1) + 4R_u(i) + R_u(i+1) = 3[R(i+1) - R(i-1)] \tag{16}$$

where the two individual segments are expressed in terms of parametric intervals $[i-1, i]$ and $[i, i+1]$ (see Figure 7.8).

If there are n segments to be combined into a single composite curve, then there will be $n-1$ equations of the form of (16) which need to be solved in order to express $n-1$ values of the derivative vectors in terms of the $n+1$ position vectors, plus the remaining two derivative values $R_u(0)$ and $R_u(n)$ at the ends of the composite curve. The total parameter interval for the complete curve is now $[0, n]$. The matrix of the equations turns out to be positive definite and of bandwidth three, and can therefore be easily and reliably solved by standard iterative methods.

The resulting composite curve is termed a **parametric cubic spline** curve. This particular formulation is a *uniform* spline, because the joints between the segments occur at integer values of the parameter u. It is a convenient automatic way of fitting a smooth curve through a set of given data points, and is satisfactory provided that the distances between successive data points are not too uneven. If, however, this uniform parameterisation is used with irregularly spaced data points, there is a tendency to generate smooth but oscillatory curves.

The usual way to deal with this problem is to change the parameterisation of the data points to one in which the parametric intervals are in proportion to the chord lengths between adjacent data points. This leads to a more general form of the equations (16):

$$h_{i+1}t_{i-1} + 2(h_i + h_{i+1})t_i + h_it_{i+1}$$

$$= \frac{3h_{i+1}(z_i - z_{i-1})}{h_i} + \frac{3h_i(z_{i+1} - z_i)}{h_{i+1}} \qquad (17)$$

where $h_i = y_i - u_{i-1}$ is the length of the parametric interval for the ith segment, and t_i is the vector $\mathbf{R}_u$ at the join between the ith and $(i+1)$th segment. It can be shown that the use of non-uniform parameterisation of this kind is equivalent to relaxing the continuity of the derivatives $\mathbf{R}_u$ and $\mathbf{R}_{uu}$ to allow a magnitude ratio of α_i in $\mathbf{R}_u$ and α_i^2 in $\mathbf{R}_{uu}$ at the join between segments i and $i+1$, for all interior values of i.

The overall effect is to enable less oscillatory curves to be fitted to a highly irregular set of data points, and to avoid the possible occurrence of loops in curves fitted to such data.

Alternative end-conditions, such as setting the second derivative $\mathbf{R}_{uu}$ to zero at each end, or choosing quadratic functions for the end-segments, are sometimes used to avoid the necessity for providing values of the tangent vectors at the ends of the composite curve.

Local adjustment of composite curves

Composite curves can be adjusted in a number of ways to effect local shape modifications.

In the case of B-spline curves, we have seen that any control point can be changed without affecting slope and curvature continuity, and this will alter only four spans of the curve.

Another method which can be used is to split a segment at some intermediate parameter value, and then to alter the position and/or the tangent vector at the 'split point'.

A third method involves replacing a segment by an identical degenerate segment of a higher degree, and then using the extra 'degrees of freedom' of the more complex curve to adjust the shape of the segment.

Full details of these and other local curve modification methods are given in Faux and Pratt [1979].

4.4 Parameterisation of composite curves

It has been noted that changes in parameterisation can be important when using spline curves to fit irregular data points.

Once a composite curve has been assembled, either as a spline or by simply combining a collection of individual segments, it is still possible to apply linear parameter transformations of the form $u^* = au + b$ to each segment which does not alter the type or the geometric properties of the segments. By adjusting the coefficients a and b in these transformations, it is possible to retain continuity of parameter value along the curve. Such global reparameterisation of curves can be useful when creating surfaces which interpolate between corresponding parametric points on these curves, as will be seen in the following chapter.

A less elegant, but more pragmatic way of providing some physical meaning to the global parameterisation of a curve is obtained by calculating the values of some attribute of a given set of points on the curve — arc length, projection on a given straight line, angle relative to some axis — and then treating this attribute as the parameter. The relationship between the original parameter and the new attribute is recorded as a spline function.

Fig. 8.1 Parametric description of a sphere in terms of the Euler angles θ and ϕ

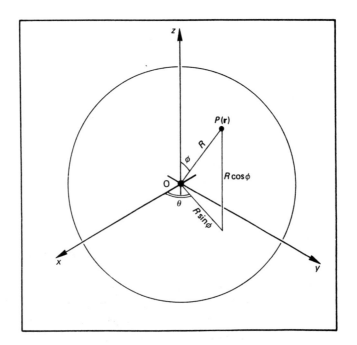

Geometry of surfaces 8

I D Faux

1 Representation of surfaces

A surface can be defined as the locus of points in Euclidean space which satisfy a constraint equation of the form $F(x, y, z) = 0$. This constraint equation then provides an *implicit* representation of the surface (cf. the corresponding implicit description of curves considered in the previous chapter).

Since the points of this locus have two degrees of freedom (rather than one in the case of a curve), it is natural that we might seek to describe the surface by equations of the form

$$x = X(u, v), \; y = Y(u, v), \; z = Z(u, v)$$

where X, Y and Z are suitable functions of the two parameters u and v.

Physically, we might imagine such parameters as arising from a grid of lines constructed on the surface and used to label points on the surface. The most familiar example is the use of two-dimensional coordinate systems on a plane, but it is perhaps more instructive to consider the case of polar coordinates on the surface of a sphere, which create an orthogonal grid of 'lines of longitude and latitude' on the surface. The corresponding parameter equations, for a sphere with its centre at the origin of coordinates, are

$$x = X(\theta, \phi) = R \sin \phi \cos \theta$$

$$y = Y(\theta, \phi) = R \sin \phi \sin \theta$$

$$z = Z(\theta, \phi) = R \cos \phi \tag{1}$$

where the u and v parameters in this case are the Euler angles θ and ϕ as shown in Figure 8.1.

Such equations are known as *parametric* or *freedom equations* of the surface, and the corresponding implicit equations can be derived from them, in principle, by elimination of the parameters u and v (that is, θ and ϕ here) in the three equations for x, y and z.

In our example, it is easy to derive $x^2 + y^2 + z^2 = R^2$, which is the corresponding implicit equation for the sphere, thus eliminating the parameters θ and ϕ. In other examples, however, this may not be straightforward, and quite low degree polynomial equations in the parametric form may correspond to much higher degree implicit equations. Moreover, the derived implicit equation resulting from the elimination process may represent a surface with more than one connected component, for example a hyperboloid of more than one sheet, whereas the parametric equation may have corresponded to one component only [see Willmore 1959].

In vector notation, the implicit equation of the surface would be written in the form $F(\mathbf{r}) = 0$, and the parametric equations as $\mathbf{r} = \mathbf{R}(u, v)$. We shall see that the partial derivatives $\mathbf{R}_u$ and $\mathbf{R}_v$ (that is, $\partial \mathbf{R}/\partial u$ and $\partial \mathbf{R}/\partial v$) determine tangent directions in the surface. If the surface normal is well-defined and the parameterisation itself is well-behaved at a given point, then the vector product $\mathbf{R}_u \times \mathbf{R}_v$ will be non-zero there. Such points are known as *regular points*, and the reader will recognise the similarity with the corresponding definition related to curves (see previous chapter). It will be assumed that singularities arising from cusps and ridges in the surface (*essential singularities*) and those *artificial* singularities arising from the particular parameterisation will not occur in the domain of interest on the surfaces we consider here. We shall normally expect the function $\mathbf{R}$ to be at least continuous with respect to the variables u and v.

In the sphere example we have chosen, there is an artificial singularity at each pole (north and south) due to the convergence of the lines of longitude there. We shall therefore treat these points with care.

The implicitly defined surface cannot have artificial singularities, but there can be essential singularities where the gradient vector, **grad** F, is zero, does not exist, or is not continuous. An example of this occurs at the vertex of a cone.

The parametric equations (1) can be converted into exact rational biquadratic parametric equations by the substitutions $u = \tan \frac{1}{2}\phi$ and $v = \tan \frac{1}{2}\theta$, giving

$$x = X^*(u, v) = \frac{2Ru(1 - v^2)}{(1 + u^2)(1 + v^2)}$$

$$y = Y^*(u, v) = \frac{4Ruv}{(1 + u^2)(1 + v^2)}$$

$$z = Z^*(u, v) = \frac{R(1 - u^2)}{(1 + u^2)} \tag{2}$$

As with the trigonometric parametric form, this equation possesses an artificial singularity, at $u = 0$. We can see this in Figure 8.2, where the rectangular region of uv-space given by $0 \leqslant u \leqslant 1$ and $0 \leqslant v \leqslant 1$ corresponds to a triangular region on the surface owing to the convergence of the constant v-lines at the pole of the sphere.

Before continuing with our example, we will briefly discuss the equations of a plane, since we will want to develop the equation of the plane tangent to a curved surface (that is, the *tangent plane*).

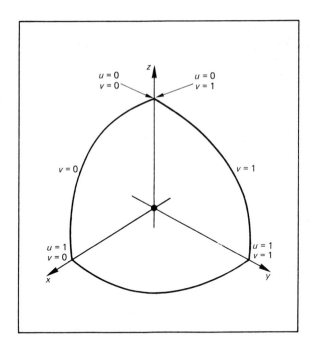

Fig. 8.2 The artificial singularity at $u = 0$ for a sphere parameterised in terms of u and v, where $u = \tan \frac{1}{2}\phi$ and $v = \tan \frac{1}{2}\theta$

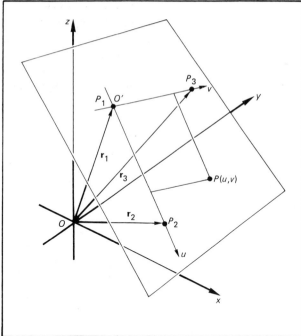

Fig. 8.3 Parametric description of a plane through the three points P_1, P_2 and P_3

1.1 The plane

The general implicit equation of a plane is given by the expression $ax + by + cz + d = 0$, and if a, b and c are normalised such that $a^2 + b^2 + c^2 = 1$, they then represent the direction cosines of the normal to the plane, and, in addition, the displacement of the plane from the origin is $-d$ in the direction of this normal (see Figure 8.3).

We can combine a, b and c as the components of a *unit normal vector,*

$$\mathbf{n} = a\mathbf{i} + b\mathbf{j} + c\mathbf{k}$$

and rewrite the above expression in vector form, giving the following vector equation for the plane:

$$\mathbf{n} \cdot \mathbf{r} = -d \tag{3}$$

where $\mathbf{r} = x\mathbf{i} + y\mathbf{j} + z\mathbf{k}$ is the position vector of any general point on this plane.

A parametric equation for the plane can be written in terms of any three points $P_1(\mathbf{r}_1)$, $P_2(\mathbf{r}_2)$, $P_3(\mathbf{r}_3)$ lying in the plane, as follows:

$$\mathbf{r} = \mathbf{R}(u) = (1 - u - v)\mathbf{r}_1 + u\mathbf{r}_2 + v\mathbf{r}_3 \tag{4}$$

where the parameters u and v vary linearly in the directions P_1P_2 and P_1P_3 respectively, as shown in Figure 8.3.

This parameterisation covers the plane with a grid of straight lines corresponding to lines of constant parameter u or v. The constant u parameter lines are parallel to P_1P_3, and those of constant v are parallel to P_1P_2. We have, essentially, set up an oblique (that is, non-orthogonal) coordinate system in the plane.

The direction of a normal to a plane can be obtained by taking the cross-product of two different vectors lying in the plane, and we will conveniently choose the vectors from P_1 to P_2 and from P_1 to P_3, namely $(\mathbf{r}_2 - \mathbf{r}_1)$ and $(\mathbf{r}_3 - \mathbf{r}_1)$ respectively. We then wish to show that

$$\mathbf{n} \propto (\mathbf{r}_2 - \mathbf{r}_1) \times (\mathbf{r}_3 - \mathbf{r}_1)$$

To verify this we choose points P_1, P_2 and P_3 to have position vectors

$$\mathbf{r}_1 = \frac{-d}{a}\,\mathbf{i}, \qquad \mathbf{r}_2 = \frac{-d}{b}\,\mathbf{j}, \qquad \mathbf{r}_3 = \frac{-d}{c}\,\mathbf{k}$$

respectively. It is then easily shown that with these particular values all three of these vectors $\mathbf{r}_1$, $\mathbf{r}_2$ and $\mathbf{r}_3$ satisfy equation (3), and hence lie on the plane. Using these, the above expression becomes

$$\mathbf{n} \propto \frac{d^2}{bc}\,\mathbf{i} + \frac{d^2}{ca}\,\mathbf{j} + \frac{d^2}{ab}\,\mathbf{k}$$

So $\mathbf{n} \propto a\mathbf{i} + b\mathbf{j} + c\mathbf{k}$ as required.

Note that the partial derivatives $\mathbf{R}_u$ and $\mathbf{R}_v$ which can be obtained from equation (4) by differentiation are equal to $(\mathbf{r}_2 - \mathbf{r}_1)$ and $(\mathbf{r}_3 - \mathbf{r}_1)$ respectively, so that the normal $\mathbf{n}$ is in the direction of $\mathbf{R}_u \times \mathbf{R}_v$. We will see that this result is true for general parametric surfaces.

1.2   Equations for a general curved surface

For the general surface $\mathbf{r} = \mathbf{R}(u, v)$, we consider first its *parametric curves*. These are the space curves of constant u and v, such as $\mathbf{r} = \mathbf{R}(u, v_0)$ where v_0 is fixed in value and u varies along the curve. The tangent at any point on this space curve is also tangential to the surface at that point (but the curve normal $\mathbf{N}$ is generally not parallel to the surface normal $\mathbf{n}$). We have seen that the (first) derivative vector of a space curve is in the direction of the tangent, so that it follows that the partial derivative $\mathbf{R}_u(u, v_0)$ is tangential to the u-parameter space curve $v = v_0$ at any given point on it. In a similar way, the partial derivative $\mathbf{R}_v(u_0, v)$ is tangential to the v-parameter curve $u = u_0$ at any given point on it. Consequently, at the point (u_0, v_0), both partial derivatives are tangential to the respective curves and hence to the surface. Both are thus vectors lying in the tangent plane at this point, and their cross-product is in the direction of the normal to this plane, provided it is non-zero.

We again denote the unit vector normal to the surface by $\mathbf{n}$, so

$$\mathbf{n} = \frac{\mathbf{R}_u \times \mathbf{R}_v}{|\mathbf{R}_u \times \mathbf{R}_v|} \tag{5}$$

which is well-defined at all regular points on the surface.

To derive the unit normal vector for a surface expressed in implicit form

$F(\mathbf{r}) = 0$, we note that this normal is perpendicular to the tangent to *any* curve $\mathbf{r} = \mathbf{R}(s)$ lying in the surface, where s is the arc-length parameter. The vector equation expressing this property is

$$\mathbf{n} \cdot \mathbf{R}_s(s) = 0$$

For any such curve, we also note that $F(\mathbf{R}(s)) \equiv 0$ since the curve lies entirely in the surface, so that $F_s = \mathrm{d}F/\mathrm{d}s = 0$, giving

$$F_s = F_x x_s(s) + F_y y_s(s) + F_z z_s(s) = 0$$

Thus the gradient vector

$$\mathbf{grad}\ F\ (= F_x \mathbf{i} + F_y \mathbf{j} + F_z \mathbf{k})$$

is also perpendicular to the tangent vector

$$\mathbf{R}_s(s)(= x_s \mathbf{i} + y_s \mathbf{j} + z_s \mathbf{k})$$

for every surface curve passing through the given point. It follows that $\mathbf{n}$ is proportional to the gradient vector, giving

$$\mathbf{n} = \frac{\mathbf{grad}\ F}{|\mathbf{grad}\ F|} \tag{6}$$

We should note, however, that the sense of the surface normal determined by either (5) or (6) is arbitrary, since the sign of $\mathbf{n}$ is reversed if we take the parameters in the reverse order, or if we take the equation $-F(\mathbf{r}) = 0$ as the implicit form. The usual practice in surface design is to choose a conventional sense for each surface type, and then to indicate separately whether this conventional sense is applicable to a given design or whether the opposite sense should be used.

In our sphere example, the parameters are ϕ and θ and we note that

$$\mathbf{R}_\phi = R \cos\theta \cos\phi\ \mathbf{i} + R \sin\theta \cos\phi\ \mathbf{j} - R\ \sin\phi\ \mathbf{k}$$

and

$$\mathbf{R}_\theta = -R \sin\theta \sin\phi\ \mathbf{i} + R \cos\theta \sin\phi\ \mathbf{j}$$

so that the unit normal vector

$$\mathbf{n} = \frac{\mathbf{R}_\phi \times \mathbf{R}_\theta}{|\mathbf{R}_\phi \times \mathbf{R}_\theta|}$$

$$= \frac{R^2 \sin^2\phi \cos\theta\ \mathbf{i} + R^2 \sin^2\phi \sin\theta\ \mathbf{j} + R^2 \cos\phi \sin\phi\ \mathbf{k}}{R^2 \sin\phi}$$

$$= \sin\phi \cos\theta\ \mathbf{i} + \sin\phi \sin\theta\ \mathbf{j} + \cos\phi\ \mathbf{k}$$

$$= \frac{x}{R} \mathbf{i} + \frac{y}{R} \mathbf{j} + \frac{z}{R} \mathbf{k}$$

$$= \frac{\mathbf{grad}\ F}{|\mathbf{grad}\ F|}$$

where $F(\mathbf{r}) = x^2 + y^2 + z^2 - R^2 = 0$

Note that the normal vector $\mathbf{R}_\phi \times \mathbf{R}_\theta$ is zero at the point where $\phi = 0$, and had we not cancelled out the factor $\sin\theta$, we would have arrived at an indeterminate expression for $\mathbf{n}$. When carrying out the calculation on a computer, we usually have to make special provision for this artificial singularity. In general, we may need to resort to deriving higher-order derivatives to obtain the normal vector.

The *tangent plane* Π, at any given point P_0 (with position vector $\mathbf{r}_0$) of the surface, is easily obtained by noting that if $\mathbf{r}$ is the position vector of a point in this plane then $(\mathbf{r} - \mathbf{r}_0)$ must lie in the plane and so must be orthogonal to the normal $\mathbf{n}$ at $\mathbf{r}_0$. The vector equation describing the tangent plane is therefore

$$\Pi(\mathbf{r}) = \mathbf{n} \cdot (\mathbf{r} - \mathbf{r}_0) = 0 \tag{7}$$

In our sphere example, at the point $\mathbf{r}_0 = (R, R, R)/3^{0.5}$ on the sphere,

$$\mathbf{n} = (1, 1, 1)/3^{0.5}$$

and the tangent plane is thus defined by the equation

$$x + y + z - 3^{0.5}R = 0$$

Points (with position vector $\mathbf{r}$) on the *parallel* or *offset surface* at distance d from a given surface with parametric form $\mathbf{R}(u, v)$, can be evaluated from the equation

$$\mathbf{r} = \mathbf{R}^*(u, v) = \mathbf{R}(u, v) \pm d\mathbf{n}(u, v) \tag{8}$$

the sign being dependent on the sense of the offset relative to the original surface.

Curvature properties of a parametrically (or implicitly) defined surface are obtained from expressions involving the second derivatives of $\mathbf{R}(u, v)$ (or of $F(\mathbf{r})$), and details are given in Faux and Pratt [1979]. More extensive coverage of the differential geometry of surfaces will be found in Willmore [1959].

We now proceed to discuss the more commonly used parametric surface representations, although it should be noted that geometric modellers usually represent the simpler planar, quadric and toroidal surfaces by their implicit forms. The representation and properties of these classical surfaces are very thoroughly discussed in traditional texts such as Sommerville [1934].

2 Parametric surface design methods

Parametric surfaces can be defined either in terms of point data (positions, tangents, normals) or in terms of data on a number of space curves lying in these surfaces (again, positions, cross-slopes and normals may be given).

The resulting surface will then either interpolate or approximate the data, or the data may be used to define (rather less directly) related surfaces as in the case of the B-spline. (The reader will recall that B-spline curves do not generally pass through any of the control points used to define them. We will therefore regard this as an approximation of the data.)

Surfaces are normally defined in *patches*, each patch corresponding to a rectangular domain in *uv*-space. Most often, this is the unit square domain $0 \leqslant u \leqslant 1, 0 \leqslant v \leqslant 1$, although this parameterisation is often modified on composite surfaces, especially when non-uniform parameterisation is used. We shall therefore first consider single patches of surface defined over this unit square domain.

Fig. 8.4 The parameter curves on a surface patch defined by a rectangular array of data points

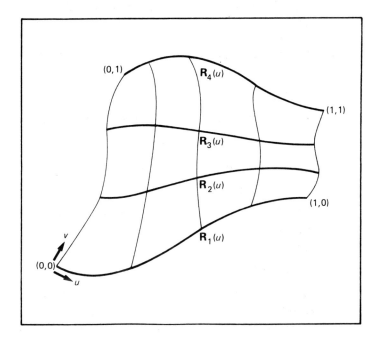

A surface patch defined in terms of point data will usually be based on a rectangular array of data points which may be regarded as defining a series of curves in one parameter direction which in turn are interpolated or approximated in the direction of the other parameter to generate the surface (see Figure 8.4). The definition is, however, symmetric, in that the curves may first be defined either by the rows or by the columns of the array of data points.

In the case of curve interpolation, the curves are assumed to be already defined, and interpolation or approximation between corresponding points on the set of curves takes place. This means that each curve must be parameterised over the same domain in *u* (say), and points on each curve having the same parameter value will be used to define intermediate points between these defining curves.

2.1 Bicubic polynomial surface patches

The description of a parametric **bicubic surface** involves up to the third power of both parameters, *u* and *v*. There are sixteen possible combinations of powers, $u^n v^m (0 \leqslant n, m \leqslant 3)$, for two parameters, so a general bicubic form involves sixteen vector coefficients, say $\mathbf{a}_{ij}(i, j = 0, 1, 2, 3)$. The most straightforward expression for a bicubic surface patch is therefore the power series form

$$\mathbf{r} = \mathbf{R}(u, v)$$

$$= (\mathbf{a}_{11} + \mathbf{a}_{12}v + \mathbf{a}_{13}v^2 + \mathbf{a}_{14}v^3)$$

$$+ (\mathbf{a}_{21} + \mathbf{a}_{22}v + \mathbf{a}_{23}v^2 + \mathbf{a}_{24}v^3)u$$

$$+ (\mathbf{a}_{31} + \mathbf{a}_{32}v + \mathbf{a}_{33}v^2 + \mathbf{a}_{34}v^3)u^2$$

$$+ (\mathbf{a}_{41} + \mathbf{a}_{42}v + \mathbf{a}_{43}v^2 + \mathbf{a}_{44}v^3)u^3$$

This is usually presented in the more convenient matrix form

$$\mathbf{r} = \mathbf{R}(u, v) = \mathbf{UAV} = [1 \ u \ u^2 \ u^3] \, [\mathbf{a}_{ij}] \begin{bmatrix} 1 \\ v \\ v^2 \\ v^3 \end{bmatrix} \tag{9}$$

$$\begin{array}{ccc} \uparrow & \uparrow & \uparrow \\ \mathbf{U} & \mathbf{A} & \mathbf{V} \end{array}$$

where $[\mathbf{a}_{ij}]$ $(i, j = 0, 1, 2, 3)$ is the (4×4) matrix of the vector coefficients.

As with the simpler power series form of the parametric cubic curve (considered in the previous chapter), it is usual to choose basis functions other than $1, v, v^2, v^3, u, vu, v^2u, \ldots, u^3, vu^3, v^2u^3$ and v^3u^3, for the bicubic polynomials in u and v, in order to give more geometrical meaning to the vector coefficients, and to aid in assembling several patches into a composite surface, with the desired order of continuity between the patches. A change of basis functions (or bases) is effected with an appropriate basis matrix $\mathbf{M}$, which relates each 'new' basis function to the set of 'old' basis functions (cf. the previous chapter for curves).

Thus, the general representation for a bicubic patch may be expressed in matrix form as

$$\mathbf{r} = \mathbf{R}(u, v) = \mathbf{UMAM}^{\mathrm{T}}\mathbf{V}^{\mathrm{T}}$$

where $\mathbf{M}$ is the basis matrix, $\mathbf{U} = [1 \ u \ u^2 \ u^3]$, $\mathbf{V} = [1 \ v \ v^2 \ v^3]$, and $\mathbf{A}$ is now the corresponding (4×4) matrix of (more meaningful) vector coefficients. The superscript T indicates matrix transpose.

Ferguson bicubic surface patches

For a Ferguson bicubic (Coons') patch, the new basis functions are identical to those of the Ferguson cubic segment (see previous chapter), so that

$$\mathbf{M} = \begin{bmatrix} 1 & 0 & 0 & 0 \\ 0 & 0 & 1 & 0 \\ -3 & 3 & -2 & -1 \\ 2 & -2 & 1 & 1 \end{bmatrix}$$

and the vector coefficents are analogous to those for the Ferguson curve since the matrix $\mathbf{A}$ has the form

$$\mathbf{A} = \begin{bmatrix} \mathbf{R}(0, 0) & \mathbf{R}(0, 1) & \mathbf{R}_v(0, 0) & \mathbf{R}_v(0, 1) \\ \mathbf{R}(1, 0) & \mathbf{R}(1, 1) & \mathbf{R}_v(1, 0) & \mathbf{R}_v(1, 1) \\ \mathbf{R}_u(0, 0) & \mathbf{R}_u(0, 1) & \mathbf{R}_{uv}(0, 0) & \mathbf{R}_{uv}(0, 1) \\ \mathbf{R}_u(1, 0) & \mathbf{R}_u(1, 1) & \mathbf{R}_{uv}(1, 0) & \mathbf{R}_{uv}(1, 1) \end{bmatrix} \tag{10}$$

Just as the cubic curve segment required position and first derivative data at each end, for the bicubic surface patch we now require position, first derivative and mixed derivative data at the four corners of the patch. We are therefore using a Hermite interpolation in the two variables u and v.

Since the (position and derivative) data on two adjacent corners effectively defines not only the edge curve which joins them, but also the 'cross-slope' at each point on the edge, we can see that we may combine two or more patches with continuity of position and slope simply by ensuring that the common corners share the same position and derivative data.

Fig. 8.5 The cross-slopes and cross-derivatives for a Ferguson bicubic surface patch

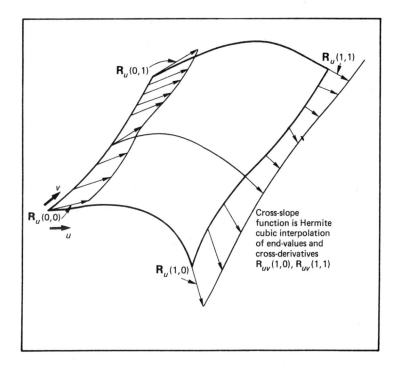

The problem with the Ferguson bicubic form is the need to supply values for the derivative vectors, since these depend as much on the parameterisation as on the shape of the desired surface. As with curves, the first derivatives correspond to tangents in the two parametric directions, but their magnitudes affect the fullness of the edge curves as described in the preceding chapter on curves. Moreover, the shape of the patch interior depends not only on these edge curves, but also on the direction and magnitude of the cross-slope functions defined by the cross-slopes at each end, and by the values of the cross-derivatives $\mathbf{R}_{uv}$ as illustrated in Figure 8.5. The cross-derivative $\mathbf{R}_{uv}$ is often referred to as the *twist vector*, but this is something of a misnomer, since it depends on both the surface *and* the parameterisation and so can be non-zero even on a plane surface if the parameterisation is irregular.

The Ferguson/Coons' bicubic patch was used by Ferguson [1964] in a surface-fitting procedure for rectangular arrays of point position data. Although his procedure allowed the user to enter first derivative values, these were usually conveniently estimated by the program, from the position values of adjacent points, and the cross-derivatives were set to zero.

Composite Ferguson surfaces can be obtained by splining the 'rows and columns' of such an array of points to obtain the required derivative data, and by ensuring curvature continuity between patches, much in the same way as was described for composite Ferguson curves in the preceding chapter. A full description will be found in Faux and Pratt [1979].

Bézier bicubic surface patches
This form of the bicubic patch uses the Bernstein basis functions described in the previous chapter for curves, so that in this case for a surface patch the basis matrix is

$$\mathbf{M} = \begin{bmatrix} 1 & 0 & 0 & 0 \\ -3 & 3 & 0 & 0 \\ 3 & -6 & 3 & 0 \\ -1 & 3 & -3 & 1 \end{bmatrix}$$

and the vector coefficients are now given by a (4×4) matrix of position vectors for sixteen points forming a *characteristic polyhedron* (or *net*) analogous to the polygon described for Bézier curves. Thus

$$\mathbf{A} = [\mathbf{r}_{ij}] \quad \text{where} \quad 0 \leqslant i \leqslant 3 \quad \text{and} \quad 0 \leqslant j \leqslant 3$$

As is shown in Figure 8.6, the four corner points P_{00}, P_{03}, P_{30} and P_{33} lie at the corners of the surface patch itself, whereas the remaining points do not lie on the patch. The four points along each edge of the net define the four edge curves of the patch as Bézier space curves. The interior four points determine the cross-derivatives at the corners and the cross-slopes along the nearest edges to them, and hence influence the nature of the interpolation of the edge curves in the interior of the patch.

Fig. 8.6 The characteristic polyhedron for a Bézier bicubic surface patch

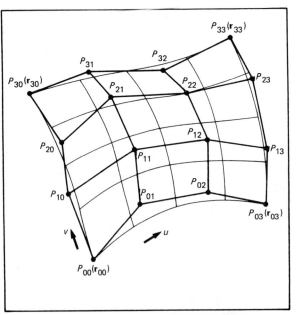

Uniform cubic B-spline surfaces
The uniform cubic B-spline surface is defined in terms of the same basis functions as the corresponding uniform cubic B-spline curves, so that

$$\mathbf{M} = \tfrac{1}{6} \begin{bmatrix} 1 & 4 & 1 & 0 \\ -3 & 0 & 3 & 0 \\ 3 & -6 & 3 & 0 \\ -1 & 3 & -3 & 1 \end{bmatrix}$$

and the vector coefficients now form a net of control points, none of which lies on the surface, as with the B-spline curve described in the preceding chapter.

This surface has slope and curvature continuity provided that none of the control points are coincident. Discontinuities of slope or curvature can be created by coincidence of control points in much the same way as for curves.

Extensions to non-uniform rational B-spline surfaces are carried out in a natural way, by analogy with the situation for curves.

2.2 Surface design by interpolation of general curves

As noted above, the symmetric cubic patch definitions may be regarded as interpolations between curves (and/or cross-slope functions) defined either by rows or by columns of coefficients in the matrix $\mathbf{A}$. In general, however, neither the curves themselves nor the interpolations between them need be restricted to the cubic form, and Coons [1967] has shown just how general this interpolation can be.

Ruled surfaces
Given two general curves $\mathbf{R}_1(u)$ and $\mathbf{R}_2(u)$, we can define a ruled surface as a linear interpolation between the two curves as follows:

$$\mathbf{r} = \mathbf{R}(u, v) = (1 - v)\mathbf{R}_1(u) + v\mathbf{R}_2(u) \tag{11}$$

Fig. 8.7 Two different ruled surfaces formed from the same two curves with different parameterisations

where we assume that the parameter interval for u is the same for both curves. Then the above surface is formed essentially by drawing straight lines between corresponding parameter points on the two curves. If each curve is a single segment defined over the interval $0 \leqslant u \leqslant 1$, the result will be a single surface patch, whereas if each curve is a uniform spline with n segments, we will obtain n ruled surface patches with slope and curvature continuity. In general,

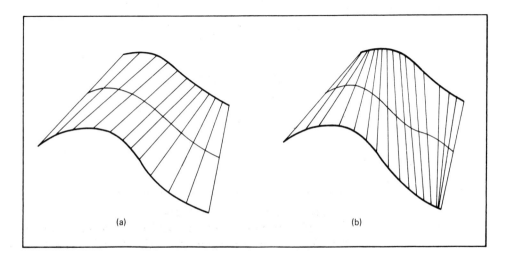

(a) (b)

the two curves may be dissimilar simple or composite curves, provided only that they are defined over the same (parameter) interval.

It is important to note that the resulting surface is determined by the parameterisation of the two curves as well as by their shape, location and orientation, as shown in Figure 8.7.

Hermitian interpolation of two curves

If, in addition to the two general edge curves, we are also given the cross-slopes $S_1(u)$ and $S_2(u)$ as functions of the same parameter u used for the curve definitions, where S_1 and S_2 each represent a vector function describing the magnitude as well as the direction of the cross-slopes, then these 'augmented' curves are known as *curve strips*. We can create a cubic Hermite interpolation between the two curve strips by using the following extension of the Ferguson curve formula (Figure 8.8):

$$\mathbf{r} = \mathbf{R}(u, v) = [1 \ v \ v^2 \ v^3]\mathbf{M}\begin{bmatrix} \mathbf{R}_1(u) \\ \mathbf{R}_2(u) \\ \mathbf{S}_1(u) \\ \mathbf{S}_2(u) \end{bmatrix} \tag{12}$$

where $\mathbf{M}$ is the Ferguson (Hermite) basis matrix.

Fig. 8.8 Hermitian interpolation between two curve strips

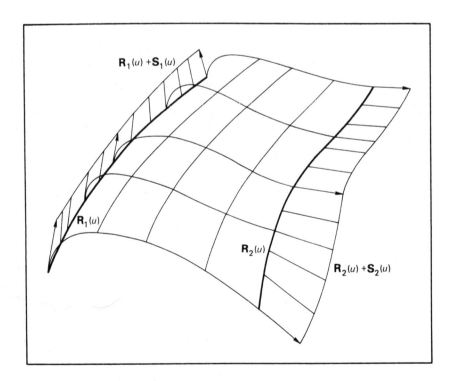

Bilinear interpolation of four boundary curves

If we have four general curves $\mathbf{R}_1(u), \mathbf{R}_2(u), \mathbf{R}_3(v)$ and $\mathbf{R}_4(v)$, which form a closed boundary as illustrated in Figure 8.9, then we may define the bilinear interpolation between them as

Fig. 8.9 Bilinear interpolation between four boundary curves

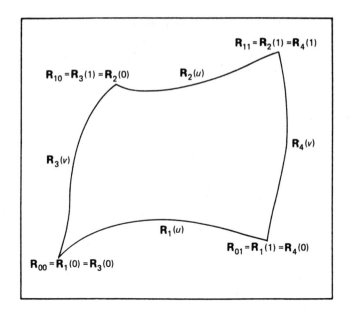

$$r = R(u, v) = (1 - v)R_1(u) + vR_2(u)$$
$$+ (1 - u)R_3(v) + uR_4(v)$$
$$- [(1 - u)\ \ u] \begin{bmatrix} R_{00} & R_{01} \\ R_{10} & R_{11} \end{bmatrix} \begin{bmatrix} (1 - v) \\ v \end{bmatrix} \tag{13}$$

where the patch corners are given by $R_{00} = R_1(0) = R_3(0)$, etc.

This surface fits all four boundary curves, as can be verified by setting $u = 0$, for example, giving

$$r = (1 - v)R_1(0) + vR_2(0) + R_3(v) - (1 - v)R_{00} - vR_{01}$$
$$= R_3(v)$$

Hermite interpolation of four boundary curves and slope functions

If the four general boundary curves have associated slope functions $S_1(u), S_2(u), S_3(v)$ and $S_4(v)$, then we can form a Hermite interpolation of the four curve strips as follows:

$$r = VM \begin{bmatrix} R_1(u) \\ R_2(u) \\ S_1(u) \\ S_2(u) \end{bmatrix} + [R_3(v)\ R_4(v)\ S_3(v)\ S_4(v)]M^TU^T - VMA^TM^TU^T \tag{14}$$

Apart from requiring the curves to meet at the corners, the cross-slope functions must also match the derivatives along the curves they meet at the corners, and the rates of change of the cross-slope functions of the strips must be equal at the corners where they meet.

If both the boundary curves and the cross-slope functions are defined by Hermite interpolation of end values and derivatives, each of the first terms becomes equal to the last, and we recover the simple bicubic Coons' patch.

As we noted in discussing the ruled surface example, the parameterisation of the curve strips is important in determining the shape of the resulting surface.

The most general form of Hermite interpolation is obtained when equation (14) is modified by replacing the cubic interpolation functions by more general Hermite interpolation functions as described in Faux and Pratt [1979].

2.3 Composite surfaces

As with the corresponding composite curves, it is possible to combine: Bézier bicubic patches, with guaranteed position continuity; Coons' patches (bicubic or general), with guaranteed slope and position continuity; and uniform B-spline patches, with guaranteed second-order continuity, in u across the v-boundaries and in v across the u-boundaries. These results are achieved by sharing common data between the patches.

If we wish to fit a set of Ferguson bicubic patches to a rectangular array of data points, we may use conditions for second-order continuity to set up equations for the slope and cross-derivative values required to define the patches. The procedure is similar to that described in the preceding chapter for curves, and once again we must specify boundary data to supply enough conditions to solve the equations. This is equivalent, for example, to providing the cross-slopes at all the peripheral data points of the array, together with cross-derivatives at the four corners.

As with composite spline curves, it is often advantageous to use non-uniform parametrisation in order to avoid wrinkles in the surface due to irregular spacing of the data points.

2.4 Other types of parametric surface definition

As we have mentioned, it is possible to combine different types of interpolation in the two parametric directions, and this may be useful when the characteristics of the surface are different in these two directions, as it is, for

Fig. 8.10 Triangular and pentagonal patches occurring at internal and external corners of a surface

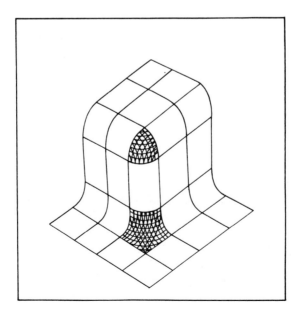

example, in the design of aircraft fuselages, ships' hulls, ducting, etc. Several computer-aided design systems adopt this asymmetric approach to meet the requirements of the types of surface for which they are intended.

All the surface patches described so far cover a rectangular domain in *uv*-space. However, there have been several schemes proposed for interpolation on triangular and pentagonal domains, and these are reviewed in Barnhill [1985]. These patches address some of the problems which occur at external and internal corners of a surface, as illustrated in Figure 8.10.

Another approach to this 'corner' problem is given by defining surfaces in terms of recursive sub-division, by means of which a three- or five-sided 'gap' in a surface can be filled with progressively smaller rectangular patches until the remaining unfilled region can be considered negligible.

On the whole, commercial systems have avoided both of these solutions, and have settled for the less elegant method of allowing two adjacent corners of a four-sided patch to coincide, and of dealing with the resulting artificial singularity by special branching in the software.

Apart from references given in Faux and Pratt [1979], a more recent update and review of these surface design techniques will be found in *CAGD* [1985].

Solid modelling

9

G E M Jared and J R Dodsworth

1 Background

The early role of computers in engineering was as relatively sophisticated calculating machines. It was not until the early 1960s that the advent of cathode ray tube (CRT) hardware connected to computers allowed the growth of graphical interaction. The traditional medium for the communication of data in design and manufacture has been the paper drawing and it was as an aid to drawing preparation that computer graphics first came to be used. Computerised systems, on which drawings could be created and edited on screen and then turned into hard copy by outputting them to a plotter, could produce dramatic increases in productivity. The early systems in this field manipulated a two-dimensional model of a product, just like drawings had before. Then later systems were able to handle a three-dimensional wire-frame representation. However, these computer-aided draughting systems could not eliminate errors by the draughtsman, and moreover the main means of communication of data remained the paper drawing. Further, these systems could not produce realistic pictorial images of a product nor could data for design calculations or generation of manufacturing instructions be extracted from them without considerable human interaction. Lastly, tasks such as interference checking between components of an assembly had still to be done by visual inspection of the computerised drawing, just as it had been with paper drawings previously. Thus these wire-frame systems were well adapted to computerising the production of drawings, but they had not been designed to provide a computerised description of products and it is in fact possible to use them to describe objects with non-realisable geometry or to describe objects in an ambiguous manner (see Chapter 5).

Several disparate strands of research led to the development of computer programs for the representation and manipulation of solid objects. One of these was an approach to the design of mechanical parts by treating them as combinations of simple building blocks such as cuboids and cylinders. Such programs are known as **solid modellers** or **volume modellers** and can hold complete unambiguous representations of the geometry of a wide range of solid objects. The completeness of the information contained in a solid model allows the automatic production of realistic images of a shape and automation of the process of interference checking. Furthermore, interfaces can and have been devised in order that existing computer application programs for design and manufacturing tasks can interrogate the solid model to extract data. Finally, new applications programs may be written which exploit the completeness of the solid model to decrease or eliminate the necessity for user intervention in design, analysis (such as finite element analysis) or manufacturing tasks (such as the generation of instructions for numerically-controlled machining).

2 Representation schemes for solid models

All solid modelling systems provide facilities for creating, modifying and inspecting models of three-dimensional solid objects, but there are a large number of different possible methods for representing such models in a computer. However, representation schemes may be divided into six general classes as follows:

- Pure primitive instancing
- Generalised sweeps
- Spatial occupancy enumeration
- Cellular decomposition
- Constructive solid geometry (CSG)
- Boundary representation (B-rep).

Before describing each of these in detail we set out some possible criteria for comparing representation schemes. First, there are formal theoretical criteria based on the mathematical properties of a scheme:

- *Domain* What class of objects can be represented?
- *Uniqueness* Is there a one-to-one correspondence between an object and its representation?
- *Validity* Does the fact that an object can be represented mean that it is valid in some way; for example, does it have realisable geometry?

Secondly, there are more 'practical' criteria for comparison, based on qualities more dependent on implementation:

- *Conciseness* How much computer store is occupied by the model of a shape?
- *Efficiency* How much computer time is used in creating, interrogating or modifying the model of a shape?

In general, we find that there is a trade-off between usage of store and usage of time. For example, if we use up storage 'remembering' the properties of a shape, then we do not need to spend a lot of time recalculating these properties every time we need the information. Representation schemes where the elements of a shape are explicitly held in the model are termed **evaluated representations.** Conversely, those where the elements must be calculated from implicit instructions for construction of the shape are known as **unevaluated representations.** Clearly, the criteria of conciseness and efficiency can directly affect the usefulness of a representation scheme for a particular application. If we have an application that continually needs to access the edges and faces of a shape, then a solid modeller which uses an evaluated representation is likely to be the most useful. However, if we can devise *algorithms* that interrogate an unevaluated structure directly then we can save on store and time. An example of such an algorithm is the so-called 'ray-firing' technique for producing realistic images of a shape directly from a CSG model.

We now describe the six types of representation scheme. Each representation is illustrated by a figure depicting a plan view of a simple three-dimensional prismatic part.

Pure primitive instancing Modellers using this technique can handle a number of families of objects, each defined parametrically (Figure 9.1). A particular solid is specified completely by giving the family to which it belongs together with a limited set of parameter values. Clearly, a disadvantage of such systems is that the range of objects that can be handled is restricted to those in the families pre-defined in the system.

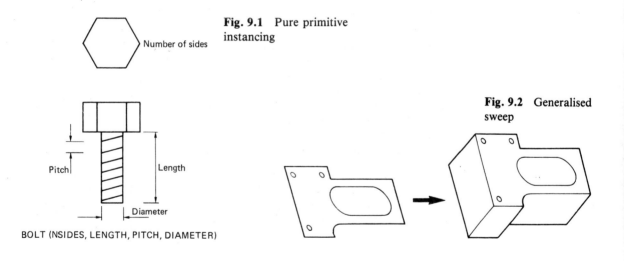

Fig. 9.1 Pure primitive instancing

Fig. 9.2 Generalised sweep

BOLT (NSIDES, LENGTH, PITCH, DIAMETER)

Generalised sweeps A solid is defined in this scheme in terms of volumes swept out by two-dimensional or three-dimensional laminae as they move along a curve (Figure 9.2).

Spatial occupancy enumeration For this technique three-dimensional space is divided up into cubical cells at a particular resolution and objects are modelled by listing the cells that they occupy (Figure 9.3). This representation scheme needs large amounts of store for reasonable resolution and thus has not been generally favoured for practical systems. However, this problem has been

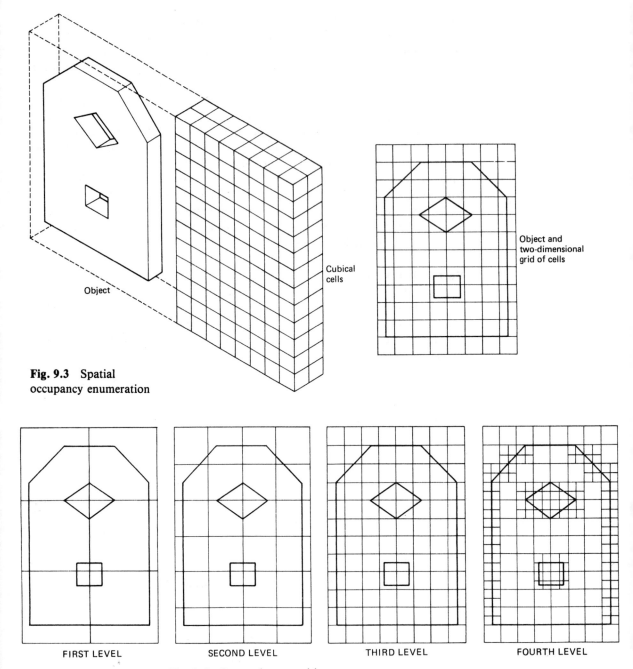

Fig. 9.3 Spatial
occupancy enumeration

Object

Cubical
cells

Object and
two-dimensional
grid of cells

FIRST LEVEL

SECOND LEVEL

THIRD LEVEL

FOURTH LEVEL

Fig. 9.4 Octree decomposition

alleviated in a recent development of this scheme known as *octree decomposition* (Figure 9.4). The spatial sub-division is divided into a hierarchy of levels. In each succeeding level the resolution doubles in each coordinate (x, y and z) so that a cube at one level will be divided into eight sub-cubes at the next. The space occupied by the model for a given resolution is significantly reduced since only those cells that are occupied at each level are stored and sub-division is only necessary for partially occupied cells.

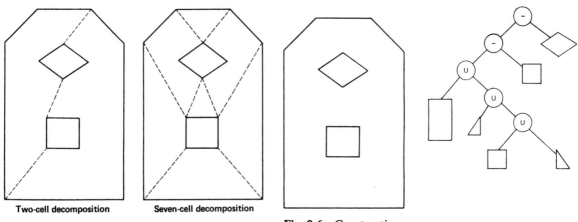

Two-cell decomposition　　　**Seven-cell decomposition**

Fig. 9.5 Cellular decomposition

Fig. 9.6 Constructive solid geometry

Cellular decomposition An object is represented in this scheme by a list of the cells it occupies, but the cells are not necessarily cubes, nor are they necessarily identical (Figure 9.5).

Constructive solid geometry(CSG) An object is represented in terms of a combination of so-called primitive volumes such as cuboids, cylinders, cones or spheres (Figure 9.6).

Fig. 9.7 Boundary representation

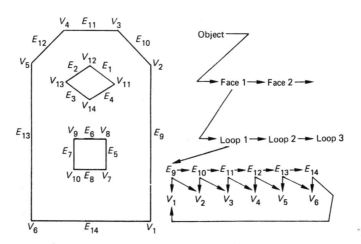

Boundary representation (B-rep) Objects are represented in this scheme by their enclosing surfaces or boundaries (Figure 9.7).

The representation schemes most widely used in commercial modellers are cellular decomposition, CSG and B-rep. These are examined in more detail in the following sections.

3 Cellular decomposition

A solid object can be represented in a computer by dividing or *decomposing* its volume into smaller volumes or *cells* which are mutually contiguous and do not interpenetrate. This process essentially produces a three-dimensional *tessellation* of volume cells. The cell shape is not necessarily cuboid, nor are the cells all necessarily identical in shape (Figure 9.5). However, it is often convenient to choose the cell shape to be cuboid (Figure 9.4) and, in addition, to choose all cells to be identical (Figure 9.3).

In general, a cellular decomposition produces an approximate representation of an object, since, for example, some cells will straddle the object boundary, so that they are partly in and partly out of the object. Representing the object by all cells (those entirely in, those entirely out, and those partially in the object volume) will therefore include some 'empty space' in the description. Such an approximate representation is often troublesome, because it can (amongst other things) change the 'topology' of the object. Thus a small hole or void in the object may not be included in the cellular model, if it lies entirely within one of the cells — it will be replaced by the cell enclosing it (Figure 9.8).

Fig. 9.8 'Topology' changed by a cellular decomposition

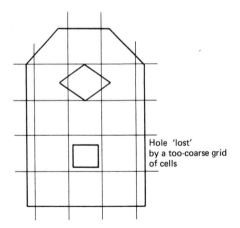

Hole 'lost'
by a too-coarse grid
of cells

We can obviate many of the problems associated with these approximations by allowing the cell shape and size to vary, so that it conforms to the object boundary. However, this usually leads to other problems in describing complex sculptured cell shapes, and it is computationally expensive. A simpler approach is to designate a cell as being *empty*, *full* or *partial*, depending on whether it is entirely outside, entirely inside, or partially inside the object. A list of cells, and the relative sizes and numbers of each type would indicate the extent of the approximation. Notice that, unless more information is associated with the partial cells, this approximate representation is not unique. It can equally well represent any one of a whole class of objects — all those objects which have some part of their boundary somewhere within every partial cell and, of course, also share the same full and empty cells (Figure 9.9).

We now examine three particular types of grid for cellular decomposition.

Fig. 9.9 Equivalent objects under a particular cellular decomposition

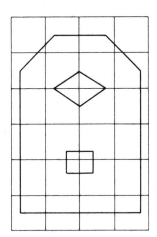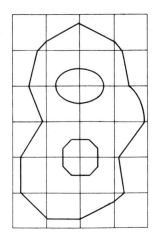

Simple regular grid

This grid is produced by dividing three-dimensional space into a regular array of mutually contiguous *cubical* volumes, forming a regular tessellation of cells (a similar grid in two-dimensional space consists of the regular tessellation of *squares*).

A representation based on this type of cellular decomposition is known as a *spatial occupancy enumeration* (Figure 9.3). This latter is often treated as a separate simple solid modelling technique, as previously discussed in Section 2.

With a regular grid, an approximate value for the volume of a solid can be obtained from the cellular representation. The volume lies somewhere between the sum of the volumes of all the full cells, and the sum of the volumes of all the full and partially full cells. More concisely, if V_{obj} is the total volume of the object to be represented, then

$$V_{full} \leqslant V_{obj} \leqslant V_{full} + V_{part}$$

where V_{full} is the total volume of all the full cells, and V_{part} is the total volume of all the partially full cells.

The regular grid produces a representation which is very inefficient in terms of computer storage, since many contiguous cells have the same designated status (full, empty or partial) and need not all be stored individually. Moreover, the storage problem is further exacerbated by reducing the grid and cell size in order to improve the resolution of the representation. The storage required is directly proportional to the third power of the linear resolution of the grid. Thus a doubling of resolution (by halving the grid spacing, and hence cell edges) leads to an eight-fold increase in the number of cells and hence in the amount of storage space required.

Octree adaptive grid

Instead of dividing three-dimensional space into an array of equally-sized and regularly-spaced cells, a more sophisticated *hierarchical* spatial sub-division is possible. The scheme is based on a hierarchy of different cell sizes. The first level contains the largest cells, and at the second level these cells may be sub-divided into smaller cells. At each subsequent level further sub-divisions may be performed, giving rise to smaller and smaller cell sizes and hence to

159

higher and higher spatial resolution. Usually the linear resolution doubles at each successive level, and always the set of smaller cells derived from a given cell on the previous level 'just fills' the volume of this 'parent' cell.

Cells which are designated as full (or empty), because they are entirely within (or entirely outside) the object to be represented, are *not* sub-divided further. Cells which are designated as partially full *are* sub-divided and hence taken to the next level.

The whole sub-division process can be viewed as forming a (rooted) *tree* structure with the root node representing a single enclosing cell (the universe), and the first-level branch nodes representing a sub-division into the largest cells. Some (but usually not all) first-level nodes then have branches to second-level nodes, and so on for each subsequent level in the tree. The cells are usually cubes and they are often sub-divided into *eight* sub-cubes of half the linear dimensions, so this hierarchical scheme is known as *octree* decomposition (Figure 9.4). (In two-dimensional space the hierarchical grid is based on squares, each of which may be sub-divided into *four* half-size squares, so the scheme is then termed *quadtree* decomposition.) Other types of sub-division (say, into *two* half-cubes) are possible of course, but currently they are less common.

The octree grid approach can adapt very easily to complex object shapes. The adaptive process usually results in an 'explosion' of smaller and smaller cells at the boundary of the object, and these cover the boundary at the higher levels of resolution. Meanwhile, the interior of the object is covered at much lower resolution since it has no significant (shape) features. The number of cells and hence the amount of computer storage required for an octree representation is thus proportional to the surface area of the object rather than to its volume.

General adaptive grid

In the octree decomposition scheme, space is sub-divided until a cell is either full or empty, or (if a cell is partially full) until a sufficient level of resolution has been reached. However, it is more space-efficient if the sub-division process stops when one of the following conditions is achieved (Figure 9.10):

a cell is full;
a cell contains a single surface;
a cell contains a single edge;
a cell contains a single vertex;
a cell is empty.

A sub-division scheme based on these criteria can be considered to form a *spatial directory* of the solid. Of course, in this case it is necessary to record the detailed contents of each partial cell. Such a scheme has a great deal of flexibility because more resolution can always be obtained (at the expense of more storage or computing time) or discarded as required. Notice that, with this type of adaptive grid, sub-division is not always eight-fold (or four-fold in two-dimensional space) and the amount of computer storage needed is dependent on the particular criterion of division.

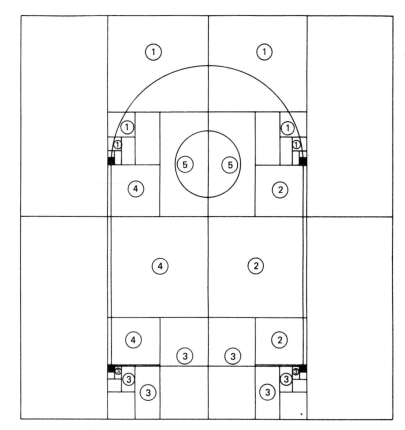

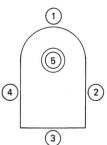

4 Constructive solid geometry

In the constructive solid geometry (CSG) approach, a solid object is represented in a computer as a combination of simpler solid objects. The simplest solid objects are termed **primitives** and often these are themselves combinations of even simpler entities known as **half-spaces.** The types of combination available are the (Boolean) set operations of *union*, *intersection* and *difference*, and the complete solid object is *constructed* from the solid primitives using these operations.

Fig. 9.11 A solid object and its CSG tree

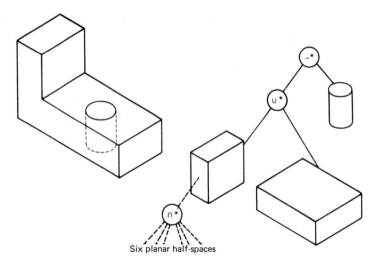

Six planar half-spaces

The data structure representing the complete object consists of a (binary) tree (Figure 9.11) in which the leaf nodes represent the primitives, and the internal nodes represent the Boolean operators for combining these. In such a scheme, the edges and faces of the objects are implied rather than appearing explicitly in the data structure (although the objects represented are guaranteed to be realisable, if not manufacturable). Thus, in the terminology introduced in Section 2, the data structure of a CSG representation is *unevaluated*.

Fig. 9.12 Boolean operations on two-dimensional shapes

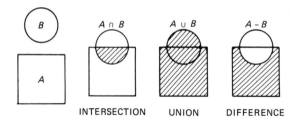

INTERSECTION   UNION   DIFFERENCE

The operations used to combine solids in CSG are known as **Boolean operations** and these are illustrated in terms of two-dimensional shapes by Figure 9.12. However, the strict application of the ordinary mathematical set operators of union, intersection, difference and negation to primitive solids would lead to anomalous objects such as the one illustrated in Figure 9.13(b). Therefore, the required 'Boolean' operations on solids in CSG modellers are modified in such a way that they produce 'regular sets'. These omit pendant (or 'dangling') faces, edges and vertices if they arise.

Fig. 9.13 (a) Two shapes, denoted by different shading. (b) Intersection of shapes in (a)

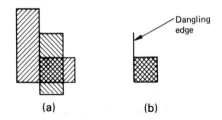

(a)   (b)

The primitive solids that form the leaves of a CSG tree may be represented either by simple functions which define a volume in space or (as indicated in Figure 9.11) by an extension of the CSG tree, in which (regularised) Boolean operations are applied to lower-level entities such as half-spaces. The concept of a half-space is illustrated in Figure 9.14. Essentially it consists of a surface (usually of infinite extent) which completely divides three-dimensional space into a *solid* region and a *void* region. Any given point is then either in the solid, in the void, or on the dividing surface.

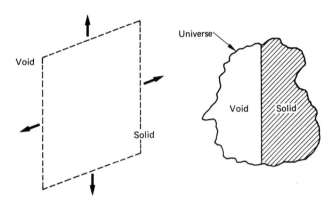

Fig. 9.14 'Plane' half-spaces

Several such half-spaces can be combined to produce more complicated solid and void sub-divisions of space, such as the enclosed volumes forming the solid primitives, used as the basis of CSG. For example, a unit cube may be constructed using the six half-spaces defined by the following inequalities:

$$x \geqslant 0 \qquad x \leqslant 1$$

$$y \geqslant 0 \qquad y \leqslant 1$$

$$z \geqslant 0 \qquad z \leqslant 1$$

These divide space up into twenty-seven regions, but only one of these (the central enclosed unit cube) lies entirely within the solid regions of *all* six half-spaces. Hence the six half-spaces define this cube uniquely.

A half-space is alternatively defined in some systems as a connected region of space whose boundary is an *analytic surface* again dividing space into solid and void regions. Any point is then either 'inside', 'outside' or 'on' the boundary surface of any such given half-space according as it is in solid, in void or in neither. With this definition of a half-space the boundary surface is specified in terms of its implicit form (see Chapter 8).

For example, a half-space disc is given by the implicit inequality:

$$x^2 + y^2 \leqslant R^2$$

where R is the radius of the disc. Any point P with coordinates (x, y) is then inside (*in*), outside (*out*) or *on* the boundary of this half-space, according as the expression $(x^2 + y^2 - R^2)$ is negative, positive or zero (Figure 9.15).

In order to determine the faces, edges or vertices of a solid from a CSG representation, the CSG tree must first be evaluated; that is, the (regularised)

Fig. 9.15 Disc half-spaces

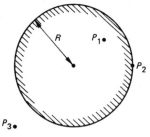

Half-space disc $P = x^2 + y^2 - R^2$

$P < 0$ in $P = 0$ on $P > 0$ out

$P_1 = (R/2, R/2)$	P evaluates to $\dfrac{R^2}{4} + \dfrac{R^2}{4} - R^2 = \dfrac{-R^2}{2}$	in
$P_2 = (R, 0)$	P evaluates to $R^2 + 0 - R^2 = 0$	on
$P_3 = (-R, -R)$	P evaluates to $R^2 + R^2 - R^2 = R^2$	out

Boolean operations must be applied to the primitives or intermediate objects that form their operands. This process, known as *boundary evaluation*, is often very expensive in computer time and techniques have therefore been developed to minimise or eliminate completely the necessity for its use. One simple strategy is to retain the results of evaluation after it has been performed and to attempt to update these incrementally as the CSG tree is further modified. A second possibility is the development of algorithms which interrogate the CSG tree directly.

5 Boundary representation

In a boundary representation (B-rep) modeller, a solid is represented by an evaluated data structure containing the elements which describe its boundary. These elements are divided into two categories: topological and geometric. The topological elements are linked together in a network or *graph* which represents their interconnections or *connectivity* in terms of vertices, edges and faces. This **face-edge-vertex graph** contains no geometric information about an object — the geometric elements (points, curves and surfaces) which give it form and fix it in space are separate. They are linked to the appropriate topological elements as follows:

    face   ⟷ surface
    edge   ⟷ curve
    vertex   ⟷ point

An example of a practical data structure, known as a **winged-edge**, which is often used for boundary representation, is shown in Figure 9.16. It can be seen that the winged-edge structure for a given edge contains more pointers to surrounding edges, faces and vertices than the bare minimum necessary to specify the topological relationships; the structure is said to be 'redundant'.

Fig. 9.16 Winged-edge data structure

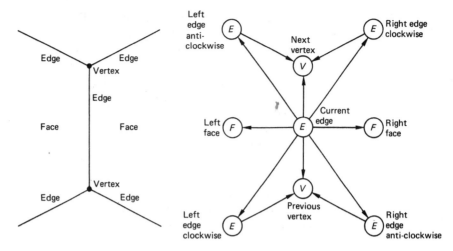

This topological redundancy is in-built in order to reduce the time spent in searching the data structure for a particular topological or geometric entity. In many modellers the redundancy also extends, to a greater or lesser extent, to the geometric data structure, since only the surface geometry actually needs to be stored: the edge equations and vertex positions can be calculated from it. This strategy aims to use more computer store to remember information instead of spending time in recalculating it when necessary. The main disadvantage in using such a redundant geometric data structure is that, as the geometry of a model is changed when the object is modified, numerical errors in the calculations may introduce inconsistencies, so that, for example, a vertex point will no longer necessarily lie precisely on all the surfaces of the faces surrounding it.

A face in a B-rep model is simply a bounded (that is, finite) area of surface. The geometric description of the surface need not be an infinite half-space as often occurs in CSG, and several different geometric forms may be used to describe the surface geometry. In some modellers, a **facetted** representation of curved surfaces is used (Figure 9.17) in order to avoid complex algorithms for geometric calculations. It is then only necessary to devise routines for straight lines and planes. Facetting has the disadvantage that it may lead to false results in some circumstances. For example, in checking for interference between two solids, the facetted approximations to their surfaces may not intersect when more exact representations would.

Since there is no requirement that the surface geometry be described by an infinite (or analytic) half-space, it is possible to introduce surfaces of limited extent with limited regions of validity (such as those used in free-form or

Fig. 9.17 Facetting of a solid

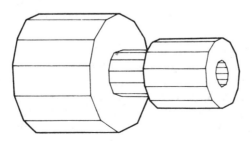

sculptured surface packages) into a B-rep modeller. A B-rep modeller therefore may have a considerable range of surface descriptions available, ranging from simple planes, through curved surfaces (such as spheres, cones, cylinders and toroids), to free-form surface patches.

Creating solids by constructing their boundary topology and specifying the appropriate three-dimensional geometry 'manually' does not provide a convenient user interface to a solid modeller. In practical systems the user is provided instead with a set of higher-level operations which manipulate the model data structure. Boolean operations similar to those used in CSG modellers are often provided (but here the evaluation of the result of combining two objects is usually carried out immediately). It is also common to provide *sweeping* operations to generate prismatic shapes and *swinging* operations (rotational sweeps) to produce turned parts. Both of these types of operation take a description of a two-dimensional profile together with a

Fig. 9.18 Tweaking operation

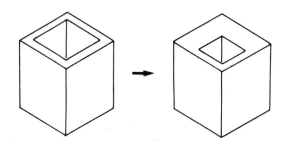

direction, or an axis of rotation, and produce a complete surface boundary for the resulting object. Finally, another class of operation is often provided. This makes localised changes to the elements of a boundary model. An example of this type of operation, known as *tweaking*, is shown in Figure 9.18.

5.1 Types of object modelled with B-reps

In order to construct practical B-rep solid modellers it is necessary to restrict the types of objects modelled to a subset of all possible three-dimensional objects. The first restriction (common to almost all current B-rep modellers) is that only *rigid*, *homogeneous* three-dimensional solids can be modelled. Of course, there are non-homogeneous parts that we might wish to model, and certainly no part that we might wish to manufacture is perfectly rigid. Consequently this restriction that parts must be idealised as rigid and homogeneous solids will be a serious restriction on the wider use of solid modellers for certain applications, such as, for example, where we wish to model the behaviour of moving mechanisms containing flexible elements such as springs.

A further important restriction is that modellers are currently constrained to handle a class of three-dimensional solids known as *manifolds*. This imposes conditions which rule out those objects that are joined to one another or to themselves at an edge or vertex. Examples of non-manifold objects are shown in Figure 9.19. Although this restriction arises from the mathematical properties of the data structures, the class of manifolds conveniently corresponds intuitively to manufacturable objects — it being beyond the bounds current technology to make a part that joins another along an infinitely thin edge!

Fig. 9.19 Examples of non-manifold objects

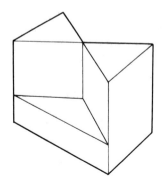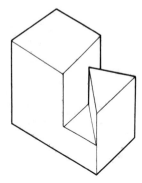

5.2 Data structures for B-reps

As previously stated, the data structure used to model a solid in a B-rep modeller represents the bounding surface of the object and the structure is divided into two types of entity: one representing the topology and the other representing the geometry. The topology is represented by a network or graph of interconnected faces, edges and vertices. A physical analogue of this network would be a 'floppy structure' made up of nodes (corresponding to vertices) connected by pieces of string (corresponding to edges) which enclose areas of flexible membrane (corresponding to faces). The geometric data give this floppy structure rigidity and form in space by specifying:

coordinates for the vertices,
curve geometry for the edges,
surface geometry for the faces.

The face-edge-vertex graph has certain intrinsic properties and obeys well-understood rules. These can be used both to ensure consistency of the model and to aid the implementation of operations on solids. The most important fundamental relationship that applies to the face-edge-vertex graph is known as the Euler–Poincaré formula

$$V - E + F - H = 2(M - G) \qquad (1)$$

where V = number of vertices in the object
E = number of edges in the object
F = number of faces in the object
H = number of hole loops in the object
M = multiplicity of the object (that is, the number of disjoint pieces)
G = genus of the object (that is, number of 'handles' or through holes)

The faces in graphs obeying this formula may be *multiply connected*. This means that they have an outer boundary or perimeter loop and may also have inner boundaries or 'hole loops' (Figure 9.20).

Fig. 9.20 Hole loops on a face

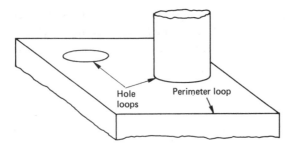

Some additional constraints are necessary for graphs which are to represent solid objects in a B-rep modeller. In terms of the variables in the Euler–Poincaré formula these are:

V, E, F, H, M, G are all $\geqslant 0$

if $V = E = F = H = 0$, then $G = M = 0$

if $M > 0$, then $V \geqslant M$ and $F \geqslant M$

If a model of a solid is constructed according to the formula (equation (1)) and it obeys the above additional constraints, it can represent a real solid. However, it should be noted that this is a necessary but *not* a sufficient condition.

In many B-rep modellers the face-edge-vertex graph is represented in the computer by the winged-edge data structure illustrated in Figure 9.16. In its basic form the winged-edge contains references only to the edges (clockwise and anti-clockwise) in the loops on either side of it and to the vertices at either end of it. However, as mentioned earlier, most implementations include many more references to other related entities in the model, in order to reduce the time spent in searching the data structure for a particular item.

An important feature in the development of B-rep modellers was the separation of geometric elements from topological elements in both algorithms and data structures. This allowed all the functions in the modeller to be implemented in a geometry-independent manner. For example, a procedure to find possible intersections between two faces should not have any in-built assumptions about the geometric properties of the surfaces in which the faces lay: it must handle the most general case of two 'arbitrarily shaped' regions in three-dimensional space. The adoption of this separation technique has the advantage that geometric routines can be developed independently from the implementation of modeller functions and thus new geometric representations and algorithms can be introduced without the need for comprehensive rewriting of the modeller. The main drawback to the geometry/topology separation is the effort needed in the early stages of development to design a geometric interface which will cover all future needs as the modeller evolves.

In order to separate the geometry from the topology, certain assumptions have to be made about the geometric elements that may be used. For example, it is assumed that surfaces and curves do not contain discontinuities in position or derivatives (slope, curvature, etc.) in the region of the piece of surface or curve that is used in the model. It is also assumed that curves are in a parametric form or may be converted to one. This is necessary in order that positions along an edge may be distinguished easily by comparing their parameter values. There is, however, no need to make the same assumption about surface representations, since both explicit $[\mathbf{r} = \mathbf{R}(u, v)]$ and implicit $[F(x, y, z) = 0]$ forms may be used (see Chapter 8).

5.3 Operations in B-rep modellers

In using a B-rep modeller a designer requires some tools for operating interactively on the designs. These tools should enable a design to be constructed and/or altered with relative ease. A range of such interfaces has been provided, and, in addition to being available to the user, most of them are utilised internally as part of data structures, etc. We present a selection of the (currently) most common and useful types.

Euler operations

The Euler–Poincaré formula (equation (1)) may be thought of as describing a six-dimensional space or, more correctly, since only integer values of V, E, F, H, M and G are easy to interpret, a six-dimensional grid. We can represent changes to a solid model in which faces, edges or vertices are added or removed as transitions between points on this grid. The operations which implement such transitions are known as *Euler operations*. An example of how Euler operations can be used to build up the face-edge-vertex graph of a simple solid is shown in Figure 9.21. A system providing only Euler operations would offer a poor interface for the creation and manipulation of solid models by a user. However, these operations constitute the basic elements from which more 'natural' operations can be built.

Fig. 9.21 Constructing a cube using Euler operations

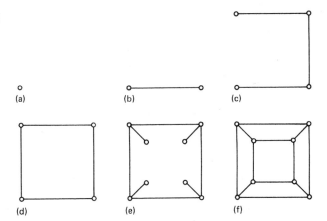

Boolean operations

It is possible to implement Boolean operations in a B-rep modeller (similar to those used for CSG representations) and they provide a useful facility for combining and constructing solids.

In a CSG modeller, Boolean operations form part of the fundamental data structure and operate on primitive solids, etc. In a B-rep modeller they are operations which act on two boundaries and combine them together into one or more new boundaries.

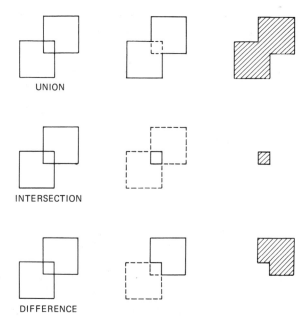

Fig. 9.22 Boolean operations for B-reps

UNION

INTERSECTION

DIFFERENCE

The two-dimensional examples in Figure 9.22 illustrate three types of Boolean operation: *union* (∪), *intersection* (∩), and *difference* (−).

Combining a pair of shapes by using any one of these operations produces a resultant combined shape. If the original pair of shapes do not overlap or interpenetrate then the resultant shape is easily derived. However, if the original pair do overlap then the resultant shape is more complicated, and in general involves new vertices and new edges. Overlaps between the two-dimensional laminae are found by pairwise comparison of the edges of each against those of the other. New vertices in the laminae resulting from the Boolean operations will occur at any intersections between edges, so the edges of the original laminae are split at such points and the segments of the split edge can be marked (to be kept or to be deleted) depending on the Boolean operation being performed and depending on whether each such partial edge lies inside or outside the other lamina. If laminae with curved edges are allowed then there are further problems to be dealt with, which occur in cases such as those shown in Figure 9.23.

Fig. 9.23 Special cases of Boolean operations for some two-dimensional shapes

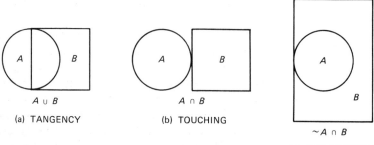

$A \cup B$

(a) TANGENCY

$A \cap B$

(b) TOUCHING

$\sim A \cap B$

(c) NON-MANIFOLD RESULT

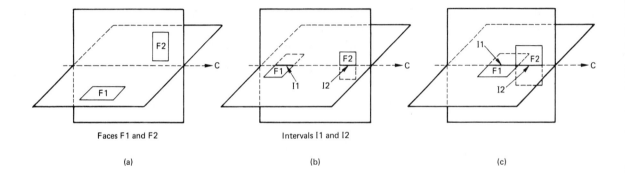

Faces F 1 and F 2   Intervals I1 and I2

(a)   (b)   (c)

Fig. 9.24 Face–face comparison in three-dimensional space

A similar algorithm to that outlined above for two-dimensional laminae is used for Boolean operations on three-dimensional solids in many B-rep modellers, and similar problems arise in dealing with objects containing curved surfaces. In three-dimensional space, potential overlaps between solids are identified by pairwise comparison of each face of one object with each face of the other. The principles used in face–face comparison are shown in Figure 9.24. Note that only in case (c) is there an intersection between the bounded regions of surface which are the two faces involved in the comparison. The 'intervals' where the faces may overlap are generated by first finding the curves of intersection between the two extended surfaces in which the faces are embedded and then testing whether any one of these curves crosses the region of surface defined by the edges of each of the faces. The places where such intervals overlap are the possible sites of new edges in the object resulting from the Boolean operation.

There are many special cases to be covered in analysing the results of face–face comparison, even when only planar geometry is present in the solids concerned. An example is the case where an interval lies along the edge of one of the faces. Moreover, if curved faces are allowed by the modeller then further complications can arise, with, for example, intervals on closed curves which lie entirely inside a face and so cannot be detected by searching for edge–interval intersection points. The remainder of the work involved in a three-dimensional Boolean operation consists in collecting together new edges (as well as the existing edges of the two solids), which occur in the resulting new object. Again the decision as to whether an edge appears in the result is based on the operation being performed and on whether the edge lies inside or outside the other object.

The process of face–face comparison is expensive because of the large number of geometric derivations, such as that of finding the intersection curve of the two surfaces, which is carried out in each comparison. In many modellers an attempt is made to avoid unnecessary geometric calculations by associating with each face in the model a box or a sphere that completely encloses it. When two faces are to be compared, the bounding boxes or spheres may be compared first and the full intersection calculation performed only when these clash. Since box vs. box or sphere vs. sphere intersection involves much less calculation than, for example, more general surface–surface intersection, the Boolean operation will be much cheaper in the cases where only a few faces interact.

Similar problems arise in three-dimensional Boolean operations as for the two-dimensional case where there are tangency points between curved surfaces (see Figure 9.23). However, there is an additional problem which was not mentioned in the two-dimensional case above, and this concerns curved surfaces which contain points where the surface normal (or other derived entities) cannot be determined, such as the apex point of a cone, or so-called 'umbilical points' on other surfaces. Algorithms for Boolean operations that rely on surface derivatives for edge ordering will fail at such points. Currently, the only reliable method available to overcome this problem is to isolate such points beforehand and to deal with them by 'marching' around that locality in order to gain some indication of local surface properties.

Sweeping and swinging operations

Fig. 9.25 (*left*) An example of a sweep operation

Fig. 9.26 (*right*) An example of a swing operation on the face of a solid

In B-rep modellers, prismatic or translational objects can be created by a compound Euler operation termed *sweeping* and rotationally symmetric ones by *swinging* or rotational sweeps. Both these operations use a two-dimensional description as the definition of the plan or profile of the desired result. In the case of sweeping, the two-dimensional profile represents a cross-section; for swinging, it represents the axial profile. Simple examples of these operations are illustrated in Figures 9.25 and 9.26.

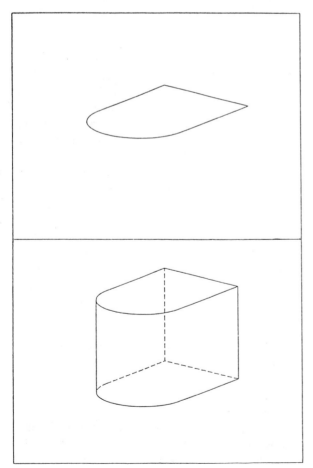

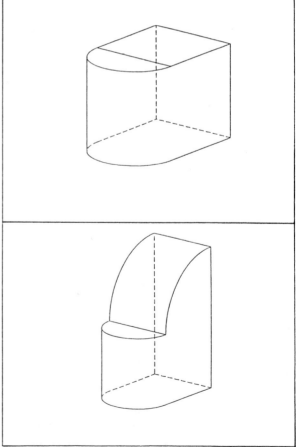

Sweeping and swinging are essentially similar operations: the fundamental concept is that of a face travelling along a defined path, with lateral faces being traced out as it goes. The path geometry, and the curves of the edges of the face being operated on, both determine the surface geometry of the generated lateral faces. The edge-curves of the lateral faces may be determined either from the path swept out by vertices, or (more expensively and less sensibly) by finding the intersection of the surfaces of the lateral faces.

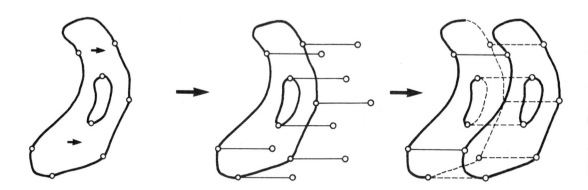

Fig. 9.27 The use of Euler operations for a sweep

Both sweeping and swinging are essentially compound Euler operations — they are carried out by performing a sequence of different basic Euler operations. Figure 9.27 shows how the new edges and faces resulting from a sweeping operation on a lamina are created using the basic 'make edge and vertex' and 'make face and edge' Euler operations.

Although sweeping and swinging operations are defined in generalised topological terms, the objects that can be produced are limited by the modeller's geometric capabilities. For example, in the swing operation, straight edges in the profile will produce planar surfaces if they are perpendicular to the axis of rotation, but cylindrical surfaces if they are parallel to the axis, and conical surfaces if they intersect the axis. There is, however, one special case which does not produce a planar, cylindrical or conical surface. This occurs when the straight edge is not coplanar with the axis of rotation. In this case a quadric surface known as a hyperboloid (of one sheet) will result and this may be outside the range of surfaces that the modeller can handle. Furthermore, swinging or sweeping operations applied to faces that contain edges whose curves are more complex than straight lines or arcs of circles may easily produce relatively complex surfaces that are not in the vocabulary of many modellers.

Tweaking and chamfering

A large amount of interaction with any design tool (whether or not it is a solid modeller) is concerned with making small adjustments to an existing shape. Boolean operations tend to be an expensive tool for this purpose, mainly because they scan the whole data structure of the models involved in an operation, even when the end-result of the operation is only a minor change to one object. However, B-rep modellers have an evaluated data structure, so the elements that represent a particular feature of a shape are immediately available. It is thus possible to devise other, less expensive operations that make small localised changes. These operations fall into two categories: those that make small changes to the geometric elements of the solid model; and those which add or remove topological elements.

An example of an operation that adjusts the geometry of faces is *tweaking*. There are two varieties of tweaking. In the first the geometry of a face is modified by a linear transformation, such as a rotation or a translation (an example of this was shown in Figure 9.18). In the second variety of tweaking operation, the surface of a face is replaced by one of a different type. For example, in Figure 9.28 the plane surface of the top face of the object is replaced by a cylindrical surface. Both varieties of tweaking may be implemented by a similar algorithm: the new surface, specified by the user or obtained by transforming the old one, is intersected with all the surrounding faces and edges to discover the new edge curves and new vertex positions. A 'safe' version may be implemented by calculating the new geometry separately and checking the new configuration before modifying the solid model.

Fig. 9.28 Tweaking which involves a change of surface type

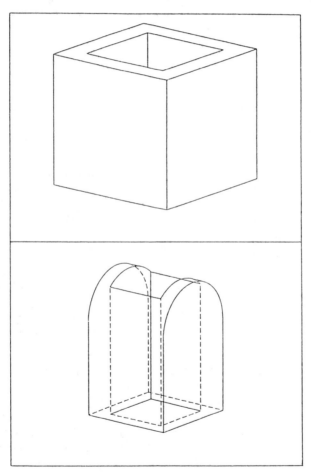

An example of a localised operation that makes a topological change to an object is *chamfering*. As the name implies, this is analogous to the process of rubbing off a sharp corner of a shape. In a modeller it corresponds to replacing a vertex or an edge with a new, small, planar face. The algorithm that implements a chamfering operation uses basic Euler operations to make the

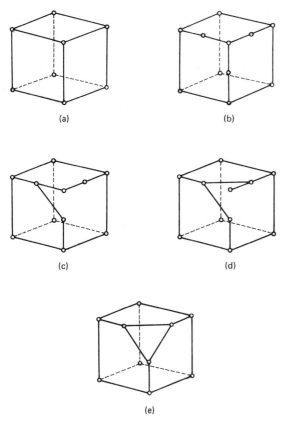

Fig. 9.29 Topological changes in the chamfering operation

(a)

(b)

(c)

(d)

(e)

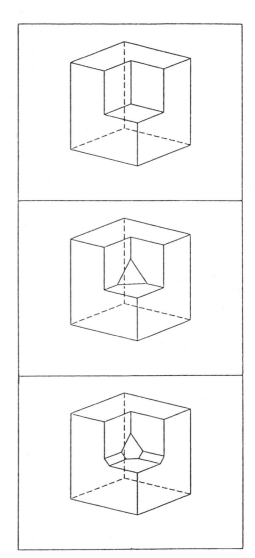

Fig. 9.30 An example of vertex and edge chamfering operations

local changes to the face-edge-vertex graph. An example of this, for the case of chamfering a vertex, is shown in Figure 9.29. Figure 9.30 similarly gives a further illustration of chamfering operations.

The use of Euler operations in local operations, to make the topological changes, ensures that objects remain topologically valid. However, because of the separation of geometry and topology in the B-rep model it is possible to produce objects with valid topology and inconsistent geometry unless further checks are performed. Two levels of checking may be distinguished:

(a) *Local checking* of faces and edges immediately adjacent to the area of the operation.

(b) *Global checking* of the geometry after the local operation for clashes with faces and edges which are remote from the area being changed.

Local checks are cheap and easy to implement, but the more difficult global checking is necessary to guarantee the consistency of the object after a local operation. Global checking may be considered to defeat the purpose of local operations and to make them as expensive as the equivalent Boolean operations. However, because of the extra information that can be implied from the use of a local operation, the global checking can be made less costly than a Boolean operation.

5.4 Visualisation

A designer using a solid modeller needs to interact with the system in the simplest and most natural way. To satisfy this requirement the system usually provides some means for visualising the designed objects. The production of wire-frame images from a B-rep modeller is comparatively easy to implement since all the necessary data is immediately available from the model. All that is necessary in order to produce an image is to follow the references in the data structure, from one edge to another, tracing the projection of each edge curve as we proceed, until the whole model has been scanned. Wire-frame views of objects containing curved surfaces can be considerably enhanced by adding the *silhouette*, *horizon* or *profile* curves of these surfaces (see Chapter 5). In practice, the calculation of silhouette curves for surfaces is much more expensive than the projection of curves from object coordinates to screen coordinates, and thus this activity takes up a major proportion of the computer time needed to produce wire-frame views of curved shapes. Further enhancement of wire-frame views can be achieved by removing the lines that are 'hidden' or by showing them in a different line-style. A varied selection of well-known and well-documented algorithms are used for this purpose (see Chapter 14).

More realistic images of shapes, with appropriate shading of surfaces, can also be generated relatively easily from B-rep models and again many different algorithms are used. Very high quality images may be obtained at considerable further expense by using *scan-line* (sometimes called 'breadslicing') or *depth buffer* (ray-firing) algorithms. In this context 'ray-firing' means tracing the line (ray) corresponding to each pixel in the image, back through object space to discover which face of the object it encounters first. The pixel can then be coloured according to the illumination and surface properties of that face. Scan-line methods use a similar technique, but instead of tracing the line corresponding to a pixel back to the object they slice the object with a plane corresponding to a whole row of pixels. The boundary curve of the slice is then scanned and the visible portions found and drawn into the image in the appropriate colour and brightness.

Other methods for producing shaded images which use facetting techniques are now becoming more popular since they use simple algorithms dealing with planar geometry which may be implemented locally in the display hardware. For these methods the surface of the object has first to be tessellated into small planar *facets*. Those facets that face away from the viewpoint are discarded and the rest sorted and then displayed in order, rearmost first. The final shaded image is generated automatically as nearer facets 'paint over' the more distant ones that they obscure (which will have been displayed first).

Neither the facetting nor the scan-line and depth buffer algorithms as described above are capable of producing shaded images with shadows. In order to perform a shadow computation a representation of the image seen from the viewpoint has to be retained so that the shadows cast can be calculated and imprinted on it. In the case of the facetting algorithm, this means that the computation of which surfaces are hidden, must be performed on the list of potentially visible facets rather than allowing overwriting effects to produce the hidden surface effect.

As an alternative to separate hidden surface and shadow calculations, techniques known as *ray-tracing* can be employed (see Chapter 14). In this method each ray of light is followed from the source of illumination to the object and on to the viewpoint in order to perform both the hidden surface calculation and to determine the appropriate shading. Such methods can permit multiple light sources and can take account of light reflected from one body to another in cases where more than one object is present. However, ray-tracing methods produce images with a high degree of realism, at the expense of a large amount of computing resources!

Finite element analysis 10

R J Goult

1 Introduction

Finite element methods are essentially methods of finding approximate solutions to a physical problem defined in a finite region or domain [Zienkiewicz 1977]. Generally the unknown in the given problem varies continuously over this domain, but the approximate solution found by finite element methods does not possess the same degree of continuity. The method is based on the technique of dividing the region or domain of the problem into a number of **finite elements** and then finding the best possible solution which is continuous and 'smooth' inside the elements (with a simple expression within each element) but which may not be smooth where the individual elements fit together. The accuracy of the solution is dependent upon the number and size of the elements and on the types of approximation function used within the elements.

Finite element methods have their origin in the *displacement method* or *matrix analysis of structures* used in the 1950s to solve structural problems in the aircraft industry [Timoshenko & Goodier 1951; Martin 1966]. In these early applications the elements represented physical components of the structure and the problem was formulated as a system of equations (usually linear) in the displacements of the **nodes** or interconnection points of the elements. Frequently the formulation of the problem involved expressing the strain energy of the structure (i.e. the elastic energy stored when the structure is stretched, compressed or twisted) in terms of nodal displacements and then applying the standard minimum-energy principle to find the equilibrium position. For a large structure, the number of equations could be very large and a computer was usually required for their solution.

As the power of computers increased, the range and complexity of problems that could be tackled by finite element methods also increased. Not surprisingly the early applications of the method were all in structural mechanics and many of the commercial finite element packages were originally designed to make the finite element solution of structural problems more readily available to engineers. However, it was soon realised that finite element methods could be combined with variational calculus and applied more generally to other problems which could also be formulated in terms of minimising an integral function over the domain of the problem. In this way finite element methods could be used to solve heat transfer problems or electrostatic potential problems. In these problems the appropriate integral function has a role which is analogous to that of the strain energy in elastic structural problems.

During the past twenty years many books and papers have been written on finite element methods [Norrie & De Vries 1976; Whitman 1975]. The subject is too vast to be covered comprehensively in the following sections but some of the basic principles and potential applications of the method will be illustrated by simple examples.

In a typical finite element problem the solution is usually derived in four separate phases in the following order:

1 Formulation phase The physical region of interest is divided into *elements* and *element types*, and appropriate *interpolation functions* are selected.

2 Evaluation phase The contribution of each element to the problem formulation is computed and this generally involves evaluating *stiffness matrices* and *generalised force vectors*.

3 Assembly phase The contributions from the individual elements are assembled to produce a large *system of equations* for solution.

4 Solution phase These equations are solved to find the primary unknowns of the problem. These unknowns are generally values of some physical quantity (such as displacement) at the nodes of the elements.

2 The elastic string problem

As a simple one-dimensional example, the problem of finding the displaced equilibrium position of a transversely loaded elastic string will be considered. Initially (for comparison later) we analyse the problem and solve it without using finite element methods. It is assumed that the tension T in the string is large by comparison with the applied load and that the resulting displacements are therefore small. Assume the string is of length L, with fixed ends, and that there is an applied load distributed along the string (Figure 10.1). Such a distributed load (i.e. one that is not concentrated only at specific points) is usually specified in terms of a load per unit length, w, at each point along the string. If the distance along the string from one end is denoted by x, then the corresponding load per unit length at position x is denoted by $w(x)$, to indicate that it is a function of x. Similarly, the transverse displacement ϕ of the string at position x is denoted by $\phi(x)$ since this also depends on x.

Fig. 10.1 A transversely loaded elastic string

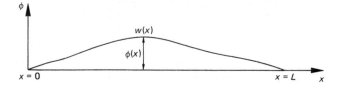

Physically the problem of determining $\phi(x)$, given $w(x)$, can be formulated in one of two ways: either by equating forces on a short segment of string in the equilibrium position; or by considering the total energy stored in the system when the string is displaced transversely (and therefore stretched) by the applied load.

1 The method of equating forces in the equilibrium position leads to the differential equation

$$T\frac{d^2\phi(x)}{dx^2} = w(x)$$

which is usually written more concisely (by not showing the explicit dependence of ϕ and w on x) in the form

$$T\frac{d^2\phi}{dx^2} = w \tag{1}$$

This states mathematically that, at each distance, x, along the string, the rate of change of the rate of change (with respect to x) of the transverse displacement ϕ is directly proportional to the applied load per unit length at that point when the system is in equilibrium. Thus, for example, if we double the load per unit length at each point, we find that the new equilibrium position is such that the rate of change of the rate of change (with respect to x) of the transverse displacement ϕ will also double, and so on. The constant of proportionality is the tension T.

Generally, unless w has a particularly simple form as a function of x, the second-order ordinary differential equation (1) is difficult to solve analytically and so must be solved using numerical techniques.

2 The alternative method for determining $\phi(x)$ given $w(x)$ involves considering the total energy stored in the system when the string is displaced transversely. This total energy consists of the elastic energy due to the stretching of the string together with the potential energy due to the applied load (Figure 10.2).

Fig. 10.2 A stretched short segment of string

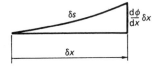

In order to determine an expression for the elastic energy we consider a short segment of the string, initially of length δx. The stretched length δs is then given approximately by

$$\delta s = \left[1 + \left(\frac{d\phi}{dx}\right)^2\right]^{0.5} \delta x$$

$$\approx \left[1 + \frac{1}{2}\left(\frac{d\phi}{dx}\right)^2\right] \delta x \qquad \text{provided } \frac{d\phi}{dx} \text{ is small}$$

The elastic energy, or work done in stretching this segment against the tension T from its initial length δx to its final length δs, is

$$T(\delta s - \delta x)$$

Using the above approximate expression for δs, the elastic energy is therefore

$$T\left\{\left[1 + \frac{1}{2}\left(\frac{d\phi}{dx}\right)^2\right]\delta x - \delta x\right\}$$

which simplifies to the expression

$$\frac{1}{2}T\left(\frac{d\phi}{dx}\right)^2 \delta x$$

Taking the sum for all such segments along the string, and the limit as $\delta x \rightarrow 0$, gives the total elastic energy E_E for the string as the integral

$$E_E = \int_0^L \frac{1}{2}T\left(\frac{d\phi}{dx}\right)^2 dx$$

An expression for the potential energy is also required. The potential energy E_W is equal to the work done against the applied load, and this can be expressed as the integral

$$E_W = \int_0^L \phi(x)w(x)\,dx$$

The total energy E for the string is now obtained by adding the elastic energy and the potential energy expressions together, to give

$$E = E_E + E_W$$
$$= \int_0^L \frac{1}{2}T\left(\frac{d\phi}{dx}\right)^2 dx + \int_0^L \phi w\,dx$$
$$= \int_0^L \left[\frac{1}{2}T\left(\frac{d\phi}{dx}\right)^2 + \phi w\right] dx \tag{2}$$

As a reference for the finite element method of solution used below, we state the solution here for the particular example where $L = 4$ and $w(x) = 1 + \frac{1}{4}x^2$. By integrating (1) with boundary conditions $\phi(0) = \phi(4) = 0$ the exact solution of this problem can be shown to be

$$\phi(x) = [\tfrac{1}{48}x^4 + \tfrac{1}{2}x^2 - \tfrac{10}{3}x]/T \tag{3}$$

---

3   One-dimensional elements

We now analyse and solve the elastic string problem using one-dimensional finite elements. Two types of element will be considered, namely *linear* elements and *quadratic* elements, and for each type the four phases of *formulation, evaluation, assembly* and *solution* will be performed. We assess the accuracy of the solutions obtained by comparing them with the exact solution given in (3) above.

3.1 Linear elements

As outlined above, the finite element method relies firstly on a sub-division of the domain (the one-dimensional string) into elements. We first consider linear elements. For this example the string is divided into four equal elements of length 1.

Formulation

Within each element a simple linear variation of transverse displacement ϕ with length x is assumed. This could be expressed as $\phi = a_i x + b_i$, with particular values of the coefficients a_i and b_i arising for each element ($i = 1, 2, 3, 4$). Since the transverse displacement should not be discontinuous in moving from one element to the next, the value of a_i and b_i on the ith element and a_{i+1} and b_{i+1} on the $(i + 1)$th element must be related.

For this reason it is more convenient to express the value of ϕ at any point within the element in terms of its values at the two nodes at the ends of the element. By convention, the ith element then extends from node i to node $i + 1$, and on this element

$$\phi(x) = \phi_i B_i(x) + \phi_{i+1} B_{i+1}(x) \tag{4}$$

where $B_i(x)$ and $B_{i+1}(x)$ are the linear interpolation (or basis) functions with the properties:

$$B_i(x_i) = 1 \qquad B_i(x_{i+1}) = 0$$

$$B_{i+1}(x_i) = 0 \qquad B_{i+1}(x_{i+1}) = 1$$

and where x_i and x_{i+1} are the x-coordinates of node i and node $i + 1$ respectively.

To simplify the calculations we introduce a change of variable, from x to u; in this case a simple 'shift' given by $x = u + p_i$ (implying $u = x - p_i$), where p_i is a constant, different for each element. This effectively transforms each element into a 'standard element' extending from $u = 0$ to $u = 1$ between two *local nodes* 1 and 2. For this *standard linear element*

$$\phi(u) = \phi_1 B_1(u) + \phi_2 B_2(u)$$

and

$$B_1(u) = 1 - u \qquad B_2(u) = u \tag{5}$$

Figure 10.3 shows the interpolated function $\phi(u)$ for this standard element and the associated basis functions $B_1(u)$ and $B_2(u)$. Each element is then

Fig. 10.3 The standard element with linear displacement and basis functions

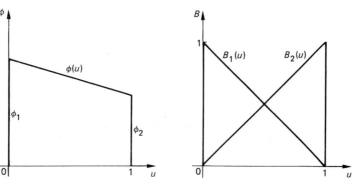

183

associated with a particular transformation from x to the local coordinates u (determined by p_i) and a correspondence between local and global node numbers.

Figure 10.4 shows the elements and associated node numbers and displacements, with the element numbers boxed, and the node numbers ringed. For these elements the correspondence with the standard element can be tabulated as in Table 10.1.

Fig. 10.4 Node numbers and nodal displacements for four (linear) elements

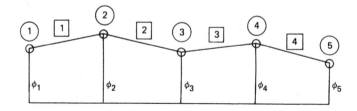

Table 10.1

Element number	Transformation		Node numbers	
			local 1	local 2
1	$x = u,$	$u = x$	1	2
2	$x = u + 1,$	$u = x - 1$	2	3
3	$x = u + 2,$	$u = x - 2$	3	4
4	$x = u + 3,$	$u = x - 3$	4	5

The problem is now formulated by re-introducing equation (2) for the total energy E in the string:

$$E = \int_0^L \left[\frac{1}{2} T \left(\frac{d\phi}{dx} \right)^2 + \phi w \right] dx$$

Within each element, the transverse displacement ϕ is given by equation (4) and the individual contribution to E from each element (that is, E_i) can be identified by sub-dividing the range of integration thus:

$$E = \sum_{i=1}^4 E_i = \sum_{i=1}^4 \int_{x_i}^{x_{i+1}} \left[\frac{1}{2} T \left(\frac{d\phi}{dx} \right)^2 + \phi w \right] dx$$

Evaluation
Each integral

$$E_i = \int_{x_i}^{x_{i+1}} \left[\frac{1}{2} T \left(\frac{d\phi}{dx} \right)^2 + \phi w \right] dx$$

can then be evaluated after substituting for ϕ from equation (4), to give a quadratic function of ϕ_i and ϕ_{i+1}. The integrals E_i are most easily evaluated by transforming to the local coordinate u and integrating over the standard range 0 to 1:

$$E_i = \int_{x_i}^{x_{i+1}} \left[\frac{1}{2} T \left(\phi_i \frac{dB_i}{dx} + \phi_{i+1} \frac{dB_{i+1}}{dx} \right)^2 + (\phi_i B_i(x) + \phi_{i+1} B_{i+1}(x)) w(x) \right] dx$$

$$= \int_0^1 \left[\frac{1}{2} T \left(\phi_1 \frac{dB_1}{du} + \phi_2 \frac{dB_2}{du} \right)^2 + (\phi_1 B_1(u) + \phi_2 B_2(u)) w(u + p_i) \right] du$$

where the node numbers are now local to the element. After expanding brackets and re-arranging terms the above integral takes the form

$$E_i = \int_0^1 \frac{1}{2} T \left[\left(\frac{dB_1}{du} \right)^2 \phi_1^2 + \left(\frac{dB_2}{du} \right)^2 \phi_2^2 + 2 \left(\frac{dB_1}{du} \right) \left(\frac{dB_2}{du} \right) \phi_1 \phi_2 \right] du$$

$$+ \int_0^1 [B_1(u) w(u + p_i) \phi_1 + B_2(u) w(u + p_i) \phi_2] \, du$$

The total energy E_i for the ith element is thus finally expressible in the local form

$$E_i = \frac{1}{2} \sum_{m=1}^{2} \sum_{n=1}^{2} K_{mn} \phi_m \phi_n + \sum_{m=1}^{2} F_m \phi_m \tag{6}$$

where $\quad K_{mn} = \int_0^1 T \left(\frac{dB_m}{du} \right) \left(\frac{dB_n}{du} \right) du$

and $\quad F_m = \int_0^1 B_m(u) w(u + p_i) \, du$

The above expression for K_{mn} is actually a condensed expression for four different terms, namely K_{11}, K_{12}, K_{21} and K_{22}, obtained by choosing the (counting) indices m and n to be equal to 1 or 2 in turn. These four terms may be arranged in a square array and treated together as a single matrix $\mathbf{K}^{(i)}$, depending on i and having the form

$$\mathbf{K}^{(i)} = \begin{bmatrix} K_{11} & K_{12} \\ K_{21} & K_{22} \end{bmatrix}$$

The matrix $\mathbf{K}^{(i)}$ is referred to as the **element stiffness matrix** since it can easily be shown that it contains all the information necessary for specifying the *stiffness* of the ith element.

Similarly, the above expression for F_m is a condensed expression for two different terms, namely F_1 and F_2, obtained by choosing m to be equal to 1 or 2 in turn. These two terms can be arranged in a column and treated together as a vector $\mathbf{F}^{(i)}$, depending on i and having the form

$$\mathbf{F}^{(i)} = \begin{bmatrix} F_1 \\ F_2 \end{bmatrix}$$

The vector $\mathbf{F}^{(i)}$ is referred to as the **element force vector** since it can easily be shown that it contains all the information relating to the *forces* on the ith element.

For the particular one-dimensional example (divided into four elements) considered here, we have, from equation (5), that

$$\frac{dB_1}{du} = -1 \quad \text{and} \quad \frac{dB_2}{du} = 1$$

Since these are both constants, the terms K_{11}, K_{12}, K_{21} and K_{22} can be obtained here without complicated integrations, giving the stiffness matrix

$$\mathbf{K}^{(i)} = \begin{bmatrix} T & -T \\ -T & T \end{bmatrix} = T \begin{bmatrix} 1 & -1 \\ -1 & 1 \end{bmatrix}$$

This does not depend on i in this case and so is the same for each of the four elements considered here.

The components F_1 and F_2 of each force vector $\mathbf{F}^{(i)}$, however, depend on a variable term p_i which differs for each element and so they also differ. The p_i term enters in the expression for w:

$$w(x) = 1 + \tfrac{1}{4}x^2$$

that is

$$w(u + p_i) = 1 + \tfrac{1}{4}(u + p_i)^2$$

Reference to Table 10.1 shows that in the current example $p_1 = 0$, $p_2 = 1$, $p_3 = 2$ and $p_4 = 3$, so that, for instance, the components of $\mathbf{F}^{(2)}$ for the second ($i = 2$) element are

$$F_1 = \int_0^1 (1 - u)[1 + \tfrac{1}{4}(u + 1)^2]\ du$$

$$F_2 = \int_0^1 u[1 + \tfrac{1}{4}(u + 1)^2]\ du$$

Evaluating these definite integrals gives

$$F_1 = \tfrac{35}{48} \quad \text{and} \quad F_2 = \tfrac{41}{48}$$

Thus $\mathbf{F}^{(2)}$ takes the form

$$\mathbf{F}^{(2)} = \tfrac{1}{48} \begin{bmatrix} 35 \\ 41 \end{bmatrix}$$

Performing the same procedure for the other elements (with $i = 1$, 3 and 4) gives finally the full set of force vectors $\mathbf{F}^{(1)}$, $\mathbf{F}^{(2)}$, $\mathbf{F}^{(3)}$ and $\mathbf{F}^{(4)}$ for the four elements of the string, in the form

$$\mathbf{F}^{(1)} = \tfrac{1}{48} \begin{bmatrix} 25 \\ 27 \end{bmatrix}$$

$$\mathbf{F}^{(2)} = \tfrac{1}{48} \begin{bmatrix} 35 \\ 41 \end{bmatrix}$$

$$\mathbf{F}^{(3)} = \tfrac{1}{48} \begin{bmatrix} 57 \\ 67 \end{bmatrix}$$

$$\mathbf{F}^{(4)} = \tfrac{1}{48} \begin{bmatrix} 91 \\ 105 \end{bmatrix}$$

In this simple one-dimensional example all the required integrals have been evaluated explicitly using standard formulae. However, in many situations the expressions for $w(x)$ and for the basis functions $B_1(x)$ and $B_2(x)$ are more complicated than this, and in general it is necessary to use numerical integration techniques.

Assembly

In the next phase of the solution to the problem, the individual elements are assembled together. The assembly process entails the addition of the individual element (energy) contributions E_i, to obtain the total energy E of the system; that is, we require

$$E = \sum_{i=1}^{4} E_i = E_1 + E_2 + E_3 + E_4 \tag{7}$$

However, the expressions for E_i derived in the previous section were evaluated in local form (equation (6)), but for the assembly process we require them in 'global' form. This is now easily achieved by reverting to the original range for the counting indices, to give E_i in the form

$$E_i = \frac{1}{2} \sum_{m=i}^{i+1} \sum_{n=i}^{i+1} K_{mn} \phi_m \phi_n + \sum_{m=i}^{i+1} F_m \phi_m \tag{8}$$

From equations (7) and (8) the expression for E is therefore

$$E = \frac{1}{2} \sum_{m=1}^{2} \sum_{n=1}^{2} K_{mn} \phi_m \phi_n + \sum_{m=1}^{2} F_m \phi_m$$

$$+ \frac{1}{2} \sum_{m=2}^{3} \sum_{n=2}^{3} K_{mn} \phi_m \phi_n + \sum_{m=2}^{3} F_m \phi_m$$

$$+ \frac{1}{2} \sum_{m=3}^{4} \sum_{n=3}^{4} K_{mn} \phi_m \phi_n + \sum_{m=3}^{4} F_m \phi_m$$

$$+ \frac{1}{2} \sum_{m=4}^{5} \sum_{n=4}^{5} K_{mn} \phi_m \phi_n + \sum_{m=4}^{5} F_m \phi_m$$

The terms in this equation can be regrouped to give, finally,

$$E = \frac{1}{2} \sum_{m=1}^{5} \sum_{n=1}^{5} K_{mn} \phi_m \phi_n + \sum_{m=1}^{5} F_m \phi_m \tag{9}$$

This has a similar form to that for E_i except now the stiffness matrix with components K_{mn} is a (5×5) **global stiffness matrix** relating to the whole string (rather than a (2×2) element stiffness matrix relating only to an individual element). Similarly, the force vector with components F_m is now a five-component **global force vector** also relating to the whole string (rather than a two-component element force vector relating only to an individual element).

We use $\mathbf{K}$ and $\mathbf{F}$ to denote the global stiffness matrix and global force vector respectively, and continue to use the bracketed superscripts to indicate individual stiffness matrices $\mathbf{K}^{(i)}$ and force vectors $\mathbf{F}^{(i)}$.

Each component of the global stiffness matrix $\mathbf{K}$ is then easily seen to be the sum of appropriate components of the element stiffness matrices and each component of $\mathbf{F}$ is the sum of appropriate components from $\mathbf{F}^{(i)}$. For example, identifying node 3 with local node 2 of element 2 and also with local node 1 of element 3, we see that

$$K_{33} = K_{22}^{(2)} + K_{11}^{(3)} = 1 + 1 = 2$$

and

$$F_3 = F_2^{(2)} + F_1^{(3)} = \tfrac{41}{48} + \tfrac{57}{48} = \tfrac{98}{48}$$

If we do this for each component K_{mn} of $\mathbf{K}$ and for each component F_m of $\mathbf{F}$ we obtain finally

$$\mathbf{K} = T \begin{bmatrix} 1 & -1 & 0 & 0 & 0 \\ -1 & 2 & -1 & 0 & 0 \\ 0 & -1 & 2 & -1 & 0 \\ 0 & 0 & -1 & 2 & -1 \\ 0 & 0 & 0 & -1 & 1 \end{bmatrix} \quad \text{and} \quad \mathbf{F} = \tfrac{1}{48} \begin{bmatrix} 25 \\ 62 \\ 98 \\ 158 \\ 105 \end{bmatrix}$$

Solution

All the coefficients in equation (9) have now been determined, and it is clear that the expression for E (the total energy) is a quadratic function of the five nodal displacements, $\phi_1, \phi_2, \phi_3, \phi_4$ and ϕ_5. The objective is to determine a set of values for these nodal displacements which will minimise the total energy E. These values should then approximate those occurring in a real string under the same loading conditions.

Mathematically, a necessary condition for E to be minimised is that the partial derivatives of E, with respect to each of the five nodal displacements, should all be zero. Thus, differentiating equation (9) partially with respect to ϕ_m and equating to zero,

$$\frac{\partial E}{\partial \phi_m} = \sum_{n=1}^{5} K_{mn} \phi_n + F_m = 0 \tag{10}$$

Equation (10) represents five separate equations (obtained by setting $m = 1, 2, 3, 4$ and 5 respectively), and as such is equivalent to the following system of linear algebraic equations, written in matrix form:

$$\begin{bmatrix} K_{11} & K_{12} & K_{13} & K_{14} & K_{15} \\ K_{21} & K_{22} & K_{23} & K_{24} & K_{25} \\ K_{31} & K_{32} & K_{33} & K_{34} & K_{35} \\ K_{41} & K_{42} & K_{43} & K_{44} & K_{45} \\ K_{51} & K_{52} & K_{53} & K_{54} & K_{55} \end{bmatrix} \begin{bmatrix} \phi_1 \\ \phi_2 \\ \phi_3 \\ \phi_4 \\ \phi_5 \end{bmatrix} + \begin{bmatrix} F_1 \\ F_2 \\ F_3 \\ F_4 \\ F_5 \end{bmatrix} = \begin{bmatrix} 0 \\ 0 \\ 0 \\ 0 \\ 0 \end{bmatrix}$$

That is $\qquad \mathbf{K}\phi + \mathbf{F} = 0$

or $\qquad \mathbf{K}\phi = -\mathbf{F} \tag{11}$

The differential equations (10) can be solved for ϕ_m by solving the equivalent algebraic equations (11). However, it is first necessary to specify *boundary conditions* since otherwise the system of equations (11) would be singular, corresponding to the non-uniqueness of differential equation solutions without such boundary conditions.

For this current problem the boundary conditions derive from the physical constraints on the string, namely that its two ends are always fixed, so that $\phi_1 = 0$ and $\phi_5 = 0$. Introducing these constraints, together with the values previously specified for the components of **K** and **F**, into the system (11), produces the following set of three linear equations in the remaining three unknown nodal displacements, ϕ_2, ϕ_3 and ϕ_4 (remember $\phi_1 = \phi_5 = 0$):

$$2\phi_2 - \phi_3 + 0\phi_4 = -\frac{62}{48T}$$

$$-\phi_2 + 2\phi_3 - \phi_4 = -\frac{98}{48T}$$

$$0\phi_2 - \phi_3 + 2\phi_4 = -\frac{158}{48T} \tag{12}$$

This is a symmetric positive definite system of linear equations which can be solved by any standard method such as triangular factorisation or Gaussian elimination [Goult et al. 1974].

The solution is finally

$$\phi_2 = -\frac{135}{48T}$$

$$\phi_3 = -\frac{208}{48T}$$

$$\phi_4 = -\frac{183}{48T}$$

This solution gives directly the displacements of the string at nodal points. At intermediate points the corresponding displacements are found by linear interpolation using equation (4), or geometrically, by drawing a straight line between the above nodal displacements. Figure 10.5 compares this solution with the analytic solution given by equation (3). On this occasion the nodal values are in fact correct but there are errors of as much as 9% at intermediate points using the finite element solution.

The accuracy of the finite element solution can be improved either by increasing the number of elements or by introducing higher-order (that is, non-linear) interpolation functions into the assumed solution. If the number of elements is increased to more than four linear elements (say, eight), the method is essentially the same, though lengthier. We will not pursue this further here.

Similarly, if the order of the interpolation functions is increased, the method is again essentially the same, though there is now more freedom to achieve a closer approximation with fewer elements. We briefly discuss this approach below.

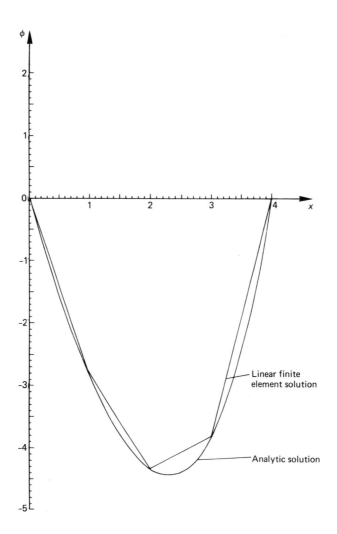

Fig. 10.5 Comparison of analytic with linear finite element solution for the stretched string

Linear finite element solution

Analytic solution

3.2 Quadratic elements

Using the same approach and the same nodes as in the linear case above, a more accurate solution to the one-dimensional string problem is obtainable by dividing the string into two elements of length 2 (rather than the four elements of length 1, used previously).

Formulation

We assume that the transverse displacement ϕ is a quadratic function of x within each element. After a change of variable from x to u, the *standard quadratic element* is then of length 2, with three local nodes at $u = 0$, $u = 1$ and $u = 2$ (Figure 10.6).

There are three (rather than two) corresponding basis functions which are now quadratic functions. These are zero at two of the three nodes and have value 1 at the remaining node. For this standard quadratic element, the appropriate equation corresponding to equation (5) is

Fig. 10.6 The three quadratic basis functions for the stretched string

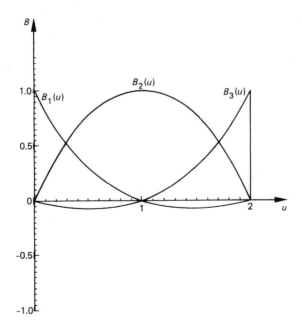

$$\phi(u) = \phi_1 B_1(u) + \phi_2 B_2(u) + \phi_3 B_3(u)$$

where $B_1(u) = \frac{1}{2}(u-1)(u-2)$

$$B_2(u) = u(2-u)$$

$$B_3(u) = \frac{1}{2}u(u-1) \tag{13}$$

Note that $B_1(0) = 1$, $B_1(1) = 0$ and $B_1(2) = 0$, and that the other basis functions $B_2(u)$ and $B_3(u)$ have similar properties as previously stated.

For the first of the two elements used in this problem $u = x$ and the local and global node numbers coincide, whereas for the second element $u = x - 2$ and local node numbers 1, 2 and 3 correspond to global numbers 3, 4 and 5 respectively.

The formulation is essentially similar to the linear case

$$E = \sum_{i=1}^{2} E_i = \sum_{i=1}^{2} \int_{x_i}^{x_{i+1}} \left[\frac{1}{2} T \left(\frac{d\phi}{dx} \right)^2 + \phi w \right] dx$$

Evaluation

After the variable change $x = u + p_i$ to the local coordinate u, the contribution from element i is

$$E_i = \int_0^2 \left[\frac{1}{2} T \left(\phi_1 \frac{dB_1}{du} + \phi_2 \frac{dB_2}{du} + \phi_3 \frac{dB_3}{du} \right)^2 \right.$$

$$\left. + (\phi_1 B_1(u) + \phi_2 B_2(u) + \phi_3 B_3(u)) w(u + p_i) \right] du$$

After expanding and rearranging terms, this simplifies to

$$E_i = \frac{1}{2} \sum_{m=1}^{3} \sum_{n=1}^{3} K_{mn} \phi_m \phi_n + \sum_{m=1}^{3} F_m \phi_m \tag{14}$$

191

where
$$K_{mn} = \int_0^2 T\left(\frac{dB_m}{du}\right)\left(\frac{dB_n}{du}\right) du$$

and
$$F_m = \int_0^2 B_m(u)w(u + p_i)\, du$$

The close similarity between equation (14) and the corresponding formula equation (6) for linear elements should be noted. The extension to cubic or quartic interpolation functions would also follow a similar pattern.

For the quadratic elements, the element stiffness matrices are (3×3) matrices which require simple integration for their evaluation, but the evaluation of the element force vectors is slightly more complicated than in the linear case. The results are

$$\mathbf{K}^{(1)} = \mathbf{K}^{(2)} = \tfrac{1}{6}T \begin{bmatrix} 7 & -8 & 1 \\ -8 & 16 & -8 \\ 1 & -8 & 7 \end{bmatrix}$$

and

$$\mathbf{F}^{(1)} = \tfrac{1}{30}\begin{bmatrix} 54 \\ 52 \\ 19 \end{bmatrix} \qquad \mathbf{F}^{(2)} = \tfrac{1}{30}\begin{bmatrix} 19 \\ 132 \\ 49 \end{bmatrix}$$

Assembly

After assembly of the two quadratic elements, the global stiffness matrix $\mathbf{K}$ and the global force vector $\mathbf{F}$ then become

$$\mathbf{K} = \tfrac{1}{6}T \begin{bmatrix} 7 & -8 & 1 & 0 & 0 \\ -8 & 16 & -8 & 0 & 0 \\ 1 & -8 & 14 & -8 & 1 \\ 0 & 0 & -8 & 16 & -8 \\ 0 & 0 & 1 & -8 & 7 \end{bmatrix} \qquad \mathbf{F} = \tfrac{1}{30}\begin{bmatrix} 54 \\ 52 \\ 38 \\ 132 \\ 49 \end{bmatrix}$$

Solution

After introducing the constraints $\phi_1 = \phi_5 = 0$ (the ends of the string are fixed, as with the linear case) the equations $\mathbf{K}\phi = -\mathbf{F}$, which are again derived from the minimisation of E, finally reduce to the three linear equations

$$16\phi_2 - 8\phi_3 + 0\phi_4 = -\frac{52}{5T}$$

$$-8\phi_2 + 14\phi_3 - 8\phi_4 = -\frac{38}{5T}$$

$$0\phi_2 - 8\phi_3 + 16\phi_4 = -\frac{132}{5T} \qquad (15)$$

(Compare these with equations (12) obtained for linear elements.) The solution of equation (15) gives

$$\phi_2 = -\frac{169}{60T}$$

$$\phi_3 = -\frac{13}{3T}$$

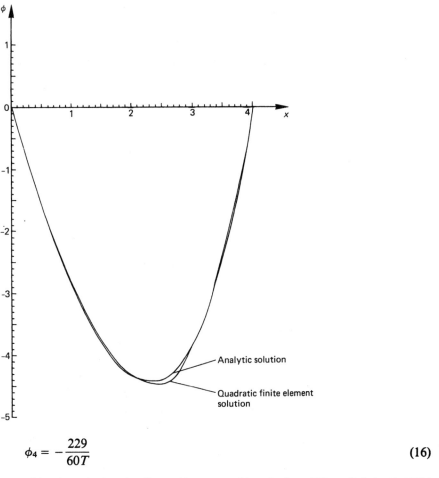

Fig. 10.7 Comparison of analytic with quadratic finite element solution for the stretched string

Analytic solution

Quadratic finite element solution

$$\phi_4 = -\frac{229}{60T} \tag{16}$$

Unlike the solution for linear elements, this solution differs slightly (0.15%) from the analytic solution (equation (3)) at nodes 2 and 4 but, as Figure 10.7 shows, the accuracy over the entire range obtained from the quadratic interpolation functions is much better than in the linear case. It is also interesting to compare this accuracy with the results obtainable with eight linear elements.

4 Variational principles

The stretched string problem considered above was analysed using one-dimensional finite elements, and the method was dependent on minimising the total (that is, elastic and potential) energy of the system, at the *solution* phase of the procedure. The approach is a specific example of a powerful technique based on the *calculus of variations* (or *variational calculus*).

In the case of the one-dimensional string, the initial problem was posed in terms of an ordinary differential equation relating the transverse displacements to the applied load (equation (1)). This required a solution $\phi(x)$, satisfying the boundary conditions $\phi(0) = \phi(L) = 0$ (that is, the end-points were fixed). The problem was then transformed into an equivalent one in terms of an integral equation, again relating the transverse displacement to the applied load, but now also involving the total energy, E (equation (2)). The required solution of equation (1) was then that function $\phi(x)$ which produced the minimum value for E, in equation (2). In other words, of all the possible different functional forms that $\phi(x)$ could take (such as $\sin x$, $1 + 2x^3$, $4x/(1 - x)^2$, and so on) only that form given by the exact solution (equation (3)) minimised E and hence satisfied the original differential equation (1). Any other form for $\phi(x)$ will yield a larger value for E when the integral (equation (2)) is evaluated.

In general, the calculus of variations provides mathematical techniques for performing the above 'search' through possible functional forms (i.e. *variations*) for $\phi(x)$, in order to find a form which minimises an 'appropriate' integral. The method is crucially dependent on an identification of this appropriate integral and hence on an identification of a *variational principle* such as: *the total energy is always to be minimised*. Once the integral has been determined it must be differentiated and equated to zero to obtain an expression for the minimum.

We solved the (one-dimensional) stretched string problem by minimising the total energy. For the analogous two- and three-dimensional problems involving elastic energy (such as stretched membranes, etc.) we can adopt a similar approach, though the expression for the total energy is now a multiple integral involving two or three variables of integration, respectively. Similarly, for more general physical problems such as those concerned with heat transfer, electrostatic potential, or the irrotational flow of an ideal fluid, there is often an identifiable variational principle which leads to an appropriate integral expression. The derivation of such general variational principles for one-, two- and three-dimensional problems is beyond the scope of this chapter but in many cases they arise when the problem can be stated in terms of a particular type of differential equation.

4.1 One dimension

For one-dimensional problems this is an ordinary differential equation and has the form

$$\frac{d}{dx}\left[f\frac{d\phi}{dx} \right] + h\phi = W \tag{17}$$

where f, h and W are each some function of x, and where the boundary conditions are

$$\phi(0) = \phi_0 \quad \text{and} \quad \phi(L) = \phi_1$$

The associated integral expression has the form

$$E = \int_0^L \left\{ \frac{1}{2}\left[f\left(\frac{d\phi}{dx}\right)^2 - h\phi^2 \right] + \phi W \right\} dx \tag{18}$$

where E is itself considered to be a function of the function ϕ, that is $E(\phi)$. The particular function ϕ which minimises the expression for E (equation (18)) is then the solution of the differential equation (17) with the above boundary conditions.

We will not prove this powerful result from the calculus of variations but merely justify it by referring the reader back to equations (1) and (2) which can easily be put into this form: these represent the special case in which the function f has the constant value T, the function h is identically zero, and the function $W = w = 1 + \frac{1}{4} x^2$. The expression for E then represents the energy of the elastic string considered earlier.

4.2 Two dimensions

For two-dimensional problems an analogous situation arises if they can be described in terms of a partial differential equation of the form

$$\frac{\partial}{\partial x} \left[f \frac{\partial \phi}{\partial x} \right] + \frac{\partial}{\partial y} \left[g \frac{\partial \phi}{\partial y} \right] - h\phi = W \tag{19}$$

where again f, g, h and W are each some function of x and y. As with the one-dimensional case, the problem is not well-defined until appropriate boundary conditions are specified. For the one-dimensional string the 'boundary' consisted of two separate points along a line (i.e. the end-points of the string). For a two-dimensional situation (such as a stretched membrane) the boundary consists of one or more curves representing the 'edge' of the region, as illustrated by Figure 10.8.

Fig. 10.8 Boundary curves and boundary conditions for a two-dimensional region

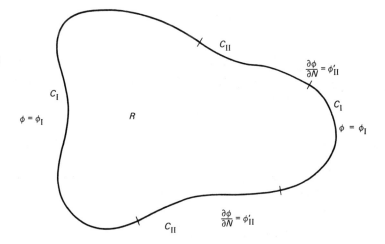

The boundary conditions can now be of two types. In the first type we specify the values of ϕ at all points along the boundary. In the second type we specify the values of $\partial\phi/\partial N$ (i.e. the rate of change of ϕ in a direction normal to the boundary curve) at all points along the boundary. As an example consider the system in Figure 10.8. Assume the region of interest is R with a boundary curve divided into four segments as shown. Along the two segments labelled as C_{I} we specify $\phi(x, y)$ to be a particular function ϕ_{I}, whereas along the two segments labelled as C_{II} we specify $\partial\phi/\partial N(x, y)$ to be another particular function, ϕ'_{II}.

It can then be shown that of all possible functions $\phi(x, y)$ satisfying these boundary conditions, the particular function which is a solution of the partial differential equation (19) is that function which minimises the associated integral expression

$$E = \int\int\left\{\frac{1}{2}\left[f\left(\frac{\partial\phi}{\partial x}\right)^2 + g\left(\frac{\partial\phi}{\partial y}\right)^2 + h\phi^2\right] + W\phi\right\} dx\,dy$$

$$- \int_{C_{II}} \phi_{II}\phi\,ds \tag{20}$$

The interpretation of E depends on the particular problem area and may or may not represent an energy expression.

4.3 Three dimensions

The variational approach can also be applied to three-dimensional problems giving similar expressions to those above. The approach differs only in the complexity of the equations and in the boundary conditions. Thus for a three-dimensional region the partial differential equation corresponding to equations (17) and (19) would have a similar form but would involve an extra term relating to derivatives of ϕ with respect to the third independent variable z. Similarly, the appropriate integral expression corresponding to equations (18) and (20) would involve a triple integral with respect to x, y and z. Finally the boundary conditions would be specified as constraints on $\phi(x, y, z)$ or $\partial\phi/\partial N(x, y, z)$ at all points on the surface(s) bounding the three-dimensional region.

5 Two-dimensional elements

Consider the stretched membrane problem, which is the two-dimensional analogue of the one-dimensional stretched string problem of Section 2. It is required to find the displaced equilibrium position of a transversely loaded elastic membrane. In general the problem would be stated in terms of the partial differential equation

$$T\left(\frac{\partial^2\phi}{\partial x^2}\right) + T\left(\frac{\partial^2\phi}{\partial y^2}\right) = w(x, y)$$

where T is the tension in the membrane and w is the applied load. However, we will restrict our treatment here to the simple case given by

$$\frac{\partial^2\phi}{\partial x^2} + \frac{\partial^2\phi}{\partial y^2} = 2 \tag{21}$$

where $\phi(x, y)$ is the transverse displacement, and the membrane is confined to a rectangular region R, bounded by a boundary curve consisting of four straight-line segments, $x = 0$, $x = 1.5$, $y = 0$, $y = 1$, with boundary conditions

$\phi = 3$ on the line $y = 0$

$\dfrac{\partial\phi}{\partial N} = \dfrac{\partial\phi}{\partial y} = 2x + 2$ on the line $y = 1$

$$\frac{\partial \phi}{\partial N} = -\frac{\partial \phi}{\partial x} = -2y \quad \text{on the line } x = 0$$

$$\frac{\partial \phi}{\partial N} = \frac{\partial \phi}{\partial x} = 2y \quad \text{on the line } x = 1.5$$

It is relatively easy to verify by substitution that the exact solution of this equation is

$$\phi = 3 + 2xy + y^2$$

We will use this for comparison with the finite element solution derived below.

5.1 Triangular elements

For a two-dimensional region there is an enormous variety of possible element shapes that might be chosen. However, triangular elements are frequently used in finite element solutions because any region with polygonal boundaries can always be sub-divided into triangular elements.

Formulation
In this example we divide the rectangular region R into eight equal triangular elements, as shown in Figure 10.9. In this figure, element numbers are boxed, global node numbers are circled and local node numbers are shown as simple numbers.

Fig. 10.9 Element numbers and node numbers for eight triangular elements

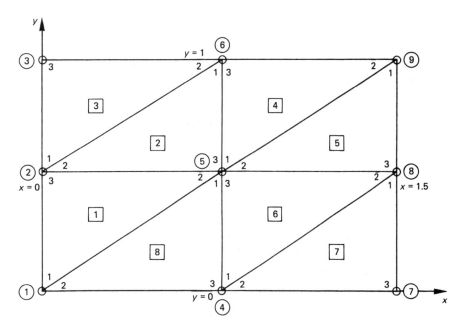

In the one-dimensional finite element approach (Section 3.1) we considered first a linear interpolation of ϕ along each (line segment) element between adjacent pairs of nodes, so that we chose $\phi = ax + b$ (linear in x). In the present two-dimensional case we have triangular elements and we similarly choose a linear interpolation function $\phi = ax + by + c$ (linear in x and y), across each element, between the three nodes defining the vertices of the triangle. Since this function depends on just three independent parameters (a, b and c), it is completely defined by the three values of ϕ at the three nodes, that is ϕ_1, ϕ_2 and ϕ_3.

Three basis functions, B_1, B_2 and B_3, are required for a triangular element and, analogously to the one-dimensional case, these should each have value 1 at one node and value zero at the remaining (two) nodes. If the triangular element has local nodes labelled 1, 2 and 3 with coordinates (x_1, y_1), (x_2, y_2) and (x_3, y_3) respectively, an appropriate set of three linear basis functions can easily be derived in terms of x_1, y_1, x_2, y_2, x_3 and y_3. In our case, reference to Figure 10.9 shows that for the particular element labelled 1 we have $y_3 = y_2$ and $x_3 = x_1$ so that our three nodes have coordinates (x_1, y_1), (x_2, y_2) and (x_1, y_2) respectively. A suitable set of basis functions is therefore

$$B_1(x, y) = \frac{(y - y_2)}{(y_1 - y_2)}$$

$$B_2(x, y) = \frac{(x - x_1)}{(x_2 - x_1)}$$

$$B_3(x, y) = \frac{(x - x_1)(y_2 - y_1) + (y - y_1)(x_1 - x_2)}{(y_2 - y_1)(x_1 - x_2)} \tag{22}$$

(Note that each of these basis functions can be derived from the equation of the line joining the remaining two nodes.)

Within the triangular element 1, ϕ is then given by

$$\phi = \phi_1 B_1(x, y) + \phi_2 B_2(x, y) + \phi_3 B_3(x, y) \tag{23}$$

The continuity of ϕ between adjacent elements is ensured by the fact that along each edge of the triangle, ϕ is given by a simple linear interpolation of the nodal values.

The finite element formulation is now obtained by using the variational calculus discussed in Section 4. Our partial differential equation (21) can easily be transformed into the form given by equation (19) and so our variational principle is based on the integral expression for E in equation (20). For our problem we have $f = 1$, $g = 1$, $h = 0$ and $W = 2$. So the expression for E that we require is

$$E = \int \int \left\{ \frac{1}{2} \left[\left(\frac{\partial \phi}{\partial x} \right)^2 + \left(\frac{\partial \phi}{\partial y} \right)^2 \right] + 2\phi \right\} \, dx \, dy - \int_{C_{II}} \phi'_{II} \phi \, ds \tag{24}$$

This can be sub-divided to give the individual contribution to E from each element (that is, E_i) in the form

$$E_i = \int \int_{R^{(i)}} \left\{ \frac{1}{2} \left[\left(\frac{\partial \phi}{\partial x} \right)^2 + \left(\frac{\partial \phi}{\partial y} \right)^2 \right] + 2\phi \right\} \, dx \, dy - \int_{C_{II}^{(i)}} \phi'_{II}{}^{(i)} \phi \, ds \tag{25}$$

where $R^{(i)}$ is the interior region of the ith element and $C_{II}^{(i)}$ is that part (if any) of the boundary of the ith element to which derivative boundary conditions are applied.

Evaluation

Using local node numbers, ϕ may be expressed in the following form within each element:

$$\phi = \sum_{m=1}^{3} \phi_m B_m$$

This enables us to rewrite the expression for E_i (equation (25)) eventually in the form

$$E_i = \frac{1}{2} \sum_{m=1}^{3} \sum_{n=1}^{3} K_{mn}^{(i)} \phi_m \phi + \sum_{m=1}^{3} F_m^{(i)} \phi_m \tag{26}$$

where $\quad K_{mn}^{(i)} = \int\int_{R^{(i)}} \left[\left(\frac{\partial B_m}{\partial x}\right)\left(\frac{\partial B_n}{\partial x}\right) + \left(\frac{\partial B_m}{\partial y}\right)\left(\frac{\partial B_n}{\partial y}\right) \right] dx \, dy$

and $\quad F_m^{(i)} = \int\int_{R^{(i)}} 2B_m \, dx \, dy - \int_{C_{\mathrm{II}}^{(i)}} \phi_{\mathrm{II}}'^{(i)} B_m \, ds$

The above expressions define the *element stiffness matrix* $\mathbf{K}^{(i)}$ and *element force vector* $\mathbf{F}^{(i)}$ in a similar form to those arising in the one-dimensional case (compare equation (26) with equation (6)).

The evaluation of the element stiffness matrices and element force vectors requires the evaluation of the integrals in equation (26). All the elements have the same shape and size and since for each element $\partial B_m/\partial x$ and $\partial B_m/\partial y$ are constant the element stiffness matrix $\mathbf{K}^{(i)}$ is the same for each element and therefore requires no integration. Note, however, that each element force vector requires the addition of two integrals, namely the double integral term which is the same for all elements and

$$\int_{C_{\mathrm{II}}^{(i)}} \phi_{\mathrm{II}}'^{(i)} B_m \, ds$$

which varies from element to element.

This latter term will not be required for elements such as element 2 which have no part of their boundary on which a derivative constraint applies.

Considering element 1 in detail:

$$B_1(x, y) = 1 - 2y$$

$$B_2(x, y) = \tfrac{4}{3} x$$

$$B_3(x, y) = 2y - \tfrac{4}{3} x$$

Thus $\quad \dfrac{\partial B_1}{\partial x} = 0, \qquad \dfrac{\partial B_1}{\partial y} = -2, \qquad \dfrac{\partial B_2}{\partial x} = \tfrac{4}{3}, \qquad \dfrac{\partial B_2}{\partial y} = 0$

$$\dfrac{\partial B_3}{\partial x} = -\tfrac{4}{3}, \qquad \dfrac{\partial B_3}{\partial y} = 2$$

For $\mathbf{K}^{(1)}$ we then obtain

$$K_{11}^{(1)} = \int\int_{R^{(1)}} \left[\left(\frac{\partial B_1}{\partial x}\right)^2 + \left(\frac{\partial B_1}{\partial y}\right)^2 \right] dx \, dy$$

$$= \int\int_{R^{(1)}} 4 \, dx \, dy$$

$$= \tfrac{3}{4}$$

since area of $R^{(1)} = \frac{3}{16}$

$$K_{13}^{(1)} = \int\int_{R^{(1)}} \left[\left(\frac{\partial B_1}{\partial x}\right)\left(\frac{\partial B_3}{\partial x}\right) + \left(\frac{\partial B_1}{\partial y}\right)\left(\frac{\partial B_3}{\partial y}\right) \right] \, dx \, dy$$

$$= \int\int_{R_{(1)}} -4 \, dx \, dy$$

$$= -\tfrac{3}{4}$$

Other components of the stiffness matrix are obtained in a similar manner to give finally

$$\mathbf{K}^{(1)} = \tfrac{1}{12} \begin{bmatrix} 9 & 0 & -9 \\ 0 & 4 & -4 \\ -9 & -4 & 13 \end{bmatrix}$$

For all other elements the stiffness matrix is identical.

The element force vector $\mathbf{F}^{(1)}$ requires the evaluation of a double integral and a line integral. For $F_1^{(1)}$ these integrals are

$$\int_0^{\tfrac{1}{2}} \int_0^{3y/2} 2(1-2y) \, dx \, dy = \int_0^{\tfrac{1}{2}} 3y(1-2y) \, dy = \tfrac{1}{8}$$

and

$$\int_{C_{II}} -\phi_{II}' B_1 \, ds = \int_{\tfrac{1}{2}}^0 2y(1-2y)(-dy) = \int_0^{\tfrac{1}{2}} 2y(1-2y) \, dy = \tfrac{1}{12}$$

Note that for convenience this integral is evaluated by taking ds in the anti-clockwise sense round the boundary of R.

Thus finally

$$F_1^{(1)} = \tfrac{5}{24}$$

The remaining components of $\mathbf{F}^{(1)}$ are evaluated in a similar manner to give

$$\mathbf{F}^{(1)} = \tfrac{1}{24} \begin{bmatrix} 5 \\ 3 \\ 7 \end{bmatrix}$$

For each triangular element the element force vector requires similar integrations, and the results are

$$\mathbf{F}^{(2)} = \tfrac{1}{8} \begin{bmatrix} 1 \\ 1 \\ 1 \end{bmatrix} \qquad \mathbf{F}^{(3)} = \tfrac{1}{48} \begin{bmatrix} 22 \\ -48 \\ -19 \end{bmatrix}$$

$$\mathbf{F}^{(4)} = \tfrac{1}{16} \begin{bmatrix} 2 \\ -25 \\ -22 \end{bmatrix} \qquad \mathbf{F}^{(5)} = \tfrac{1}{24} \begin{bmatrix} -7 \\ 3 \\ -5 \end{bmatrix}$$

$$\mathbf{F}^{(6)} = \tfrac{1}{8} \begin{bmatrix} 1 \\ 1 \\ 1 \end{bmatrix} \qquad \mathbf{F}^{(7)} = \tfrac{1}{24} \begin{bmatrix} 3 \\ -1 \\ 1 \end{bmatrix}$$

$$\mathbf{F}^{(8)} = \tfrac{1}{8} \begin{bmatrix} 1 \\ 1 \\ 1 \end{bmatrix}$$

Assembly

The assembly process is concerned with the construction of the global stiffness matrix and the global force vector from the contributions from the individual elements. For each element this requires a transformation from local back to global node numbers. For the current problem this data can be obtained from Figure 10.9. For large problems and computerised solutions it is normal to construct a table of equivalent local and global node numbers. Once this identification has been made the components of each element stiffness matrix and element force vector can be added cumulatively in the appropriate locations to give totals for the global stiffness matrix $\mathbf{K}$ and the global force vector $\mathbf{F}$. For the first element the stiffness matrix and force vector, in local node numbers, are

$$\mathbf{K}^{(1)} = \tfrac{1}{12} \begin{bmatrix} 9 & 0 & -9 \\ 0 & 4 & -4 \\ -9 & -4 & 13 \end{bmatrix} \quad \text{and} \quad \mathbf{F}^{(1)} = \tfrac{1}{8} \begin{bmatrix} 1 \\ 1 \\ 1 \end{bmatrix}$$

Here the equivalences between local and global node numbers are $1 \to 1$, $2 \to 5$ and $3 \to 2$. Thus, for example, the component $K_{23} = -4$ must be added into location 52 of the global stiffness matrix.

For the second element the local–global equivalences are $1 \to 6$, $2 \to 2$ and $3 \to 5$. In this instance K_{23} of $\mathbf{K}^{(2)}$ has to be added to K_{25} of $\mathbf{K}$.

After the assembly process for all eight elements has been completed in this way, the final matrix and vector are

$$\mathbf{K} = \tfrac{1}{12} \begin{bmatrix} 13 & -9 & . & -4 & 0 & . & . & . & . \\ -9 & 26 & -9 & . & -8 & 0 & . & . & . \\ . & -9 & 13 & . & . & -4 & . & . & . \\ -4 & . & . & 26 & -18 & . & -4 & 0 & . \\ 0 & -8 & . & -18 & 52 & -18 & . & -8 & 0 \\ . & 0 & -4 & . & -18 & 26 & . & . & -4 \\ . & . & . & -4 & . & . & 13 & -9 & . \\ . & . & . & 0 & -8 & . & -9 & 26 & -9 \\ . & . & . & . & 0 & -4 & . & -9 & 13 \end{bmatrix}$$

$$\mathbf{F} = \tfrac{1}{48} \begin{bmatrix} 16 \\ 42 \\ -19 \\ 10 \\ 36 \\ -108 \\ 2 \\ 2 \\ -89 \end{bmatrix} \tag{27}$$

In this global stiffness matrix $\mathbf{K}$, a dot denotes a zero where no assembly from element stiffness matrices has occurred, whereas a 0 is an assembled zero, arising from $K_{12} = 0$ in the element matrices, for example. As with the elastic string problem the final stiffness matrix is symmetric and singular with the sum of elements in each row being 0. A feature of practical significance is that it is also 'banded'; that is, the non-zero elements occur only in a few locations on either side of the leading diagonal. The semi-bandwidth β (maximum number of elements on and below the diagonal in any row) is equal to one more than the difference in node numbers within any element. This is dependent upon the way in which the nodes are numbered and in this case $\beta = 5$ (or 4 if the assembled zeros are excluded). The significance of a small bandwidth is that the banded structure is maintained in any standard method of solving the subsequent linear equations, and significant savings in computer storage requirements and computation time can be achieved with careful node numbering. For an $n \times n$ system of linear equations, solution time is proportional to n^3 but for a banded system it is proportional to $n\beta^2$.

Solution

After the assembly process has been completed we have the following expression for the total energy $E(\phi)$:

$$E(\phi) = \frac{1}{2} \sum_{m=1}^{9} \sum_{n=1}^{9} K_{mn}\phi_m\phi_n + \sum_{m=1}^{9} F_m\phi_m \tag{28}$$

As with the one-dimensional string problem we must minimise E by setting the partial derivatives $\partial E/\partial \phi_m = 0$, which gives the set of linear equations

$$\sum_{n=1}^{9} K_{mn}\phi_n + F_m = 0 \tag{29}$$

that is $\quad \mathbf{K}\phi = -\mathbf{F}$

The solution is given by solving this system of equations. As written, the system is singular but, as for the string, it becomes soluble after the simple boundary constraints on ϕ have been reintroduced. For the current problem these constraints are $\phi_1 = \phi_4 = \phi_7 = 3$, and they reduce the number of unknowns to six, transforming equation (29) into the simpler system:

$$\frac{1}{12}\begin{bmatrix} 26 & -9 & -8 & 0 & 0 & 0 \\ -9 & 13 & 0 & -4 & 0 & 0 \\ -8 & 0 & 52 & -18 & -8 & 0 \\ 0 & -4 & -18 & 26 & 0 & -4 \\ 0 & 0 & -8 & 0 & 26 & -9 \\ 0 & 0 & 0 & -4 & -9 & 13 \end{bmatrix}\begin{bmatrix} \phi_2 \\ \phi_3 \\ \phi_5 \\ \phi_6 \\ \phi_8 \\ \phi_9 \end{bmatrix} = \frac{1}{12}\begin{bmatrix} 16.5 \\ 4.75 \\ 45 \\ 27 \\ 26.5 \\ 22.25 \end{bmatrix} \tag{30}$$

After multiplying equations (30) by 12, these equations can be solved by Gaussian elimination, to give eventually the final solution:

$$\phi_9 = 6.4956 \qquad \phi_8 = 4.4866 \qquad \phi_6 = 5.4537$$

$$\phi_5 = 3.9614 \qquad \phi_3 = 4.3751 \qquad \phi_2 = 3.3680$$

For comparison, the corresponding values from the analytic solution are 7.0, 4.75, 5.5, 4.0, 4.0 and 3.25 respectively.

5.2 Rectangular elements

The same membrane problem can be solved using simple rectangular elements instead of the triangular elements used above. We briefly outline the process for comparison.

Formulation

The two-dimensional region in Figure 10.9 can be divided into four rectangular elements rather than into the eight triangular elements used previously, and this can be achieved using the same set of nodes. This alternative arrangement is illustrated by Figure 10.10.

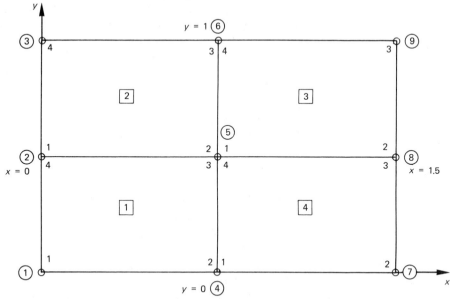

Fig. 10.10 Element numbers and node numbers for four rectangular elements

Now, each element is associated with a linear interpolation function of the form $a + bx + cy + dxy$. Once more this is expressible in terms of nodal values and basis functions as

$$\phi = \phi_1 B_1(x, y) + \phi_2 B_2(x, y) + \phi_3 B_3(x, y) + \phi_4 B_4(x, y)$$

If the local node numbering is as shown in Figure 10.10 and the nodes have coordinates (x_1, y_1), (x_2, y_2), (x_3, y_3), (x_4, y_4), then each basis function is expressible as the product of the equations of the two opposite edges (straight lines) of the rectangle. Thus, for example,

$$B_1(x, y) = \frac{(x - x_3)(y - y_3)}{(x_1 - x_3)(y_1 - y_3)}$$

(Note that along each edge of the rectangle either x or y is constant and ϕ varies linearly; this property makes it possible to mix these rectangular elements with the preceding triangular elements and still maintain continuity along the common edges.)

Evaluation

The evaluation now follows precisely the method used previously except that the stiffness matrices for the elements are now (4×4) matrices, with the integrations occurring over a rectangle rather than over a triangle. The results are

$$\mathbf{K}^{(1)} = \mathbf{K}^{(2)} = \mathbf{K}^{(3)} = \mathbf{K}^{(4)} = \frac{1}{36} \begin{bmatrix} 26 & 1 & -13 & -14 \\ 1 & 26 & -14 & -13 \\ -13 & -14 & 26 & 1 \\ -14 & -13 & 1 & 26 \end{bmatrix} \quad (32)$$

203

Similarly the element force vectors each have four components and the evaluation gives

$$\mathbf{F}^{(1)} = \frac{1}{48}\begin{bmatrix} 13 \\ 9 \\ 9 \\ 17 \end{bmatrix} \qquad \mathbf{F}^{(2)} = \frac{1}{48}\begin{bmatrix} 25 \\ 9 \\ -45 \\ -16 \end{bmatrix}$$

$$\mathbf{F}^{(3)} = \frac{1}{48}\begin{bmatrix} 9 \\ -7 \\ -92 \\ -63 \end{bmatrix} \qquad \mathbf{F}^{(4)} = \frac{1}{48}\begin{bmatrix} 9 \\ 5 \\ 1 \\ 9 \end{bmatrix} \qquad (33)$$

Assembly and solution

If the previous method of assembly and solution used for triangular elements were to be used here for rectangular elements, we would eventually arrive at a similar set of linear equations to be solved, in the form $\mathbf{K}\boldsymbol{\phi} = -\mathbf{F}$. However, there is a more efficient method known as the **frontal method,** which is designed to save computer space and time by eliminating (using Gaussian elimination) some variables from the equations before the assembly process is complete. We do not intend to present the method here, but in the frontal method the separate processes of assembling and solving the final set of equations are performed simultaneously, and variables are eliminated as soon as the last element containing the relevant node has been assembled.

The current 'working space' on the computer is never as large as the full stiffness matrix but care must be taken to record the locations of the current 'active' variables contained in the 'front'. For most variables, elimination from the front is by Gaussian elimination, which involves subtracting multiples of some appropriate row from rows both above and below it in the current matrix. Before the elimination the entire row together with the variable number and location in the front must be transferred to 'backing store'.

5.3 Higher order elements for two-dimensional problems

As in the one-dimensional string problem the accuracy of the solution obtained for a two-dimensional finite element problem can be increased either by increasing the number of elements or by using higher order interpolation functions within each element. In addition, most commercial finite element systems provide a variety of element types (triangular, rectangular, etc.) for each major area of application. The type of interpolation functions used is not always specified but can generally be deduced from the number of nodes. Thus two nodes along the edge of an element (that is, one at each end) implies linear interpolation functions. Three nodes are associated with quadratic interpolation functions and four nodes would imply cubic interpolation, and so on.

Practical problems often involve finite element solutions in regions which have curved boundaries. Such a region can always be meshed approximately with a large number of small triangular elements but an alternative is to have available some form of finite element with curved edges. The most popular types for this purpose are the so-called *iso-parametric elements* in which the

Fig. 10.11 A curvilinear four-sided element with eight nodes

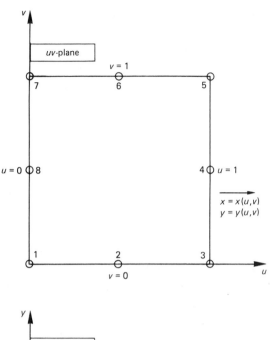

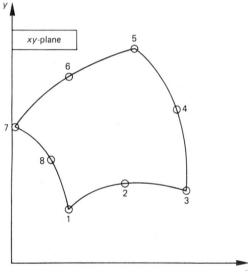

same basis or shape functions are used both for the finite element interpolation and for the geometric deformation of the element itself from its basic 'uncurved' shape in the uv parameter space. Figure 10.11 shows a simple example of a four-sided element with eight nodes; the basic element is a unit square in uv-space whereas the deformed element has curved edges in xy-space.

With suitable basis functions the geometric transformation is

$$x = \sum_{m=1}^{8} B_m(u, v) x_m \qquad y = \sum_{m=1}^{8} B_m(u, v) y_m$$

where (x_m, y_m) are the coordinates of the mth node and the finite element interpolation is

$$\phi = \sum_{m=1}^{8} B_m(u, v) \phi_m$$

where ϕ_m is the value of ϕ at the mth node. Each of the eight basis functions is obtainable from the product of the three straight lines joining the remaining seven nodes, for example

$$B_1(u, v) = -(u - 1)(v - 1)(2u + 2v - 1)$$

$$B_2(u, v) = 2u(u - 1)(v - 1)$$

and so on. The use of curvilinear elements of this type can give unsatisfactory results when such elements are deformed too far from their basic square shape.

6 Three-dimensional elements

Finite element methods can also be applied to solve three-dimensional problems using a formulation which is conceptually similar to those used for one-dimensional and two-dimensional problems. There are, however, practical difficulties associated with three-dimensional elements in that both the number of elements and the number of nodes per element will be considerably larger than with two-dimensional elements. In the first instance the problem of constructing a suitable finite element mesh is usually sufficiently complex to require some form of automatic mesh generator (which may possibly be linked to a solid modeller). Once the mesh has been generated a large amount of computer memory will be required for the formulation and solution of the problem.

Even more significantly the amount of computer time required for the solution is likely to be proportional to n^3 where n is the number of nodes. For these reasons it is sound practice to exploit any possible symmetries in the problem in order to avoid a full finite element model of the entire region, and moreover to use a fine mesh size only in those critical parts of the region where the solution is likely to be changing rapidly.

An important subset of three-dimensional problems are those which are axi-symmetric in both geometry and loads or constraints. For these problems it is only necessary to construct a two-dimensional cross-sectional version of the model — the third dimension being accommodated by the integrations arising at the element formulation phase of the solution. With appropriate axi-symmetric elements such a problem can be solved at a fraction of the cost of a full three-dimensional solution.

7 Applications of finite element methods

Historically, finite element methods originated for computing stresses and strains in complex structures and this remains the most common application area. However, such methods are now also used in many other application areas, including thermal analysis, electrostatic field analysis, fluid mechanics and vibrational analysis.

7.1 Stress problems

For an elastic material a knowledge of its elastic constants (usually Young's modulus and Poisson's ratio) is sufficient to determine the stresses from a given set of strains. From the stresses and strains the work done in deforming the specimen (its strain energy) can be computed. The strains themselves are defined in terms of changes in length and are calculated from the partial derivatives of the displacement occurring at any point in the material.

In the usual finite element formulation and solution of a stress problem (two-dimensional, three-dimensional or axi-symmetric) the body is first divided into a mesh of finite elements. Within each element a set of displacements is defined by suitable interpolation functions. These are usually expressed in terms of the unknown displacements of the nodes. The partial derivatives of the displacement functions provide the strains and, from these, the stresses and, by integration, the strain energy can be computed. The minimum energy principle (that the actual displacements occurring will be those which minimise the strain energy) is then used to produce a set of equations which can be solved for the unknown nodal displacements. Boundary conditions on the problem can take either the form of known external loads which must be matched by the stresses on the surface, or the form of fixed (frequently zero) values for certain nodal displacements.

This basic formulation process does not differ significantly from that used in the previous (string and membrane) examples — the strain energy corresponding exactly to the minimum principle. Similar element types can also be used but the number of 'degrees of freedom' associated with each node may be greater. For a two-dimensional stress problem each node has two degrees of freedom, namely, its displacement ϕ in the x-direction and its displacement θ in the y-direction. Within each element, ϕ and θ are given by the interpolation functions

$$\phi = \sum_{m=1}^{n} \phi_m B_m(x, y) \qquad \theta = \sum_{m=1}^{n} \theta_m B_m(x, y)$$

where the mth node of the n-noded element has displacement (ϕ_m, θ_m) and is associated with basis function $B_m(x, y)$.

For a three-dimensional problem the node has three degrees of freedom, namely, its displacements ϕ, θ, ψ in the x-, y- and z-directions, respectively.

It should be noted that with this type of formulation it is the displacements which are the fundamental unknowns in the problem and not the stresses. If, as is usual, the stresses are required they are calculated from these displacements, using the strains, at a later stage of the computation. Many systems provide a post-processing facility in which some form of graphical display (using contours or colour-shaded plots of maximum principal stresses) is produced. The element formulation ensures continuity of displacement from element to element but neither the strains nor the stresses will generally be continuous across element boundaries. In particular when using the simple triangular element with linear interpolation functions, the partial derivatives of the displacements (and hence the strains and the stresses) will be constant for the entire element. One commonly used simple check on the accuracy of the finite element solution of a stress problem is to compare computed stresses at the same point in adjacent elements.

In addition to the simple types of element described here a large number of special-purpose elements have been developed for the solution of specific types of stress problem. These include: beam elements, in which the end-nodes have rotational degrees of freedom associated with bending and torsion of the beam; elements for plate bending problems; axi-symmetric elements; and thin shell elements. Each element type requires special software to compute the element contribution to the strain energy, but can share general-purpose software for assembly and solution.

Finite element methods have also been applied to solve stress problems with more complex material properties. Two types of complexity can occur: the material may be anisotropic, in that the material properties are not the same in all directions; or the material may have non-linear elastic properties. For an anisotropic material the strain energy computation is more complex and requires a special type of element. For non-linear materials the elastic 'constants' are in effect variables, varying with the displacement. Such problems are usually solved by progressively increasing the loads and up-dating the material properties at each increment of the loading cycle.

7.2 Thermal problems

A common thermal problem is that of determining the temperature at different points in a body exposed to non-uniform heating, such as occurs in an exhaust manifold or turbine blade.

For steady state problems (in which the temperature ϕ at any point does not vary with time) the spatial variation of temperature is usually given by the differential equation

$$\tau\left(\frac{\partial^2\phi}{\partial x^2}\right) + \tau\left(\frac{\partial^2\phi}{\partial y^2}\right) = 0 \tag{34}$$

or, in three dimensions, by

$$\tau\left(\frac{\partial^2\phi}{\partial x^2}\right) + \tau\left(\frac{\partial^2\phi}{\partial y^2}\right) + \tau\left(\frac{\partial^2\phi}{\partial z^2}\right) = 0$$

where ϕ is the temperature and τ is the thermal conductivity.

This is clearly a special case of equation (19) and can be solved by the methods described in the earlier two-dimensional example. Frequently, stress problems are associated with thermal problems in that most materials expand when heated, and this expansion can cause stresses. In this case thermal stresses can be computed by a two-stage finite element analysis in which first the temperature distribution is computed, and secondly, with a knowledge of the expansion coefficients of the materials, the displacements and the corresponding strains and stresses are then computed, using structural elements rather than heat transfer elements.

For transient thermal problems (in which the temperatures vary with time) equation (34) must be replaced by

$$\tau\left(\frac{\partial^2\phi}{\partial x^2}\right) + \tau\left(\frac{\partial^2\phi}{\partial y^2}\right) = \frac{\partial\phi}{\partial t} \tag{35}$$

Equation (35) is essentially similar to equation (19) except that the right-hand side now contains the time derivative term $\partial\phi/\partial t$. An expression similar to that in equation (20) exists in this case though it now contains a term involving $\partial\phi/\partial t$.

The conventional finite element formulation method can be used for this transient thermal problem if it is assumed that the nodal values ϕ_m and their rates of change $\mathrm{d}\phi_m/\mathrm{d}t$ are independent of each other. The result is that, for any particular value of t, the linear equations $\mathbf{K}\boldsymbol{\phi} = -\mathbf{F}$ corresponding to equations (29) are replaced by

$$\mathbf{K}\boldsymbol{\phi} + \mathbf{C}\left(\frac{\mathrm{d}\boldsymbol{\phi}}{\mathrm{d}t}\right) = -\mathbf{F} \tag{36}$$

where $\mathbf{C}$ is a matrix which depends upon the element interpolation functions, and on certain thermal properties of the material.

Equations (36) are a system of first-order linear ordinary differential equations which can be solved by any standard method using suitably small time steps.

7.3 Irrotational fluid flow

Many other physical problems can be described by differential equations which are essentially similar to equation (34) in the steady state case, or to equation (35) in the transient case. These are known as *field problems*. Clearly for these problems precisely the same methods of finite element formulation and solution can be applied. An example is afforded by the two-dimensional irrotational flow of an ideal fluid in which a velocity potential ϕ can be introduced, such that the components of the fluid velocity in the x- and y-directions are respectively $v_x = \partial\phi/\partial x$ and $v_y = \partial\phi/\partial y$. The equation of motion of the fluid is then

$$\rho\left(\frac{\partial^2\phi}{\partial x^2}\right) + \rho\left(\frac{\partial^2\phi}{\partial y^2}\right) = 0$$

where ρ is the mass density of the fluid.

7.4 Electrostatic potential

Another field problem occurs in electrostatics. For an electrostatic problem the electrostatic potential ϕ satisfies the differential equation

$$\varepsilon\left(\frac{\partial^2\phi}{\partial x^2}\right) + \varepsilon\left(\frac{\partial^2\phi}{\partial y^2}\right) = \rho(x, y)$$

In this equation ε is the dielectric constant of the material and ρ is the density of distributed charge.

7.5 Elastic membrane

As briefly mentioned in Section 5 (where we discussed a particular example in detail), in general the transverse deflection of an elastic membrane satisfies an equation which is essentially a generalisation of that for an elastic string and is another example of a field problem. The equation is

$$T\left(\frac{\partial^2\phi}{\partial x^2}\right) + T\left(\frac{\partial^2\phi}{\partial y^2}\right) = w(x, y)$$

Note that equation (21) is a special case of this form. Here, T is the tension in the membrane and $w(x, y)$ is the applied transverse load.

7.6 Mechanical vibrations

In the limited space available in this chapter it has only been possible to consider the simplest methods available for finite element problem formulation together with a selection of the problems which can be solved by these methods. The finite element method has, however, been applied to many other types of problem.

One problem which is within the scope of most commercial finite element packages is that of computing the normal modes and frequencies for the mechanical vibrations of an elastic structure. For these problems the standard finite element formulation, as used for stress problems, produces a second-order system of linear ordinary differential equations

$$\mathbf{K}\phi + \mathbf{M}\left(\frac{\mathrm{d}^2\phi}{\mathrm{d}t^2}\right) = \mathbf{0}$$

where ϕ is now the vector of nodal displacements, $\mathbf{K}$ the stiffness matrix and $\mathbf{M}$ the mass matrix; $\mathbf{K}$ is identical to the stiffness matrix for the static problems considered previously, and $\mathbf{M}$ depends upon the element discretisation and material density. The normal modes and frequencies are found by assuming a simple harmonic motion solution of the above equation, of the form

$$\phi = (\cos \omega t)\phi_0$$

then

$$\frac{\mathrm{d}^2\phi}{\mathrm{d}t^2} = -(\omega^2 \cos \omega t)\phi_0$$

and the equation becomes

$$(\mathbf{K} - \omega^2\mathbf{M})\phi_0 = \mathbf{0}$$

This can be recognised as a generalised eigenvalue equation and solved accordingly, or can be simply transformed to a standard eigenvalue problem. These are standard problems in linear algebra for which a number of reliable computer algorithms exist [Goult *et al.* 1974].

7.7 Fluid mechanics

Finite element methods have also been used extensively to solve problems in fluid mechanics. It is only the simplest problems of this type for which a minimum principle exists and the type of finite element formulation described here can be applied. For most fluid mechanics problems the governing differential equations are non-linear and other more general methods, such as the Galerkin method [Washizu 1981], of finite element formulation must be employed.

Kinematic analysis **11**

M J Pratt

1 Introduction

In this chapter it is assumed that a computer-aided design (CAD) system is available which is capable of modelling engineering parts and, in particular, the components of a linkage or mechanism. It is also clearly desirable that the system can model not only the individual parts but also the complete mechanism. If this is so, and if there is some way of simulating the motion of the components with respect to each other, then several advantages arise. For example, it is possible to verify that a mechanism moves in the required manner, and also that its components do not collide with each other during the motion.

Consider the set of mechanical parts (from a slider-crank mechanism) shown in Figure 11.1. Any contemporary three-dimensional CAD system is capable of modelling these individually [Klosterman, Ard & Klahs 1982].

Fig. 11.1 A set of four parts of a mechanism

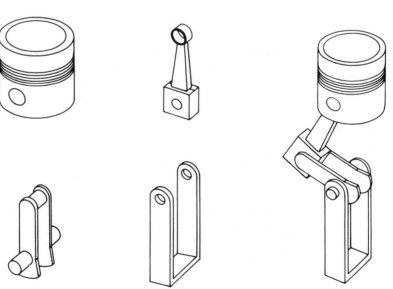

When it comes to modelling a mechanism constructed from them, however, system capabilities vary considerably [Tilove 1983]. There are several possible levels of sophistication, as follows:

1 The user can position and orientate the components appropriately so that they form a 'legal' configuration of the mechanism. Motion of the mechanism may now be simulated in an incremental manner by making small successive adjustments to the positions and orientations of the components such that a legal configuration always results. The responsibility for maintaining legality rests with the user, and involves a very tedious, time-consuming and error-prone procedure. Verification of the correctness of the motion and interference or collision checking will probably be solely visual, as depicted by the image on the screen.

2 A more advanced CAD system may permit the definition of constraints which allow relative motion between the components but which limit it in some way, so that the individual parts are always linked to form a legal configuration as the free parameters are varied. The situation is now much more straightforward for the user. Motion simulation is again incremental, but now the system provides geometrical feedback on the configurations traversed as the mechanism moves. However, the detection of collisions is again essentially visual.

3 A yet more advanced system may be capable of generating an analysis of the motion of the mechanism as and when it is required; in essence this only necessitates some geometric interrogations to be performed and the results displayed in some appropriate manner. Collision checking will still be visual if the model is just a wire-frame one, but it can be automatic in the case of a solid model. Automatic checking is computationally expensive, however, since it makes use of the Boolean operation of intersection. It is worth noting that the hidden-line or hidden-surface graphics capabilities of solid modellers greatly improve the visualisation of a complex linkage or mechanism; a wire-frame representation is often very difficult to interpret visually.

4 In the preceding three types of system the motion of the mechanism has been modelled in an incremental manner. Some early research is in progress on the modelling of time-continuous motion, but commercial implementations are probably some years in the future. In principle such a simulation is better than an incremental one since collisions may occur at intermediate positions and pass unnoticed in the latter case. The problem of continuous simulation is discussed in more detail later in this chapter.

2 The representation of mechanisms

A mechanism can be viewed conceptually as a set of rigid solid bodies interconnected with each other in a way which constrains, but does not generally prohibit, relative motion between any two of the bodies. The individual solid bodies are usually referred to as **links** (think of the links of a chain), while the relative motion constraints are referred to as **joints** (here we exclude rivetted, welded and glued joints, etc.).

2.1 Links, joints and transformations

Fig. 11.2 Some commonly occurring kinematic joints (four of the Reuleaux lower pairs)

It can be seen from Figure 11.2 (which illustrates some common types of kinematic joint) that a joint can be thought of as defining a family of rigid transformations of one of the links involved in the joint relative to the other. Indeed we can identify the joint with its associated family of transformations. In the prismatic joint, for example, if link 1 is held fixed, the family of transformations includes all translations of link 2 in the axial direction of the joint. For the revolute joint the family of transformations comprises all rotations of link 2 about the joint axis in link 1. Link 1 will not generally be fixed as to position and orientation, of course, but this presents no problem provided we are prepared to think in terms of relative motions only.

Since a single joint constrains the relative motion of precisely two links (and is therefore often referred to as a kinematic pair), it is possible to represent a mechanism by a connected undirected graph as shown in Figure 11.3. The

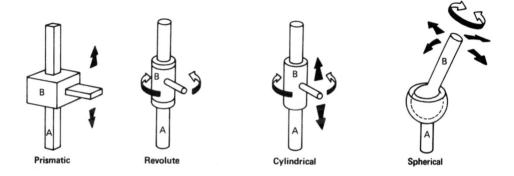

Prismatic   Revolute   Cylindrical   Spherical

Fig. 11.3 Two simple mechanisms and their graphs

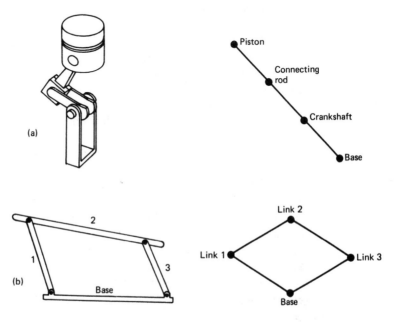

213

vertices of such a graph represent links and the edges represent joints (connecting two links) of the mechanism. Then, to each edge of the graph there corresponds a family of rigid transformations as previously discussed. If the mechanism is a **closed-loop mechanism**, such as the four-bar linkage shown in Figure 11.3(b), the graph contains cycles (that is, one or more closed loops). On the other hand, for an **open-loop mechanism**, such as a typical robot manipulator, or the piston, connecting rod, crank and base assembly shown in Figure 11.3(a), the graph is a tree (that is, it contains no loops), and so is acyclic. The open-loop case is easier to analyse and will be dealt with first; the necessary refinements required for dealing with closed-loop mechanisms will be covered later.

For the moment, then, consider the modelling of an *open-loop mechanism*. A link is a rigid solid, which may be modelled in various degrees of detail as we shall discuss later. In order to represent relative motion it is necessary to associate one or more coordinate systems with each link; these are assumed to be embedded in the link so that they move as it moves. It is customary to use cartesian coordinate frames in this context. Suppose that the coordinate frames associated with link i are F_{i1}, F_{i2} and so on. These systems are in fixed positions relative to each other, and we may therefore define fixed rigid transformations, relating F_{i1} to F_{i2} for example, such as T_{i12}, which has the property that

$$F_{i2} = T_{i12}F_{i1}$$

i.e. T_{i12} transforms F_{i1} into F_{i2}. In the above abstract form this equation does not indicate how the transformation is to be calculated. However, in practice this is most commonly achieved using matrices to represent T_{i12}, etc. and matrix multiplication to perform the transformation. This explains why the above equation is conventionally written in the form shown, as a product of terms. Figure 11.4 shows the connecting rod from the mechanism of Figure 11.1 with its two embedded coordinate systems. In this case the transformation T_{i12} represents a simple translation in the x-direction of F_{i1}, from the position of F_{i1} to the position of F_{i2}.

The T-transformations of the last paragraph relate different coordinate systems which are embedded in the same link. In order to relate coordinate systems associated with different links which are connected by a joint we need another type of transformation which will be denoted by $U_k(\alpha)$, where the suffix k denotes the type of joint and the 'vector' α denotes the array of joint variables. The components of α are the variables which express the relative position and orientation of the two links meeting at the joint. The number of components of α corresponds to the number of degrees of freedom of the joint. For example, reference to Figure 11.2 shows that a prismatic joint has one degree of freedom, so that α has only one component, that is $\alpha = (\alpha_1)$, where α_1 is a length variable. A revolute joint also has one degree of freedom, though α_1 is now an angular variable. A spherical (ball-and-socket) joint has three degrees of freedom, whence $\alpha = (\alpha_1, \alpha_2, \alpha_3)$; all three variables in this case are angles.

Each type of joint, then, has an associated characteristic transformation expressed in terms of one or more variables. The transformation not only embodies the constraints which restrict the type of relative motion between the two links but it also provides a way of quantifying the remaining degrees of

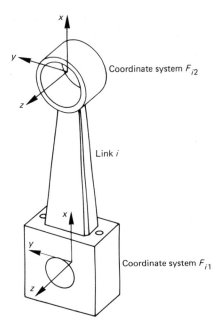

Fig. 11.4 Link with two embedded coordinate frames

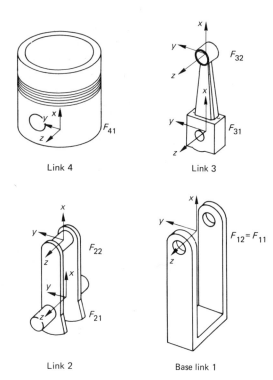

Fig. 11.5 Links of mechanism with associated coordinate systems

freedom. In addition, fixed parameters often occur in the transformation associated with a joint; for example, a screw joint has only one (say angular) degree of freedom but the transformation depends on the fixed *pitch* of the screw, which couples the translation to the rotation in a constant ratio.

Returning to the example of Figure 11.1, we show in Figure 11.5 the various links of this mechanism with their associated coordinate systems. From the foregoing we see that the coordinate system F_{41}, embedded in the piston, can be expressed as

$$F_{41} = U_r(\gamma)F_{32}$$

$$= U_r(\gamma)T_{312}F_{31}$$

$$= U_r(\gamma)T_{312}U_r(\beta)F_{22}$$

$$= U_r(\gamma)T_{312}U_r(\beta)T_{212}F_{21}$$

$$= U_r(\gamma)T_{312}U_r(\beta)T_{212}U_r(\alpha)F_{12} \qquad (1)$$

where U_r denotes the transformation associated with a revolute joint and α, β and γ are the angular displacements at the three revolute joints, measured from some datum in each case. Clearly, if F_{12} is fixed then F_{41} depends upon the three variables α, β, and γ; as they change, the coordinate systems move relative to each other and hence the links in which they are embedded must move. Thus it is possible to simulate the motion of the mechanism by incrementing the joint variables, and moving the coordinate systems.

215

In the example just given the displacement variables are all mutually independent. This is a feature characteristic of open-loop mechanisms. However, if the piston is now constrained (as it would be inside an internal combustion engine) to move in a fixed cylinder, we have a *closed-loop mechanism* since this cylinder is rigidly connected to the base. The resulting piston–cylinder combination effectively forms a prismatic joint and the system is now a slider-crank mechanism. In this case the variables α, β and γ are no longer independent and it can be shown that only one variable is required to specify the configuration (that is, only one overall degree of freedom remains).

In practice it is convenient to represent the transformations involved in this type of representation in terms of (4×4) matrices.

The following two examples illustrate the form that these (4×4) matrices take for two particular joint types.

Example 1 A revolute joint in which F_{21} results from rotation of F_{12} by α about its z-axis has an associated characteristic transformation $U_r(\alpha)$, with the (4×4) matrix form

$$
\mathbf{U}_r(\alpha) = \begin{bmatrix} \cos \alpha & \sin \alpha & 0 & 0 \\ -\sin \alpha & \cos \alpha & 0 & 0 \\ 0 & 0 & 1 & 0 \\ 0 & 0 & 0 & 1 \end{bmatrix}
$$

where the conventions used are those adopted by Faux and Pratt [1979].

Example 2 A prismatic joint in which F_{21} results from a translation of F_{12} by α along its z-direction has an associated characteristic transformation $U_p(\alpha)$ with the (4×4) matrix form

$$
\mathbf{U}_p(\alpha) = \begin{bmatrix} 1 & 0 & 0 & 0 \\ 0 & 1 & 0 & 0 \\ 0 & 0 & 1 & -\alpha \\ 0 & 0 & 0 & 1 \end{bmatrix}
$$

2.2 Modelling the links in a mechanism

So far the links in a mechanism have been represented only in terms of rigidly connected sets of coordinate systems. In an interactive graphical system the links must also be modelled in some geometrical sense for the purposes of more detailed design and display, and to permit collision detection.

The simplest form of geometric representation of a link (and also of a joint) is as one or more lines in space, leading to a 'stick' model of a mechanism. The advantage is that the complete system of links and joints can be represented in terms of a comparatively small number of line segments and it can therefore be drawn quickly. With the use of a graphical system with refresh capabilities (i.e. anything other than a storage tube), the motion of the mechanism can also be simulated on the screen in real time. This provides a rapid means for verification of programmed motions. On the other hand, such a minimal representation is not well suited to the detection of collisions between links and/or joints of the mechanism, for example, because the details of size, shape and position of the links and joints are not fully modelled.

Many CAD systems allow the links to be modelled in wire-frame form, which has few advantages but several drawbacks. A screen display will now in general be congested with line segments and difficult to interpret because no automatic hidden-line removal is provided. Owing to the much larger number of line segments (compared to the number in a stick model) a graphical image will take longer to draw, so that real-time screen animation requires much greater computing resources. Collision checks are possible, but these must be made visually by the operator and cannot be automated easily.

Currently the most sophisticated form of geometric model is, as we have seen earlier, the solid model. If the links are modelled as solids, then greater reality is attainable through the use of automatic hidden-line removal. Collision detection in any fixed configuration may also be performed automatically by the use of the Boolean intersection operation available on solid modellers. However, it must be stressed that both these operations are computationally very demanding and that the real-time simulation of the motion of a mechanism modelled in solid form is currently only possible with the use of expensive specialised hardware and models which have been simplified by the use of (for example) facetting techniques.

The detection of collisions in simulated relative motion of solid models is a current topic of research. There appear to be three modes of approach to the problem. These are:

1 Modelling the motion in discrete time-steps and making a static collision check after each incremental movement.

2 Modelling the volumes swept out by the moving links and checking for clashes between the swept volumes.

3 Modelling the kinematic situation in a continuous four-dimensional manner, the fourth dimension being time.

Each approach has its disadvantages. The first may miss clashes which occur at interim time-steps. The second is best used as a check that collisions cannot occur, since this will certainly be so if the swept volumes do not intersect. However, the intersection of the swept volumes does not necessarily imply a clash between the components concerned since they may occupy the overlapping portions of those volumes at different times during the motion (Chapter 15). The approach only gives unequivocal results in the case of relative motion between not more than two components. As for the third possibility, four-dimensional modelling is still very much in its infancy. There is much to be learnt, and the associated computations will inevitably be time-consuming and extremely expensive in terms of computing resources.

In practice, it is important to know not only when the components of a mechanism clash, but also what is the minimum distance between them when they 'nearly' clash. For example, if two links miss by 0.1 mm during the simulated motion, a Boolean collision check will give a null result. However, manufacturing tolerances and inaccuracies may give rise to a realisation of the mechanism in which the links actually clash by 0.1 mm. Furthermore in a real system the links will not be absolutely rigid so that inertial and gravitational forces will inevitably deform the components elastically, causing potential clashes in 'near miss' situations. It is important therefore that close approaches can be identified. This again is a topic of ongoing research, and current kinematic modelling systems based on solid modellers do not address the problem.

3 Open-loop mechanisms

As we have seen above, in an open-loop mechanism, the joint variables are independent of one another, so that all joint variables must be specified (i.e. be given a value) in order to define a particular configuration of the system. The piston, connecting rod, crank and base, shown connected in series in Figure 11.1, provides a simple example of such an open-loop mechanism, as does the planar robot manipulator system [Paul 1982] shown in Figure 11.6.

Fig. 11.6 Planar robot manipulator

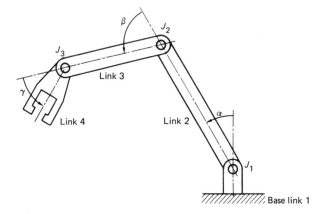

Both systems consist of four links connected serially by three revolute joints. Hence, from equation (1), and the expression for $U_r(\alpha)$ presented in example 1, we can obtain an expression for F_{41} (the coordinate frame in the end-link) in terms of the three revolute joint angles α, β and γ and F_{12} (the coordinate frame in the base-link). This has the matrix form

$$\mathbf{F}_{41} = \mathbf{U}_r(\gamma)\mathbf{T}_{312}\mathbf{U}_r(\beta)\mathbf{T}_{212}\mathbf{U}_r(\alpha)\mathbf{F}_{12}$$

where

$$\mathbf{U}_r(\gamma) = \begin{bmatrix} \cos\gamma & \sin\gamma & 0 & 0 \\ -\sin\gamma & \cos\gamma & 0 & 0 \\ 0 & 0 & 1 & 0 \\ 0 & 0 & 0 & 1 \end{bmatrix}$$

$$\mathbf{U}_r(\beta) = \begin{bmatrix} \cos\beta & \sin\beta & 0 & 0 \\ -\sin\beta & \cos\beta & 0 & 0 \\ 0 & 0 & 1 & 0 \\ 0 & 0 & 0 & 1 \end{bmatrix}$$

$$\mathbf{U}_r(\alpha) = \begin{bmatrix} \cos\alpha & \sin\alpha & 0 & 0 \\ -\sin\alpha & \cos\alpha & 0 & 0 \\ 0 & 0 & 1 & 0 \\ 0 & 0 & 0 & 1 \end{bmatrix}$$

The *T*-transformations are also easy to specify in this case since they consist of simple translations and can be expressed using (4×4) matrices with the same form as those for $U_p(\alpha)$ from example 2. The appropriate translations (i.e. the α's) are the link lengths a_2 and a_3 of links 2 and 3 respectively, but here the translations are in the x-directions, so we have

$$
\mathbf{T}_{212} = \begin{bmatrix} 1 & 0 & 0 & -a_2 \\ 0 & 1 & 0 & 0 \\ 0 & 0 & 1 & 0 \\ 0 & 0 & 0 & 1 \end{bmatrix}
$$

$$
\mathbf{T}_{312} = \begin{bmatrix} 1 & 0 & 0 & -a_3 \\ 0 & 1 & 0 & 0 \\ 0 & 0 & 1 & 0 \\ 0 & 0 & 0 & 1 \end{bmatrix}
$$

and hence, after multiplying the five matrices in sequence, we finally obtain the expression

$$
\mathbf{F}_{41} = \begin{bmatrix} \cos(\alpha+\beta+\gamma) & \sin(\alpha+\beta+\gamma) & 0 & -a_2\cos(\beta+\gamma)-a_3\cos\gamma \\ -\sin(\alpha+\beta+\gamma) & \cos(\alpha+\beta+\gamma) & 0 & a_2\sin(\beta+\gamma)+a_3\sin\gamma \\ 0 & 0 & 1 & 0 \\ 0 & 0 & 0 & 1 \end{bmatrix} \mathbf{F}_{12}
$$

$$(2)$$

relating the coordinate frames F_{41} and F_{12}. This matrix equation immediately gives the relationships between the coordinates x_1, y_1 and z_1 (specified with respect to the base-link coordinate frame F_{12}) and the coordinates x_4, y_4 and z_4 (specified with respect to the end-link coordinate frame F_{41}), of any point in space in the following form:

$$x_4 = x_1 \cos(\alpha+\beta+\gamma) + y_1 \sin(\alpha+\beta+\gamma) - a_2 \cos(\beta+\gamma) - a_3 \cos\gamma$$

$$y_4 = -x_1 \sin(\alpha+\beta+\gamma) + y_1 \cos(\alpha+\beta+\gamma) + a_2 \sin(\beta+\gamma) + a_3 \sin\gamma$$

$$z_4 = z_1 \tag{3}$$

These relationships can be 'inverted' (for example, by deriving the inverse of the matrix in equation (2)) to obtain x_1, y_1 and z_1 in terms of x_4, y_4 and z_4, giving

$$x_1 = x_4 \cos(\alpha+\beta+\gamma) - y_4 \sin(\alpha+\beta+\gamma) + a_3 \cos(\alpha+\beta) + a_2 \cos\alpha$$

$$y_1 = x_4 \sin(\alpha+\beta+\gamma) + y_4 \cos(\alpha+\beta+\gamma) + a_3 \sin(\alpha+\beta) + a_2 \sin\alpha$$

$$z_1 = z_4 \tag{4}$$

These equations enable a point on the end-link (and specified in the F_{41} frame) to be located in the 'fixed' coordinate frame F_{12} attached to the base-link, for any choice of values for the joint variables α, β and γ and hence also for any configuration of the planar manipulator in Figure 11.6.

4 Closed-loop mechanisms

In the case of an open-loop mechanism, the joint variables are independent of one another and their values must be specified individually in order to determine the configuration of the system. For closed-loop mechanisms, however, this is not the case since these have the characteristic that the mutual relationships at the joints are not independent of each other. There exists a well-established theory of closed-loop mechanisms [Suh & Radcliffe 1978; Shigley & Uicker 1980] which is particularly well developed for those systems having just one degree of freedom, and hence requiring only one joint variable to be specified in order to determine their configuration. This can be illustrated most simply in terms of the planar four-bar linkage shown in Figure 11.7.

Fig. 11.7 Planar four-bar linkage

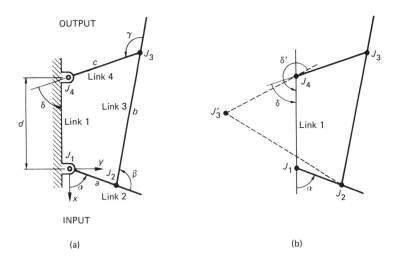

(a)

(b)

Four-bar linkage

This linkage has only a single degree of freedom. Thus if the angle α is regarded as the independent (input) variable and given a value, then the remaining three angles β, γ and δ may each be regarded as a dependent (output) variable with value determined by that of α. For simplicity we consider just one of these, namely δ, as the output variable. A straightforward trigonometrical derivation in terms of the coordinates of the points J_2 and J_3 (joint axes 2 and 3) in the coordinate frame shown at joint 1 gives

$$A \sin \delta + B \cos \delta + C = 0$$

where $A = -\sin \alpha$

$$B = \frac{d}{a} + \cos \alpha$$

$$C = \frac{d}{c} \cos \alpha + \frac{1}{2ac} (a^2 - b^2 + c^2 + d^2)$$

Using the tan-half-angle substitution for $\sin \delta$ and $\cos \delta$, namely

$$\sin \delta = \frac{2t}{(1 + t^2)} \quad \text{and} \quad \cos \delta = \frac{(1 - t^2)}{(1 + t^2)}$$

where $t = \tan \frac{1}{2}\delta$, we can rewrite the above equation as the quadratic equation

$$(C - B)t^2 + 2At + (C + B) = 0$$

This can then be solved for t (in terms of A, B and C) using the standard formula for the roots of a quadratic equation, giving

$$t = \frac{-A \pm (A^2 + B^2 - C^2)^{0.5}}{(C - B)}$$

so that, finally, we have

$$\delta = 2 \arctan \left\{ \frac{[-A \pm (A^2 + B^2 - C^2)^{0.5}]}{(C - B)} \right\} \tag{5}$$

This gives δ in terms of α and the link lengths a, b, c and d (that is, in terms of the input, and the design parameters defining the geometry of the mechanism).

Notice that this expression yields two different values for δ (these correspond to the two roots of the quadratic equation, indicated by the occurrence of the $\pm$ signs). This is physically meaningful since, for a given input value α, there are two possible configurations of the mechanism (known as *closures*) and hence two possible values for δ. Figure 11.7(b) illustrates this situation.

Slider-crank mechanism

To complete our discussion of closed-loop mechanisms we consider another simple example, namely the slider-crank system discussed earlier. Figure 11.8 shows the mechanical components from Figure 11.1, in closed-loop form, as they would occur interconnected in a slider-crank mechanism.

Fig. 11.8 Planar slider-crank mechanism

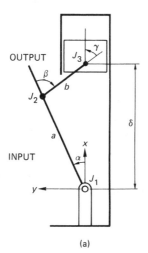 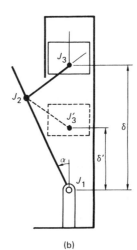

(a)   (b)

In this case we have three angular variables, α, β and γ (at the three revolute joints), together with the distance variable, δ (at the prismatic joint). If we consider the mechanism to function as a pump, rather than as an engine, we can take α as the (independent) input variable and δ as the (dependent) output variable. As with the four-bar linkage considered above, a straightforward derivation in terms of the coordinates of the points J_2 and J_3 (revolute joint axes 2 and 3) in the coordinate frame shown at joint 1 gives

$$\delta^2 + D\delta + E = 0$$

where $D = -2a \cos \alpha$ and $E = a^2 - b^2$

This time, the equation is already in quadratic form and so its solution (in terms of the usual formula) is given by

$$\delta = \tfrac{1}{2}[-D \pm (D^2 - 4E)^{0.5}] \qquad (6)$$

This gives δ directly in terms of α and the link lengths a and b (the input and the design parameters of the mechanism).

Notice, again, that there are two different values of δ, in general, for a given value of α (indicated by the $\pm$ signs). These correspond to the two possible configurations of the mechanism illustrated by Figure 11.8(b).

Results such as those obtained from equations (5) and (6) are known for a wide range of closed-loop mechanisms; computer programs and specialised subroutine libraries are available for the analysis of mechanical systems built up from such linkages. One such system is the well-known IMP (Integrated Mechanisms Package) system from the company SDRC [Sheth & Uicker 1972]. IMP is used extensively for the design of linkages, such as those found on car suspension systems, for example. Furthermore, the company also has software modules which allow the building up of models of mechanisms from solid models of their components and the subsequent examination of their properties.

5 Dynamic problems

So far the problems discussed have been mainly concerned: with modelling mechanisms in various static configurations; with checking for collisions of components with each other and with external items in their environment; and with visual simulation of motion. As we have seen, these considerations generally require the derivation and computation of the relative positions of the links in a mechanism as functions of the independent joint variables (a *displacement analysis*). However, if we specify those joint variables as functions of time we can go on to calculate relative velocities (linear or rotational) and accelerations of the links (a *kinematic analysis*). Such calculations are often very important, especially in the case of high-speed mechanisms. (Indeed they are essential for a true kinematic analysis and synthesis of any mechanical system.)

In addition, if the links in a mechanism are subjected to large accelerations the 'inertial' forces (resisting any deviation from constant velocity) are correspondingly large and a *dynamic analysis* is required. Their calculation depends not only on the detailed kinematics (involving displacement, velocity and acceleration analyses) but also on a knowledge of the masses, moments of inertia and centres of mass of the links (that is, on a detailed knowledge of their mass distribution). These dynamic parameters and properties may be automatically derived, provided a solid modeller is used, and a dynamic analysis may then be performed on the mechanism. Moreover, with a knowledge of the link geometry and the forces acting upon it we can go further and use finite element analysis to compute the deformations of the link during the motion, which if neglected may have a detrimental effect on the required performance. Similarly, vibration analysis may also be undertaken.

In fact any realistic modelling and simulation of the kinematics and dynamics of mechanisms brings together a number of the topics discussed elsewhere in this book (notably geometric modelling, simulation and finite element analysis) together with other well-established techniques of engineering mathematics and computations.

6 Applications

There are obvious applications of kinematic modelling in a variety of areas. We briefly examine just two of these, namely robot simulation, and the simulation of numerically-controlled machining processes.

It is generally considered to be desirable that a robot should be programmable as though it were some form of computer-controlled machine tool (which is in fact close to the truth for an industrial robot). Currently, robots are often programmed in *teach mode*, that is by leading them through the required sequence of actions and recording the most important joint positions, etc., at each stage of the task. When the robot is executing the stored sequence of positions, it will usually then interpolate its motion to determine the intermediate positions not specified in detail by the programmer. Often it will do this without taking account of obstacles in its workspace, or of optimum paths in terms of minimising time, energy, etc. The onus is therefore on the programmer to select an appropriate number of significant fixed positions for the robot to pass through in order to approximate as closely as possible to some trouble-free optimised path, required for achieving the task. Moreover, similar comments apply to those applications involving continuous movements (along some curve, for example) such as occur in welding. Here, as with the previous *point-to-point* case, the programmer is often involved centrally in specifying the intricate details of the motion, in order to achieve the task.

Recently, however, formal languages for the off-line programming of robots have been under development and are now in limited use. These enable the programmer to specify more sophisticated moves and tasks in a higher level (and more user-friendly) form, and they provide the robot with a pre-determined strategy and procedures for dealing with the details of its task. Such languages will greatly influence developments in the design and control of robots and should facilitate their more widespread introduction, since they will essentially hide many of the conceptually difficult aspects of kinematics from the programmer and user. Furthermore, once an off-line robot program has been written, it may be used to drive a simulated robot modelled by a CAD system. This enables verification that the required motion is achieved without taking a real robot out of service. It also permits collision checks to be made by the computer model rather than (potentially more disastrously) in situ.

For the present, however, it is in principle possible to program a robot using either one of two general approaches: by specifying the relative motion at the joints; or by specifying the required motion of the end-effector. The second approach, known as *path-following*, is the more useful in practice, and it leads to the necessity for solving what is termed the *inverse kinematic problem*. For example, suppose that a point on the end-effector is required to follow a specified space curve (perhaps for welding along a curved seam). Then the relative motion at all joints of the robot must be determined such that the desired end-effector motion results.

This inverse kinematic problem presents certain mathematical difficulties (often formidable) since in general there is more than one way of achieving each position along the path. The several possible configurations of the arm for each position of the end-effector are exemplified by the two closures derived earlier for both the four-bar mechanism and the slider-crank mechanism. The mathematical difficulties arise because the algebraic equations describing the different configurations are highly non-linear and intricately coupled.

The two alternative approaches mentioned above also illustrate the distinction between the *analysis* and the *synthesis* of a mechanism. In analysis we specify the mechanism and the relative motion of its links (at the joints) and calculate the resulting overall motion (*forward kinematics*). In synthesis we specify the desired overall motion and work backwards to the necessary relative link motions (*inverse kinematics*) or to the necessary geometry of the links required to produce a good approximation to the desired overall motion.

Clearly there are similarities between the modelling of robots and the modelling of linkages and mechanisms in general. Most of the foregoing comments apply, though the modelling of closed-loop mechanisms gives rise to some special problems as discussed in the previous section.

A less closely related application area is that of the kinematic simulation of numerically-controlled (NC) machining processes. This requires the use of a solid modeller to be most effective. The stock material can be modelled, as can the volume swept out by the cutting tool as it follows the motion specified in an NC part program. This volume is subtracted (using Boolean operations) from the stock volume to give a model of the part in process at various stages during the machining. Moreover, it is possible to check for collisions of the tool holder, for example, with other objects in the environment. In addition, this type of simulation shows up instances of undesired gouging of the workpiece or inadvertent machining of material from the clamps or fixtures used in securing it to the bed of the machine tool.

Electronics—logic and layout 12

M Dooner and P Wallace

1 Introduction

Design in electronics falls into two major sequential and connected phases (Figure 12.1). In the first phase, *logic design*, functional or logic modules are used to develop a circuit structure that satisfies a given specification. The types of logic module used and the way they are connected together determine the operation of the circuit. This is the creative phase of the design. *Physical design* comes next, and is referred to as the implementation or layout phase. In general, this phase does not demand as much intellectual skill or knowledge of electronics as the first. However, it does require experience and an appreciation of electrical design constraints. The basic problems in physical design or layout are: where to place the components (whether they are discrete components on a printed circuit board (PCB), or their silicon equivalents, the *cells*, on an integrated circuit (IC)); and how to route the connections between the components.

Two types of computer tool have been developed to aid electronics design, each corresponding to one of the major design phases. These tools are shown in Figure 12.1 as CAEE and CAED. *Computer-aided electronic design* (CAED) is the older technology, and includes facilities for developing the physical layout. CAED for PCB design provides facilities to draw schematic diagrams, logic networks and a geometrical layout of components. These systems also usually include facilities for checking that design rules are adhered to; for producing network lists (connection lists between logic components); for outputting designs to photo-plotters; and for producing drill tapes for PCB manufacture. General CAED systems are found in draughting or engineering service departments, while CAED systems specifically developed for IC design are usually located in 'silicon foundries' where the chips are actually manufactured. CAED for microelectronics is not just a tool for increasing design productivity. Its use is essential, even for the design of relatively small chips; otherwise, the vast amount of design information arising from a chip's complex layout cannot be handled.

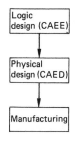

Fig. 12.1 Major phases in electronic design and manufacture

Computer-aided electronic engineering (CAEE) is a relatively recent term that refers to the first phase of the design process, where the circuit's overall structure is developed. In the USA in particular, where the term originated, CAEE is understood mainly to include tools for initial schematic design and logic simulation; it is now almost synonymous with the new generation of electronics workstation.

The CAEE workstation exemplifies the state-of-the-art in modern design tools. Some integrated workstations can be used for system design, functional design, schematics, simulation and testing and even physical layout design and the production of manufacturing information (roles traditionally carried out within CAED). Such progress with CAEE has come with the ability to provide extensive processing power for logic/circuit simulation — this is what distinguishes the previous generation of CAED systems (mainly concerned with schematics and layout) from the new generation of CAEE workstations.

Many new features of the CAEE tools have been introduced to reduce the design/development cycle time. Simulation reduces the need for 'breadboarding' (the traditional practice of checking or verifying an electronics circuit before manufacture). Breadboarding involves constructing a physical prototype using actual components so that the circuit can be tested in a number of ways. Simulation is an essential feature of IC design, since ICs cannot be breadboarded.

Electronics design tends to be hierarchically structured. Designs are initially conceived at a fairly high level which are mainly concerned with *system architectures*. With modern electronics design tools, high-level block schematics are produced using a graphics editor or a schematic language. This top-down approach permits the engineer to design the overall structure, deferring details until they are required, thus simplifying the design task. Partitioning then divides the functional blocks into lower-level blocks or sub-blocks, and so on, forming the hierarchy (Figure 12.2).

Each module or level in the design hierarchy is defined in terms of a set of lower-level modules. *Simulation techniques* have been developed to assist at all levels of the hierarchy, thereby allowing designers to verify, with some degree of confidence, each level before they progress down the structure. Several designers can in fact work on the same design more or less independently. The (logic) design is complete when each level can be expressed in terms of completed modules right down to device/transistor level.

Figure 12.3 shows the electronic design stages in more detail.

During the initial design phase, a schematic diagram of the circuit is produced, which displays information about the types of block used and how they are connected together. This circuit description is an abstract representation and, if the design is at a high level (that is, without reference to the actual logic components), little is known about how it will eventually be implemented.

In the jargon of CAEE this activity is referred to as *schematics capture*. Data 'captured' during this stage will include types of logic component used (extracted either from a library or created graphically at the terminal) and their interconnections. In a typical CAEE/CAED system, a variety of graphical commands will be available for this process, including design creation facilities (symbol/circuit extraction from libraries), line routing, editing (delete, move, rotate), viewing commands (zoom, pan, magnify) and many others. (See Chapter 3.)

Fig. 12.2 Hierarchically structured design, showing the different levels in the hierarchy

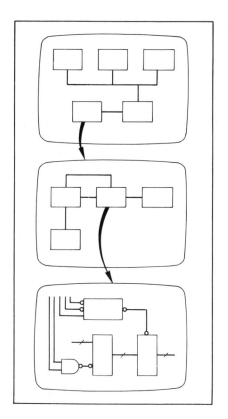

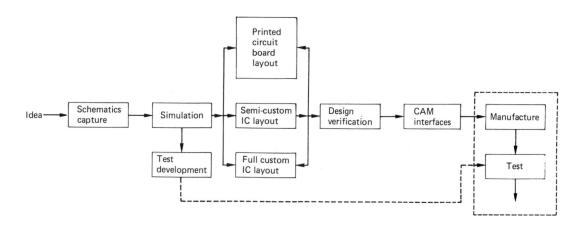

Fig. 12.3 More detailed steps in electronic design, showing the alternative implementation technologies, using PCBs and ICs

Once the design has been captured, it can be translated into another form to help verify the circuit; that is, to check that it functions as it should. Logic simulation languages are available on some CAEE systems, which enable the designer to perform the many simulation tasks (logic simulation, timing simulation, fault simulation) deemed necessary to provide confidence in the design. Once designs are simulated in some way, they are passed to the second phase which is concerned with implementation and layout.

Before CAED became widely available, PCB designs were laid out by hand on a drawing board, using coloured pencils to differentiate between the upper and lower tracking layers. Although this work could be tedious, it nevertheless required considerable skill in positioning components to ensure that adequate room was available to accommodate all the tracks. Designs were often on drawing boards for months or more, and design amendments were particularly difficult to implement. But with packing densities increasing rapidly (often using multi-layer boards) and design specification becoming more exacting, CAED became essential rather than optional. One result is that some modern board layouts appear as complex as microcircuits.

Figure 12.3 also shows where IC design fits into the overall CAEE process. With the development and easier application of microtechnology, implementing a design directly on silicon is now a real alternative to the more usual method — that of realising the design with discrete logic components and placing them onto a PCB. This new implementation route produces what are called *application specific integrated circuits* (ASICs): tailor-made chips with functions which are specific to the customer's requirements.

Logic circuits which are designed on silicon have a number of attractions. They can be more compact, contain more functions, be cheaper and (in a desire to protect proprietary designs) be almost impossible to copy. In effect, the silicon chip manufacturers themselves have significantly contributed to the development of the new generation of CAEE tools. By introducing partially designed chips, producers of gate-array and standard cell chips (both referred to as *semi-custom chips*) have created the environment for customers wishing to do their own customising (that is, producing a tailor-made finished design). Although the chip manufacturers have design facilities and offer such a service, many customers prefer to do their own design work.

2 Logic design

In the design of logic circuitry (that is, circuitry to perform various logical functions and operations), the first step usually involves the derivation of an input–output model. This identifies the input and output (logical) variables and establishes the required logical relationships between them. The usual practice is then to determine an overall logic design which will satisfy these relationships, and to construct it from a set of standard primitive logic circuits. Currently these primitives are often **logic gates**, which perform the basic lowest-level logical functions. They are treated as 'black boxes'; the details of their own internal design are essentially ignored. However, knowledge of their input–output behaviour *is* required so that they can be combined to produce more complex input–output relationships. In digital circuitry the gates most commonly used are the AND and OR gates (Figure 12.4) together with their logical complements (or inversions), the NAND and NOR gates (Figure 12.5).

The OR gate has two or more inputs and one output. Each input can have one of two states (designated 0 and 1) and the output similarly has one of these two states. The output has the state given by the logical (OR) sum of the input states, so that if any number (greater than or equal to one) of the inputs is in state 1 then the output state is 1. Otherwise, when all inputs are 0, the output is in state 0. The AND gate similarly has two or more inputs and a single

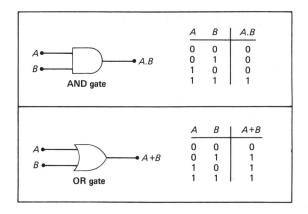

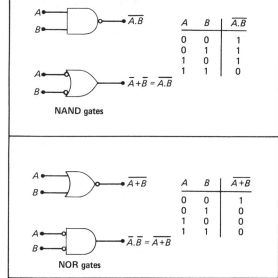

Fig. 12.4 AND and OR gates, together with their truth tables

Fig. 12.5 NAND and NOR gates, together with their truth tables

output. In this case, however, the output has state 1 only when all inputs are in state 1. Otherwise, the output is in state 0. The AND gate performs the logical (AND) product of the input states.

In practice, the NOR and NAND gates are more versatile. This is because it is possible to implement any logic expression using only NOR gates (or only NAND gates) and no other type of gate. These are essentially the same as the OR and AND gates (from which they are respectively derived), except that they include an inverter circuit which changes the original output to its logical (NOT) complement (that is, 1 is changed to 0, or 0 is changed to 1).

Logic functions are often specified in terms of a *truth table*, which lists each possible combination of input states together with the associated output states. Simple truth tables for the AND, OR, NAND and NOR gates (each having just two inputs and one output) are shown in Figures 12.4 and 12.5.

Although logic circuitry can be derived directly from simple truth tables, for more complex logic involving more variables, other methods have to be used to represent the logical relationships. Logic behaviour can be described algebraically using *logic equations*. These involve the logical AND, OR and NOT operators, and are expressed in terms of Boolean algebra (a branch of mathematics dealing with two-state logic). In Boolean algebra the basic operators are conventionally represented as follows:

AND by .
OR by +
NOT by an overbar $^{-}$

Thus for example, the algebraic statement

$$A \cdot B = C$$

means that if *A and B* are true then *C* must also be true. Logical variables can only take on two 'values' — *true* or *false* (designated 1 or 0 respectively).

Rules of Boolean algebra allow the equations initially specified to be manipulated and simplified, making the result easier to implement.

The input–output model shown in Figure 12.6 is a *full-adder* logic network. The network has three inputs; two are binary bits and the third is a 'carry' arising from a previous adder, say. The outputs are a *sum* and a new *carry*. The truth table (Figure 12.6(b)) defines the desired function for this network. By referring to this table line-by-line, the corresponding logic equations can be written down.

Fig. 12.6 (a) Full-adder input–output model. (b) Truth table for full-adder

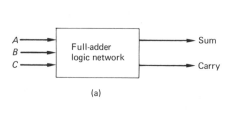

(a)

Input			Output	
A	B	C	Sum	Carry
0	0	0	0	0
0	0	1	1	0
0	1	0	1	0
0	1	1	0	1
1	0	0	1	0
1	0	1	0	1
1	1	0	0	1
1	1	1	1	1

(b)

A relationship (or *occurrence*) is produced each time 1 occurs in the output variables, making a total of eight occurrences: four in *sum* and four in *carry*. (Refer to Figure 12.6(b).)

$$sum = \bar{A}.\bar{B}.C + \bar{A}.B.\bar{C} + A.\bar{B}.\bar{C} + A.B.C$$

$$carry = \bar{A}.B.C + A.\bar{B}.C + A.B.\bar{C} + A.B.C$$

Thus the logic is expressed by these Boolean equations. The next step is to implement the design defined by these equations using basic logic gates. This procedure is illustrated by the following example. For a fuller description of digital logic design refer to Gault and Pimmel [1982].

2.1 Design example

We introduce the following example to demonstrate the processes of deriving circuitry with NAND/NOR logic gates to fulfill a particular function.

Logic circuitry is required to convert binary coded decimal (BCD) information, shown as input to the circuit diagram, into another form suitable to drive a seven-segment display, shown on the right of Figure 12.7(a) and appearing as a shaded **8** figure. Combinations of segments can be illuminated to display any decimal digit, from **0** to **9**. Converters or decoders of this kind are frequently used in practice to drive light-emitting diodes and incandescent filaments in electronic instruments.

This decoder should accept a four-bit BCD input which would normally be supplied from an adjacent module (not shown). Logic circuitry is required to convert the BCD into 'decimal digits' and output the information to appropriate segments on the seven-segment display. The logic for this type of circuit is fairly complex because each output is activated for more than one combination of inputs.

Fig. 12.7 (a) Decoder circuit diagram. (b) Truth table for decoder circuit

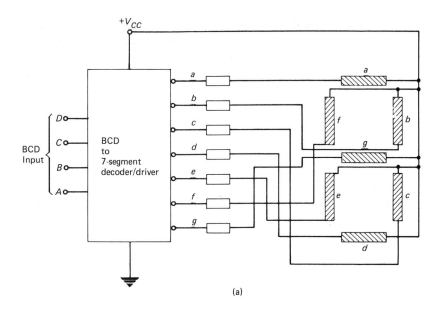

(a)

| Inputs | | | | Outputs | | | | | | | Decimal |
A	B	C	D	a	b	c	d	e	f	g	digit displayed
0	0	0	0	1	1	1	1	1	1	0	0
0	0	0	1	0	1	1	0	0	0	0	1
0	0	1	0	1	1	0	1	1	0	1	2
0	0	1	1	1	1	1	1	0	0	1	3
0	1	0	0	0	1	1	0	0	1	1	4
0	1	0	1	1	0	1	1	0	1	1	5
0	1	1	0	1	0	1	1	1	1	1	6
0	1	1	1	1	1	1	0	0	0	0	7
1	0	0	0	1	1	1	1	1	1	1	8
1	0	0	1	1	1	1	1	0	1	1	9
1	0	1	0	0	0	0	0	0	0	0	
1	0	1	1	0	0	0	0	0	0	0	'Don't care'
⋮						⋮					conditions
1	1	1	1	0	0	0	0	0	0	0	

(b)

For example, the e segment (see Figure 12.7(a)) must be activated in displaying any of the decimal numbers **0, 2, 6** and **8**; that is, whenever any of the input codes 0000, 0010, 0110 or 1000 occur at the input. Clearly, using this procedure it is possible to define the active cases for each segment. For example, a is required to display **0, 2, 3, 5, 7, 8** or **9**.

The entries in the truth table (Figure 12.7(b)) are defined by identifying the segments that must be activated to display the symbol corresponding to the input BCD. For example, for the value **0** to be indicated on the display, the input condition is as shown in the first row of the truth table, displaying segments a, b, c, d, e and f. In the truth table, a 1 represents an activation and 0 a deactivation. This procedure is repeated for the other nine rows.

Unused input cases 1010 to 1111 can be treated so as to produce no active segments (blank display) — these are referred to as 'don't care' conditions.

Once the truth table has been set up, Boolean expressions for each output relating to each segment can be obtained, simplified and then implemented. Only the relationship for segment a is produced here, in logic equation form:

$$a = \bar{A} . \bar{B} . \bar{C} . \bar{D} + \bar{A} . \bar{B} . C . \bar{D} + \bar{A} . \bar{B} . C . D + \bar{A} . B . \bar{C} . D +$$
$$\bar{A} . B . C . \bar{D} + \bar{A} . B . C . D + A . \bar{B} . \bar{C} . \bar{D} + A . \bar{B} . \bar{C} . D$$

It is now necessary to implement these relationships in actual digital logic gates. The gates have to be connected in the ways determined by the logic equations. However, it is important in good electronics design to aim for an efficient implementation. Thus, although the above equation for a is a valid expression describing the required functional relationship, it is not in the most economical form for implementation. The expression can be *minimised* by using Boolean algebra or graphics; one widely used graphical technique is *Karnaugh map reduction*. K-maps are frequently applied to five- and six-variable problems, but with problems of greater complexity, computational reduction techniques have to be used.

After applying K-map minimisation, the equation for a reduces to

$$a = A + B . D + C + B$$

The relationships for the remaining display segments, from b to g, are developed and minimised using the same techniques.

Figure 12.8 shows the full NAND gate implementation logic diagram for the complete seven-segment decoder network.

---

3 Logic simulation

The breadboarding approach to logic design can suffer from several disadvantages.

- It leads to an excessive development phase.
- It establishes only that the design works with a particular set of components operating within their own respective tolerances. There is the possibility therefore, which should be checked out, that the design may not work with a different set of components.

With adequate simulation facilities many of these disadvantages are overcome, although, as yet, simulation techniques have not replaced completely the need for building prototypes. In many instances, simulation precedes and reduces the breadboarding phase.

Early simulation programs were applied at *device* or *transistor level*. Extensive circuit analysis programs like SPICE (now an industrial standard) model analogue circuits and transistor parameters but require large computing support, and tend to have specialised applications. However, more manageable programs now exist for logic simulation, often referred to as *gate-level simulation*. Such programs are widely used and are an integral part of many CAEE workstations.

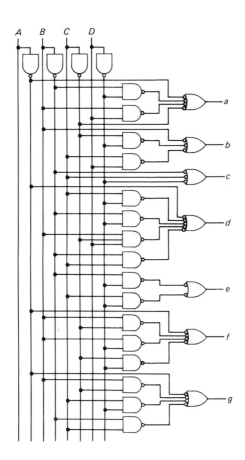

Fig. 12.8 NAND-gate logic diagram for the seven-segment decoder

Logic design, as pointed out earlier, is a hierarchical activity and the application of simulation has moved up through the hierarchy from device level to nearly all levels of the design process. At the top level, the *system architecture specification*, a suitable general-purpose language is sometimes used to predict high-level behaviour. Hardware description languages are used slightly below this level to describe the system structure and predict its behaviour — simulation at this level is referred to as *functional simulation*.

Gate-level simulation (for flip-flops, adders) uses a program that mimics the behaviour of logic elements. It can be used with different inputs to test the logic of the circuit, and the resultant outputs can be examined for correctness. While logic simulators are ideal for initial logic development, in practice the more detailed (device-level) model is important for eventual validation of the circuit.

Logic simulation programs contain built-in knowledge of how the basic logic devices (sometimes called *primitives*) behave. The user can supply information about the behaviour of more complex devices by representing them with models built up from the basic gates. Given a knowledge of the behaviour of the elements of the circuit, the simulation program needs the interconnections between these elements, and the behaviour of the circuit inputs during the time of simulation. The *net-list* provides the information about interconnections. If the circuit diagram has been drawn on a computer graphics terminal (schematics capture), it is possible to derive the net-list automatically from the information stored within the terminal. Otherwise, it is a tedious and error-prone job to create the net-list by hand.

3.1 Simulation example

Here we discuss an example which shows a simulation program being applied to a simple design; that of *half-adder* logic circuitry. The code (the program statements) is taken from the HILO system, a proprietary logic simulator, and a widely used program.

Figure 12.9 identifies the half-adder inputs and outputs and the truth table establishes the logical relationships.

A design for the half-adder is shown in Figure 12.10; it comprises one OR gate, two ANDs and one NAND.

Fig. 12.9 (a) Half-adder input–output model. (b) Truth table for half-adder

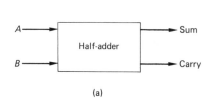

Inputs		Outputs	
A	B	Sum	Carry
0	0	0	0
0	1	1	0
1	0	1	0
1	1	0	1

(b)

Fig. 12.10 Half-adder circuit with 'identifiers' for the gates and input–output signals

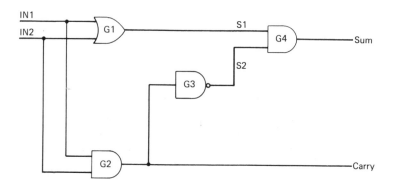

In order to simulate this logic network, each logic gate has to be given an identity, as have the input and output signals, as indicated in Figure 12.10. Next, the simulator requires a description of the connections or relationships between logic gates. The half-adder circuit can be described by the following statements which are specific to the HILO system:

```
CCT HADD (SUM, CARRY, IN1, IN2)
NAND (10, 10) G3 (S2, CARRY)
OR (10, 10) G1 (S1, IN1, IN2)
AND (10, 10) G2 (CARRY, IN1, IN2)
              G4 (SUM, S1, S2)
INPUT (IN1, IN2)
```

The first statement declares that the circuit is named HADD with outputs SUM, CARRY, and inputs IN1 and IN2. Each type of logic gate in the circuit is declared, together with its occurrence name (G1, G2, ...) and the input and output signals associated with each gate occurrence. The numbers in brackets after the gate type indicate the time taken for the output of the gate to change in response to an input change (Figure 12.11). The times may be different for the output to rise or fall, although it has been shown here as the same in both cases for convenience.

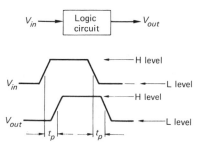

Fig. 12.11 Timing diagram, showing the propagation time t_p for example between the gate's input and output voltages

It is then necessary to specify input conditions: with the HILO system the particular code is

WAVEFORM	HADDTEST
STIMULUS	IN1, IN2 = 0;
50	IN1 = 1;
100	IN1 = 0, IN2 = 1;
150	IN1 = 1, IN2 = 1;
200	FINISH

These statements declare that we are describing a set of waveforms named HADDTEST. The input stimuli IN1 and IN2 are to start in logic state 0 and then change as shown at the specified times. The whole simulation is to end at time 200. (Note: the time units are arbitrary and are assigned by the user. Typically, however, they are nano-seconds, 10^{-9} seconds.)

The result of simulating the circuit with these input stimuli (and specifying that the behaviour of input and output signals only is to be shown) would be

TIME	IN1	IN2	SUM	CARRY
0	0	0	0	0
50	1	0	0	0
70	1	0	1	0
100	0	1	1	0
150	1	1	1	0
160	1	1	1	1
180	1	1	0	1

Interpreting these results, it is possible to check whether the logic network is behaving as required. Comparing the output results with the specified truth table (Figure 12.9(b)) shows how propagation delays affect the performance of the logic. It is up to the designer to decide whether this is satisfactory or not.

235

In practice, the propagation delay through a gate is not a fixed value but lies between fixed minimum and maximum values. This can be specified in the circuit description by replacing each single number by a pair of numbers. Correspondingly, the simulation results will show the earliest and latest possible times at which a signal will change.

Primitives within a logic simulator (AND, OR, NAND, NOR gates, etc.) are not usually inclusive of the whole range of logic devices found in electronics circuits. Devices not identified as primitives have to be modelled in terms of the primitives available in the simulator. Such models can be stored in a computer library and used as required, in much the same way as the half-adder circuit might become a stored device. It is usually not difficult to create models for medium-scale integration (MSI) devices, particularly since the manufacturers often explain the action of these devices in terms of simpler devices. However, when it comes to the more complex large-scale integration (LSI) devices, such information is not usually available and it may take several weeks of effort to devise a model for such a device. Furthermore, putting much effort into a model definition which then has infrequent use obviously negates some of the advantages of simulation. A way round this problem is being sought by using a sample of the actual device in the simulation — perhaps a contradiction in terms!

The device is plugged into a special unit connected to the computer carrying out the simulation. Reference to the model is effectively removed from the circuit net-list so that a model is not sought. The computer takes simulated signal values from the circuit, applies them as real signals to the device, monitors the device's response, and injects the response back into the simulated circuit. The timing characteristics of the device are given as data to the simulation program so that it treats the response signals as having arrived at the appropriate time, irrespective of how long it took to obtain and measure the actual response from the actual device. Most simulators will allow several actual devices to be connected in this way during simulation. This approach to modelling is one of the major differences between simulating a circuit to be built as a PCB assembly and one to be made as an integrated chip. The logic building-blocks or cells within a chip are simpler and their logical structure is known so that the modelling problem is much reduced. Conversely, timing is much more important within a chip and it is often necessary to take into account signal path delays which are ignored in a printed circuit board.

3.2 Fault simulation and test generation

As yet we have considered simulation only as a means of establishing the logical correctness of a circuit. However, it can also be used to assess the testability of the circuit. In fact many of the logic simulators can also be applied to develop and validate test programs. In PCB design, functional testing accesses only the inputs and outputs of the board. For effective testing a set of test inputs should provide a high level of test coverage. Thus many CAED design packages for PCBs come with simulators that provide both logic and fault simulation.

Many physical faults within a logic gate or on a printed circuit board have an effect which is equivalent to a signal being held in a fixed state — 'stuck-at-1' or 'stuck-at-0', generally abbreviated to SA1 and SA0. The circuit is first simulated with a given set of input stimuli and the circuit response determined assuming a fault-free circuit. The simulation is then repeated with the same inputs but with each signal to each gate in turn being held fixed at 1 and 0 successively. If any signal being held fixed (SA1, SA0) causes the circuit response to differ at any time from the fault-free response, then the presence of a fault equivalent to that signal being SA1 or SA0 can be detected with those inputs.

However, other faults may cause the same difference from the fault-free response and then the particular set of test inputs being used indicate only that one of that set of faults is present. For the presence of a fault to be detected and for that fault to be uniquely identified it is necessary for the test inputs to cause the circuit response to differ uniquely from the fault-free response.

By carrying out the above exercise the designer can establish:

(a) whether any potential 'stuck-at' faults cannot be detected;
(b) whether there are any large groups of faults which cannot be distinguished;
(c) whether unduly large numbers of test inputs are required to avoid the previous two problems.

The resolution of these conflicts is often a management decision based on the nature of the product and on the amount of subsequent system testing which a PCB assembly will receive. A test program for a board to be used in a large system will typically aim to detect 90–95% of potential stuck-at faults on a board, since the cost of detecting a fault increases by a factor of ten at each successive stage of assembly. (This factor of ten is only a rule of thumb but it is borne out remarkably consistently in practice.) The test inputs are usually devised manually and so there are strong incentives to keep the number of input patterns as small as possible. Although some fault simulators will generate test patterns, they are more successful in dealing with combinatorial rather than sequential logic — and the majority of present-day circuits are sequential in nature. Work is being carried out on programs which will generate test patterns based on a knowledge of the circuit but this is at an early stage.

As a footnote to this section on testability, it is worth noting an alternative approach to test program generation. Within this approach, strict control is imposed on the designer of circuits, so that circuits are designed to be more easily testable. In other words, the responsibility for circuit testing is placed within the brief of the designer. The method works by introducing into the design processes a strict set of rules that should be followed for both circuit design and PCB design — rules intended to make the testing phase easier. This approach is perhaps an example of design and manufacture coming together in a more formal manner.

4 Physical layout

We now consider the problems of implementing an electronic design. We concentrate on the physical layout aspect and in particular examine two important layout areas: printed circuit boards (PCBs) and integrated circuits (ICs).

4.1 PCB design

Even though many more designs are now being implemented directly onto silicon, with the aid of the new CAEE tools, the PCB still retains its dominant role in supporting, fixing and interconnecting the components used to make an electronic circuit (after all, even ASICs have to be mounted somewhere). In itself, the PCB represents significant technological progress by replacing an otherwise tedious and error-prone task of making wired interconnections manually.

The PCB is a sheet of insulating material (paper- or glass-based laminates) with the interconnection pattern etched in copper, on one or both surfaces of the board. Multi-layer boards, with up to 32 separate layers, are bound together with links between the boards. Holes are drilled through the material to accept component mounting leads that are soldered onto the copper surface. Unwanted copper is selectively etched away to leave only the tracking required to connect components.

Actual manufacture of PCBs is essentially a two-stage process, involving initially a sequence of electro-mechanical processes and mechanical operations which produce a bare board. After that the unpopulated boards are fitted-out with electronic components. Although the latter assembly operation can be carried out manually, and often is, it is a process which is increasingly being automated, particularly for volume production. In practice, a variety of semi-automatic and dedicated automatic machines assist in PCB manufacture. New and more flexible technologies being applied include the use of surface mounted devices (which are smaller, cheaper and easier to manipulate) and robotics for automated assembly.

Modern PCB design systems have features similar to those found in logic design systems. Included in many such CAED systems are schematics and draughting facilities which can capture data. Libraries are available with standard parts, symbols, and component descriptions. Layering techniques are used where different layers (or files) within the computer separately model electrical items such as route tracks, copper areas and edge connections. Other layers can be used for documentation and the production of part lists for manufacture. Design rule checking is performed automatically by many systems. Typically systems check tracks, pads, etc. for spacing violations against user-defined parameters.

With modern CAEE tools, layout (the placement and routing of track) can be done interactively (manually) or automatically — many systems allow both options to be used at appropriate times by the designer. Automatic routines rely on placement and routing algorithms to determine (with varying degrees of success) the optimum positions for components and track. Current design practice suggests that a combination of the two (interactive and automatic) is most efficient for the majority of layouts.

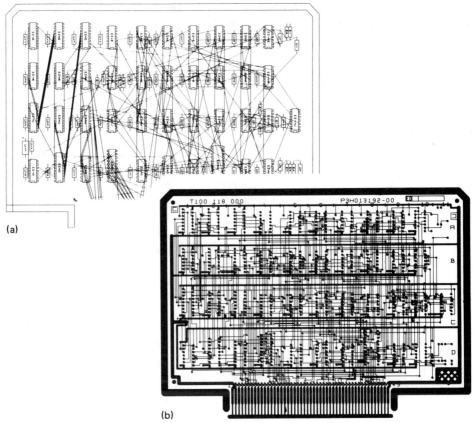

(a)

(b)

Fig. 12.12 (a) Rubber-banding and rats-nest. (b) Actual layout showing pins and track

Interactive design involves the designer intuitively placing the components in some sensible positions. Frequently components are initially placed to optimise the interconnection routing, so minimising the total track length. Placement procedures, whether manual (interactive) or automatic, must consider the design constraints, which are mainly electrical, but which can include mechanical and thermal considerations. Designs should also try to account for the problems of manufacturing, such as the provision of tooling, and whether a design can be manufactured economically.

Rubber-banding (Figure 12.12(a)) is a technique which facilitates and displays the designer's logical connections between components. Such connections, usually shown as dotted lines on the VDU, are 'elastic' connections: when components are interactively moved around the board, their connectivity is maintained. The screen image of such connectivity is often called the **rats-nest**. These rubber-band connections form the basis of the routing of the track. It is the designer's task to manipulate and translate the logical connections into physical track, bearing in mind electrical constraints such as non-coincident tracks, minimal track clearances, etc. (Figure 12.12(b)).

The problem of devising appropriate component placement and routing of track is one amenable to computer solution. A lot of research effort has been put into the development of *routing algorithms* to automate this process, much of the work originating from large-scale integrated circuit design.

Traditionally, the task of layout by automatic means is split into three stages: the placement, the 'loose' routing, and the final routing. At each stage, mainly heuristic methods are used, and approaches similar to the procedures used in interactive design are often applied.

Loose routing, or global routing, is in effect a preliminary stage before final routing. It is concerned with laying down channels, through which individual connections are later made. Only during the final routing is the actual detail included, and frequently at that stage not all the routing can fit into available areas. In such situations, it is often left to the designer to 'clean up' after the router has finished, trying to squeeze extra connections into impossible areas.

Good placement is regarded as the key ingredient to a successful design. In early CAED systems, the minimum total routing length was a major placement objective. Experience has shown that while compactness is a worthy aim, this objective leads to crowded and unroutable channels.

Some routes may often be found quickly by a 'line search' algorithm which starts at the source and moves in an x- or y-direction towards the destination. When it meets an obstacle it changes direction orthogonally and repeats this until it either reaches the destination or gives up. Although line routing algorithms can be very fast, they are often very inflexible and not particularly well able to deal with complex boards.

An algorithm which will find a route if one exists, but often at a high price in computing time, is Lee's algorithm. Most proprietary autorouters are based on Lee's algorithm, though many differences exist in its actual implementation. This algorithm divides the areas into a grid of squares. Each square touching the square containing the source is 'marked' with a number 1. Each unmarked square touching a square numbered 1 is marked 2. This process, which is equivalent to propagating a diamond-shaped wavefront from the source, is continued with successive numbers until either the destination square is numbered, or there are no free squares left. If the destination is reached then any path of sequentially numbered squares from source to destination is a potential route. Most commercial routing programs use more than one algorithm in a strategy to optimise the number of successful routings in a reasonable time.

4.2 IC layout

Logic design on silicon is supported by a whole range of computer tools, carefully structured so that they match existing design practices. These include the software equivalents of the familiar standard logic components, catalogued to be called upon and used in the design. The problem of producing the geometrical configurations corresponding to the design has been made easier by severely limiting the possible range of silicon geometry in advance. In the **gate-array** approach, the design is completely determined except for the final layer of metallisation which the user then specifies in order to implant the design. With **standard cells**, the silicon structures of the various cells are pre-designed and held in software form.

Semi-custom technologies, the gate-array and standard cell, have been developed to reduce the chip design time and to bring customising within the bounds of the user. (Design and fabrication for full custom chips can take between nine months and two years.)

Unlike the gate-array, the standard cell with its partially constrained geometry does not in fact reduce the number of fabrication processes as all the layers on the chip still have to be fabricated for each individual ASIC. It does, however, speed up the design process and reduce errors. To a designer, it is similar to PCB layout. A library of pre-defined cells (logic elements, gates, counters, etc.) stored as software macros are contained within the layout design system. The designer tells the system which cells and which interconnections are required. The logic cells selected by the designer are translated and positioned by the layout software in rows, between which are wiring channels. With some standard cell systems, the user can enter placement information, if say several cells should be placed close together. Otherwise design rules determine the precise placement of the cells, such as that all inputs and outputs lie on the edge of a cell. Routing algorithms select connection paths corresponding to the designer's functional specification. Where possible the algorithms try to minimise wiring length, although this does not always guarantee minimum chip area. Often the automatic placement and routing system will not produce a chip of the desired size or performance. When this occurs the designer must intervene to modify the placement and wiring. Many commercial systems allow both automatic and interactive design.

The *gate-array* (uncommitted logic array) consists of a regular matrix of identical components or functional elements (Figure 12.13). This chip has been through all fabrication processes except the final metallic coating (the interconnection stage) — used for tailoring to the customer's specific needs. Using a gate-array is rather like forming a circuit from a PCB containing hundreds of identical transistors by connecting them together to provide the required circuit.

Fig. 12.13 (*Left*) Uncommitted logic array. (*Right*) Completed logic array chip

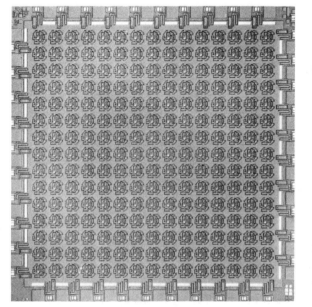
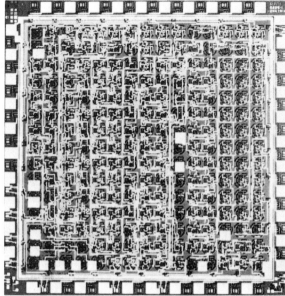

Fig. 12.14 (a) A (4 × 4) cell section of a gate-array, showing uncommitted cells. (b) One array cell, showing an overlaid grid for reference

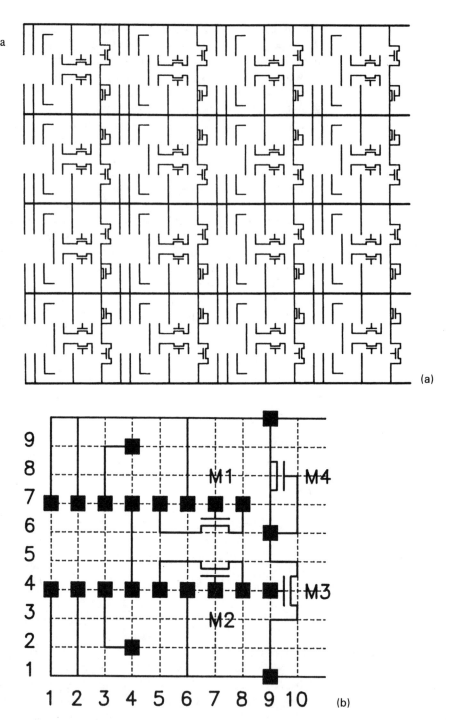

Gate-array layout, pioneered and known as a 'master slice layout' by IBM (where the technology is extensively used in their computers), is a variant of standard cell layout that takes advantage of manufacturing economies of scale. Internal structures can be sets of transistors, complete NAND gates (the usual form), or other functional elements. Gate-array layouts are more constrained than standard cells because in the array all cells are identical and the amount of wiring space available is pre-defined.

A section of a gate-array, one specially designed for educational and teaching purposes, is shown in Figure 12.14. It shows the pre-defined structures and identical cells in more detail. These cells of transistors can be configured in many ways to perform a range of logic functions. To implement a previously defined logic circuit, the task for the designer is to select and form the interconnections within the cells. Figure 12.14(b) shows, in schematic form, a basic gate-array cell with an overlaid grid provided by a graphics editor (part of a CAED system) to allow identification of the features to which the connections should be made.

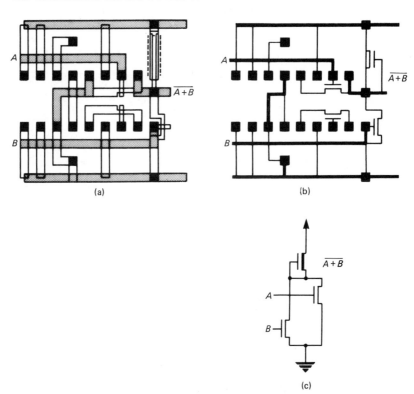

Fig. 12.15 (a) NOR gate configuration: metallisation routes (shown in heavy shaded lines). (b) Schematic with connections and grid. (c) Cell circuit diagram

In configuring a cell to produce, say, a NOR gate implementation, corresponding track or connections need to be made between certain transistors (Figure 12.15). Metallic tracking is shown as shaded lines in Figure 12.15(a). Defining the metal connections in this way effectively 'commits' the gate-array cells to, in this example, a NOR gate. Naturally, in this instance, a knowledge of how the transistor devices operate and what connections should be made is necessary to produce the implementation.

With this particular cell, it is necessary to make use of the 'cross-unders' where the signals descend into and through the underlying silicon structure, leaving room for metal to be routed straight through the cell. Also, this cell has metal power-supply lines pre-defined and cannot be reconfigured. The only way to achieve these connections is to make use of cross-unders.

Gate-array layout is frequently performed automatically, unlike the exercise above, which has been developed to demonstrate the process of IC gate-array design. Layout algorithms which map logic specifications onto the logic gates require correspondence between the functional description and the physical structures on the chip, thus specifying the wiring between the gates.

Designing directly onto silicon is likely to predominate in the future. Many would argue that, since silicon is a fundamentally different medium from the PCB, the tools should be developed to emphasise this direct approach, rather than translating some of the limitations of PCB technology into the new tools. In their most developed form, the tools adopt the approach which emphasises hierarchy and structure, so that a design can be specified at a high level in a structured format, relying on software to translate the design directly onto silicon. The *silicon compiler*, a concept that owes much to software engineering, is used to describe such systems.

Architecture—spatial layout

13

P Steadman

1 Introduction

Many of the types of computer method and computer-aided design package described in previous chapters have found applications in computer-aided architectural design. Thus two-dimensional draughting systems are now widely used by architects; there is some use of three-dimensional modelling systems; and a great variety of separate programs have been developed for analysing building designs and for simulating their performance.

The greatest emphasis in analysis has been on structural calculations and on the prediction of heat flow through buildings. But other programs have been produced, for example: for modelling ventilation and air movement in buildings; for modelling the penetration of natural light and the shadows cast by buildings; for measuring the acoustic properties of rooms; and for predicting the movement of people and goods through buildings and estimating the patterns of use of corridors and lifts. Advanced computer graphic techniques have been applied to the production of architectural perspectives, some examples of which are illustrated in colour plates 11,12. Another large field for computer applications in building has been for making cost estimates and drawing up schedules of materials, components and labour; indeed some of the earliest users of computers in the building industry were the quantity surveyors whose job this is.

2 The nature of building geometry

In this chapter we will concentrate very selectively on some problems and approaches in computer-aided design which are peculiar to architecture. These problems arise from the special nature of the geometry of buildings, and the particular kinds of functions which buildings fulfil. In mechanical or electronic design the focus is on the forms and materials of the physical components from which the machine or circuit is built up. In buildings by contrast the principal functions are met by the *spaces* which the physical components enclose: the architect is as concerned with designing voids as with designing solids.

We can think of building design, then, in two ways. Either it is a process of putting together the solid components of construction — bricks, beams, tiles — so as to form walls, floors, ceilings and roofs which in turn are assembled to enclose the rooms. Or it is a process of manipulating spaces, arranging them together, and then inserting walls, floors, ceilings and roofs between and around these spaces. Of course the two ways of seeing the matter are quite complementary, and in practice the architect moves backwards and forwards between thinking about the solids and thinking about the voids. But the distinction is a useful one for computer-aided design, and different programs for aiding the process of spatial layout in architecture have tended to emphasise one or the other view.

Thinking about the solids first, the great majority of buildings have an overall rectangular geometry, and many of their constructional components — timber joists, bricks and blocks, concrete planks and panels — approximate to cuboids. The average building comprises a very large number of separate components, but the geometry of these individual parts tends to be simple. Those components or fixtures which *do* have more complicated three-dimensional forms — wash-basins, radiators, baths — can, for the purposes of building design, still be represented as if 'boxed' within cuboids (Figure 13.1). For computer draughting of plans and elevations it is sufficient to store just orthographic projections of their shapes onto the faces of the containing box. In this way it is possible to avoid all the problems of representing sculptured surfaces and complex polyhedra which commonly occur in mechanical engineering.

This restriction to a rectangular 'box geometry' is the main reason for the otherwise perhaps surprising fact that architecture was one of the first areas of application for which three-dimensional modellers were developed in the early 1970s. Another reason was that the later 1960s and early 1970s marked the peak of popularity for prefabrication in building, and prefabrication systems lent themselves especially well to representation in tailor-made computer-aided design programs. This was because such systems are generally organised on modular rectangular grids, and put severe limits on the numbers of different types and sizes of components used in design. (At that time the fashion was also for flat roofs, which further simplified the geometrical problem!)

3 Floor plan layout

There is another obvious feature of the geometry of most buildings, and that is that they are *layered* horizontally. They are organised on one or more floor

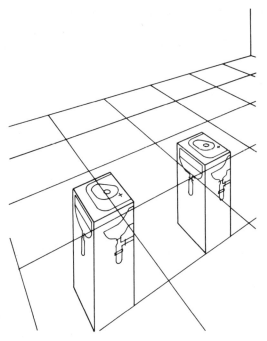

Fig. 13.1 Component of complex three-dimensional form 'boxed' in a cuboid, with orthographic projections of shape on faces of box. [From the OXSYS system developed for the Oxford Regional Health Authority by Applied Research of Cambridge Ltd.]

levels, such that on each level most if not all rooms have the same floor-to-ceiling height. The process of arranging rooms can therefore be resolved essentially into a two-dimensional task, that of organising room shapes in plan. This fact has been exploited in the many attempts made, from the mid 1960s onwards, with varying degrees of success, to generate room layouts *automatically* (although there are certainly many types of building with rooms of widely differing heights — theatres, railway terminals — whose spatial layout must be imagined and manipulated wholly in three dimensions).

Many functional and aesthetic criteria can govern the placing of rooms in plans. But one consideration of obvious practical importance is the pattern of circulation of people from one room to another. It will be convenient if rooms between which people are expected to move frequently or in large numbers are placed near to each other in the plan. That is to say this criterion relates to the *propinquity* of spaces.

In many automatic layout programs the attempt is made to construct the layout in such a way as to minimise its total 'circulation cost'. This cost objective can be stated quantitatively as follows.

Let d_{ij} be the distance between two rooms labelled with i and j in the plan. Let c_{ij} be a measure of circulation cost per unit distance between rooms i and j. Then total circulation cost is

$$\sum_{i=1}^{n} \sum_{j=1}^{n} d_{ij} c_{ij}$$

where n is the total number of rooms.

Stated in this way, the architectural layout process becomes an instance of the more general **assignment** problem. There are other practical tasks in spatial arrangement, where some similar 'cost' objective related to distance is to be minimised, which have been formulated in an analogous way: the placing of machines on a factory floor, the location of warehouses in relation to road and rail networks, and the placing of components on electronic circuit boards.

3.1 Measuring circulation costs and distances

Some questions arise immediately in the architectural case as to how to measure the distances and circulation costs. The costs are usually related to the estimated average number of journeys made, over some representative period such as a day or week, between each pair of locations. The implied assumption is that people will be using the building according to some regular, repetitive routine. These data would be obtained perhaps from surveys of people's behaviour in existing buildings of a similar functional type to the one being designed. Figure 13.2 shows an example of such data for a hospital operating suite.

The total circulation cost which is then to be minimised by the assignment is taken to be equal in this case to half the total distance travelled by all occupants of the building during the specified time period. It is only half the distance because we are counting the number of journeys, each of which involves an outward and a return trip. Alternatively, the total distance could be divided by an average walking speed and multiplied by a monetary cost per unit time (for example an average salary rate) to arrive at a total circulation cost for the layout in pounds.

A refinement of this approach might involve costing the time of different groups of occupants of the building at different rates. For example, more value might be placed in a hospital on reducing the movement of patients than on minimising the distances travelled by staff.

Another approach would be not to rely on data on journey frequencies from surveys, but instead for the architect to ask the building's future occupants to make some subjective assessments of the desired degree of 'association' between each pair of rooms. This association would be expressed as a numerical value, such that the higher the value the closer those rooms should ideally be placed in the plan.

As for the calculation of distances, the simplest way to measure these is, naturally, as straight-line distances between pairs of room centres or room entrances (Figure 13.3). However, in the final layout it is unlikely that these will be equal to the actual distances travelled. This is because in buildings of rectangular geometry the corridors will normally be aligned with the building's axes. So the actual distances people would travel between rooms would be more properly measured as *rectangular* or *taxi-cab* distances (Figure 13.4). Moreover, it is possible that in some real buildings the circulation system would involve routes more circuitous even than this.

There is a chicken-and-egg type of difficulty here. We need to estimate distances between rooms in order to construct the layout on the basis of the circulation-minimising criterion. But we can only obtain accurate measurements of those distances off the final resulting layout itself.

		1	2	3	4	5	6	7	8	9	10	11	12	13	14	15	16	17	18	19	20	21
1	Sisters' changing room																					
2	Nurses' changing room	41																				
3	Surgeons' rest room	8	4																			
4	Surgeons' changing room	0	0	295'																		
5	Superintendent's room	2	1	6	0																	
6	Medical store	0	0	0	0	3																
7	Small theatre	2	6	7	0	0	2															
8	Anaesthetic room no. 1	0	2	22	1	0	3	56														
9	Theatre no. 1	0	2	40	0	0	1	9	85													
10	Sink room	3	8	0	0	0	0	24	7	123												
11	Sterilising room	1	3	0	1	0	0	16	4	123	151											
12	Scrub up room	3	3	12	11	0	0	52	13	111	22	16										
13	Ante-space & nurses' station	5	5	85	43	11	4	113	51	111	20	13	182									
14	Theatre no. 2	0	2	40	0	0	1	9	39	32	123	123	111	111								
15	Anaesthetic room no. 2	0	2	22	1	0	3	8	56	39	7	4	13	51	85							
16	Emergency theatre	2	6	7	0	0	2	62	8	9	24	16	52	113	9	56						
17	Workroom & clean supply	7	32	7	6	3	3	13	1	15	10	13	13	31	15	1	13					
18	Sterile supply room	3	9	0	4	1	0	3	0	0	3	0	49	10	0	0	3	26				
19	Male staff changing room	9	1	11	7	0	0	2	7	8	3	1	6	50	8	7	2	27	2			
20	Nurses' station	21	14	130	2	13	2	8	14	3	0	3	8	90	3	14	8	13	33	48		
21	Entrance	10	30	21	28	6	0	3	7	0	0	0	0	16	0	7	3	5	0	50	119	

Fig. 13.2 Measures of 'association' between spaces in an operating theatre suite. These are derived from survey data on the numbers of journeys made between each pair of spaces in an existing building, over a representative period, weighted according to the salary costs of the staff involved. [Adapted from Whitehead and Eldars 1964.]

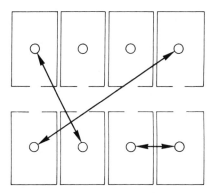

Fig. 13.3 Straight-line distances between room centres in a plan

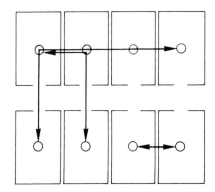

Fig. 13.4 Rectangular or taxi-cab distances between room centres in a plan

Some programs for automated architectural layout have got round this difficulty by fixing a pattern of circulation routes — a kind of 'skeleton' of corridors and lifts — in advance. One such system was developed for the 'Harness' hospitals designed by the British Department of Health and Social Security in the 1970s. The name 'Harness' referred to a predetermined structure of corridors in a branching pattern, designed such that 16-metre square structural modules could be assembled into different arrangements to form departments, wards and so on strung out along these corridors (Figure 13.5). The placement of the departments was based on a calculation of circulation costs, with the distances of trips measured along the 'Harness'.

It is clear, however, that such a procedure will have very marked consequences for the general character of the plans produced. Given a different fixed

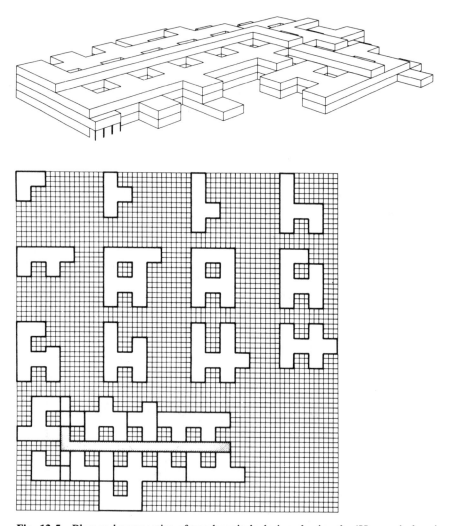

Fig. 13.5 Plan and perspective of two hospitals designed using the 'Harness' planning principles developed by the UK Department of Health and Social Security in the 1970s. Departments of standard design are arranged along a central 'harness' of circulation routes (shown shaded in the plan)

pattern of circulation routes, correspondingly different plans would result. Some of those who have developed other layout programs have tried not to constrain the process of design so rigidly at the outset. They have defined just a square grid on which the rooms are to be placed. Distances between rooms are then measured as straight-line distances or rectangular distances, with all the approximations these necessarily entail.

3.2 Grid representations of floor plans

One further problem is that in most buildings there will be requirements for rooms with different floor areas. These rooms must in general pack closely together into the plan without producing 'holes' (that is, extraneous spaces which are not rooms). In order to achieve this the shape of each room may be allowed to vary, within limits. In the layout process we also want to shuffle or permute the positions of rooms, so as to find the arrangement with least cost. The task is thus something like solving a jigsaw puzzle whose pieces have variable shapes, and may go together in many different ways.

Most programs for automated layout approach this problem by taking the unit dimension of the square grid, on which the plan is laid out, to be something like two or three metres. This is about the minimum width which any small room would take. Each room is then approximated as a set of square modules of appropriate total area. In the allocation process precautions are taken to ensure that all the modules belonging to one room are placed directly adjacent to each other. This strategy has the further advantage of allowing for the plan to be represented very simply in the machine as a two-dimensional array. The positions of modules, and hence rooms, can be labelled by integers (Figure 13.6). The automatic layout process consists then of assigning integers to suitable locations in this array.

Fig. 13.6 Rectangular plan represented by array of integers

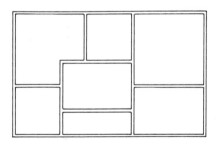

1	1	1	2	2	3	3	3
1	1	1	2	2	3	3	3
1	1	4	4	4	3	3	3
5	5	4	4	4	6	6	6
5	5	7	7	7	6	6	6

Unfortunately, the general assignment problem is currently not amenable to analytical solution, nor are there any efficient algorithms known by which arrangements of minimum cost may be found with certainty. It is therefore necessary to search for low-cost layouts by methods which involve an element of trial and error.

3.3 A worked example

Let us consider a very simplified case to explore the difficulties involved. Imagine that our problem is to design an office building with eight equal-sized rooms. These rooms are to be arranged on either side of a corridor, in the positions labelled a to h shown in Figure 13.7. Each room is to accommodate one person. Let us label the occupants themselves with the capital letters A to H. (There is not really therefore any element of spatial design here: the basic geometry of the layout is given from the start. The problem is equivalent to that of allocating eight rooms to eight individuals, in an existing building.)

Fig. 13.7 Office plan for the worked example. Distances are measured along the network marked in heavy line

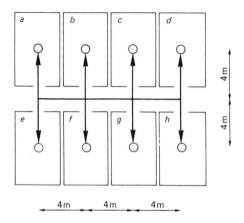

Let us suppose that, on the basis of a survey, we have data on the frequency of journeys which the occupants will make per day between the rooms in a plan, as below:

	A	B	C	D	E	F	G	H
A	.	0	0	0	5	2	0	1
B	0	.	0	4	1	0	5	0
C	0	0	.	0	0	0	0	0
D	2	3	0	.	1	0	1	0
E	4	1	0	1	.	2	1	3
F	1	0	0	0	2	.	0	1
G	0	1	0	0	0	0	.	0
H	0	0	0	0	3	2	0	.

The entry 5 in row A, column E for example shows that occupant A visits occupant E five times a day. Similarly the entry 4 in row E, column A shows that occupant E visits occupant A four times.

Adding the two triangular halves (upper right and lower left) of this table together to sum the total number of journeys in both directions between each pair of occupants, we obtain

Cost/distance table

	A	B	C	D	E	F	G	H
A	.							
B	0	.						
C	0	0	.					
D	2	7	0	.				
E	9	2	0	2	.			
F	3	0	0	0	4	.		
G	0	6	0	1	1	0	.	
H	1	0	0	0	6	3	0	.

The entry 9 in column A, row E now shows that nine journeys are made each day between the pair of rooms occupied by A and E. Let us take these values to express the 'costs' of circulation per unit distance c_{ij} between rooms i and j in the assignment.

The distances d_{ij} between the possible locations a to h for the eight rooms in the plan are as below:

Distance table

	a	b	c	d	e	f	g	h
a	.							
b	12	.						
c	16	12	.					
d	20	16	12	.				
e	8	12	16	20	.			
f	12	8	12	16	12	.		
g	16	12	8	12	16	12	.	
h	20	16	12	8	20	16	12	.

These distances are measured in metres between room centres taking routes along the corridor, as shown in Figure 13.7. They are not (all) rectangular distances, since in some cases the routes double back. They are (rather schematic and idealised) measurements of the actual distances travelled.

For any given assignment of occupants to room locations we can now calculate the total circulation cost, by evaluating the expression

$$\sum_{i=1}^{8} \sum_{j=1}^{8} d_{ij} c_{ij}$$

This involves multiplying each entry in the cost/distance table by the corresponding entry in the distance table. Let us suppose that occupant A is in location a, occupant B in location b, and so on in alphabetical order. We then obtain a third cost table as below:

Cost table	Aa	Bb	Cc	Dd	Ee	Ff	Gg	Hh
Aa	.							
Bb	0	.						
Cc	0	0	.					
Dd	40	112	0	.				
Ee	72	24	0	40	.			
Ff	36	0	0	0	48	.		
Gg	0	72	0	12	16	0	.	
Hh	20	0	0	0	120	48	0	.

Thus the cost/distance value 9 in column A, row E is multiplied by the distance 8 in column a, row e, to give a cost value of 72 in column Aa, row Ee above.

All entries in this cost table must now be summed, to give a total circulation cost for the layout of 660 (expressed in metres, and equal to half the total distance travelled by all occupants per day, as explained previously).

In principle at least, the simplest way of finding that assignment of rooms to locations which has *lowest* total cost would be to generate exhaustively all possible permutations of arrangement, calculate the cost in every case, and identify the 'cheapest'. The main objection to this approach is that the numbers of such permutations grow very rapidly with the numbers of rooms involved. The number of different possible assignments of n items to n locations is given by $n!$. Values of $n!$ for $n = 1$ to 10 are shown below:

n	$n!$	n	$n!$
1	1	6	720
2	2	7	5040
3	6	8	40 320
4	24	9	362 880
5	120	10	3 628 800

Even in our illustrative example the number of arrangements to be compared is over forty thousand, although this number can be reduced to nearer ten thousand by considerations of symmetry, since in this particular plan-form many possible arrangements will be mirror-image reflections of others. For eleven rooms the number would be nearly forty million. Clearly even using computers such a method of exhaustively generating and testing arrangements becomes impractical for larger numbers of rooms or floor-space modules.

4 Random sampling layout methods

Obviously many of the plans generated as suggested in the last section would only differ trivially from one another, and their circulation costs would be almost equivalent. It is not essential therefore to search for the *absolute* least cost solution. Perhaps it will be quite adequate to find some arrangement with *relatively* low cost. One simple way to do this is to generate a sample of different arrangements by assigning floor-space modules or rooms to grid locations *at random*. Each of these random arrangements is then costed and the cheapest chosen. A method of this kind has been published by Nugent, Vollmann & Ruml [1968].

Other methods, such as the ALDEP program of Seehof & Evans [1967], use some simple rules to generate part of each candidate solution formally, while generating the remainder of the arrangement randomly.

The success of the random sampling approach depends on two things: the size of the sample taken, relative to the size of the 'space' of all possible arrangements; and how evenly, or otherwise, solutions of reasonably low cost are distributed throughout this space. Let us imagine such a space, in a rather informal way, as if it consisted of a continuous curved surface somewhat like a landscape of hills and valleys. Solutions which are similar (let us say they differ only by the positions of a pair of rooms or floor-space modules) lie adjacent in x or y to each other on the surface. Meanwhile the dimension z of height represents cost, decreasing upwards. Thus relatively low-cost solutions are represented by the peaks of the hills in this 'landscape'. The absolutely lowest cost arrangement is on the top of the highest peak.

If the landscape is flattish with many low hills, then a random search process has a good chance of finding a good low-cost solution. If the landscape has only one or a few steep peaks however, then the chances of finding these at random are poor. Fortunately architectural and similar layout problems seem to be of the former flattish character.

5   Improvement layout methods

Another class of computer layout methods can be conceived as carrying out searches in a more systematic way across such surfaces. At each stage small changes are made in the layout, and measurements made to see whether the total cost decreases or increases as a result. If the cost decreases, the change is retained. This is equivalent in our landscape analogy to moving small distances across the surface to find the slope of the ground, and then moving always *up* the slope. Indeed such methods are referred to as **hill-climbing** procedures.

Returning to the earlier worked example, let us suppose that a search of this kind starts from the arrangement shown in Figure 13.8, where occupant A is assigned a room in location a, etc.

Now suppose that the positions of each pair of room occupants are swapped in turn, and the costs calculated for every new layout. If the change results in an increased cost, the occupants are returned to their original positions. If the change results in a decreased cost, however, the new positions are retained and the search goes on. The number of possible pairwise swaps of n items is given by

$$\frac{n!}{2(n-2)!}$$

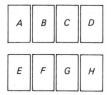

Fig. 13.8 Assignment of occupants to rooms, used as starting point for worked example of 'improvement' procedure (see Figure 13.9)

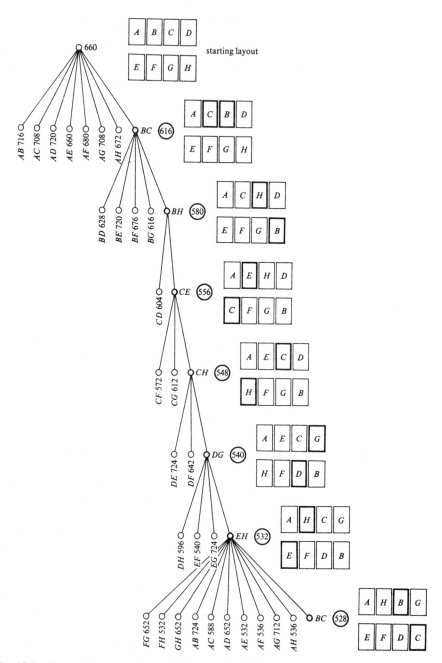

Fig. 13.9 Successive steps in worked example of 'improvement' layout procedure. The sequence of swaps of room occupants is illustrated as a tree. *AB* indicates a possible swap of *A* with *B*, etc. The figures give total layout costs for each permutation of arrangement. Successful swaps, resulting in decreased costs (ringed figures), are shown by heavy outlines round the respective rooms in the plan

For our eight-room example this represents 28 swaps. Even if the complete cycle of swaps has to be repeated several times, this still obviously represents a very restricted search compared with going through all ten thousand or so distinct possible arrangements exhaustively.

Let us assume that the order chosen for making the exchanges is A with B, A with C, etc., up to A with H; then B with C, B with D, etc., up to B with H; then C with D, etc. The results are illustrated in the form of a tree in Figure 13.9. Each node of the tree represents a room layout, and each branch the swapping of two rooms. The process continues until a complete cycle of swaps is tried without effecting any further decrease in cost. This happens in the example after only seven swaps have been made. The circulation cost is reduced from 660 at the start to 528 at the end.

Unfortunately this is not the arrangement of lowest possible cost. Figure 13.10 shows a solution whose cost is 492 units, produced by a method we shall examine shortly. (Even this may not be the cheapest possible.) The present method has climbed the wrong hill. The result it has produced is determined by the particular arrangement chosen as the starting point. If we look closer we can see why this is so.

Occupants A and E both start at the *end* of the corridor. They make numerous trips between each other's rooms. So when the effort is made to move *either A or E* away from these locations, the result is always an increase in cost. Both occupants, but E in particular, also make many visits and are visited frequently themselves by other occupants, as the cost/distance table shows. It would be better for this reason if E and A were both located in the centre of the plan. If they were so positioned, as in the arrangement of Figure 13.10, the total cost would be significantly lowered. But this could only be achieved by moving both A and E *together* — something of course the present method can never do.

There are several ways of getting round this difficulty. Either a number of different starting arrangements might be generated at random, so effectively combining random sampling with this kind of 'improvement' procedure. Or else the starting arrangement might be produced by the architect intuitively, and the computer method then used to try to make improvements.

The worked example has illustrated the principles behind a number of actual floor plan layout programs, starting with Armour & Buffa's CRAFT system [1963]. One difference between CRAFT and the worked example is that in CRAFT the complete cycle of pairwise swaps is evaluated first. Then that exchange which produces the greatest decrease in cost is made, the complete cycle of swaps evaluated again and so on, until no further improvement results. Figure 13.11 illustrates a sample layout for an industrial building, generated by CRAFT. Each department is approximated as a number of ten-foot-square floor-space modules. The cost to be minimised is the annual cost of moving materials between departments. The figure shows the starting layout produced by hand, and the final layout, giving a cost reduction of 23%. Notice how roughly half the departments remain completely unchanged.

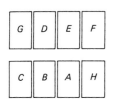

Fig. 13.10 Assignment of occupants to rooms in worked example, with total circulation cost of 492 units

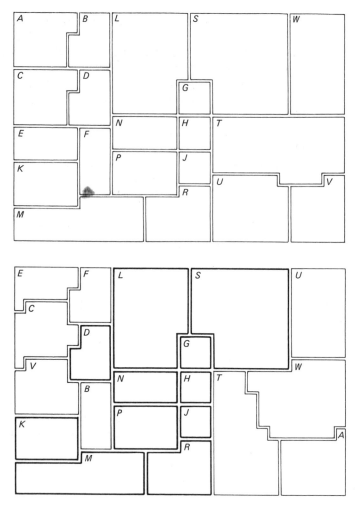

Fig. 13.11 Sample layout for an industrial plant layout problem, generated by the CRAFT system [from Armour & Buffa 1963]. The cost to be minimised is that of moving materials between departments. The starting layout (produced by hand) is shown above, and the final layout (produced by CRAFT) shown below. Departments in heavy outline have not been moved

6 Additive layout methods

Programs embodying improvement procedures such as CRAFT start from a complete layout and try to lower its cost by making incremental changes. They are perhaps best suited to problems such as office or factory layout, where the shape of the building envelope and possibly also the positions of corridors and lifts can be fixed at the outset, and the job of the designer is to arrange or rearrange rooms or machinery within these constraints. Authors of other programs have sought to assemble plans piecewise, one room or floor-space module at a time, without constraining the overall form of the plan so rigidly from the start. These have been called *additive* procedures.

We can illustrate some of the principles of additive layout methods with our worked example. Imagine in this case that the same eight rooms are to be placed along a corridor as before, but starting with a single room and adding others around it one at a time. The first decision to be made is what *order* to place the rooms in.

Let us define the measure of *association* between any pair or group of occupants, in this case, as the total number of journeys made daily by these individuals to each other. It would seem reasonable to position a room first, in the centre of the plan, for that occupant who has the strongest association with all others. In the example this is occupant E. The second room will be allocated to that occupant who has the strongest association with E. This is occupant A. The third room will be allocated to the occupant who has the strongest association with those already placed, i.e. with *both* E and A together; and so on. In the example this means that the order of placing is E, A, F, H, D, B, G, C.

Figure 13.12 shows successive steps in the placing of the eight rooms. The criterion for *where* to place each room, is in that place, adjacent to those already placed, which results in the least increase in total circulation cost (measured as before). Occupant E is placed first, and occupant A in a room opposite, since this minimises the distance between them. There are four potential positions for occupant F, in each of which the cost increase is the same. One of these is therefore selected arbitrarily. There are again four potential positions for occupant H, but they vary in their incremental cost; and so the position producing least cost increase is selected. The figure illustrates at the bottom the completed layout, whose total circulation cost is 492.

This procedure is similar to one employed in the earliest published additive method, that of Whitehead & Eldars [1964]. In the worked example we have constrained the layout along a predetermined circulation route; but many authors of these methods have, as mentioned, sought to avoid such prior constraints.

Whitehead and Eldars' method, for example, assembles layouts on a square grid of indefinite extent. Figure 13.13 shows a layout for a hospital operating theatre suite produced by their program, on the basis of the journey data shown earlier in Figure 13.2. Twenty-one rooms are each approximated by a number of ten-foot-square floor-space modules. As this plan illustrates, it is a natural tendency for such a method to cluster rooms concentrically around the space or spaces with highest association values.

Other programs take very similar approaches, but rather than positioning rooms using a travel-minimising criterion, they work instead to satisfy a series of *adjacency* requirements, that spaces be located next to each other. The DOMINO program of Mitchell & Dillon [1972] is of this type. Figure 13.14 shows a large 'landscape' office layout produced by DOMINO, laid out within a fixed perimeter and with the positions of lifts, staircases and other services also preassigned.

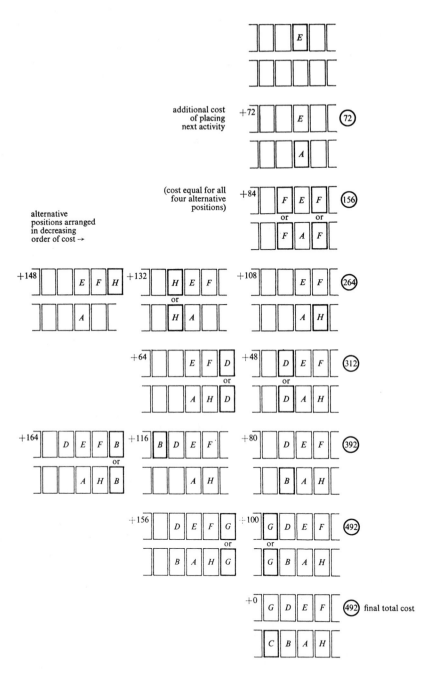

Fig. 13.12 Successive steps in worked example of 'additive' layout procedure. Each level in the figure corresponds to the placing of one room occupant. The plan diagrams indicate in heavy outline the alternative rooms available, with their associated costs in each case. The ringed figure gives the cumulative cost of the partial layout

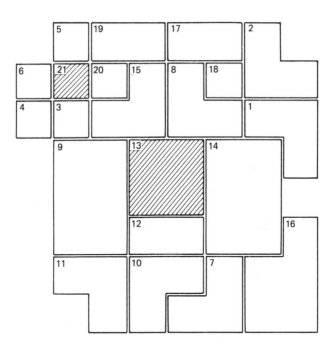

Fig. 13.13 Layout for hospital operating suite produced by the program of Whitehead & Eldars [1964]. Circulation spaces are shown shaded. Rooms are clustered concentrically around the principal circulation space (13) and the two theatres (9 and 14)

7   Reasons for failure of automated layout methods

It is in the field of large-scale office planning that automated layout programs have found most commercial application. Otherwise, it has to be said, the history of these programs has not been one of great success. Many have not got beyond the research and development stage. It is still well worth looking at these techniques however, and the reasons for their failure, because they throw light on the more general and very profound problems which are likely to beset all attempts to automate synthesis, to be discussed in Chapter 16.

There seem to be at least three causes of failure. The first is that architects do not find it difficult to produce layouts of reasonably low circulation cost by hand, especially for smaller buildings. If equipped with an interactive computer aid, allowing the designer to generate layouts intuitively, with the machine then evaluating their circulation cost, the designer can compete effectively with automated layout procedures.

The second failing is that most layout programs seek to optimise the plan on the basis of a single criterion of performance, that of circulation of people or the movement of materials. This may possibly be the overriding criterion in, say, the placement of machines on a factory floor, but in architecture more generally the designer's job is to reconcile many different functional criteria (not to mention aesthetic considerations). For example, the additive type of layout program tends, as we have seen, to produce deep concentric plans. In most buildings, however, the fact that the majority of rooms need windows

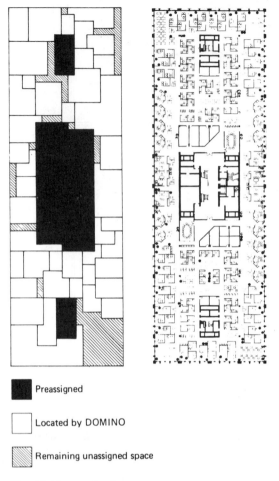

Preassigned

Located by DOMINO

Remaining unassigned space

Fig. 13.14 (*Left*) Floor plan of an office block, generated by the DOMINO program of Mitchell & Dillon [1972] for Morganelli-Heumann and Associates, Los Angeles. The positions of circulation and service cores (shown in black) are preassigned. (*Right*) The plan developed in detail by hand

for natural lighting and to provide views means that their forms are elongated into blocks or wings. The satisfaction of these other requirements can thus often work against the absolute minimisation of circulation cost.

A third weakness of many layout programs is that they generate large numbers of unsatisfactory permutations of arrangement blindly, like monkeys failing to type Shakespeare. An experienced designer would never consider most of these possibilities, since they fail rather elementary tests of performance. What is required is some means for generating much more restricted classes of candidate solutions, all of which can be guaranteed to meet certain minimal criteria of performance. This question is pursued further in Chapter 16.

Recommended reading
Eastman [1975] and Mitchell [1977].

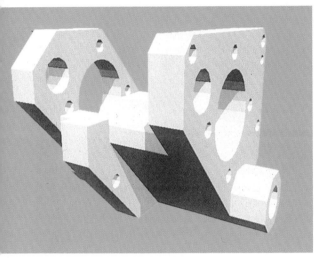

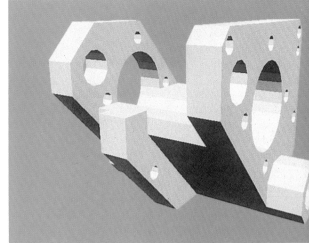

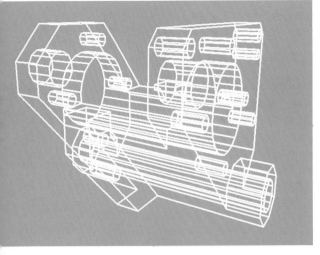

1. (*Top left*) Perspective view of wire-frame model

2. (*Top right*) Surfaces shaded and hidden surfaces removed

3. (*Bottom left*) Cast shadows, calculated by ray-tracing

4. (*Bottom right*) Appearances of rust created by fractal techniques

Plates 1–4 produced with the DORA solid modeller, by John Woodwark and Adrian Bowyer, School of Engineering, Bath University. See Woodwark and Bowyer 1986.

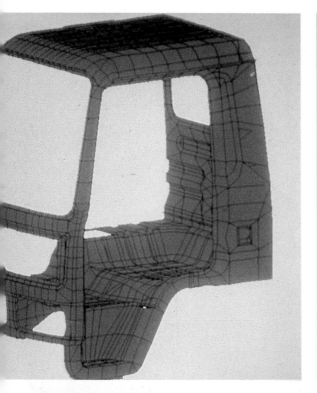
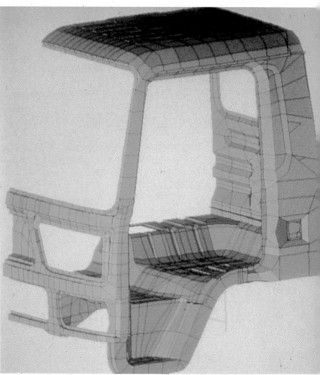
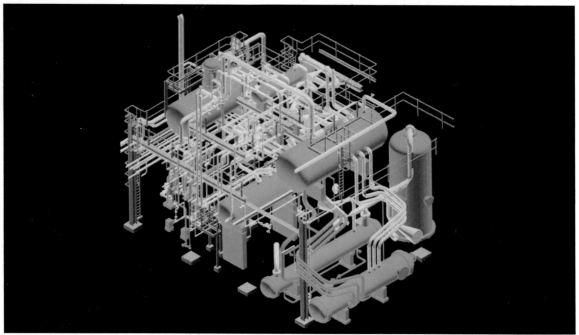

5. (*Top left*) Finite element mesh for lorry cab (*PAFEC*)

6. (*Top right*) Colour-shaded lorry cab (*PAFEC*)

Symbolic use of colour (Plates 7 and 8)

7. (*Bottom*) Colour to aid visualisation in isometric view of plant and pipe layout. (*Computervision*)

8. Use of colour in integrated circuit design, showing
graphics workstation with display, keyboard and
graphics tablet. The operator uses a stylus to select
commands from a menu. (*Computervision*)

Aircraft simulators
(Plates 9 and 10)

9. Landscape from Sogitec GI 10000 simulator system, intended for training helicopter pilots and gunners in tanks. The images of other vehicles can be made to move through the landscape. (*Sogitec Document*)

10. Harrier jump-jet refuelling. Notice cloud effects, solar shadows, surface patterns on the ground and on the truck bodies, tyre-marks on the runway and leaves on the trees. (*Rediffusion Simulation*)

Architectural interiors
(Plates 11 and 12)

11. A computer room
lit by a window. The
window is treated as an
area source.
(*Top*) Direct illumina-
tion only.
(*Bottom*) With direct
illumination, plus
indirect illumination
produced by inter-
reflection.

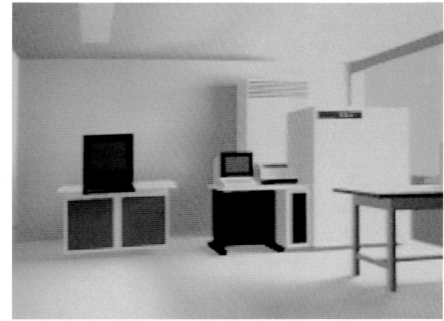

12. (*Top*) Traditional Japanese room illuminated by a point source of artificial light. Note the shadows (including the shadow of the plant), and the fall-off of illumination levels with distance from the source. Patterns on the mats, table cloth, sliding doors and hanging picture are produced by texture mapping.

Plates 11 and 12 by E. Nakamae and T. Nishita, Faculty of Engineering, Hiroshima University.

Photomontage

13. (*Bottom*) Waste incineration plant in Norway. Computer-generated image of the building super-imposed on a photograph of the actual site. (*Architecture and Building Aids Computer Unit, Strathclyde University*)

Fractal landscapes

14. Fractal landscapes generated by the Fast Fourier Transform filtering method. The two images are produced by varying the surface roughness effect for the same basic landscape. The surface height variations are scaled (relative to water level) by a power law: (*above*) Height^3, (*bottom*) Height$^{1/3}$.
(*Richard M. Voss, IBM Thomas J. Watson Research Centre*)

Ray-tracing

15. Ray-traced image showing shadows, highlights,
specular reflections and refraction at curved surfaces.
(*Apollo Computer*)

Realism in computer graphics

P Steadman

1 Introduction

Many of the drawings of solid objects seen in previous chapters are *wire-frame* images, in which all edges are visible, even those on the far sides of the objects. This is a consequence of the fact that *all* (edge) lines in the model are projected to produce the image. In reality of course most objects are opaque, and we do not see the *hidden lines* on their back faces. Furthermore one object may well obscure other objects or parts of objects beyond it.

This 'transparency' of a wire-frame image can make it difficult to interpret, both because of the confusion of superimposed lines, and because there is ambiguity as to the relative distances away from the viewpoint (depths) of different points on the object. One of the most famous of optical illusions, the Necker cube (Figure 14.1), illustrates this point. It can be perceived in two distinct ways, and the eye and brain hesitate between the alternative interpretations.

For many purposes in computer graphics it is desirable to have more realistic images, in which the hidden lines are removed and in which solid objects are shown with properly opaque surfaces. To increase the realism further, these surfaces may be naturalistically coloured and textured, and the effects of light and shadow may also be simulated.

One area of application in which the quest for realism has been pushed perhaps furthest of all is in cockpit simulators for training the pilots of aircraft and spacecraft (colour plates 9,10). Similar training equipment has been developed for the captains of large ships. The 'windows' of the simulated bridge or cockpit consist of computer displays, giving views of the simulated scene 'outside'. These views are updated continuously in response to the pilot's actions at the controls, so as to give an animated illusion of the vehicle's movements over land or sea. Since pilots often rely on subtle visual cues to guide them, it is important to simulate real appearances with some accuracy. The simulator may be capable of showing night-time as well as day-time views, and may even reproduce the effects of haze, fog or smoke.

Fig. 14.1 The Necker
cube (*left*) and its
alternative readings

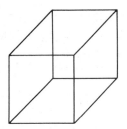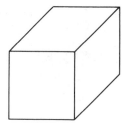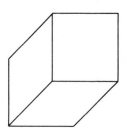

Another field in which spectacular computer graphics effects have been pioneered is film animation, in a number of space epics and technological fantasies. However, in one respect film animation is *less* demanding on computer resources than cockpit simulation, since the frames of the film can be generated and photographed individually, over a period of many months. In the flight simulator the images must be generated and displayed *in real time*, as fast as they are viewed, typically at a rate of 24 frames per second. This needs special and powerful computer hardware, and creates considerable storage requirements.

In some areas of design — electronics, or mechanical engineering, for example — the demand for such highly realistic images is currently not so pressing. But there are other fields in which aesthetics plays a larger part — such as industrial design, architecture and town planning — where the potential of high quality graphics in design is very great. For consumer products, computer-generated images can be used to study styling and ergonomics (colour plate 6). In architecture the appearances of buildings can be simulated from many viewpoints, in sunlight and in shadow. Some impressive work has been done to depict buildings artificially and naturally lit (colour plates 11,12), and to simulate the appearances of interiors viewed through large areas of glazing. Such kinds of effects would be very difficult indeed to represent in traditional architectural drawings.

The clients for a building might be taken through the interior, using computer animation to give them an 'electronic guided tour'. The same might be done for the exterior spaces in large new building complexes or town plans. The visual impact of a new building might be assessed by superimposing computer-generated views onto photographic or video images of the existing surroundings (colour plate 13). All these developments in computer graphics have potentially profound implications for the greater involvement of clients and users in the design of their own environments. The design process can, at least in principle, become more open to members of the public, who may be able to 'see what they are getting' in a much more complete and vivid way through computer images than they ever could from manually produced drawings.

All this is not to say that shaded, coloured or animated images have no place in engineering design. Colour can be used in a *symbolic* rather than in a naturalistic way, to distinguish different features in a complex electronic layout or mechanical assembly drawing (colour plates 7,8). This can be a great help in understanding the arrangement. The three-dimensional form of a mechanical component may be difficult to appreciate from a single static wire-frame perspective image. The removal of hidden lines and the addition of shading will in general make the shape much more comprehensible, since we rely heavily in our perception of depth and form on interpreting the shadows cast on and by solid objects.

One relatively simple technique which has been used to aid depth perception, without resorting to the computational expense of hidden-line removal, is that known as **intensity depth cueing.** Lines which are nearest to the viewpoint are displayed with the greatest intensity; those further away are made progressively fainter. Draughtsmen sometimes use a similar trick in perspectives drawn by hand. The effect is roughly comparable with the phenomenon of 'aerial perspective' by which distant objects appear less bright than nearer ones because of the scattering of light by dust in the atmosphere. (Normally this is only noticeable over distances of several kilometres, not over the depth of a few metres depicted for example in the view of the aeroplane in Figure 14.2.) Another possibility is for the model to be *clipped* against a back plane positioned passing through the object, such that further parts of the model are discarded and only a foreground slice is displayed.

Another powerful way to aid three-dimensional understanding is through *animation*. If the perspective viewpoint is moved in small steps laterally around an object, the effect of displaying the resulting views in sequence will be for the object to appear to rotate about a vertical axis. Different points on the object will move at different relative speeds, and much of the depth ambiguity of static pictures will be removed. Animation is also of course extremely valuable in kinematic analysis, and for detecting the potential spatial clash of moving parts, as described in Chapter 15.

Fig. 14.2 Image (*left*) without and (*right*) with intensity depth cueing [McDonnell Douglas Corp.]

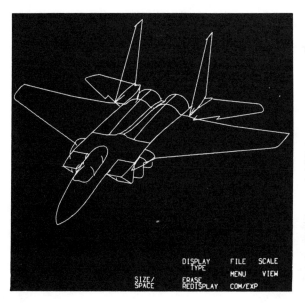 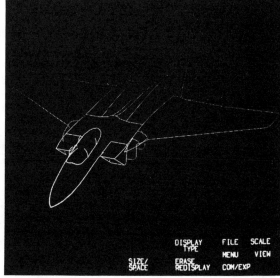

2 Hidden line and hidden surface removal

We now consider in more technical detail various methods for removing from views those lines and surfaces which are hidden behind other surfaces. Let us take first the case of parallel projection. Suppose that some object or objects have been positioned for viewing as shown in Figure 14.3. We can define a **view volume** which takes the form of a parallelepiped extended in the direction of view (i.e. perpendicular to the screen). The rectangular transverse cross-section of this view volume corresponds to the shape and size of the required window.

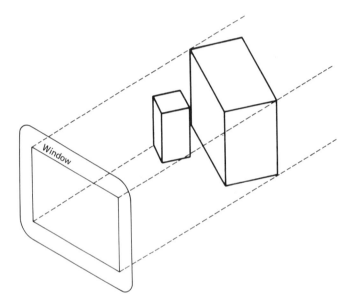

Fig. 14.3 Objects positioned for viewing in parallel projection, with window defining rectangular cross-section of view volume

We can identify points in this volume by reference to the screen coordinate system (x_s, y_s), which we now extend into the third dimension to give z_s values for the *depths* of points (Figure 14.4). The depth of the view volume overall can be limited to the minimum and maximum depths (z_s values) of points in the scene to be viewed. These define respectively **front** and **back clipping planes** (sometimes called *hither* and *yon* planes). Parts of objects falling outside the view volume will not be visible in the view, and must be clipped before the projection is made.

Now if two points P_1 and P_2 in the view volume share the same x_s and y_s values, this means they must lie on the same projector (Figure 14.5). The point with the larger z_s value will be further away from the viewer, and so will be hidden behind the (nearer) point with the smaller z_s value.

A similar argument applies to perspective projection (Figure 14.6). Again, given two points P_1 and P_2 lying on the same projector, the one nearer to the eye-point will be visible and the further one obscured. The difference between this and parallel projection is that points on the same projector do *not* now share the same (x_s, y_s) values.

Fig. 14.4 Screen coordinate system extended into third dimension to give z_s values for depths of points; and front and back clipping planes, defined by minimum and maximum z_s values of points in scene

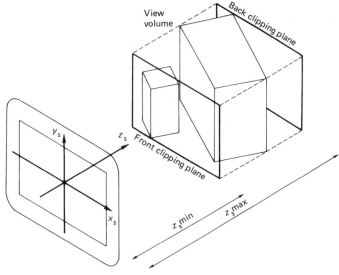

Fig. 14.5 Two points P_1 and P_2 on the same projector in parallel projection, sharing the same (x_s, y_s) values

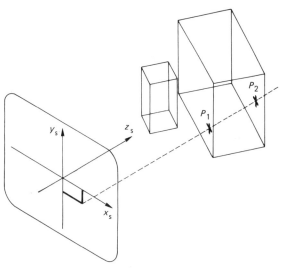

Fig. 14.6 Two points P_1 and P_2 on the same projector in perspective projection

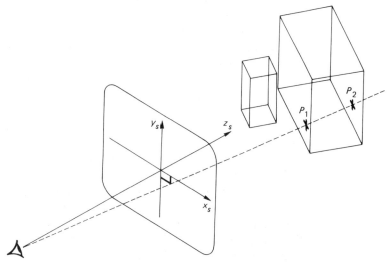

Fig. 14.7 View volume in perspective projection, defined by four projectors through corners of window, and by front and back clipping planes

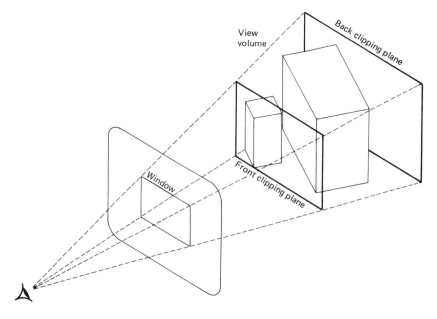

The view volume in the perspective case takes the form of a truncated pyramid whose apex is at the viewpoint (Figure 14.7). The four projectors through the corners of the window define the sloping edges and faces of the pyramid. The $x_s y_s$-plane whose z_s-coordinate is that of the nearest point in the scene truncates the pyramid; the $x_s y_s$-plane whose z_s-coordinate is that of the furthest (deepest) point on the object(s) forms the base of the pyramid. These are the front and back clipping planes, as with parallel projection. Again, parts of objects lying outside the viewing pyramid will not appear in the view and must be clipped.

Detection of hidden points — and hence of hidden lines and surfaces — is clearly much simpler in the case of parallel projection. A direct comparison of (x_s, y_s) coordinate values can decide whether projected points will coincide in the view; and if they do, then a comparion of z_s values will determine which is visible and which is hidden. For this reason it is usual in calculating hidden features in perspectives, to *transform the model of the object(s)* in such a way that the required view can be produced by parallel projection.

This is achieved by performing a three-dimensional **perspective transformation** on the model of the object in situ before the parallel projection onto the (two-dimensional) plane of the screen is carried out.

Figure 14.8 shows this perspective transformation applied to a cuboid. In this particular orientation relative to the viewpoint, the cuboid is transformed to become a truncated pyramid, whose base faces towards the viewer. The perspective transformation in three-dimensional space has the effect that the *parallel projection of the transformed object onto the screen is the same as the perspective projection of the original (untransformed) object onto the screen.* Now the detection of hidden points can proceed by the simple comparison of (x_s, y_s, z_s) values as before.

Fig. 14.8 Cuboid subjected to perspective transformation to become a truncated pyramid. All points in the shaded zone beyond this pyramid must be hidden from view

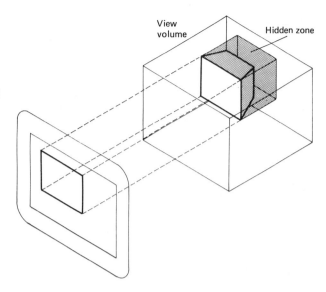

The in-situ three-dimensional perspective transformation is identical to the one used in Chapter 3 (see equation (1) of that chapter) except that it also produces a 'z' screen coordinate, z_s, which retains the required depth information. The screen coordinates (x_s, y_s, z_s), of a point on the model of the object, are therefore expressed in terms of the eye coordinates (x_e, y_e, z_e), of the same point, by the relationships

$$x_s = \frac{Dx_e}{z_e}$$

$$y_s = \frac{Dy_e}{z_e}$$

$$z_s = \frac{B(z_e - D)}{(B - D)z_e} \tag{1}$$

where D is the distance from the viewpoint to the screen (as in Chapter 3) and B is the distance from the viewpoint to the back clipping plane. If the screen size S is introduced, the above equations can be written in dimensionless form as

$$x_s = \frac{Dx_e}{Sz_e}$$

$$y_s = \frac{Dy_e}{Sz_e}$$

$$z_s = \frac{B(z_e - D)}{(B - D)z_e} \tag{2}$$

Consider the rectangular plane of the nearer face of the transformed cuboid in Figure 14.8. (It is the base of the truncated pyramid.) This plane hides a shaded zone beyond it. All points lying in this zone must be hidden by the front plane.

269

Several different methods have been devised for detecting and removing hidden lines and hidden surfaces. In raster displays the surfaces of objects can readily be shown shaded or coloured, and so their introduction has brought new interest in techniques for hidden surface elimination. The performance of some algorithms is dependent on the character and complexity of the scene in question and on the number of polygonal faces to be processed; the performance of others is related to the resolution of the screen. There is no one 'best' approach.

Depth buffer algorithm

Conceptually perhaps the simplest technique is the so-called *depth buffer* algorithm, which is applicable only to raster graphics. Recall that in a raster display each image is stored in a *frame buffer,* as a matrix of values for the intensity of each pixel. For this algorithm a second buffer of the same size is created, the *depth buffer* (sometimes called a *z-buffer*), whose purpose is to store for each pixel a z_s value for the depth of some corresponding point in the scene.

Initially all pixels are set to the background intensity value in the frame buffer, and set to the *maximum* z_s value of the scene (that is, the depth of the back clipping plane) in the depth buffer. Each polygon (face or facet) in the scene is then projected in turn, and the (x_s, y_s) coordinates of all pixels falling inside the projected polygon boundary are found. For each such pixel, the z_s depth value and the intensity value of the corresponding point in the polygon are determined. If the depth is *less* than the currently recorded z_s value in the depth buffer, this means that the new point must be nearer to the viewer than points with the same (x_s, y_s) coordinates on other polygons previously considered. The pixel value in the depth buffer is reset to this new z_s value, and the pixel value in the frame buffer is reset to the appropriate intensity for the shading of the polygon under consideration.

If the depth z_s is *greater* than the currently recorded z_s value in the frame buffer, this means that the point under consideration must be further away than points with the same (x_s, y_s) values on polygons already processed, and hence must be obscured by them; so no action is taken.

There is no need here, as with some other algorithms, to sort all polygons in order of depth beforehand. Whatever order the polygons are considered in, the images of those nearer to the viewer will be progressively 'painted over' those further away. One advantage of the depth buffer algorithm is that its performance is related not to the number of polygons in the scene, but to the number of pixels in the display. The disadvantage is that large amounts of storage space are needed for the depth buffer; and this requirement of course increases as the resolution of the screen increases.

2.1   Scan-line coherence and area coherence in the image

The depth buffer algorithm takes a 'brute force' approach, treating faces in no particular order, and considering each pixel in isolation. It will work for absolutely any kind of object or scene. In practice, however, most ordinary real-world objects and scenes, and most views of such scenes, have certain properties of *coherence* which can be exploited in algorithms for eliminating hidden surfaces. Projected polygons will occupy discrete continuous areas of

Fig. 14.9 (*Left*) Scan-line coherence. Within the polygon boundary all pixels on a scan-line share the same intensity value.
(*Right*) Area coherence. Within the polygon boundary most pixels on adjacent scan-lines share the same intensity value

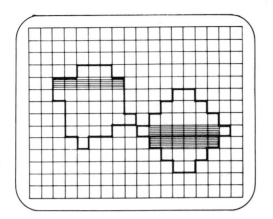

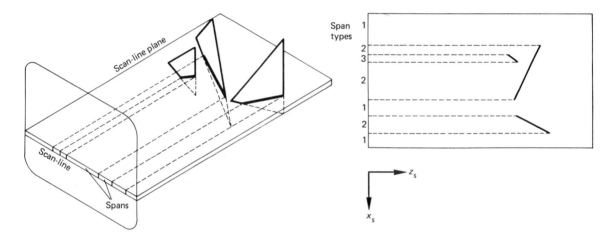

Fig. 14.10 Scan-line algorithm. An (x_s, z_s) scan-line plane cuts through the scene. The plane cuts linear segments from polygonal faces in the scene. These segments are projected onto *spans* in the scan-line, as shown in top view (*below*). Spans may be of three types, 1, 2 and 3 (see text)

the screen. Within each projected polygon boundary, all pixels on the same scan-line will share the same intensity value — the portion of the image in question displays **scan-line coherence** (Figure 14.9, left). Similarly, most pixels on adjacent scan-lines within the given polygon boundary will share the same intensity value — the portion of the image displays **area coherence** (Figure 14.9, right).

Scan-line algorithms

Scan-line algorithms, as the name indicates, solve the hidden surface problem one scan-line at a time, usually working from the bottom of the screen upwards. We can think of the process as that of considering a succession of planar horizontal (x_s, z_s) slices through the scene, each corresponding to a single scan-line (Figure 14.10). Consider the intersection of one of these **scan-line planes** with a number of polygons in the scene. The plane will cut a linear *segment* out of each polygon. When these segments are projected onto the scan-line they divide it into a number of discrete lengths or **spans.** Within each span the intensities of all pixels are the same: the span corresponds to a part, or the whole of, some visible segment (or else to part of the background).

For any span, there are three possible situations:

1 No segment is projected onto the span. This means that only the background will be visible, and so all pixels are set to the background intensity.
2 Only one segment is projected onto the span. The segment must be visible, and all pixels are set to the appropriate intensity for that polygon.
3 Several segments are projected onto the span. It is necessary to determine which is the nearest and hence the visible segment.

Lines are scanned from left to right. Thus the beginnings and ends of spans correspond to the edges of polygons. The algorithm keeps, and continually updates, a list of these edges for all 'active' polygons which intersect the current scan-line plane. It keeps another list of the active polygons themselves, sorted by their depths. As each span is entered, the depths of the relevant polygons are compared; the visible polygon is determined; and appropriate intensity values are assigned to all succeeding pixels, until the next span is reached.

The algorithm thus takes advantage of scan-line coherence in order to determine the intensity values of rows of pixels (the spans) rather than of single pixels. The calculation of depth priority is confined just to that small number of polygons which are 'active' at any time. What is more, there will in general be a close similarity, in terms of polygons visible, between one scan-line and the next; and this fact too can be exploited in the design of such algorithms.

Area sub-division algorithms
Area sub-division algorithms sub-divide the screen into successively smaller areas or windows. Suppose these windows are rectangular. We can imagine in this case that the scene is intersected by a series of rectangular-section tubes, corresponding to the windows (Figure 14.11). The smaller the window, the greater the chance that, within the window, only *one* polygon will be visible. When this is found to be the case, the corresponding pixels in the window can be set to the appropriate intensity. At the limit the window will become reduced to the size of a single pixel. (There may still be several polygons visible, but only one intensity value can be displayed. This is taken to be either that of the polygon opposite the centre of the pixel, or better, an averaged value for all the visible polygons.) Because of area coherence in the view, however, it will often be the case that much larger windows will contain only a single polygon.

Consider the possible relationships of polygons in the scene to such a rectangular tube (Figure 14.12):

(a) the polygon may completely *surround* the tube (Figure 14.12(a)).
(b) the polygon may *intersect* the tube (Figure 14.12(b)).
(c) the polygon may be wholly *contained* within the tube (Figure 14.12(c)).
(d) the polygon may be *disjoint* from the tube (Figure 14.12(d)).

It is the surrounding polygons which are critical to the elimination of hidden surfaces.

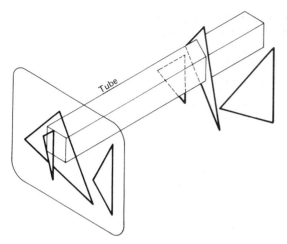

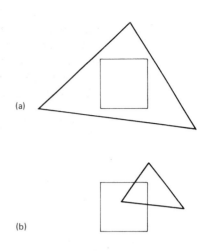

(a)

(b)

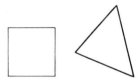

(c)

(d)

Fig. 14.11 Area sub-division algorithm. A rectangular-section tube, corresponding to a window, intersects polygonal faces in the scene

Fig. 14.12 Possible relationship of polygonal faces in the scene to a rectangular tube (compare Figure 14.11)

For any tube and window various situations can arise:

1 All polygons are disjoint. Only the background will be visible, and all pixels in the window are set to the background intensity.

2 There is a single contained polygon. This must be visible. It is projected, the corresponding pixels set to the appropriate intensity, and the remaining pixels set to the background intensity.

3 There is a single intersecting polygon. The intersecting part must be visible. The algorithm proceeds as in step **2.**

4 There is more than one intersecting polygon, but the projections of the intersecting parts of these do not overlap. The algorithm proceeds as in step **2.**

5 There is a single surrounding polygon. The part seen through the window must be visible. All pixels in the window must be visible. All pixels in the window are set to the appropriate intensity.

6 There is more than one intersecting, contained or surrounding polygon; of these at least one is surrounding; and all z_s coordinates of one surrounding polygon are less than all z_s coordinates of all the other polygons. It follows that this *surrounder* must hide all the others, and the algorithm proceeds as in step **5.**

Fig. 14.13 Recursive sub-division of screen into square windows and sub-windows, in Warnock's algorithm

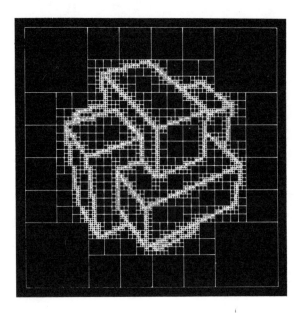

In all other circumstances the window must be sub-divided. It is only contained and intersecting polygons which now need to be identified, since disjoint polygons and surrounding polygons must remain disjoint and surrounding relative to the smaller window. The sub-division ceases either when one or other of the six cases has arisen, or when the window reaches the size of a single pixel.

One of the first algorithms of this kind was developed by Warnock [1969]. It employs square windows, each divided into four square sub-windows (Figure 14.13). Another potentially more efficient approach is to make the sub-windows match the projected shapes of the polygons found in the larger window.

2.2 Depth priority of faces in the scene

The depth buffer algorithm uses no 'intelligence' to anticipate whether or not the projections of polygons might overlap, or in what order of priority. But it is possible to make calculations about the geometrical relationship of polygons in the (x_s, y_s, z_s) coordinate system which can determine these priorities, and can avoid unnecessary comparisons between polygons.

For example, no polygon facing away from the viewer on the far side of some opaque solid object can ever be visible. These **back faces** can therefore be eliminated from consideration at the outset. Back faces can be distinguished from other faces by examining *face normals*. A face normal is a vector perpendicular to the plane of the face, pointing 'outwards' (Figure 14.14). If the angle between the face normal and the direction of view is less than $90°$, then the face is a back face and must be invisible.

If the scene contains only one convex polyhedron, then all hidden surfaces are completely eliminated by removing back faces. In more complex scenes, the removal of back faces will typically halve the number of polygons to be considered in hidden surface calculations.

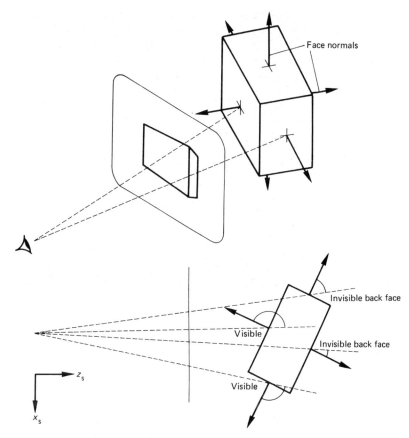

Fig. 14.14 Back face elimination. (*Above*) Face normals on the faces of a convex polyhedron (a cuboid) and (*below*) the same shown in top view. If the angle between the face normal and the direction of view is less than 90°, the face is a back face and must be invisible

Fig. 14.15 Bounding box or three-dimensional extent of a face, and the corresponding screen extent

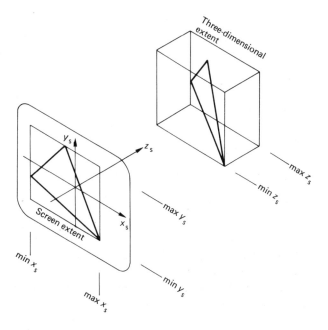

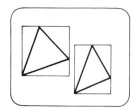

Fig. 14.16 Screen extents of two faces do not overlap

Another means for limiting the computations involved in comparing faces is to surround each face by a **bounding box** or three-dimensional **extent**, whose coordinates are those of the maximum and minimum x_s, y_s and z_s values of the face itself (Figure 14.15). If the extents of two faces do not overlap in the x_s and y_s directions (their **screen extents** do not overlap), then the projections of those faces cannot overlap in the view, and hence one cannot obscure the other in part or in whole (Figure 14.16).

Fig. 14.17 Screen extents of two faces overlap, but the faces do not overlap in x_s and y_s

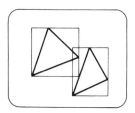

Fig. 14.18 Two faces overlap in x_s and y_s

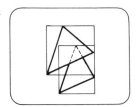

On the other hand, if the extents of two faces *do* overlap in x_s and y_s, it is possible that the faces themselves overlap (Figures 14.17 and 14.18), in which case it becomes necessary to compare the relative depths of those faces. If there is no overlap of the extents of the faces in the z_s direction, all points on one face must be deeper than all points on the other, and it is possible that the further face may be hidden either in whole or in part by the nearer. If there *is* overlap of the extents in the z_s direction, the situation is potentially more complex, and needs to be examined further. It may be that one face lies in front of the other and conceals it in whole or in part, as before. But an alternative possibility is that the two faces *mutually overlap each other*. This can occur where one face penetrates the second (Figure 14.19). Another possible situation is the *cyclic overlap* of three or more faces (Figure 14.20). Special precautions may be needed to take care of such cases.

Fig. 14.19 Mutual overlap of two faces

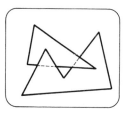

Fig. 14.20 Cyclic overlap of three faces

Depth-sort algorithms

Both scan-line and area sub-division algorithms work by taking small areas of the image, scan-lines, or windows, at a time; they then consider the relative depths in the scene of polygons visible within each area. Depth-sort algorithms work the other way round. They first arrange all polygons throughout the whole scene in the order of their depth; and only then do they consider their projected images in the required view.

One example of a depth-sort approach is provided by the algorithm of Newell, Newell & Sancha [1972]. The procedure here is to sort all polygons in the scene by depth, into an *order of priority,* with the highest priority nearest the viewer and the lowest priority furthest away. Once this order is established the polygons can then be projected and displayed one by one, from the lowest to the highest. In this process higher priority polygons will be 'painted over' those of lower priority which are partly or completely hidden in the view.

An initial ordering of polygons is made by sorting them in terms of their maximum z_s-coordinates, that is, by the point on each polygon furthest from the viewer. There will in general be groups of polygons whose extents overlap in depth. Here further examination is required. For every pair of polygons A and B the algorithm must decide which lies in front of and so hides the other in whole or in part. It is not necessarily the case that a polygon with a smaller value for its maximum z_s-coordinate will have higher priority.

Polygon A will *not* hide polygon B, in the following circumstances:

1   The extents of A and B do not overlap in depth, and A is deeper than B. This relationship is established in the initial sorting.
2   The extents of A and B do not overlap in x_s or y_s, that is their screen extents do not overlap (Figure 14.16).
3   Every vertex of A is deeper than the corresponding point with the same (x_s, y_s) coordinates in the plane of B (Figure 14.21).
4   Every vertex of B is less deep than the corresponding point with the same (x_s, y_s) coordinates in the plane of A (Figure 14.22).
5   The screen extents of A and B overlap; nevertheless A and B themselves do not overlap in x_s or y_s (Figure 14.17).

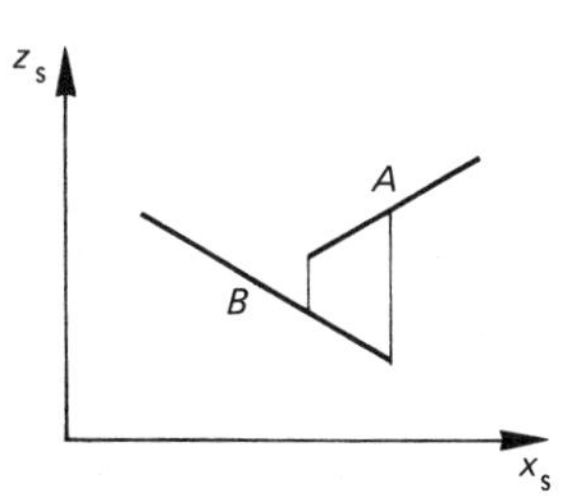

Fig. 14.21 Test 3 in the algorithm of Newell, Newell & Sancha. *A* does not hide *B*

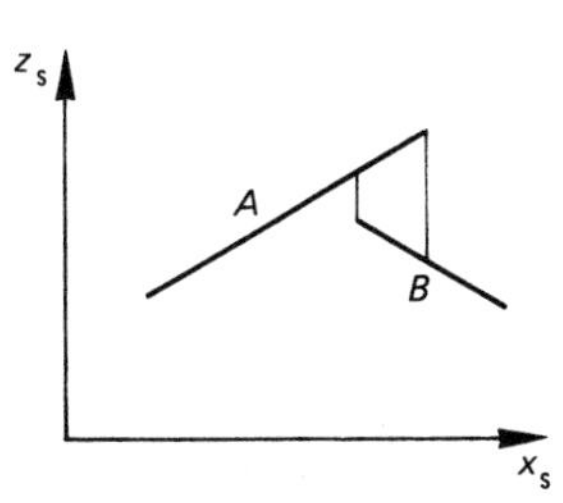

Fig. 14.22 Test 4 in the algorithm of Newell, Newell & Sancha. *A* does not hide *B*

Fig. 14.23 Priority is established for mutually overlapping faces in the algorithm of Newell, Newell & Sancha, by cutting one face into two parts

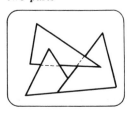

Because these tests increase in computational complexity from **1** to **5**, they are applied in that order. Once the initial sorting of the polygons is made, the more detailed tests are carried out where applicable, and the positions of polygons are shuffled in the list where necessary. If the algorithm attempts to move the same polygon repeatedly, this signals the presence of the special cases of *mutual* or *cyclic overlap* illustrated in Figures 14.19 and 14.20. The algorithm resolves these difficulties by cutting one of the polygons involved into two parts (Figure 14.23).

3 Effects of light and shade

The next step towards realism in computer-generated images, after hidden surface removal, is to take account of the effects of *light and shade* on the visible surfaces. These effects are dependent both on the properties of the surfaces themselves, and on the nature and position of the sources of light.

Most normal day-time scenes are lit by a combination of *diffuse illumination* or *ambient light* coming from all directions, with *point sources* such as direct sunlight or artificial lights. If diffuse illumination were the only lighting, the shading of objects would be uniform over their entire visible surfaces, and their appearance would lack the 'modelling' of brighter and darker tones which is produced by the differential lighting of one side or the other. Such conditions are rare in practice.

At the other extreme, where there is just one artificial point source of light, the effect is that of a searchlight or torch beam, and the modelling is very harsh with bright illuminated parts and deep black shadows. To achieve realistic effects in most cases therefore it is necessary to allow for some combination of diffuse and point sources of light.

The appearance of a plane surface illuminated by a single point light source will depend on the brightness of that light, on the angle which each ray of light makes with the plane, and on the *reflectance* of the surface. If the surface is dull or matte — it has a *low* reflectance — it will reflect light in all directions. The reflection is **diffuse**. The surface will appear brighter if the light falls perpendicularly than if it strikes at a shallower angle. This effect can be seen by holding a flat object such as a book up to a table lamp and turning it through $90°$.

These properties are related together by Lambert's *cosine law* which expresses the intensity I_d of the diffuse light reflected from a surface lit by one point source (Figure 14.24):

$$I_d = I_p k \cos \theta$$

where I_p is the intensity of the light falling on the surface from the point source

k is the coefficient of reflectance, which can vary between 0 and 1 depending on the material of the surface

θ is the angle between the surface normal and the direction to the light source. (If $\theta > 90°$, then the surface is hidden from the light, and I_d must be set to zero.)

Fig. 14.24 Lambert's cosine law

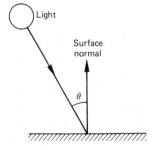

Where the same surface is illuminated by several point sources, the diffusely reflected light must be summed from all of these to find the resulting intensity ΣI_d. The intensity of illumination received from any given point source will fall off (according to an inverse square law) with the distance from that source. This fact might need to be taken account of in views of interiors lit by electric light for example; but for outdoor scenes in sunshine the distance from the sun to all surfaces in the scene can be taken as equal, and the value of I_p as the same throughout.

If the surface is polished and shiny — it has a *high* reflectance — then light from a point source is reflected off it in a particular direction; the angle θ between the reflected ray and the surface normal is equal or nearly equal to the angle between the surface normal and the direction to the light source (Figure 14.25). This is **specular** reflection, of which reflection in a mirror is the extreme case. It is specular reflection which produces the bright *highlights* on polished objects. Figure 14.25 shows the angle α between the direction in which light is reflected off a shiny surface, and the direction from the surface to the viewpoint. Highlights are only seen when this angle α is small. The effect can be observed with any shiny spheroid such as an apple or orange. Notice that the highlight takes its colour from the light source (and is usually therefore white or yellow) rather than from the surface itself. This is in contrast with diffuse reflection, where the colour seen depends both on the colour of the incident light *and* on the properties of the surface.

Fig. 14.25 Specular reflection

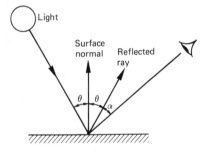

The phenomenon of specular reflection has been modelled for computer graphics by Phong Bui-Tuong [1975], using an empirically-derived formula for the fall-off of intensity with the angle α. An alternative model based more closely on the theoretical optics has been implemented by Blinn [1977]. This gives rather different results especially for light falling at shallow angles of incidence (that is, where θ in Figure 14.25 is large).

For objects made of *transparent* materials, there may be light transmitted through their surfaces from sources beyond them. We will consider this possibility shortly. Meanwhile for opaque materials the intensity of the reflected light from any surface can be calculated from the sum of diffuse and specular reflections from all point sources, together with a further contribution of diffuse reflection from ambient light. If the image is to be coloured then these calculations must be made separately for different colours. For example in the red, green, blue (RGB) system used in colour television and in most colour computer displays, three calculations would be made with appropriate values of I_p and reflectance k in each case. The calculations would be made *after* the elimination of hidden surfaces, in order to decide pixel values to display for each remaining visible surface.

3.1 Smooth shading

So far we have considered the shading of plane surfaces. Where a curved surface is approximated by a mesh of plane polygons the result is a facetted appearance (Figure 14.26). This however can be **smooth-shaded** to restore the effect of continuous curvature. One method for doing this has been developed by Gouraud [1971]. For each vertex in the polygon mesh a *vertex normal* is calculated; this is done by averaging the face normals of the adjacent faces (Figure 14.27). These vertex normals are used to compute shading values (as discussed previously) at each vertex. Shading values for the remainder of the surface are then interpolated linearly between these vertex values. If the

Fig. 14.26 (*Above*) Approximation of curved surface by mesh of uniformly shaded plane polygons. (*Below*) The same surface shaded by Gouraud's method [University of Utah]

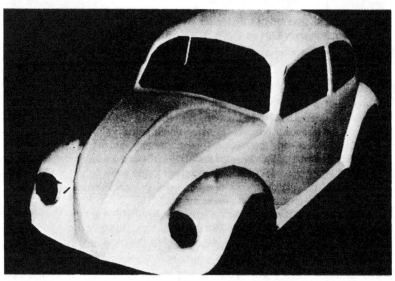

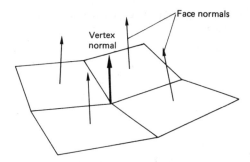

Fig. 14.27 Vertex normal (heavy line) calculated by averaging face normals of adjacent faces in polygon mesh

Vertex normal

Face normals

appearance of a sharp crease is to be retained in the surface, then vertex normals are derived by averaging face normals along each side of the creased boundary, but not across this boundary.

Gouraud shading is simple but has some drawbacks. It produces anomalous highlights. Discontinuities in the rate of change of shading can generate the perceptual phenomenon known as the *Mach band effect*, whereby a surface, supposedly of smooth curvature, appears to have light and dark stripes. This type of shading is also unsatisfactory for computer animation. These defects are largely remedied in a somewhat more complex method due to Phong Bui-Tuong [1975], which interpolates normal vectors between the vertex normals, instead of interpolating intensity values. The one mildly unsatisfactory feature remaining is that the outside edges of the polygon mesh still exhibit facetted contours.

3.2 Shadows

Although calculating the positions of *shadows* cast by lights in a scene is a complex matter in practice, the geometrical principles involved are quite straightforward. Indeed the problem of finding the shadows cast by a point source of light is essentially identical with the problem of finding hidden surfaces in a perspective projection. The same algorithms can be used for both purposes. We can imagine a 'viewpoint' at the position of the light (Figure 14.28). All surfaces 'visible' from the light will be brightly illuminated, with

Fig. 14.28 Shadow cast by point source of light (compare Figure 14.6)

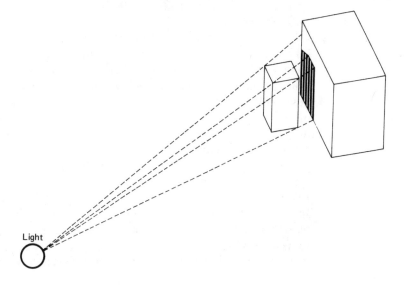

Light

highlights on any shiny surfaces. All surfaces not 'visible' from the light must be in shadow, and will show only the diffuse reflection of ambient light. Some polygons may be partly in the shadow, partly in the light. These must be subdivided into shadow polygons and illuminated polygons for the purpose of assigning intensity and colour values.

Where a scene is lit by several point sources, these calculations must be made in turn for each source, taking account of its particular intensity and colour. If the source of light itself cannot be treated as a point but has some appreciable area, as for example a window, or an array of bulbs behind a diffusing panel, then the problem becomes more difficult. The area of total shadow or *umbra* will now be fringed with a partial shadow or *penumbra*, and the boundaries of each must be calculated separately (colour plate 11).

In the case of shadows cast by the sun, the 'point source' is, in effect, infinitely distant. The rays of light can thus be taken to be parallel; and so the problem of computing solar shadows is equivalent to determining hidden surfaces in *parallel projection*.

Although it is time-consuming to compute the positions of shadows from many sources of light in a complex scene, there is at least the advantage that (so long as the lights do not move) the shadows remain the same, whatever viewpoint is then taken for the picture. In practice the positions of shadows would be determined first, and then the hidden surfaces eliminated for the chosen viewpoint. The algorithm of Newell, Newell & Sancha [1972] is well-suited for integrating with shadow calculations.

3.3 Ray tracing

The technique of **ray tracing**, described in Whitted [1980] and Kay & Greenberg [1979], can be used both to determine shadows and reflections, and to take account of the special properties of *transparent* materials. The method returns to the basic optics of the situation, and considers the paths of individual light rays as they pass through the scene on their way to the eye. Each ray originates in a light source. It may be reflected off one or more surfaces. And where it passes through a transparent object it will in general be *refracted*. The intensity of the light will be attenuated where it travels through materials of imperfect transparency, such as coloured glass.

Where the reflection is diffuse, the notional single ray becomes split into an infinite number of rays moving off in different directions. Similarly where a light ray meets a *translucent* material like alabaster or milky glass it is again split into many rays: the *transmission* of the light is also *diffuse*. It is obviously impossible to follow the separate paths of these infinities of rays. The method of ray tracing applies then only to *specular reflection,* and to *direct* (not diffuse) *transmission* of light. (Diffuse reflection and the contribution made by ambient light are treated separately.)

For any view we are interested only in those rays which reach the viewpoint. The rays are therefore traced *backwards*, starting from the viewpoint and followed back through the scene. In theory even this number of rays is infinite. In practice the method considers only rays passing through the *corners* of pixels. The intensity for each pixel is then taken as an average of its four corner values.

A ray coming from a transparent surface may be made up from the

Fig. 14.29 Ray tracing. Ray traced back through transparent object is divided into two rays, one refracted and one reflected, at each surface. N = surface normal

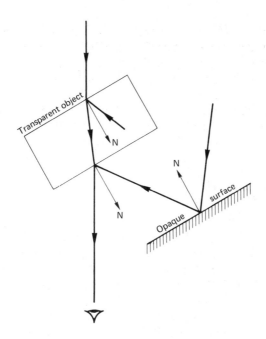

combination of two rays, one reflected and one transmitted and refracted (Figure 14.29). *Both* of these contributing rays must be followed further back; and so in principle each ray traced back from the eye may branch into a (binary) tree of rays all of which must be followed to their sources. At each stage calculations must be made of the changes in intensity and colour of each light ray due to the reflective properties of the opaque surfaces from which it is reflected and the transmissive and refractive properties of the transparent materials through which it passes. For these reasons ray tracing is currently a very slow and costly technique in computing terms; but the effects which have been achieved with it are extraordinarily impressive (colour plate 15).

4 Surface detail and texture

The plane or curved surfaces of an object shown in a computer image need not be uniformly coloured. It is possible to place patterns or coloured shapes on a surface by specifying extra **surface detail polygons** lying in the same plane as the face polygon. Another possibility is to digitise some photographed pattern and map this geometrically onto the surface (colour plate 12). However, this still leaves the surface smooth.

A further step in the search for realism is to represent the characteristic **textures** of materials. Quite apart from enhancing the illusion of natural appearances, the texturing of surfaces can be a powerful additional aid to depth perception: for example we can detect the perspective recession of a grassy field or of a gravelled road surface because the texture becomes finer with increasing distance.

It would be far too costly in terms of memory resources to model many kinds of knobbly or wrinkled surfaces explicitly. But the visual effect of texture can still be simulated in a number of different ways. One possibility is that the shading of a plane surface can be varied from pixel to pixel to give the appearance of roughness. Another possibility proposed by Blinn [1978] is to vary the surface normal over the surface, either in a random way or in some regular repetitive pattern. Depending on how great is this perturbation, the resulting appearance can range from a slight roughening to a highly corrugated effect. One minor problem here is that the silhouetted edges of the object still appear smooth.

In design we deal always with objects whose geometrical forms are *relatively* simple and well-defined. They must be so, otherwise the objects could not be modelled and manufactured. In nature, however, there are forms of very great complexity such as those of mountains, trees or clouds, which the designer of computer images might want to show in an animated film, or in the background to a perspective of a new building. One way to do this is in a **montage**, combining together computer-generated images with still photographs or video sequences of the natural surroundings.

Another approach, inspired by the work of the mathematician Mandelbrot [1982], is to model such forms in a semi-random or probabilistic way, using **fractal surfaces**. For example, in the case of a view of mountains there is no real virtue in reproducing every minute feature of the actual ground surface. What is required is some specific overall shape which is then given a generally craggy and rocky effect in the detail (colour plate 14).

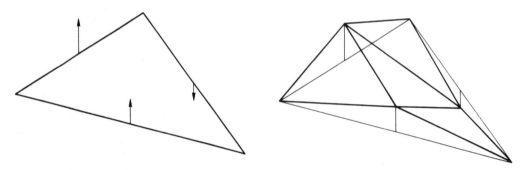

Fig. 14.30 Sub-division of triangle into four smaller triangles by randomly displacing the mid-points of its three edges. Repeated recursively, this process generates a corrugated surface

This can be achieved by digitising a polygon mesh to describe the overall form approximately. Suppose this mesh is made up of triangles. The mid-points of the edges of each triangle are randomly displaced from the plane of the triangle, so as to create four new smaller triangles, and so corrugate the surface (Figure 14.30). This process is repeated recursively for each smaller triangle to produce a texture of the desired fineness. A similar approach can be taken using a quadrilateral mesh, recursively sub-divided into smaller quadrilaterals. Appropriate control of the randomising function used can change the character of the resulting surface, from slightly rough to very jagged. Hidden surfaces are then eliminated and the surfaces shaded to generate the final picture.

Geometry in motion **15**

J Rooney

1 Introduction

In previous chapters we introduced several different types of representation or model in the context of design, analysis and synthesis. The main emphasis in most of these was on the representation of spatial forms, and in particular on the geometry of these forms. Naturally, much effort has been directed towards the modelling of 'static' (that is, non-moving) systems, components, schemes, and so on. Not surprisingly, the resulting techniques are generally adequate for the spatial representation of buildings, mechanical parts and electronic layouts, since their spatial forms are essentially 'fixed'. However, when designing systems which necessarily involve movement and/or change of shape as part of their function, we must address the problems of representing the resulting 'dynamic' geometry, and the changing spatial structure. Such systems obviously include the kinematic systems of Chapter 11 (the slider-crank mechanism, the robot manipulator arm, and so on), but in addition, since all physical objects are embedded in space and *time*, any given system may require a *temporal* as well as a spatial description as it moves, changes or evolves in form. In particular, if a spatial form is to be *animated* in some way, such as to provide a continual sequence of images from different viewpoints or from a moving viewpoint (Chapters 3 and 14), or to generate an assembly sequence of parts coming together to form a whole (Chapters 2 and 9), or to generate a sequence of incremental changes in shape such as occur in vibrations, strain deformations and so on (Chapter 10), then a temporal description is essential.

The representation of this 'geometry in motion' requires the construction of both spatial and temporal forms. Often the temporal aspect may be modelled relatively simply by associating a single extra parameter (time) with each spatial form, so that each 'element' of the latter essentially becomes a function of time. However, it is more likely to be the case that this approach is inadequate. In general, the spatio-temporal *interrelationships* of all components of a system must be modelled. For example, in order to determine whether or not two moving objects collide or interpenetrate it is necessary to know (or to be able to derive) their relative spatial position at each instant of the motion. It is *not* sufficient just to know whether or not they occupy the same spatial position (or neighbourhood) since they may do this at widely different times.

General spatio-temporal modelling is still in its infancy and we do not intend to discuss it in great detail here. Instead, in this chapter, we present a brief introduction to some of the problems and ideas that arise in this field.

2 Kinematic synthesis

Kinematics is the archetypal subject which is directly concerned with *motion*, divorced from any associated forces 'causing' that motion (the word 'cinema' is derived from the same root — the Greek word '$\varkappa\iota\nu\eta\mu\alpha$' meaning 'movement'). The motion of an object is specified with respect to another object or with respect to a frame of reference. It is specified in terms of movements or *spatial displacements* (involving both translations and rotations in general), and often also in terms of various rates of change of displacement (with respect to time), such as *velocities* (linear and angular), and *accelerations* (linear and angular). *Kinematic synthesis* is primarily concerned with the design of kinematic systems capable of achieving particular required motions. We consider two simple examples of this type of synthesis as an illustration of geometry in motion.

Two-position synthesis
The kinematic problem of moving an object from one location to a second location in two-dimensional space is illustrated by Figure 15.1.

At the first location, the (rigid) object is in position and orientation A, and a mechanical system must be designed to displace the object to the second position and orientation B. To simplify the situation we ignore the speed of the required movement at this stage. This simplification does *not* reduce the problem from a spatio-temporal one to a purely spatial one, as may be thought. The temporal aspect is still present since we require the object to be at A, *before* it is at B. We have merely not specified a time-scale for measuring the time interval between the two events 'object at A' and 'object at B'.

Perhaps the simplest mechanical system for achieving the displacement is the 'hinge' mechanism shown in Figure 15.2. This relies on the fact that, in general, for any two positions and orientations A and B in two-dimensional space, there exists some unique fixed point such that an object can be displaced from A to B by a simple rotation about the fixed point. This special fixed point is termed the **pole** for the displacement. The hinge is constructed so that it pivots about this pole, and it is attached to the object at any two distinct points P and Q, thereby forming a rigid attachment.

Reference to Figure 15.2 shows that the hinge pivot is easily located geometrically, for any two positions A and B, by considering the two attachment points P and Q. Since the object moves from A to B by a simple rotation about the pivot, all of its points (including P and Q) move on circular

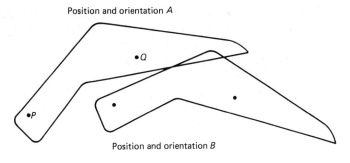

Fig. 15.1 Moving an object from position and orientation A to position and orientation B in two-dimensional space

Position and orientation A

•Q

•P

Position and orientation B

y

x

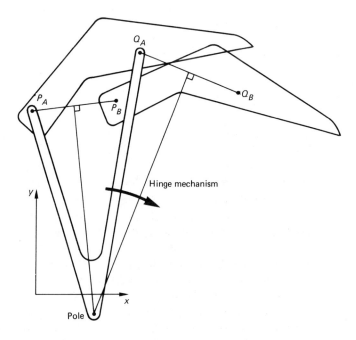

Fig. 15.2 Single-hinge solution to the two-position problem in two-dimensional space

Q_A

Q_B

P_A

P_B

Hinge mechanism

y

x

Pole

arcs centred on the pivot point. The latter must therefore lie on the perpendicular bisector of the chord $P_A P_B$, and also on the perpendicular bisector of the chord $Q_A Q_B$. In general, these two perpendicular bisector lines are not parallel and so they intersect in the required pivot point. Having obtained a suitable hinge and appropriate pivot point, this kinematic system can then be refined by introducing a time-scale and so specifying a speed of movement (say, an angular velocity about the pivot) from A to B.

From the designer's point of view this simple hinge solution may not be satisfactory, in that it is unduly restrictive. Thus for many two-position problems, the derived hinge pivot point may be inaccessible (for example, inside another object), inconveniently placed (for example, too close to other components, or outside the specified confines of the system) or totally unreachable (for example, orders of magnitude too far away from the rest of the system). Furthermore, there is not much design expertise required, other than that associated with the choice of attachment points P and Q, with the detailed shape of the hinge, and with the size and type of joint.

Fig. 15.3 Two-hinge solution to the two-position problem in two-dimensional space

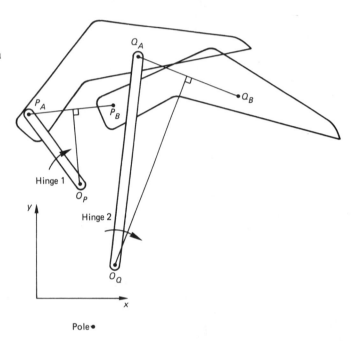

A more 'flexible' approach to the two-position problem is based on the use of two hinges rather than on just one. The situation is illustrated by Figure 15.3. This time, instead of choosing just one pivot point at the intersection of the two perpendicular bisectors, we choose two separate pivot points O_P and O_Q — one on each bisector. A hinge or link (Chapter 11) is attached to the object at point P only (forming a revolute or pin joint), and to the fixed pivot point O_P (again forming a revolute joint). A second link is similarly attached between the point Q on the object and the second pivot point O_Q. The complete system of object, two hinge links and frame of reference, now forms a *four-bar linkage* which can move the object from position A to position B.

This solution to the two-position problem provides designers with much more freedom of choice. They can now select either pivot point to be in a more suitable position; the only restriction being that each must lie on its respective bisector line. However, the resulting motion of the object is now no longer just a simple rotation about a pole (as it was for the single hinge solution) but instead it is a more complicated general motion which is dependent on the choice of location for the pivots. Furthermore, although this kinematic system does move the object from position A to position B, the range (and sequence) of 'intermediate' positions is not the only one available, and it can be changed to satisfy other constraints by choosing different pivot points.

Clearly, introducing a time-scale and specifying or deriving velocities and accelerations for the object, or kinematic system, is now a more difficult task than with the previous solution to the two-position problem. We will not pursue this further.

Three-position synthesis

We now consider the obvious extension of two-position synthesis, namely three-position synthesis. Here the kinematic problem is that of moving an object through three prescribed positions (and orientations) A, B and C in two-dimensional space. The situation is illustrated by Figure 15.4.

Fig. 15.4 Moving an object through three positions and orientations, A, B and C, in two-dimensional space

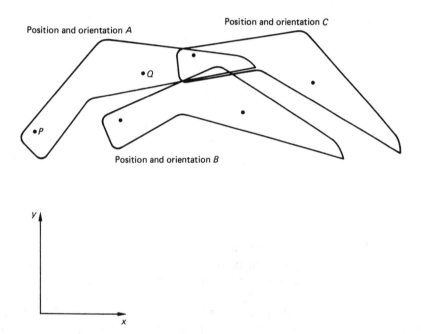

If we restrict our attention to just two of these positions (say A and B), then the previously discussed two-position synthesis approach will yield a kinematic system to move the object from one position to the other. However, it is unlikely that such a system will also move the object through the third specified position. Moreover, in general it is impossible to achieve a single-hinge solution to the three-position problem. Nevetheless, it is possible to derive a two-hinge kinematic system which will perform the required displacement through these three positions. The solution is illustrated by Figure 15.5.

The approach is again based on perpendicular bisectors. We choose two points, P and Q, on the object to be moved. For a two-hinge solution we require P to move on one circular arc and Q to move on a different circular arc. The pivot points O_P and O_Q are obtained as the centres of the respective arcs. Thus O_P is located at the intersection of the perpendicular bisector of the chord $P_A P_B$ with the perpendicular bisector of the chord $P_B P_C$. The other

Fig. 15.5 Two-hinge
solution to the
three-position problem
in two-dimensional
space

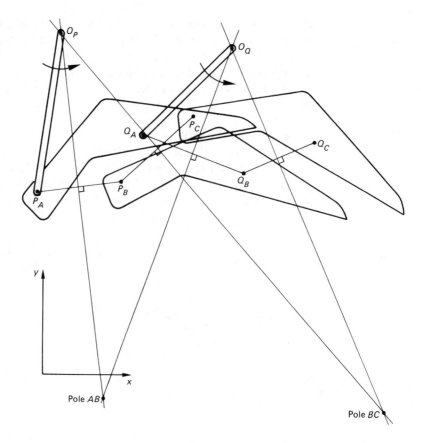

pivot point O_Q is obtained similarly using the chords Q_AQ_B and Q_BQ_C. A
unique four-bar linkage is thus formed from the object, the two hinge links
and the frame of reference, and this linkage achieves the required
displacements. However, as with the single-hinge solution to the two-position
problem, the designer is severely restricted in choice since having chosen the
attachment points P and Q, the pivot points O_P and O_Q are determined
essentially by the *three* positions A, B and C, so that the kinematic system is
also determined, but may be unsuitable. There is now no freedom to choose
O_P or O_Q anywhere along a bisector line — each pivot *must* lie at the (unique)
intersection of the appropriate *two* bisectors.

3 Spatial and temporal forms

The kinematic systems of the previous section, as well as those in Chapter 11,
all involve the displacement of objects and component parts, through two or
more positions in space. These objects and their spatial positions can be
represented in the normal way using the various types of geometric modelling
considered in Chapters 5–9. The resulting spatial forms then describe the static

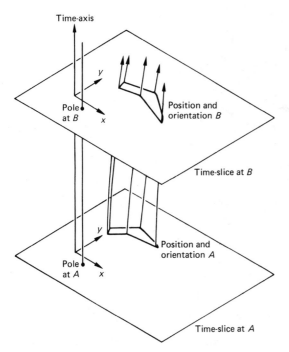

Fig. 15.6 A two-dimensional shape 'extruded' in three-dimensional space–time

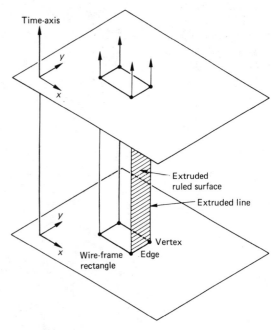

Fig. 15.7 A two-dimensional wire-frame model of an object (a rectangle) extruded into a three-dimensional surface model in space–time

geometry of the systems. However, the temporal aspects can also be described geometrically by considering 'time' to be just another spatial dimension. Figure 15.6 illustrates the situation for the single-hinge solution to the two-position problem.

The two-dimensional shape of the object in space becomes a three-dimensional 'extruded' shape in space–time. The two specified positions A and B of the object are then represented by the 'bottom' and 'top' faces of this extruded shape, respectively. Any intermediate position is obtained by taking a 'time-slice' at the appropriate intermediate time, to obtain a two-dimensional spatial cross-section. The geometry of the extruded shape itself depends on the motion of the two-dimensional object as it moves from A to B.

Wire-frame, surface, and solid models in space–time

A simple wire-frame model of an object in space becomes a surface model in space–time as can be seen from Figure 15.7.

The vertices of the two-dimensional shape shown in Figure 15.7 are extruded into lines and the edges are extruded into ruled surfaces. The resulting space–time 'object' is then a hollow tube. In general, this tube will not be a

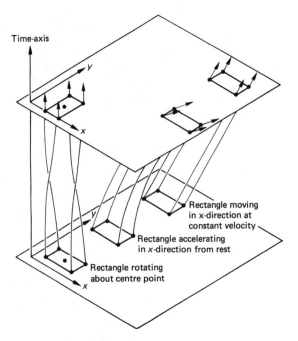

Fig. 15.8 Three rectangles moving in two-dimensional space. The first is rotating about its centre point and generates a twisted tube in space—time. The second is accelerating from rest in the x-direction and generates a bent tube in space—time. The third is moving at constant velocity in the x-direction and generates a prismatic tube

prism since the two-dimensional object may have been rotating (thereby giving the tube a twist), or translating non-uniformly (thereby giving the tube a bend). The tube is a prism only in the case of uniform motion in a straight line (Figure 15.8).

For a three-dimensional wire-frame model, similar comments apply, though now the space—time is four-dimensional and not easily visualised. Again the vertices and edges become extruded lines and surfaces, but care must be taken in interpreting the result as a surface model since surfaces in four-dimensional space(—time) have different properties from those in three-dimensional space, and several of these are counter-intuitive — for example, a surface in four-dimensional space does not possess a unique 'normal' direction at each of its points.

In a similar way to the wire-frame situation above, a surface model of an object in space becomes a solid model in space—time, as each of its vertices, edges and faces is extruded into a line, a surface and a volume, respectively. As before, care must be taken in interpreting the result as a 'solid' model, since amongst other things the 'volume' of such a solid is a space—time volume and its shape and size depend on how the spatial object has moved.

Finally, a solid model of an object in space becomes a hyper-solid model in space—time, as each of its vertices, edges, surfaces and volumes is extruded into a line, a surface, a volume and a hyper-volume respectively. Such models have yet to be studied extensively.

Despite all the problems of visualisation associated with the extension of purely spatial models into spatio-temporal models it seems clear that very similar approaches can be used, and furthermore essentially the same types of data structure arise, involving vertex lists, edge lists, face lists, surfaces, solids, and so on. The required generalisations of concepts are not inherently more problematical for computational purposes than are those currently in use.

Collision of moving shapes

One of the most useful applications of spatio-temporal modelling is in the representation of changing spatial relations. In particular, the determination of whether or not two moving objects will physically collide or interpenetrate is an obvious problem area. Figure 15.9 illustrates a situation in which two simple one-dimensional 'objects' (just line segments) move relative to each other, in straight-line motion at constant speed.

In space–time, the objects sweep out space–time 'areas', and if these areas overlap, then clearly the one-dimensional objects collide or interpenetrate at some time value. Thus in Figure 15.9(a) the two objects occupy the same space, but at different times, so there is no collision, and their space–time areas do not intersect. But in Figure 15.9(b) the objects occupy the same space at the same time, so they collide, and their space–time areas do overlap.

Fig. 15.9 Two simple one-dimensional objects in relative constant straight-line motion in one-dimensional space (a) The objects occupy the same space but at different times (b) The objects occupy the same space at the same time

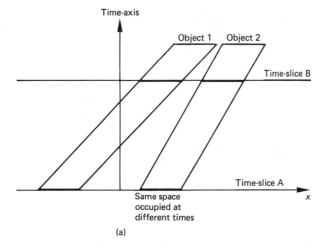

(a)

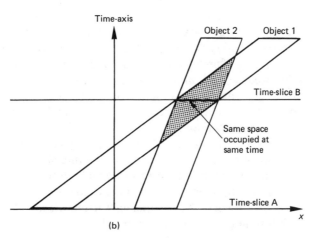

(b)

Determining whether or not two objects collide is therefore possible in terms of their space–time 'intersection'. However, this intersection is not the usual Boolean intersection of the two objects in space. Rather it is the Boolean intersection of the regions swept out by the objects in space–time.

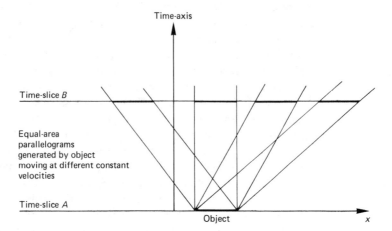

Fig. 15.10 Equal-area parallelograms generated by a one-dimensional object moving in one-dimensional space at different constant velocities

Unfortunately, such regions are not unique. A given object can sweep out a large range of differently sized, shaped and located regions depending on the complexity of its motion. A single object in space therefore gives rise to a whole class of potential regions in space–time.

In the case of straight-line motion at constant speed it is easy to identify the class of regions for a given object. Figure 15.10 shows that all such regions swept out by a one-dimensional moving object are parallelograms, and that for any given time interval they all have the same space–time area. This is easily generalised to two-dimensional and three-dimensional objects moving at constant speed in straight-line motion.

4 Discrete vs. continuous

Throughout this book it has been assumed that physical objects are continuous in form: in other words that their shapes are infinitely resolvable at finer and finer detail. This assumption is implicit in our geometrical representations, since we use real numbers liberally to represent lengths, areas, volumes, distances, angles, positions, coordinate values, and so on. In practice, however, this is something of a fiction, and we routinely approximate our 'exact' representations.

In particular, any data structure residing in a digital computer memory must necessarily be specified in terms of a *finite* string of characters or digits and so it cannot actually involve real numbers (which in general require infinite strings of digits, for non-recurring decimals, etc.) unless these can be specified finitely. Consequently, most geometric models in CAD contain a finite amount of information, expressed essentially in terms of *discrete* data structures.

As an example, consider perhaps the simplest geometric data structure, namely that representing a point in three-dimensional space. This is expressed as an ordered triple of coordinate values, say (x, y, z). A particular point would have coordinate values within a certain range and specified to a certain number of decimal places or to a certain number of significant figures. Thus suppose we consider the point (1.24, 3.51, 9.07), whose coordinates lie within the range zero to ten, and are specified to just two decimal places. The order information distinguishes this point from the point (3.51, 9.07, 1.24), for example, whereas the numerical information distinguishes this from the point (1.23, 3.51, 9.07). Since there are one thousand (0, ..., 999) possible three-digit numbers, the above point data structure can represent any one of a total of $1000 \times 1000 \times 1000$ possible points — a large but not an infinite range of possibilities.

A (discrete) wire-frame modeller based on this data structure can only represent $(1000 \times 1000 \times 1000)^4$ possible different tetrahedra, for example, since each tetrahedron has four vertex points. Any tetrahedron whose vertices have one or more coordinate value lying outside the range, or specified to more than two decimal places, cannot be modelled faithfully by the system, though the 'nearest' approximation may suffice.

The above discussion illustrates some aspects of discrete modelling in CAD. Such discreteness may not be apparent to the user if the resolution is high. However, much coarser resolutions are in common use particularly on smaller and less powerful systems. The most widespread example occurs in computer graphics where an image of an object is displayed on a graphics terminal or screen. A point on the screen is located relatively coarsely in terms of integer (screen) coordinates (typically in the range 0–1024), and on raster-scan screens this 'point' is actually a pixel with some shape — usually rectangular or square (Chapter 3). The number of distinct images possible on a graphics screen is therefore limited — though still relatively large.

As a final example of discrete modelling we consider another fairly common occurrence, namely sequences of graphical images, such as occur in animations and simulations. These are just sequences of 'snapshot' frames at regular time intervals and so they are essentially just a discrete version of 'geometry in motion'. In practice, of course, the latter would be modelled just in this way, though it might involve very short time intervals between frames and so be discretely modelled to a high degree of temporal resolution.

For the purposes of CAD it seems very likely that discrete modelling will predominate for representing both spatial and temporal forms, although finer and finer resolution will lead to a greater and greater illusion of continuity in the 'approximate' forms. The implication here is that forms should be created and generated from the outset as discrete objects, for the purposes of computer-aided design.

Shape grammars and the generation of designs

16

C F Earl

1 Introduction

At this stage in the book we draw together different areas in computer-aided design and put them into perspective by looking at the ways they may develop in the future. These areas may be divided into two types, as reflected in the structure of the book, namely: those concerned with the representation of spatial form; and those concerned with the analysis of function. The former is seen as the prelude to the latter.

In general there are two driving forces behind the description of form in the progression from wire-frame, through surface to full three-dimensional solid modellers: the first, in providing input to analysis of the design; and the second, in providing input to synthesis, manufacture or construction of the design. These may overlap in the sense that the results of analysis may concern the processes of synthesis.

2 Representations

A broad picture of these two aspects of CAD can be given in terms of the general notion of representations. A design has many different representations or descriptions in its passage from conceptual development, to formal realisation, analysis and production. No one representation deals with all features of the design explicitly, but the features arising in one representation may be consequences of features in other representations. For example, in generating the mesh representation of an object for finite element analysis, the choice of mesh type and of mesh size is partly dependent on the shape features created in the geometric description of the object. Certain geometric features can pose problems for automatic mesh generation and should be avoided, if possible, at the shape generation phase of the design process. This example illustrates the need to understand the relationships amongst the different representations used in design.

The idea that understanding design is essentially about understanding the relationships amongst various representations is emphasised by the links relating product design, manufacture and marketing. The descriptions of a product in terms of shape, colour and material, in terms of manufacturing operations, and in terms of market 'forces' are all interrelated. They are each very different descriptions of the same object. The links between representations lie at the heart of good design practice and are consequently aspects of design to which CAD should attend. For example, the geometrical representation of an object by a solid modeller and the sequential list of machining operations (and the consequent analysis of possible machining sequences) required to make the object, should not be thought of as separate representations following one another, but rather as closely interrelated descriptions of the same object. Decisions made in terms of one representation should not be made in isolation from their effect on the other representation.

The development of CAD will move increasingly towards providing the means to elucidate and to understand the relationships amongst representations. Previous chapters of the book have shown how various representations are generated. This chapter will examine the framework in which these representations can be brought closer together. This enterprise, which attempts to examine the relationships between pairs of representations, is founded on the understanding that the essence of design lies in these relationships. However, some of the emphasis in CAD has neglected its importance. The reason is simple. In the move to develop representations of shape and physical properties for use in analysis, the fact that these representations refer to whole classes of designs has not been exploited. Thus for example in developing solid modellers, the emphasis has been on creating the detailed description of a *single* design, rather than on providing the tools for exploring *classes* of possible designs.

The relationships between two individual designs within each representation can only be understood fully in terms of whole *classes* of possible designs. More crudely, properties of particular designs only have significance if we know the properties of other, perhaps 'closely related' designs. Evaluation and modification of designs is thus dependent on the relationships between possibilities. The nature of progress in this field depends on the extension of knowledge of *possible designs*. In referring to possible designs we mean the possible designs within the various representations. For example, a mechanical part may correspond to a number of possible designs in the machining sequence description. These are just as much different possible designs as are those described by explicitly different spatial and geometric characteristics of possible parts. The relationships amongst the sets of possibilities form the core of design knowledge for the machining of parts. We do not just want to know how to machine a part, once it has been designed, but we also want to know how to design the shape of the part so that it can be machined efficiently and economically. This is yet another representation of the part.

This chapter will consider the formal representation of possible designs at the level of spatial descriptions. The relationship to possibilities within other representations will be considered towards the end of the chapter.

Current (geometric) solid modellers do not encourage the formalisation, let alone the exploration, of formal possibilities. Their approach tends to direct the designer progressively closer to the details of the individual design and generally does not provide a suitable framework for generating classes of designs from which different design solutions can be selected in response to a specification. The geometric modeller thus provides at best an individual manifestation of design ideas as a basis for modification and improvement. However, it is by no means certain that design ideas are best expressed by a single manifestation. Indeed these ideas are not likely to be single examples of configurations of spatial elements. It appears more likely that such broad conceptual notions are about how the parts of the design are to be interrelated. There may be many ways in which these relations can be realised in a complete design. It seems inadequate to provide a design tool in CAD which encourages only the single solution representation of design ideas which are essentially about a range of possible designs that the designer may wish to explore. On the other hand it is often necessary to examine an individual formal possibility to assess how different relations affect one another. However, this should be done in an experimental fashion, namely that of examining examples of the possibilities, to assess the best use of available generating relations between the parts.

We propose to examine a formalism which addresses the representation of design possibilities directly. It takes as its premise that these possibilities be defined by relationships between parts. It formalises these relationships and expresses them in terms of rules which are then used for generating possible designs in which the required relationships are displayed.

3 Generating form

We concentrate on the generation of formal possibilities. The potential for some such methods of generation in architectural design has been introduced in Chapter 13. It is instructive to note that much of the research in the generation of spatial forms has taken place in the field of architectural design. In traditional areas of engineering design, although spatial form and its detailed representation are essential for communication and manufacture, the process of design is closer to the generation of functional descriptions for which there are associated formal solutions. However, in architectural design the idea of formal composition is central to the generation of new designs.

The method of form generation described below has found its main inspiration and application in architectural design. However, if the programme for design as the interrelationship of representations is to be effective then the concentration on single representations will not be appropriate in other contexts. The generation of formal possibilities will have as much a place in engineering design as it has in architectural design.

To summarise, we view the generation of design possibilities within the different representations of designs as the central aim in the future development of CAD. Designs are chosen from these possibilities and the generation process is controlled and directed towards designs meeting a given specification. Secondly, we regard the generation of *formal* possibilities as representative of this enterprise, as well as being an essential feature in any area of design.

The generation of form in architectural design has tended to concentrate on two areas. Firstly, on the definition of **vocabulary elements,** and secondly, on conditions or constraints on how these elements can be put together or *composed.* The vocabulary elements tend to be relatively simple collections of formal features, as for example columns, walls and doorways. The constraints are attempts to define the kinds of compositions of these elements which are permissible. There is great difficulty here since the definition of permissible compositions is either given by examples of complete building designs, or by some vaguely stated architectural intention, such as that the building should have a 'grand' or 'religious' appearance, or by the definition of a 'style' which is often a mixture of the previous two. These are important but do not give an explicit formal description of how the architectural elements can be composed. We will attempt to remedy this by defining rules for composition which comprise **grammars** for languages of architectural forms. The choice of rules defines a language. In some cases it is possible to identify rule systems with particular architectural styles. They are the explicit representation of the rules of formal composition of designs in that style. The style is the set of rules.

4 Shape

Earlier chapters, particularly Chapters 5 to 9, have dealt at length with the representation of shape. We will consider the simple wire-frame representation to illustrate the ideas of rule-based generative systems. This does not imply that these ideas are only appropriate to the wire-frame representation of shape, but there are difficult problems which arise in applying rule-based systems to solid models of shape. Furthermore, there is another reason for concentrating on the wire-frame representation. Traditionally designers have used line drawings as the basis for interpreting surface and volume information. One of the advantages of the surface and solid modellers available in current CAD systems has been that these interpretations have been made explicit from the initial stages of design (although the detailed definition and interpretation may be inappropriate at the early conceptual stages, especially if we are concerned with exploring possibilities).

A wire-frame representation of a shape is a set of line segments which generally indicate the edges of the shape. However, this can suggest an interpretation of the 'regions' bounded by the line segments as surfaces. We will consider the wire-frame representation to be the shape itself rather than a partial representation of a more detailed description. As such the shape is simply a configuration of line segments. A drawing of a shape is just this, with indications and keys for the interpretation of certain configurations as surfaces, volumes and voids.

A shape is a set of line segments. Each line segment can be represented by its pair of end-points. A single shape may have many representations as sets of line segments because each line can be composed of numerous overlapping segments. In order to provide a *canonical* (unique) description of a shape we introduce the idea of a *maximal line* as a line segment which is (strictly) not contained in any other segment in the shape. The maximal lines are put together by the unions of overlapping line segments. A shape is defined canonically by its set of maximal lines. It is now possible to compare two shapes for equality, since they will consist of the same set of lines. A suitable data structure for representing these sets of lines will be described later.

We saw previously that shapes are the same if they are (pseudo) rigid transformations of one another, without being necessarily identically 'equal'. Thus two shapes S_1 and S_2 are the same if there is a transformation τ consisting of either a translation, a rotation, a reflection or some combination of these, such that the transformed shape $\tau S_1 = S_2$. The transformation preserves the configuration of lines in the shape but changes their position relative to the reference frame in which the shapes are described. For the purposes of this chapter we will also allow transformations which change the scale. The reason is that a change of scale does not change the configuration of lines in the shape but only their absolute sizes.

Suppose that for a shape S there is a transformation τ such that $\tau S = S$; then τ is called a *symmetry* (transformation) of the shape. For example, a square has a number of symmetry transformations generated by $90°$ rotations about the centre and reflections in either diagonal (Figure 16.1).

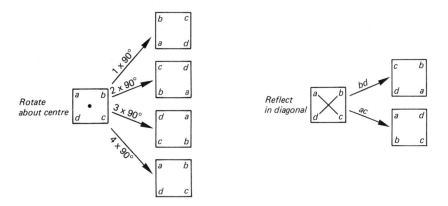

Fig. 16.1 Symmetry transformations of the square

To describe the set of maximal lines composing a shape we construct a *descriptor* for each line which effectively gives its position and its direction. In this way collinear lines have the same descriptor. The data structure for the maximal lines in a shape first lists the lines according to the 6-tuples (three entries describing position and three entries describing direction) forming their descriptors. Note that the descriptor for a two-dimensional line will be shorter (a 3-tuple), but we consider the general case of a three-dimensional shape. The data structure then orders the collinear lines corresponding to each descriptor value according to the values of their end-points. This gives the representation of the lines in a shape as an ordered list of ordered lists. This data structure allows the efficient comparison of two shapes for equality.

5 Spatial relations

Each shape is a configuration of line segments in some defined mutual relationships. The basis for generating shapes is the definition of relations between shapes. How are these spatial relations defined? Most simply a spatial relation between two shapes is defined explicitly by the representations of the two shapes. Thus, just as the relations between the lines in a single shape are represented by specifying the line segments which compose the shape, the representation of a spatial relation between two shapes is just the ordered pair of representations of the two shapes. More generally a spatial relation amongst any number of shapes is specified by the representations of the constituent shapes. For two shapes S_1 and S_2 a spatial relation is represented by the ordered pair (S_1, S_2). In general the spatial relations $(\tau S_1, S_2)$ and $(S_1, \tau S_2)$ are relations distinct from (S_1, S_2) where τ is a transformation, although $(\tau S_1, \tau S_2)$ represents the same relation as (S_1, S_2).

Recall from Chapter 2 that objects (shapes) may be defined relative to a local coordinate frame, which, together with the relation between the local frame and the reference frame, is sufficient to define the shape. Observe that the notion of spatial relation is not dependent on the absolute position of the shapes in the reference frame, but is a function of their relative position. The relative positions of the two shapes may be defined by the relation between their local coordinate frames. Thus a spatial relation may be described more conveniently by the ordered triple (S_1, S_2, τ) where S_1 and S_2 are descriptions of the two shapes with respect to their local frames and τ represents the transformation between the two local frames. The transformation τ is described in the local frame of the first shape S_1.

An interesting feature of this representation of spatial relations is the way in which it enables us to deal with symmetrical shapes. Observe that if a shape S_1 is symmetrical then there are essentially a number of ways that the spatial

Fig. 16.2 Equivalent spatial relations. Local frames F_1 and F_2 are defined in each of the component shapes S_1 and S_2

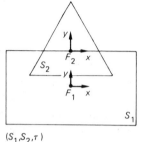

(S_1, S_2, τ)

$\tau \equiv$ translation along y-axis

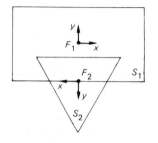

$(S_1, S_2, \tau * \alpha)$

$\alpha \equiv$ rotation through $180°$

relation (S_1, S_2, τ) may be realised. If the shape S_1 has a symmetry transformation α, that is $\alpha S_1 = S_1$, then the spatial relation $(S_1, S_2, \tau * \alpha)$ is equivalent to (S_1, S_2, τ). An example is shown in Figure 16.2. The two shapes still have the same spatial relation, because the configuration of lines in the combined shape is still the same although the combined shape has been transformed.

6 Shape rules

The generation of spatial forms is accomplished by shape rules, based on spatial relations. We have already argued that generation should be based on the relations between parts of the design. The rules express the desired relations between parts and provide the means to incorporate them into designs. The rule systems which we describe form grammars which are essentially examples of the kinds of **production systems** used in expert systems. Such rule systems are used to generate properties and attributes of the 'world' under consideration, and to make inferences from available knowledge of the world using the rules. The shape grammars we describe are similar to such systems except that they work directly with the objects of design rather than with propositions about them. Each set of rules encapsulates knowledge about a 'world' of spatial designs. This knowledge is derived from the kinds of spatial relation we require to hold between the component shapes in the design.

Before defining any shape rules, another feature of shapes is described which can be used to control the ways that spatial relations are realised in a shape generation. The positions and the combinations of spatial relations which emerge in the final design can then be controlled. This control is introduced by the use of **labels** or **markers** on the shape. We concentrate on labels. Points on shapes can be labelled, so that some rules can apply only if the correct configuration of labels is present. The application of certain rules will then build up configurations of labels to control the application of subsequent rules.

A labelled shape is thus a combination of a set of maximal line segments, together with a set of labelled points. The points can be labelled by a convenient set of symbols — we choose upper-case letters. Alternatively the labels themselves may be special marker shapes. These have the advantage of allowing the whole shape description to be specified solely in terms of spatial elements, although we must distinguish between the two types of shapes. Generally we will require the final design to be free of labels or marker shapes, since their function is just to guide and to control the generation. The labels or markers are referred to as non-terminal elements of the shape, since they do not appear in the final productions of valid designs. The absence of labels or markers provides a condition on which to base the decision to halt a generation of shapes using the shape rules.

A shape rule is based on a spatial relation which may involve any number of shapes, but for simplicity we consider two-shape relations. Given a spatial relation (S_1, S_2, τ) a number of rules can be derived. The simplest is the additive rule, where shape S_1 is replaced by the combination of S_1 and S_2 in the relation (S_1, S_2, τ). This is written as

$$S_1 \mapsto S_1 \cup \tau S_2$$

where $S_1 \cup \tau S_2$ denotes the union of the shapes S_1 and τS_2. The shape S_1 is in the same position before and after application of the rule. A pictorial representation is shown in Figure 16.3(a).

If the shape S_1 is symmetrical under the transformation α, such that $\alpha S_1 = S_1$, then since the spatial relation $(S_1, S_2, \tau * \alpha)$ is equivalent to (S_1, S_2, τ) the above shape rule is equivalent to the rule (Figure 16.3(b))

$$S_1 \mapsto S_1 \cup \tau * \alpha S_2$$

or alternatively

$$S_1 \mapsto \alpha S_1 \cup \tau S_2$$

When we write the rule in the original form it is assumed that it can apply in the equivalent ways for symmetrical shapes S_1. Similarly if the shape S_2 has symmetry transformation β then the original form of the rule has the equivalent (Figure 16.3(c)).

$$S_1 \mapsto \alpha S_1 \cup \beta * \tau S_2$$

The spatial relation (S_1, S_2, τ) also gives rise to another rule which involves the replacement of the shape S_2 by the combination of S_2 and S_1 in the given relation. To represent this, an alternative description of the spatial relation is needed which gives the relation in terms of the local frame of the shape S_2 as (S_2, S_1, τ') where τ' is the inverse transformation of τ expressed in the local frame of S_2. The shape rule is

$$S_2 \mapsto S_2 \cup \tau' S_1$$

There are also subtractive shape rules which can be defined, based on the relation (S_1, S_2, τ). These rules apply to shapes in the specified relation and remove one of the shapes. They are described by the rules

$$S_1 \cup \tau S_2 \mapsto S_1$$

$$S_1 \cup \tau S_2 \mapsto \tau S_2$$

The second rule is shown in Figure 16.4.

Suppose that we require the two 'sides' of a shape rule to be quite different shapes. That is, one shape is to be replaced by another shape. This type of rule may be achieved by applying two of the above rules in sequence (Figure 16.5):

$$S_1 \mapsto S_1 \cup \tau S_2 \mapsto \tau S_2$$

This replaces the shape S_1 by the shape τS_2 described in the local frame of S_1. In effect the shape S_1 is replaced by the shape S_2.

If the local frames of the shapes S_1 and S_2 coincide then we use the spatial relation (S_1, S_2, ι) where ι is the identity transformation. The corresponding shape rules are

Fig. 16.3 Shape rules based on spatial relation in Figure 16.2

Fig. 16.4 Subtractive shape rule based on spatial relation in Figure 16.2

Fig. 16.5 Combination of additive and subtractive rules to replace shape S_1 by shape S_2

$$S_1 \mapsto S_1 \cup S_2 \qquad S_1 \cup S_2 \mapsto S_1$$

$$S_2 \mapsto S_1 \cup S_2 \qquad S_1 \cup S_2 \mapsto S_2$$

This form of the shape rules will be used if each of the shapes is described with respect to a global coordinate frame. The shape rule which replaces the shape S_1 by the shape S_2 is then represented by the composite rule

$$S_1 \mapsto S_1 \cup S_2 \mapsto S_2$$

Any shape rule can be represented by a sequence of additive and subtractive rules.

---

7   Generating designs

Rules are used to generate shapes. An **initial shape** is required from which the generation can start. A shape at any intermediate stage of generation is termed the **current shape**. We now examine how shape rules are applied. Essentially a particular rule can be applied when the left-hand shape in this rule is the same as a subshape of the current shape.

A shape S_1 is a subshape of S_2 if there is a part of S_2 which is equal to S_1. Formally S_1 is a subshape of S_2 if each of the maximal lines in S_1 is contained in a maximal line of S_2 and if the labelled points in S_1 are a subset of the labelled points in S_2. The labels attached to the points must also be subsets of the total set of labels (Figure 16.6).

Fig. 16.6 S_1 is a subshape of S_2

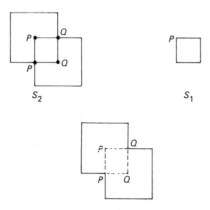

Operations can conveniently be defined on shapes which are analogous to the ideas of union, intersection and difference operations mentioned in the treatment of solid modellers (Chapter 9). We have already introduced shape union in the definition of shape rules. A formal definition of the **shape union** of two shapes S_1 and S_2 is as that shape consisting of the line segments in S_1 and S_2 together with the union of the labels attached to S_1 and S_2 (Figure 16.7). The shape union is denoted as $S_1 \cup S_2$. The representation of this shape union is given in terms of maximal line segments. Thus overlapping lines from S_1 and S_2 are combined to form new maximal lines in $S_1 \cup S_2$.

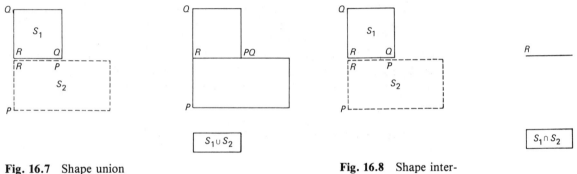

Fig. 16.7 Shape union of S_1 and S_2. The top line of rectangle S_2 (broken line) is aligned with the bottom of the square S_1

Fig. 16.8 Shape intersection of S_1 and S_2, which consists of a single line segment. The label R is common to S_1 and S_2

Fig. 16.9 Shape difference of S_1 and S_2. Note that label R does not appear in either difference

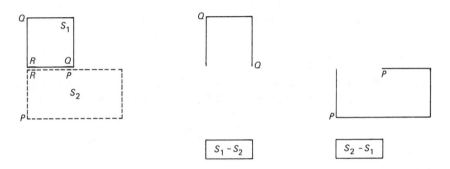

The **shape intersection** (Figure 16.8) $S_1 \cap S_2$ is the shape consisting of all those line segments and labelled points which are in *both* S_1 and S_2. Thus for a line in S_1 which overlaps a line in S_2, the common portion of the two lines is in the intersection. The **shape difference** (Figure 16.9) $S_1 - S_2$ consists of all those line segments, or portions of line segments, and labelled points which are in S_1 but *not* in S_2. Similarly, $S_2 - S_1$ consists of all those line segments and labelled points in S_2 but not in S_1.

A rule $S_1 \mapsto S_1 \cup \tau S_2$ can be applied to a current shape S if there is a transformation α (translation, rotation, reflection or scaling) such that αS_1 is a subshape of S. The result of applying the shape rule is the shape

$$(S - \alpha S_1) \cup \alpha S_1 \cup \alpha * \tau S_2$$

The major problem arising in implementing shape rules is that of finding whether there exists a transformation α such that αS_1 is a subshape of S. These subshapes S_1 do not always appear as explicit instances of the shape S_1 in the sense that they have been created directly by a rule which produces the shape S_1. There is as yet no means of inferring whether, and if so, where these *emergent* instances of shapes will arise in a generation sequence. The problem is solved by searching each current shape for all possible places at which the rule can apply. The particular ways in which this is done will not be covered here, but we remark that the data structure for the lines in the shape which facilitated checking for shape equality is also appropriate for recognising subshapes.

Some examples of shape generation using rules are now given which illustrate both the basic principles of rule application and the ways in which labels are used to control or guide rule application to give designs of widely differing characteristics.

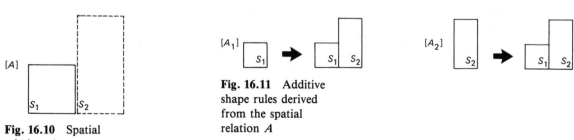

Fig. 16.10 Spatial relation A

Fig. 16.11 Additive shape rules derived from the spatial relation A

Fig. 16.12 Generations using the shape rule A_1 (see Figure 16.11)

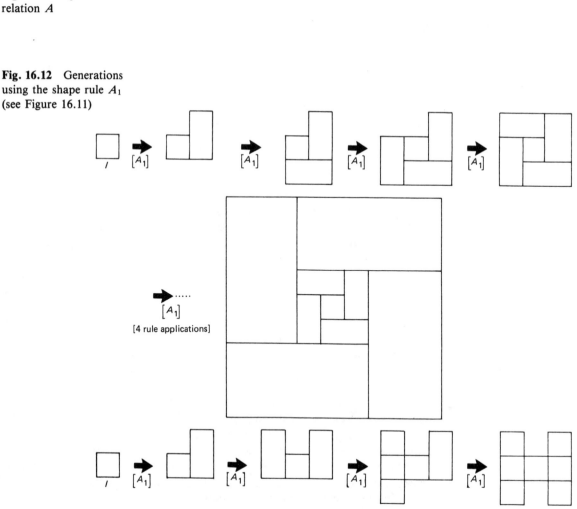

Figure 16.10 shows a spatial relation A which is used here as the basis for grammars. The spatial relation A gives rise to the additive rules shown in Figure 16.11. With an initial shape which is a square, the rule A_1 can be applied to generate the designs shown in Figure 16.12.

The symmetry of the shape S_1, a square, gives many possible rule applications which realise the spatial relation A. We now introduce some complexity into the generation by inserting labelled points in the shapes. The introduction of the labels also limits the number of rule applications which arise from the symmetry of the shapes. Figure 16.13 shows the rule A_1 now modified by the addition of a label P at the corners of the component square and rectangle. Two possible generations are shown in Figure 16.14. Note that the initial shape must have a label P if the rule is to apply.

If we now introduce a rule for selectively erasing the label P, valid shapes without labels can be obtained. For the rule shown in Figure 16.15 only the final shape in the first generation shown in Figure 16.14 is a valid shape in the language defined by the rules. It is a valid shape as can be seen by applying the erasing rule five times. Note that the erasing rule can be applied to the bounding square in each case, but that it cannot be applied to all the labels at the intermediate stages because the labels do not all lie at the corners of squares.

Fig. 16.13 Modification of rule A_1 by addition of labels P

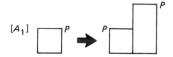

Fig. 16.14 Generations using modified rule A_1 (Figure 16.13) starting with initial shape with label P at its corner

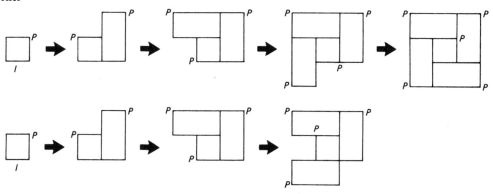

Fig. 16.15 Example of a label-erasing rule

Fig. 16.16 Further modification of rules A_1 and A_2, with two label-erasing rules

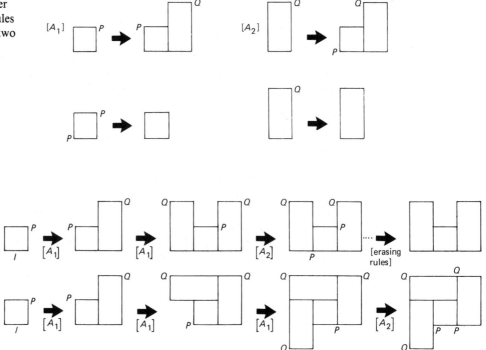

Fig. 16.17 Two generations using rules in Figure 16.16. The first generation produces a valid design in the language but labels in the final design of the second generation cannot all be erased

Building on these simple examples, we take both additive rules A_1 and A_2 derived from the spatial relation A with labels P and Q, and erasing rules as shown in Figure 16.16. Possible generations are shown in Figure 16.17, starting from the initial shape — a square with a label P at a corner. Valid designs in the language defined by the rules may be derived from the final design in the first generation, but not in the second generation, by suitable applications of the label-erasing rules.

There are a great many possibilities arising from the use of these rules even when they are constrained by the use of labels. The range and variety of rule applications arises from the symmetry of the component shapes as well as from the ability to apply rules to the emergent shapes. Let us look at the effect of 'removing' symmetry in the components by using suitably placed labels. Placing the labels in the corners of the square shape still leaves a reflection symmetry about the diagonal. But we can remove this symmetry by placing the label P one-third of the way along a side of the square (Figure 16.18). A generation is shown in Figure 16.19. This is the only generation possible using the rules shown and the final design is the *unique* valid design in this language.

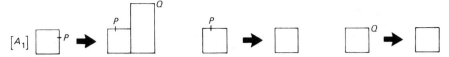

Fig. 16.18 Further modification of rule A_1 with label P one-third of the way along the side of the square. Appropriate label-erasing rules are shown. Note that the erasing rule for label Q is relative to a square shape

Fig. 16.19 Generating the unique valid design produced by rules in Figure 16.18

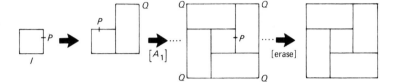

8 An architectural example

As an example of using shape grammars in generating designs we look at a set of rules for house layout. Although these are based on a set of rules for generating the layouts of a particular group of actual nineteenth-century houses in Pittsburgh (USA), the resulting spatial organisations occur more widely. The grammar we examine essentially provides ways of arranging reception rooms around a hall. This occurs in many styles of house both in Europe and in North America. The different styles result from dimensional constraints on the spaces, from the 'articulation' of the plan boundary by extending rooms beyond the rectangular outline of the basic arrangement, and from more detailed ornamentation and decoration.

The grammar presented here is based loosely on that developed by Flemming *et al.* [1985]. It is a simplified version of that grammar. It considers just the arrangement of hall and principal rooms, while Flemming's grammar also adds kitchen and stairs and articulates the plan boundary. The spatial organisation is represented in terms of rooms composed from 'modular' squares. For actual designs the dimensions are adjusted to fit the site and the particular requirements of the dwelling.

The grammar (Figure 16.20) has an initial shape consisting of the hall. The labels R (Room) and H (Hall) are located at the centres of the modular squares composing these spaces. The labels B and F are located at the corners of the plan, indicating the back and front respectively.

The first rule adds a room next to the hall at the front of the house. This rule embodies the fact that, in many houses of the type in question, the hall and parlour are adjacent at the front of the house. The other rules are self-explanatory, adding rooms on the sides or across the back of the hall, and sub-dividing these rooms. The label-erasing rules are not included; each stage

Fig. 16.20 Rules to generate house layouts with reception rooms around a hall

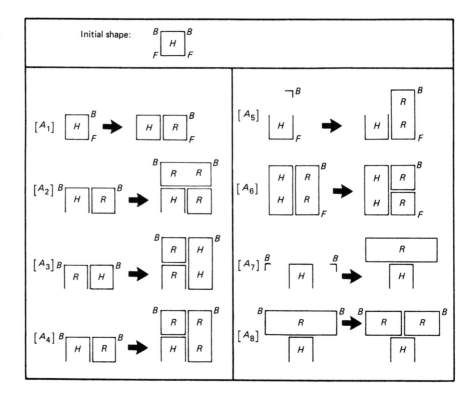

of the generation is assumed to produce a valid design. The possible layouts generated by the rules $A_1, A_2, \ldots, A_8$ are shown in Figure 16.21 in a tree structure.

9 Languages of design

It should be clear that the grammatical formalism for generating designs is essentially an 'enabling mechanism' which provides the framework for expressing the spatial relations required between the components in a design. The direction which generation takes is to some extent under the control of the user. The decisions on which paths to take in the generation depend on the degree to which knowledge of required design features can be built into the rules, particularly by the use of labels or markers.

This formalism does not necessarily imply a mechanical or deterministic approach to the production of designs; rather it provides a formalism within which production takes place. Decisions about and control of the generative process become crucial features of design within a rule system. One can think of the grammar as providing the means for producing designs within a *language*. It can be argued that design knowledge is often encapsulated in terms of 'generative rules' (although these may not be stated explicitly),

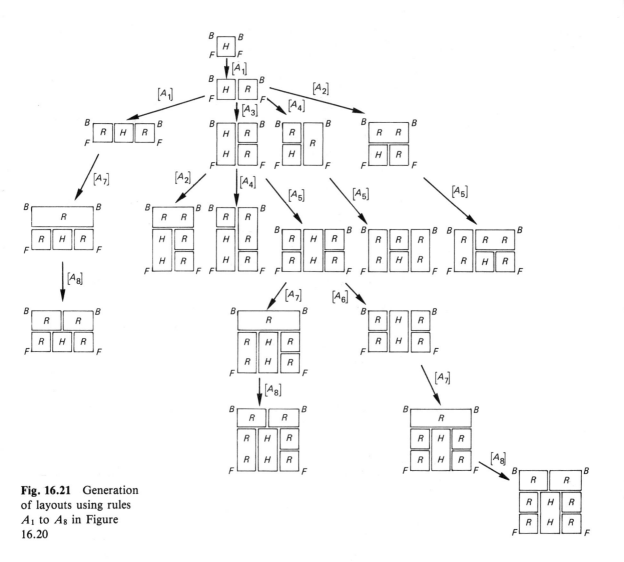

Fig. 16.21 Generation of layouts using rules A_1 to A_8 in Figure 16.20

together with an extensive knowledge of how these rules can be applied to realise specific architectural or design intentions. This knowledge is partly theoretical and partly experimental in nature. This is reflected in two major tasks which must be faced in the development of CAD systems based on a grammatical approach: firstly, the development of methods to infer properties, attributes and spatial characteristics of given sets of rules; and secondly, the empirical and experimental exploration of languages of designs and the design intentions that can be realised by different grammars. The two tasks are complementary.

This approach to design can be seen as changing the characteristics and requirements of CAD quite radically. The CAD system will become a tool at a high level in the design process for defining, creating and exploring 'worlds of design', and at a low level for controlling and deciding the paths of generation to particular design solutions.

10 Functional descriptions of designs

The aim of exploring possible designs within a defined world has led some researchers in the fields of artificial intelligence and engineering design to examine the description of designs from a *functional* point of view. Designs are generated in terms of functional descriptions.

An example of such a system is being developed as part of the Alvey Programme of research on knowledge-based systems. The project aims to produce a 'design assistant' for the whole process of product generation from design, through manufacture to field servicing and maintenance. This work is a collaborative project between the universities of Edinburgh, Leeds and Loughborough, GEC Electrical Products, National Engineering Laboratory, and Lucas.

The intention of the project is to examine the design of small electric motors given a specification [Popplestone 1984]. Possible designs are encoded in terms of their functional parts or *modules*. Thus modules might be shafts, bearings, windings and so on. Modules may be parts of other modules and modules belong to module classes. Typically a module class contains design components which have a similar function. The modules have functional inputs and outputs, which may be modules in their own right.

The interaction of modules takes place via the connection of their *ports*. These connections may have formal elements which describe the spatial relations and the layout of the connected modules. The behaviour or state of the modules is characterised by design variables.

The hierarchical structure of modules is used to represent possible designs. This representation of designs was originally developed to analyse a given design, particularly a digital electronic hardware design, for correctness of performance. The aim was to construct the functional representation of the design rather than a simulation of the digital hardware, in order to verify that the design functioned according to specification.

The attraction of this approach to the representation of possible designs lies in its ability to capture functional knowledge about a design in terms of component behaviour and in terms of component interconnections. The properties of modules and their connections can be expressed in terms of rules in a logic programming language such as PROLOG. Broadly speaking, such a system should allow the search for a design based on a specification of its desired function, by evoking clauses in the knowledge-base which are expressed relative to the module structure.

The worlds of design for which this functional description is suitable are those in which substantial knowledge is available. However, in more exploratory design work in which one wants to investigate a range of formal possibilities for which detailed knowledge is not formalised, or is still being sought (possibly through the exploration of the design world itself), the ideas of rule-based formal generation and the multiple descriptions of design discussed earlier are more appropriate.

11 Conclusion

This chapter has looked to the future of CAD and presented the point of view that it should provide systems for: the creation of new worlds of design; exploration and search in these worlds; and the accumulation of knowledge about the generated designs. A method of functional representations was described briefly, which allows knowledge, once acquired, to be used in meeting functional specifications within a given world of design. However, in design there are many representations, apart from those concerned with engineering function, which must be encompassed, ranging from those derived from cultural considerations, through those arising in the context of manufacturing, to those satisfying the requirements of the market. It is the integration of this multitude of descriptions into a computer-aided design system which we look to as the main theme in the future of CAD, with different areas of design emphasising different representations.

Integrating databases and data transfer

17

K G Pasquill and P R Wilson

1 Introduction

In 1980 there were fewer than 1000 CADCAM systems in th UK. By 1985 this had increased to well in excess of 7000 systems. This increase has been due mainly to the resulting increased productivity, reduced lead times and improved product quality with CADCAM (leading to increased profitability), and also to the sharp reduction in the costs of CADCAM equipment.

One of the problems with this increase in the adoption of CADCAM is the creation of 'islands of automation'. These arise because investment is often made in individual systems without sufficient attention being paid to the need for exchanging information in digital format amongst the various types.

It is not possible simply to send a drawing via magnetic tape or hardwire link from one system to another, since each system stores its data in a separate unique format.

2 Data mobility

With the increase in the numbers of CADCAM systems there is a desire for increased mobility of data both internally within a company and externally to and from other companies. As an example of this, consider company A which designs and manufactures body panels for a car. There is a requirement that when the headlights are fitted they must be flush with the front body panel. These headlights are designed and manufactured by company B. Company A operates a CADCAM system from vendor X and company B a system from vendor Y. Company B must transfer the design for the front body panel to their CADCAM system in order to design the correct headlight, and, as each system stores its data in a different format, a translation of data from the format of system X to that of system Y is necessary.

When only two systems are involved then only two translators are needed (X to Y and Y to X), but when the number of systems increases the number of translators required is large (for n systems, $n(n-1)$ translators are needed). From the point of view of support and maintenance this large number of translators becomes totally unmanageable. This problem is similar to that of interconnecting telephone subscribers. Without a telephone exchange a combinatorial explosion of cables (joining every pair of subscribers) is required.

To overcome this problem some sort of 'Esperanto' language (cf. the telephone exchange) is needed so that for each system only two translators are required (system X format to 'Esperanto', and 'Esperanto' to system X format). This language must not only provide the capabilities of transferring (draughting) data normally associated with engineering drawings (two-dimensional geometric data, dimensions, text, etc.), but must, in addition, be capable of transferring all product definition data (three-dimensional solid modelling data, finite element data, numerical control data, etc.).

Facilities must also be provided for users, software bureaux, and so on, to write application programs for system X that do not require major modifications should there be a need to implement them on system Y. A standard interface specification is therefore necessary which allows the application program to make calls to standard routines — the vendor ensuring that the links from these routines to the CADCAM system exist. If the application program is required to be implemented on some other system, then, if the vendor has the link from the CADCAM system to this standard interface specification, a minimal amount of work should be involved in the adaptation process.

3 Data exchange specifications

Currently there are a number of different data exchange specifications (for example, Shl, VDA-FS, FDDI, etc.), each aimed at its own specialised area, although there is only one truly international standard — the Initial Graphics Exchange Specification (IGES).

IGES is a neutral format for two- and three-dimensional CADCAM data having the support of the majority of CADCAM suppliers. It came about as a result of work initiated under the US Airforce ICAM program. Version 1 of IGES (issued in 1981) covered basic two- and three-dimensional CADCAM data; version 2 was a refinement and extension of version 1; version 3 further extended the specification which previously limited competence in the transfer of surface detail; version 4 is planned for 1987 and handles the transfer of constructive solid geometry (CSG) data for solid modelling purposes.

As the number of CADCAM systems continues to increase, the requirement for the transfer of product definition data between systems will also increase. CADCAM systems will always have dissimilar means of storing data and, as they develop and evolve, the amount and complexity of this data will also increase. CADCAM systems of the future may well be front-ended by a powerful database management system and the information stored in the database may then include all the information required to describe a part completely and unambiguously, to manufacture a part, to create an assembly of parts, and so on. Moreover, there will be a definite requirement to exchange some (or all) of this data with other systems for use by sub-contractors, analysis departments, etc.

In the very near future (now, for some companies), before a CADCAM system is purchased the vendor will have to demonstrate, and state commitment for, data exchange via the current internationally accepted standard. Exchange via other specifications, which, because of their limited area of application, may be able to react more quickly to CADCAM system developments, may be required until the development of the international standard catches up with the capabilities and facilities of the individual CADCAM systems.

As new specifications are developed for more efficient and effective transfer of product definition data, the accepted international standard may have to change. Furthermore, as the number of CADCAM systems increase, so the number of application programs will also increase. In theory the development costs associated with these programs will necessitate that, should they require implementing on many CADCAM systems, an applications interface specification must exist. In practice, however, most CADCAM systems already have their own interface specifications and if vendors were to provide a general interface specification it would be very costly and unfortunately it would also allow applications programs to be used on any CADCAM system. For this reason it will be many years before this general applications interface specification is developed.

Both of the areas described here (data exchange and applications interface specification) will enable the efficient and effective integration of CADCAM systems (and databases) which will be required for further increased profitability. Major CADCAM vendors now recognise the need, particularly for data exchange, and are committed to the development and support of the necessary software.

4 Data transfer between geometric modelling systems

Over the last ten years or so, geometric modellers have moved from the academic institutions into the industrial research and development (R & D) establishments and, in the near future, they will be used more widely in production environments. Computer-aided draughting systems went through a similar gestation period a few years ago and now there is a proliferation of these systems throughout industry. It has become essential to be able to transfer data between different computer-aided draughting systems, and the introduction of IGES [NBS 1980], now incorporated into an ANSI standard [ANSI 1981], was designed to meet this need. A similar requirement to be able to transfer data between geometric modelling systems will also arise as these are used more widely by industry.

Two interfaces have been proposed by the CAM-I Geometric Modelling Project. The first of these, called the Applications Interface (AI)[CAM-I 1980], is a specified set of subroutines intended to act as an active interface to the majority of geometric modellers. The second interface, called the Experimental Boundary File (XBF)[CAM-I 1982a], is based on the IGES format and is intended to act as a computer- and modeller-independent data transmission file.

In order to test the concepts embodied in the AI and the XBF, two experimental translators have been developed [CAM-I 1982b]. The first extracts data from a geometric modeller via calls to AI routines that have been implemented with a modeller, and then produces an XBF file as its output. The second translator reads an XBF file and makes calls on the appropriate AI routines to enable an underlying modeller to re-create the model described in the XBF. The test system is shown in Figure 17.1.

Fig. 17.1 Block diagram of translator system

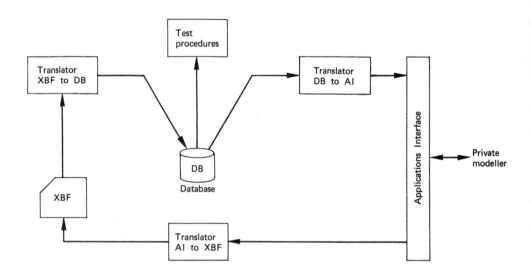

4.1 Applications Interface

The Applications Interface (AI) is a set of approximately 150 FORTRAN subroutines which, when implemented with a modeller, will enable the creation, manipulation and interrogation of geometric models. The AI was developed after a study of a range of currently available proprietary modellers, such as BUILD, EUCLID, PADL-1, ROMULUS, SYNTHAVISION and TIPS, which included both constructive solid geometry (CSG) modellers and boundary representation (B-rep) modellers. The specified functions cover at least those which are common to the majority of existing B-rep modellers and CSG modellers. Several additional facilities were specified which appeared to be desirable but which did not at that time exist in any modeller. For example, provision was made for 'sheet' and 'graph' models for constructing representations of sheet metal parts and piping systems.

The AI implies the existence of a nominal data structure for B-rep and CSG models, as shown in Figure 17.2, which has to be mapped into the actual data

Fig. 17.2 (a) AI B-rep object nominal topological data structure. (b) AI assembly and CSG nominal data structure

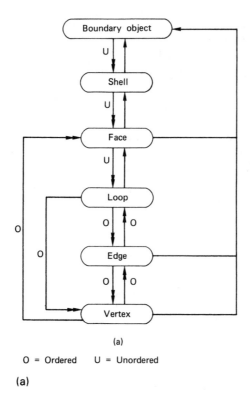

(a)

O = Ordered   U = Unordered

(a)

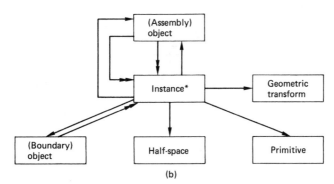

(b)

*Instance points to *one* of half-space, primitive, (boundary) object, or (assembly) object

(b)

structures used by an underlying modeller. The AI will support CSG modellers using solid primitives and/or (un-)bounded half-spaces. For B-rep models the topology is kept separate from the geometry. The geometric specifications include the normal analytic surfaces and curves as well as a variety of parametric curves and surfaces, as found in sculptured surface systems.

4.2 Experimental Boundary File

The Experimental Boundary File (XBF) is meant to meet the same requirements for data transfer between geometric modellers as IGES does for data transfer between CAD systems. The XBF was developed by extending the IGES formats to include the geometric modelling entities specified in the AI. It should be noted, though, that these were developed independently from the IGES organisation and nothing which is reported here should be construed as having emanated from (or been approved by) any IGES committee. The current XBF specifications are given in CAM-I [1982a] and a discussion on the design concepts used in developing the specification is available in Wilson, Faux and Ostrowski [in press].

An XBF file, like an IGES file, is divided into five sections:

Start
Global
Directory Entry (DE)
Parameter Data (PD)
Terminate

The overall format is that of an eighty-column card image sequential file. Each card image has a sequence number which must be unique within each section

Fig. 17.3 Defined XBF data structure

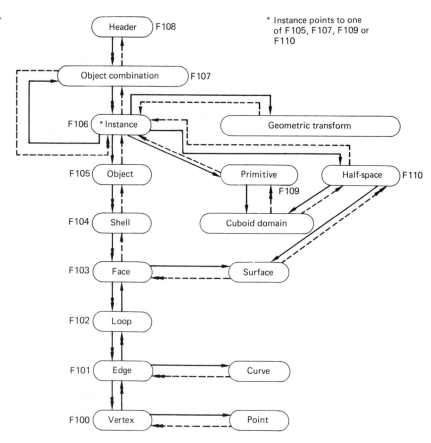

322

and is in increasing numerical order within each section. These sequence (or line) numbers act as pointer references within the file. As in IGES, each entity in the file requires a minimum of three cards for its definition, two DE cards and at least one PD card.

The topological entities are defined as IGES-type *associativities*. The data-structuring specified in the XBF is shown in Figure 17.3. No use was made of any IGES geometric definitions as these were orientated towards the transfer of graphical entities rather than towards the more general geometric entities used by the majority of geometric modellers. For example, a circular arc is defined in IGES by its centre point and the two end-points of the arc. But in the XBF, only a complete circle is defined, and this by its centre point, its axis direction and its radius. In a B-rep geometric model which includes a circular arc, the end-points can be obtained from the geometric points associated with the vertices of the edge which references the circle. However, the geometric definitions given in the XBF are more amenable to the attachment of tolerance information, when this becomes necessary. Thus, taking the circular arc again, the radius is given explicitly in the XBF, but only implicitly in IGES, and so it can be toleranced directly in the XBF.

4.3 Translator AI to XBF

This translator makes calls on the AI interrogation procedures to extract geometric model data from an underlying modeller in order to produce an XBF file as its output.

The AI interrogation routines allow geometric models to be treated as *graph* structures. For CSG models and mechanical assemblies the graph is a *tree*, but B-rep models introduce cycles into the graph. Figure 17.4 shows the type of graph arising and the following algorithm can be used to traverse such a structure, by treating it as a 'tree' with cycles.

Fig. 17.4 'Tree-with-cycles' structure

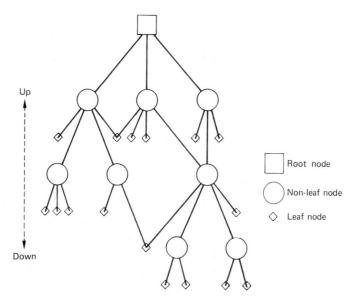

Up

Down

☐ Root node

◯ Non-leaf node

◇ Leaf node

Traversal of tree with cycles

The tree is rooted, so the algorithm steps are:

1 Start at root.

2 If all link edges are marked, then stop.

3 Descend tree by taking an unmarked link edge until either a leaf node is found or there are no further descending unmarked link edges (this will occur only at a non-leaf node).

4 If a leaf node has been reached, then mark the link edge, return to the previous node and go to step 3.

5 If the current node is the root node, then go to step 2.

6 Ascend the link edge used to reach the node, mark the link edge and go to step 3.

Figure 17.5 shows the structure shown in Figure 17.4, traversed by the above algorithm. The numbers show the order in which a leaf node is reached or in which a node is left for the last time. It will be noted that before a node is left for the last time all lower leaf nodes and non-leaf nodes will have been visited.

Fig. 17.5 Traversal of 'tree' structure

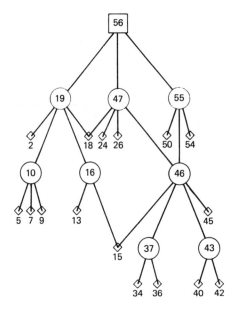

This algorithm is used twice by the AI to XBF translator. The first use of the algorithm is to examine all the model data and to calculate and store the final XBF sequence numbers for each model/XBF entity. This is necessary because, as stated earlier, line numbers are pointer references in the XBF and the data for most XBF entities includes pointer values. Hence the pointer values must be available before the entities can be written to the file. The same tree traversal algorithm is then used for a second pass over the model data and this time the entities are transferred to the file.

4.4 Translator XBF to AI

This translator reads an XBF file containing a description of a geometric model and makes calls on the appropriate AI creation procedures in order to re-create the model in an underlying geometric modeller. The AI creation procedures build a CSG model in a tree form and hence the previously described tree traversal algorithm can be utilised for this. However, the creation procedures for B-rep models imply that any particular B-rep model, both during and after its creation, should satisfy the Euler–Poincaré formula (see Chapter 9)

$$V - E + F - H = 2(M - G) \tag{1}$$

A B-rep model of a solid object essentially consists of the notion of a graph of vertices and edges embedded in a surface topologically equivalent to a sphere or to an n-fold multi-torus. The following algorithm traverses every edge in a connected graph exactly twice, once in each direction.

Graph traversal

The steps in the algorithm are:

1 Start at any vertex.

2 Travel from this vertex along any edge until the next vertex is reached. Mark the edge as having been traversed from the start vertex (that is, as an *exit* edge of that vertex). Mark the vertex just reached with the *advent* edge (an advent edge being the first edge that was travelled to reach a vertex for the first time), and make this vertex the current vertex.

3 Select an exit edge of the current vertex. (In this sense an exit edge is the first clockwise edge from the edge just travelled that has not previously been used as an exit edge for the vertex, provided also that it is not the advent edge of the vertex. No edge may be selected that has been travelled in both directions. If no edge can be found then the advent edge is selected provided that it has not been travelled in both directions.)

4 If no exit edge has been found, then stop.

5 Traverse the selected edge to the next vertex. If it is the first traverse of the edge, then mark it as an exit edge of the current vertex. Otherwise mark it as having been traversed twice. If the vertex has not been marked, then mark it with the edge as the advent edge. Make the vertex the current vertex.

6 Go to step 3.

Figure 17.6 shows the traversal of a graph by the above algorithm. The arrowed edge at each vertex shows the advent edge for the vertex and the numbered arrows alongside each edge show the order and direction of each edge traversal.

Because the graph of a B-rep model may be disconnected, it is first necessary to convert the disconnected set of sub-graphs into a a single connected graph in order to use the algorithm. This may be done by adding imaginary edges or *imedges* to the model so that all the loops in a model face are connected. Imedges are added in each face containing multiple loops, from the first vertex of one loop to the first vertex of the next loop. The imedge is anticlockwise to the first edge in the first loop and clockwise to the last edge in the next loop.

The modified model is then traversed by the above graph traversal algorithm and the model is re-created via the AI according to the following procedure.

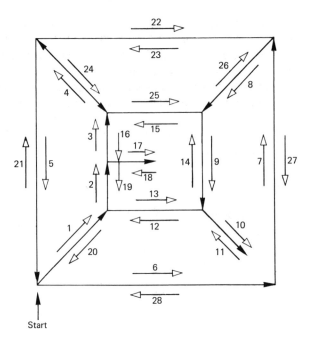

Fig. 17.6 Traversal of connected graph structure

Model re-creation procedure

This is achieved with five rules:

1 Start vertex: a 'minob' (consisting of one object, shell, face, loop and vertex) is created via the AI.

2 First traversal of an edge to a 'new' vertex: add edge and vertex to AI model.

3 First traversal of an edge to an 'old' vertex:

(a) If the AI vertices are in the same AI face: add edge to AI model (which also creates a new face and loop).

(b) If the AI vertices are in different AI faces: merge AI faces (which deletes one face and increases the genus by one) and then add edge (which creates a new face and loop).

4 Second traversal of an imedge: delete edge from AI model (which also adds one loop and deletes a face).

5 Second traversal of ordinary edge: do nothing.

During the above procedure the vertex and edge geometry can be transferred to the AI as soon as the topological entities are created. Obviously there is no geometry associated with an imedge. However, there is not a one-to-one correspondence between the XBF and AI faces during the model-building process because of rules 3 and 4 of the above procedure. The face geometry is transferred after the complete topological model is built.

4.5 Translator XBF to DB

In view of the need to add imedges to the XBF model, the XBF to AI translator was developed as a two-stage process. The first stage, termed XBF to DB, takes an XBF file as its input and transfers this data into a temporary database configured to aid geometric modelling operations. The tree traversal algorithm is used to extract the data from the XBF. In order to increase the efficiency of this process, the sequential XBF file is rewritten as two direct access files, one for the DE data and the other for the PD data. The direct access file record numbers are the same as the XBF sequence numbers in the two sections. One field in each record in the direct access file for the DE data is used to store marker information for the tree traversal procedure.

The database is configured partly as a tree structure, and for B-rep model information as a winged-edge structure [Baumgart 1974] (see also Chapter 9). The high-level access routines were written to mimic those specified in the AI and thus the database appears as a simple static read-only modeller.

4.6 Translator DB to AI

This is the second stage of the XBF to AI translator and it embodies both the tree traversal algorithm for CSG models and assemblies, and the graph traversal algorithm for B-rep models.

The tree algorithm is used to traverse the models in the database and to make calls to the appropriate AI routines to create these in the underlying modeller. When the algorithm encounters a B-rep model, imedges are added to the model, and the graph algorithm is then used to transfer the B-rep model.

5 Assessment of the AI and XBF approach

The Applications Interface (AI) was implemented with a proprietary B-rep modeller and two test parts were constructed using the modeller's own user interface. A third test part (termed 'spring' in Figure 17.7) was available as a 'hard-coded' XBF file. The spring part was transferred to the modeller via the XBF to AI translator. The modeller facilities were used to produce hidden line drawings, to take plane sections and to calculate the surface areas of the three parts. XBF files of the parts were then generated via the AI to XBF translator, and, in turn, these were put back into the modeller, via translator XBF to AI, as second generation parts. The same hidden line views and sections were taken as before and the surface areas recalculated. No 'noticeable' differences were observed between the first and the second generation drawings. The detailed B-rep descriptions of the first and the second generation models *were* different because the graph traversal algorithm does not guarantee a traversal in the same order as the original model creation. There were also some very minor discrepancies in some of the geometric values and these could be attributed to numerical round-off errors in some of the geometric routines. Table 17.1 shows the surface areas calculated for the three parts.

Table 17.1. Area calculations.

	Spring	MBB	ANC101
Area-1	189965	1163.38	104585
Area-2	189984	1163.38	104585
Error %	0.01	0	0

Table 17.2. CPU timings.

	Spring	MBB	ANC101	Normalised
AI to XBF	32	129	195	0.381
XBF to DB	230	1000	1600	3.125
DB to AI	43	189	310	0.605
Modeller				0.231
$F + E + V$	70	314	512	

Table 17.3. Storage requirements.

	Spring	MBB	ANC101
DB	7760	35715	50573
XBF	80080	295680	450560
Ratio	10.32	8.28	8.91

Fig. 17.7 Sectioned view of test parts

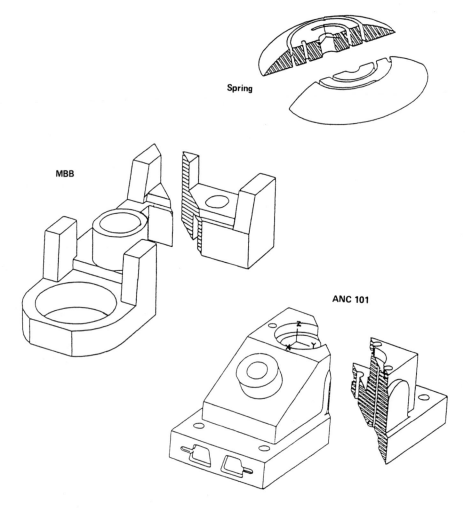

Spring

MBB

ANC 101

The translators and the modeller were run on a PRIME 550 Mark II machine. A reasonable estimate of the complexity of a B-rep model is given by the sum of the faces, edges and vertices in the model. Table 17.2 shows the CPU times for the translators, as well as the CPU time for the modeller alone, normalised with respect to the number of faces, edges and vertices. All times were linear with respect to $(F + E + V)$.

Table 17.3 shows the storage requirements for the models, assuming, for the XBF, that only one character can be stored per word. The storage requirements for the XBF are an order of magnitude greater than those for the database. Even at four characters per word storage, the XBF requires an excessive amount of storage.

The successful transfer of B-rep geometric models via the Application Interface and the Experimental Boundary File shows that the concepts embodied in these two interface specifications are valid. It was not possible to test the transfer of CSG models, owing to the unavailability of a CSG modeller, but there is no reason to suppose that the CSG concepts are not just as valid as the B-rep model concepts.

With the facilities at our disposal there was a major difficulty in comparing two boundary representations of the same object in order to determine whether these representations did actually describe the same object. Hidden line drawings and sectioning did test the topological validity of the second generation objects and the surface area calculations gave some assurance that the two generations were 'similar', but these were indirect comparisons. B-rep models are fairly low-level descriptions of solid objects and descriptions of an object may differ in detail (for example, by splitting every edge into two edges) without affecting the overall shape of the object being described. It appears that the best way of comparing two boundary descriptions would be to perform a Boolean difference operation on the two representations with an expected null result if the described objects had the same overall shape.

The efficiency of the translators (particularly of AI to XBF and of DB to AI) is comparable to that of a commercial modeller. The translator XBF to DB, though, leaves something to be desired, as does the storage requirement of the XBF file itself. Most of the time spent by the XBF to DB translator is spent in 'pointer following' in the direct-access XBF files. Pointer following is a two-stage process in that a PD record points to a DE record, which in turn points to another PD record. Thus every conceptual pointer in the XBF is realised as two actual pointers. Suggestions have been made by Wilson, Faux and Ostrowski [in press] for changes in the XBF file format which should: decrease the data storage requirements by about 60%; decrease the processing time required for writing a file by about 30%; and decrease the time for reading a file by about 50%. If these changes were incorporated, then the translator running times should compare favourably with commercial modellers.

References and further reading

ANSI (American National Standards Institute) (1981) 'Digital representation for communication of product definition data', *ANSI Standard* Y14.26M

Archer, L. B. (1965) *Systematic method for designers,* The Design Council, London

Armour, G. C. & Buffa, E. S. (1963) 'A heuristic algorithm and simulation approach to relative location of facilities', *Management Science* **9**(2), 294–309

Barnhill, R. E. (1985) 'Surfaces in computer aided geometric design: a survey with new results', *Computer Aided Geometric Design* **2**, 1–17 (a general review of modern developments)

Baumgart, B. G. (1974) 'Geometric modelling for computer vision', *Stanford Artificial Intelligence Lab. Report* STAN-CS-74-463

Bézier, P. (1971) 'Example of an existing system in the motor industry: the UNISURF system', *Proc. Roy. Soc. Lond.* **A 321**, 201–18

Bézier, P. (1982) *Numerical control: mathematics and applications,* Wiley

Blinn, J. F. (1977) 'Models of light reflection for computer synthesized pictures', *Computer Graphics* **11**(2), Summer 1977, 237–41

Blinn, J. F. (1978) 'Simulation of wrinkled surfaces', *Computer Graphics* **12**(3), August 1978, 286–92

Bui-Tuong, Phong (1975) 'Illumination for computer-generated pictures', *Communications of the ACM* **18**(6), June 1975, 311–17

CAGD (Computer Aided Geometric Design) (1985) Special issue on 'surfaces', *Computer Aided Geometric Design* **2**, nos. 1–3, September 1985

CAM-I (1980) 'An interface between geometric modellers and application programs', *CAM-I Report* R-80-GM-04

CAM-I (1982a) 'CAM-I geometric modelling project boundary file design (XBF-2)', *CAM-I Report* R-81-GM-02.1

CAM-I (1982b) 'Implementation and testing the CAM-I geometric modelling project boundary representation for solid objects', *CAM-I Report* R-82-GM-02

Clarke, A. (1982) 'APT on a micro', *Chartered Mechanical Engineer,* October 1982, 42–6

Coons', S. A. (1967) 'Surfaces for computer aided design of space forms', *Project MAC Report* TR-MAC-41, Mass. Institute of Technology

Eastman, C. M. (ed.)(1975) *Spatial synthesis in computer-aided building design,* Applied Science

Faux, I. D. & Pratt, M. J. (1979) *Computational geometry for design and manufacture,* Ellis Horwood

Ferguson, J. C. (1964) 'Multivariate curve interpolation', *Journal ACM* **11**(2), 221–8

Flemming, U., Coyne, R., Pithavadian, S. & Gindroz, R. (1985) *A pattern book for Shadyside,* Department of Architecture, Carnegie-Mellon University, Pittsburgh

Foley, J. D. & Van Dam, A. (1982) *Fundamentals of interactive computer graphics,* Addison-Wesley

Forrest, A. R. (1971) 'Computational geometry', *Proc. Roy. Soc. Lond.* **A 321**, 187–95 (an early review paper with original results)

Gault, J. W. & Pimmel, R. L. (1982) *Introduction to microcomputer-based digital systems,* McGraw-Hill

Gordon, W. J. & Riesenfeld, R. F. (1974) *Computer aided geometric design,* Barnhill & Riesenfeld (eds.), Academic Press

Goult, R. J., Hoskins, R. F., Milner, J. A. & Pratt, M. J. (1974) *Computational methods in linear algebra,* Stanley Thornes (Publishers) and Wiley Interscience

Gouraud, H. (1971) 'Continuous shading of curved surfaces', *IEEE Transactions on Computers* **C-26**(6), June 1971, 623–8

Johnson, T. E. (1963) 'SKETCHPAD III: a computer program for drawing in 3-dimensions', *MIT Electron. Syst. Lab.* ESL-TM-173, June 1963. Also in SJCC (1963), Spartan Books

Jones, J. C. (1970) *Design methods: seeds of human futures,* Wiley Interscience

Kay, D. & Greenberg, D. (1979) 'Transparency for computer synthesized images', *Computer Graphics* **13**(2), August 1979, 158–68

Klosterman, A. L., Ard, R. H. & Klahs, J. W. (1982), 'A geometric modelling program for the system designer', *Proc. Conf. on CAD/CAM Technology in Mechanical Engineering*, March 1982, Mass. Institute of Technology, MIT Press

Lidbro, N. (1956) 'Modern aircraft geometry', *Aircraft Engineering,* November 1956, 388–94

Liming, R. A. (1944) *Practical analytical geometry with applications to aircraft,* Macmillan

Mandelbrot, B. B. (1982) *The fractal geometry of nature,* Freeman

March, L. J. (1976) 'The logic of design and the question of value', *in* March, L. J. (ed.) *The architecture of form,* Cambridge University Press

Martin, H. C. (1966) *Introduction to matrix methods of structural analysis,* McGraw-Hill

Mitchell, W. J. (1977) *Computer-aided architectural design,* Applied Science

Mitchell, W. & Dillon, R. L. (1972) 'A polyomino assembly procedure for architectural floor planning', *in* Mitchell, W. (ed.) *EDRA3/AR8*, Environmental Design Research and Practice, School of Architecture and Urban Planning, University of California, Los Angeles, pp. 23/5/1–23/5/12

NBS (National Bureau of Standards) (1980) 'Initial graphics exchange specification, IGES version 1.0'

Newell, M. E., Newell, R. G. & Sancha, T. L. (1972) 'A new approach to the shaded picture problem', *Proc. ACM Nat. Conf.,* 443

Newman, W. M. & Sproull, R. F. (1981) *Principles of interactive computer graphics,* Addison-Wesley

Norrie, D. H. & De Vries, G. (1976) *A finite element bibliography,* Plenum Press

Nugent, C. E., Vollman, T. E. & Ruml, R. (1968) 'An experimental comparison of techniques for assignment of facilities to locations', *Operations Research* **16**, Jan./Feb. 1968, 150–73

Pahl, G. & Beitz, W. (1984) *Engineering design,* The Design Council, London

Paul, R. P. (1982) *Robot manipulators*, MIT Press

Popplestone, R. J. (1984) 'The application of artificial intelligence techniques to design systems', *Proceedings, International Symposium on Design and Synthesis,* Japan Society of Precision Engineering, Tokyo, 583–8

Seehof, J. M. & Evans, W. O. (1967) 'Automated layout design program', *Journal of Industrial Engineering* **189**, no. 12, 690–5

Sheth, P. N. & Uicker, J. J. (1972) 'IMP (Integrated Mechanisms Program), a computer aided design package for mechanisms and linkage', *J. Engineering for Industry, Trans. ASME* **94**, May 1972, 454–64

Shigley, J. E. & Uicker, J. J. (1980) *Theory of machines and mechanisms,* McGraw-Hill

Simon, H. A. (1969) *The sciences of the artificial,* MIT Press

Sommerville, D. M. Y. (1934) *Analytic geometry of three dimensions,* Cambridge University Press

Stiny, G. (1975) *Pictorial and formal aspects of shape and shape grammars,* Birkhauser

Sturge, D. P. (1983) 'The DUCT system of computer aided engineering', *Proc. 3rd Anglo-Hungarian Seminar on Computer Aided Geometric Design,* Cambridge University Engineering Dept.

Suh, C. H. & Radcliffe, C. W. (1978) *Kinematics and mechanism design,* J. Wiley & Sons

Sutherland, I. E. (1965) 'SKETCHPAD: a man–machine graphic communications system', *MIT Lincoln Lab. Tech. Rep.* 296, May 1965. Abridged version in SJCC (1963), Spartan Books

Tilove, R. B. (1983) 'Extending solid modeling systems for mechanism design and kinematic simulation', *IEEE Computer Graphics and Applications* **3**, 3, May/June 1983, 9–19

Timoshenko, S. P. & Goodier, J. N. (1951) *Theory of elasticity,* McGraw-Hill

Várady, T. & Pratt, M. J. (1984) 'Design techniques for the definition of solid objects with free-form geometry', *Computer-Aided Geometric Design* **1**, 207–25

Warnock, J. E. (1969) 'A hidden-surface algorithm for computer generated half-tone pictures', *Univ. Utah Computer Science Dept. Report* TR 4-15

Washizu, K. (1981) *Variational methods in elasticity and plasticity,* 3rd ed., Pergamon Press

Whitehead, B. & Eldars, M. (1964) 'An approach to the optimum layout of single storey buildings', *Architects' Journal,* 17 June 1964, 1373–80

Whitman, J. R. (1975) *A bibliography for finite elements,* Academic Press

Whitted, T. (1980) 'An improved illumination model for shaded display', *Communications of the ACM* **23**(6), June 1980, 343–9

Willmore, T. J. (1959) *Differential geometry,* Oxford University Press

Wilson, P. R., Faux, I. D. & Ostrowski, M. (to be published) 'An extension of the IGES concept of geometric modelling'

Zienkiewicz, O. C. (1977) *The finite element method,* McGraw-Hill

Index

closed-loop mechanisms 213, 214, 216, 220–2, 224
dynamic problems 222–3
and mechanism representation 212–17
open-loop mechanisms 213, 214, 216, 218–19
software packages for 7
Kinematic design, role of computers in 9
Kinematic loops 23
Kinematic synthesis 286–90
Kinematics, definition of 286
Klahs, J. W. 212
Klosterman, A. L. 212

Labelled shapes 303, 309, 310
Lambert's cosine law 278
Languages of design 312–13
Layering
in draughting systems 88–9
in PCB design 238
Lee's algorithm 240
Lidbro, N. 180
Light, effects of in computer graphics 278–83
Light-pens 83
Liming, R. A. 107
Line routing algorithms 240
Line vectors 30
Linear blending functions 110
Linear edges, wire-frame models with 96–9
Linear elements, in finite element analysis 183–9
Linear interpolation functions 204
Linear transformations 27, 61–4
in B-rep modellers 174
and coefficient matrices 33–4
Lines, removal of hidden 266–77
Links in mechanisms
dynamic problems 222–3
modelling of 216–17
representation of 213–16
Local checks, and B-rep modellers 175, 176
Local coordinate frames
and relations between objects 47–50, 51
and spatial relations 302
Local coordinate systems 24
Lofting 107, 113
Logic design 225, 226, 228–32
Logic simulation 232–7
Loose routing 240

Mach band effect 281
Mandelbrot, B. B. 284
Manifolds
and B-rep modellers 166–7
Manufacture, and design 2–10
March, L. J. 3
Martin, H. C. 179
Mathematical tools and techniques and object representation 17, 22–37
coordinates 24–8
graphs 22–3
matrices 32–4
rates of change 34–7
vectors 28–32
and surface modelling 107–8
Matrices 32–4; see also Stiffness matrices

Mechanical vibrations, and finite element analysis 210
Mechanisms and kinematic analysis 211–24
closed-loop 213, 214, 216, 220–2, 224
modelling links in 216–17
open-loop 213, 214, 216, 218–19
representation of 212–17
stick models of 216
Memory maps see Frame buffers
Menus, and computer draughting 84
Meridians 102
Mitchell, W. 259, 262
Modelling
and draughting systems 90, 91, 92
and graphical techniques 57
and object representation 17–19
see also Solid modelling; Surface modelling; Three-dimensional modelling; Wire-frame modelling
Modules, functional descriptions of designs 314
Montages 284
Motion, geometry in 285–95
discrete vs. continuous 294–5
kinematic synthesis 286–90
spatial and temporal forms 285–6, 290–4
see also Kinematic analysis
Mouse, in computer draughting 83
Moving an object 39, 40–6
Moving trihedral, in space curves 124–5

NAND gates 228, 229, 230, 234, 242
NC (Numerically-controlled) machining, kinematic simulation of 224
NC (Numerically-controlled) tools 20
and surface modelling 108, 111, 114
Necker cubes 263, 264
Newell, M. E. & R. G. 277, 282
NONAME solid modeller 91, 92
Nonsense objects, wire-frame models 103–4
NOR gates 228, 229, 230, 243
Norrie, D. H. 180

Objects
and attributes 14–16
and B-rep modellers 166–7
creating complex 39
geometry in motion 285–95
representing 13–37
declarative vs. procedural 20–1
mathematical tools and techniques 22–37
and modelling 17–19
representing relationships 39–56
assemblies 53–6
combining 52–3
moving 39, 40–6
spatial relations 39, 46–8
wire-frame models
of real objects 103–5
wire-frame representation 96–102
Oblique projection 80, 81, 82
Octree adaptive grid 159–60
Octree decomposition, in solid modelling 156
One-dimensional elements, and finite element analysis 182–93, 194–5, 197
OR gates 228–9, 234
Orthographic multi-views 76–8, 82, 93

Orthographic projection 74–5
  and perspective projection 80–2
Ostrowski, M. 322

Pahl, G. 3
Parabolas, and Bézier cubic curve segments
    130
Parallel projection
  and shadows 282
  in three-dimensional graphics 72–6
  view volume in 266, 267
Parameterised description of parts in
    draughting systems 89–90, 91
Parametric bilinear surfaces 110–11
Parametric curves
  cubic spline 133
  equations for 140–2
  in surface modelling 109–12
  of surfaces 140
Parametric equations
  and plane curves 117–22
  for a sphere 137–8
Parametric surface design methods 142–51
  bicubic polynomial surface patches 143–7
  composite surfaces 150
  interpolation of general curves 147–50
Parametric techniques, and surface modelling
    108
Part programming 2
Partial derivatives of shapes 37
Path-following, in robot simulation 224
Paths, graphs and object representation 22–3
Paul, R. P. 218
PCBs (Printed circuit boards)
  design 225, 227–8, 236–7
    physical layout 238–40
  and silicon 244
Pentagonal surface patches 150, 151
Perspective images 71–2
Perspective projection 72–6
  and orthographic projection 80–2
  view volume in 266–8
Perspective transformations 27, 268–9
Pimmel, R. L. 230
Pixels
  and depth buffer algorithms 270
  in raster graphics 59, 60
  and scan-line coherence 271, 272
Planar four-bar linkages 220–1
Planar robot manipulators 218–19
Planar slider-crank mechanisms 221–2
Plane curves
  and lofting 107
  representation of 117–22
Planes
  parametric equations for 139–40
  and surface representation 139–40
Plate bending problems, elements for 208
Plotters 58–9, 60, 84
Pointer following 329
Polar coordinate systems 25, 26
  on a sphere 137
Pole 286
Popplestone, R. J. 314
Position vectors 29–30, 31
  in Bézier cubic curve segments 130
  and parametric bilinear surfaces 110–11

Pratt, M. J. 112, 116, 126, 130, 132, 133,
    134, 142, 146, 150, 151, 216
Primitive solids in CSG 161, 162–3
Primitives (logic devices) 228, 233, 236
Principal normal vectors of space curves
    124–5
Prismatic joints in mechanisms 213, 214, 216
Procedural representations of objects 20–1
Profile curves, wire-frame models 104–5, 176
Projective geometry, and homogeneous
    coordinates 27–8
Pucks 83
Pure primitive instancing, in solid modelling
    154–5

Quadratic elements, in finite element analysis
    190–3
Quadratic interpolation functions 204

Radcliffe, C. W. 220
Raster graphics 59–60, 270
Rational biquadratic parametric equations
    138
Rational polynomial segments 132
Rational quadratic segments, and curve
    design 132
Rats-nest, in PCBs 239
Ray-firing see Depth-buffer algorithms
Ray-tracing 176, 282–3
Realism in computer graphics 263–84
  area coherence 270–4
  depth priority of faces 274–7
  effects of light and shade 278–83
  hidden line and surface removal 266–77
  scan-line coherence 270–4
  surface detail and texture 283–4
Rectangular elements, in finite element
    analysis 202–4
Recursive (iterative) synthetical formulation
    21
Reference coordinate frames, and relations
    between objects 46–50
Reflected symmetry, in two-dimensional
    graphics 65
Reflection, in two-dimensional graphics 61,
    63, 67
Representations
  in computer-aided design 297–9
  of object relationships 39–56
  of objects 13–37
Revolute joints in mechanisms 213, 214, 215,
    216
Riesenfeld, R. F. 131
Rigid transformations 27
Robots
  and computer-aided design 9
  and object manipulation 55–6
  simulation of 223–4
Rotation of objects 40, 42–6
  about the z-axis 44–6
  through right angles 42–4
  in two-dimensional graphics 61, 63, 67
Rotational symmetry, in two-dimensional
    graphics 65
Routing algorithms 240, 241
Row vectors 31–2
Rubber-banding of PCBs 239